Contested Liberalisms

Edinburgh Critical Studies in Victorian Culture
Series Editor: Julian Wolfreys

Recent books in the series:

Rudyard Kipling's Fiction: Mapping Psychic Spaces
Lizzy Welby

The Decadent Image: The Poetry of Wilde, Symons and Dowson
Kostas Boyiopoulos

British India and Victorian Literary Culture
Máire ní Fhlathúin

Anthony Trollope's Late Style: Victorian Liberalism and Literary Form
Frederik Van Dam

Dark Paradise: Pacific Islands in the Nineteenth-Century British Imagination
Jenn Fuller

Twentieth-Century Victorian: Arthur Conan Doyle and the Strand Magazine, 1891–1930
Jonathan Cranfield

The Lyric Poem and Aestheticism: Forms of Modernity
Marion Thain

Gender, Technology and the New Woman
Lena Wånggren

Self-Harm in New Woman Writing
Alexandra Gray

Suffragist Artists in Partnership: Gender, Word and Image
Lucy Ella Rose

Victorian Liberalism and Material Culture: Synergies of Thought and Place
Kevin A. Morrison

The Victorian Male Body
Joanne-Ella Parsons and Ruth Heholt

Nineteenth-Century Settler Emigration in British Literature and Art
Fariha Shaikh

The Pre-Raphaelites and Orientalism
Eleonora Sasso

The Late-Victorian Little Magazine
Koenraad Claes

Coastal Cultures of the Long Nineteenth Century
Matthew Ingleby and Matt P. M. Kerr

Dickens and Demolition: Literary Afterlives and Mid-Nineteenth-Century Urban Development
Joanna Hofer-Robinson

Artful Experiments: Ways of Knowing in Victorian Literature and Science
Philipp Erchinger

Victorian Poetry and the Poetics of the Literary Periodical
Caley Ehnes

The Victorian Actress in the Novel and on the Stage
Renata Kobetts Miller

Dickens's Clowns: Charles Dickens, Joseph Grimaldi and the Pantomime of Life
Jonathan Buckmaster

Italian Politics and Nineteenth-Century British Literature and Culture
Patricia Cove

Cultural Encounters with the Arabian Nights in Nineteenth-Century Britain
Melissa Dickson

Novel Institutions: Anachronism, Irish Novels and Nineteenth-Century Realism
Mary L. Mullen

The Fin-de-Siècle Scottish Revival: Romance, Decadence and Celtic Identity
Michael Shaw

Contested Liberalisms: Martineau, Dickens and the Victorian Press
Iain Crawford

Forthcoming volumes:

Her Father's Name: Gender, Theatricality and Spiritualism in Florence Marryat's Fiction
Tatiana Kontou

The Sculptural Body in Victorian Literature: Encrypted Sexualities
Patricia Pulham

Olive Schreiner and the Politics of Print Culture, 1883–1920
Clare Gill

Victorian Auto/Biography: Problems in Genre and Subject
Amber Regis

Gissing, Shakespeare and the Life of Writing
Thomas Ue

The Aesthetics of Space in Nineteenth-Century British Literature, 1851–1908
Giles Whiteley

Women's Mobility in Henry James
Anna Despotopoulou

The Persian Presence in Victorian Poetry
Reza Taher-Kermani

Michael Field's Revisionary Poetics
Jill Ehnenn

Plotting Disability in the Nineteenth-Century Novel
Clare Walker Gore

The Americanisation of W. T. Stead
Helena Goodwyn

Literary Illusions: Performance Magic and Victorian Literature
Christopher Pittard

For a complete list of titles published visit the Edinburgh Critical Studies in Victorian Culture web page at edinburghuniversitypress.com/series/ECVC

Also Available:
Victoriographies – A Journal of Nineteenth-Century Writing, 1790–1914, edited by Diane Piccitto and Patricia Pulham
ISSN: 2044–2416
www.eupjournals.com/vic

Contested Liberalisms

Martineau, Dickens and
the Victorian Press

Iain Crawford

EDINBURGH
University Press

For Melissa

Edinburgh University Press is one of the leading university presses in the UK. We publish academic books and journals in our selected subject areas across the humanities and social sciences, combining cutting-edge scholarship with high editorial and production values to produce academic works of lasting importance. For more information visit our website: edinburghuniversitypress.com

© Iain Crawford, 2020, 2021

Edinburgh University Press Ltd
The Tun – Holyrood Road, 12(2f) Jackson's Entry, Edinburgh EH8 8PJ

First published in hardback by Edinburgh University Press 2020

Typeset in 11/13 Adobe Sabon
by IDSUK (DataConnection) Ltd

A CIP record for this book is available from the British Library

ISBN 978 1 4744 5313 4 (hardback)
ISBN 978 1 4744 5314 1 (paperback)
ISBN 978 1 4744 5315 8 (webready PDF)
ISBN 978 1 4744 5316 5 (epub)

The right of Iain Crawford to be identified as the author of this work has been asserted in accordance with the Copyright, Designs and Patents Act 1988, and the Copyright and Related Rights Regulations 2003 (SI No. 2498).

Contents

List of Illustrations	vi
Series Editor's Preface	vii
Acknowledgements	ix
Introduction	1
1. 'The display of woman's naked mind to the gaze of the world': Harriet Martineau and the Press, 1830–1834	29
2. Martineau, the Press and Jacksonian America	50
3. *American Notes* and the 'frightful engine' of the Press	95
4. 'Yield to the mighty mind of the Popular Instructor': Print and the Press in *Martin Chuzzlewit*	137
5. 'Called hither by the commotion of the times': Martineau and the Press, 1837–1850	180
6. *The Factory Controversy*: 'What I dread is being silenced'	220
7. The End of Whig History: Dickens, Martineau and the Mid-Victorian Press	266
Conclusion: 'Likeness in unlikeness'	298
Bibliography	303
Index	319

Illustrations

2.1	*On the Ohio River.*	65
2.2	*The Southern Rose*, 14 November 1835.	84
3.1	*The Thunderer.*	101
3.2	*The Extra Boz Herald.*	121
4.1	Mr Jefferson Brick proposes an appropriate sentiment.	150
5.1	Toussaint L'Ouverture.	204
5.2	*Knight's Weekly Volume.*	208
6.1	Extract from *The Factory Controversy.*	231
6.2	Harriet Martineau to Charles Dickens, 8 March 1855.	241
C.1	Harriet Martineau's grave.	301

Series Editor's Preface

'Victorian' is a term, at once indicative of a strongly determined concept and an often notoriously vague notion, emptied of all meaningful content by the many journalistic misconceptions that persist about the inhabitants and cultures of the British Isles and Victoria's Empire in the nineteenth century. As such, it has become a byword for the assumption of various, often contradictory habits of thought, belief, behaviour and perceptions. Victorian studies and studies in nineteenth-century literature and culture have, from their institutional inception, questioned narrowness of presumption, pushed at the limits of the nominal definition, and sought to question the very grounds on which the unreflective perception of the so-called Victorian has been built; and so they continue to do. Victorian and nineteenth-century studies of literature and culture maintain a breadth and diversity of interest, of focus and inquiry, in an interrogative and intellectually open-minded and challenging manner, which are equal to the exploration and inquisitiveness of its subjects. Many of the questions asked by scholars and researchers of the innumerable productions of nineteenth-century society actively put into suspension the clichés and stereotypes of 'Victorianism', whether the approach has been sustained by historical, scientific, philosophical, empirical, ideological or theoretical concerns; indeed, it would be incorrect to assume that each of these approaches to the idea of the Victorian has been, or has remained, in the main exclusive, sealed off from the interests and engagements of other approaches. A vital interdisciplinarity has been pursued and embraced, for the most part, even as there has been contest and debate amongst Victorianists, pursued with as much fervour as the affirmative exploration between different disciplines and differing epistemologies put to work in the service of reading the nineteenth century.

Edinburgh Critical Studies in Victorian Culture aims to take up both the debates and the inventive approaches and departures from convention that studies in the nineteenth century have witnessed for the last half century at least. Aiming to maintain a 'Victorian' (in the most positive sense of that motif) spirit of inquiry, the series' purpose is to continue and augment the cross-fertilisation of interdisciplinary approaches, and to offer, in addition, a number of timely and untimely revisions of Victorian literature, culture, history and identity. At the same time, the series will ask questions concerning what has been missed or improperly received, misread, or not read at all, in order to present a multifaceted and heterogeneous kaleidoscope of representations. Drawing on the most provocative, thoughtful and original research, the series will seek to prod at the notion of the 'Victorian', and in so doing, principally through theoretically and epistemologically sophisticated close readings of the historicity of literature and culture in the nineteenth century, to offer the reader provocative insights into a world that is at once overly familiar and irreducibly different, other and strange. Working from original sources, primary documents and recent interdisciplinary theoretical models, Edinburgh Critical Studies in Victorian Culture seeks not simply to push at the boundaries of research in the nineteenth century, but also to inaugurate the persistent erasure and provisional, strategic redrawing of those borders.

Julian Wolfreys

Acknowledgements

This book has been the focus of a distinct period in my professional career, one in which I returned to the life of disciplinary scholarship after a decade and a half spent serving in a variety of roles in institutional leadership. In developing it I have been especially indebted to the support of a network of professional communities and the generosity of their members who welcomed me back into the academic fold, and I am delighted to have this opportunity to thank those friends and colleagues here.

Both my current and previous institutions have been pivotal to this project. It began during a sabbatical year provided by The College of Wooster, and I am grateful to then Board Chair James R. Wilson for making possible that leave as well as the funding that supported my first conference and archival research travel. Since I joined the University of Delaware, I have been recurringly grateful to departmental colleagues, notably Ann Ardis, Anne Boylan, Martin Brueckner, Siobhan Carroll, John Ernest, Ed Larkin, Kristen Poole, the late Charles Robinson and Julian Yates, for their encouragement and insights into the transatlantic world of nineteenth-century literary exchange. The College of Arts and Sciences and then-Dean George Watson and Deputy Provost Lynn Okagaki have also all been generous in providing financial support and encouragement for my research, even as they have enticed me back into the world of administrative responsibilities.

My colleagues in UD's Undergraduate Research Program – Lauren Barsky, Mary Ann Null and Judi Smith – have been amazingly gracious and supportive of their Faculty Director's absences on travel for research and to the conferences that have been essential proving grounds for the ideas underlying this book. In particular, the Dickens Universe has been for me, as it has for so many nineteenth-century scholars, an intellectual melting pot of all things Victorian and a rich gathering place of ideas and discussions that have constantly pushed me to rethink the claims and scope of the book's argument. Among so many in Santa Cruz, I think especially of Jim Adams, John Bowen, Jim Buzard, Jay Clayton, Ryan Fong, Holly Furneaux, Jonathan Grossman, John Jordan, Gerhard Joseph, Melisa Klimaszewski, Ruth Livesey, Tricia Lootens, Teresa Mangum, Meredith McGill, Elsie Michie, Helena Michie, Bob Patten, Rob Polhemus, Caroline Reitz, Catherine Robson, Rebecca Stern, Dan Stout, Sharon Weltman and Carolyn Williams. While I had heard of the summer Dickensfest in California long before my first trip to Santa Cruz in 2009, joining the Research Society for Victorian Periodicals that same year and attending its conference in Minneapolis opened up an entirely new aspect of the multiverse of nineteenth-century studies. In the years since that first meeting, RSVP has become central to my professional life, and I owe more than I can say to the opportunities it has offered to test and develop ideas and to the friends and colleagues I have found there. Among those at RSVP to whom I owe so much are Margaret Beetham, Laurel Brake, Marysa Demoor, Fionnuala Dillane, Alexis Easley, Maria Frawley, Natalie Houston, Anne Humpherys, Linda Hughes, David Latané, Kitty Ledbetter, Dallas Liddle, Brian Maidment, the late Linda Peterson, Jennifer Phegley and Cathy Waters. Above all, I am enormously grateful to both Patrick Leary and Joanne Shattock, who have been unstintingly generous in sharing their incomparable knowledge of nineteenth-century periodicals and given me the benefit of their wisdom throughout the writing of this book. Finally, both the Dickens Society, with which I have been affiliated for more decades than I quite like to recollect, and the Martineau Society, whose members I met for the first time in the early part of this project, have helped me immensely as I have navigated between their eponymous authors and sought to bring them together in this book. I think in particular of Diana Archibald, Joel Brattin, Sean Grass, Natalie McKnight, Lillian Nayder and David Paroissien at the Dickens Society; Elizabeth Arbuckle, Sharon Connor, Mary Fielding, Susan Hoecker-Drysdale, Shu-Fang Lai, Victorine Martineau, Valerie Sanders, Barbara Todd, Beth Torgerson, John Vint, Ruth Watts and Gaby Weiner at the Martineau Society. Finally, Deborah Logan, cited so often in this book, has both provided through her editorial work a foundation for all of us who work on Martineau and been a generous respondent to my occasionally esoteric queries.

The archival research that informs much of this book was facilitated by the professional generosity of librarians at a number of institutions. In Britain, the Bodleian Libraries, University of Oxford; the Cadbury Research Library at the University of Birmingham; the Castle Howard Archive; Dr Williams's Library; the Forster Collection at the National Art Library (with particular thanks to Doug Dodds for providing the image used in Chapter 3); the Harris Manchester College Library; the National Library of Scotland; University of Kent Library; and University of Sussex Library. In the United States, the Arthur and Elizabeth Schlesinger Library on the History of Women in America, Radcliffe Institute for Advanced Study, Harvard University; the Boston Athenaeum; the Delaware Historical Society; Hagley Museum and Library; the Historical Society of Washington, DC; the Houghton Library, Harvard University; the Huntington Library; the Massachusetts Historical Society; the Morgan Library and Museum; the New York Historical Society; the New York Public Library; Princeton University Library; the Smithsonian American Art Museum; the Stuart A. Rose Manuscript, Archives, and Rare Book Library, Emory University; the University of Delaware library; Winterthur Library; and the W. S. Hoole Special Collections Library at the University of Alabama (RTR).

Earlier versions of parts of this project appeared in a number of publications, and I am grateful to those venues for the original opportunity to present my work and for permission to draw on it here: the University of Massachusetts Press for material included in Chapter 3 and first published in *Dickens and Massachusetts: The Lasting Legacy of the Commonwealth Visits*; *Nineteenth-Century Literature* for the first working through of the great Martineau/Dickens falling out discussed in Chapter 6; and Cambridge University Press for the discussion of Martineau and Macaulay in Chapter 7 first published in *Journalism and the Periodical Press in Nineteenth-Century Britain*.

Finally, the genre expectation of these acknowledgements is that we turn at the end to those closest to us. In this case, the most important women in my life should really have come first, for, without them, this project would never have begun: my mother, Norfolk-born like Harriet Martineau and lifelong lover of Dickens's novels, who saw the beginnings of the book and who I wish were still here to see it come to fruition; my daughters Jelena and Nevena, fully realised liberal subjects flourishing in their personal and professional paths, dedicated progressive activists in their communities; and, above all, my wife Melissa Ianetta, to whom I dedicate this book, an extraordinary critical reader and editor whose remarkable genius for helping writers stretch to realise their best potential has been foundational to my journey back into creating disciplinary knowledge and whose rigorous, loving patience with and support of this book has kept me on genre and on course from the beginning. Thank you all.

Introduction

This project draws together three aspects of nineteenth-century scholarship that have not previously been brought into unified focus. During the first two decades of the current century, the development of the Victorian press has become a substantial area of critical study, the complex legacy of liberalism in both Britain and America has received extensive attention and the reciprocal dynamics of transatlantic literary exchange have come to be understood with increasing subtlety. These scholarly conversations have, however, evolved independently, and to date there has been no attempt to explore the connections between them and, by doing so, to further our understanding of all three. That is, there has been no study of the relationship between transatlantic exchange, the development of Anglo-American liberalism and the formation of the Victorian press. Indeed, as Bob Nicholson has noted, such relationships through the press constitute an area that has gone largely unexamined, and, in particular, 'the role played by periodicals in shaping Britain's relationship with the United States during the first half of the nineteenth century has received relatively little scholarly attention'.[1] *Contested Liberalisms* addresses this lacuna through focusing upon the role played in the formation of the early Victorian press by two of its essential shaping figures, both of whom were deeply invested in the liberal project and both of whom were themselves shaped by their encounters with America and American journalism. Despite their shared commitment to liberal progress, however, and notwithstanding their extensive collaborative connections within the tight-knit world of Victorian journalism and letters, Harriet Martineau and Charles Dickens embodied fundamentally incompatible aspects of liberal ideology, opposing commitments to transatlantic engagement and competing visions of the role of print culture and, in particular, of the press in shaping civil society. Using Martineau and Dickens as its focusing lens, then, this project offers a fundamentally new reading of the formation of the early Victorian press and of the ways in which that press both contributed to and was shaped by a transatlantic community of letters broadly united in support for the advance of progressive values but crucially divided over core elements of the ideology of liberalism itself.

Although modern critical studies have leaned far more heavily towards Dickens than Martineau,[2] during their lifetimes they were praised as, respectively, 'the greatest magazine editor of his own, or any other, age', and 'the first and the greatest of women journalists'.[3] Because their experiences overlapped so closely, because their encounters with America were so foundational to their subsequent work as journalists and because, ultimately, they quarrelled so bitterly and so publicly, their connections offer us an unparalleled insight into the role of the early Victorian press in advancing liberal progress, the capacity of women authors to contribute to public discourse and the resistance women encountered attempting to achieve agency in the public sphere. At times working together, at times in parallel, at times adversarially, that is, no other two major Victorian figures operate as such a binary system of mutual proximity and influence. Examining Martineau and Dickens side by side, then, and exploring the ramifications of the ways in which they were connected, provides us with an exceptional lens for understanding not only the ways in which our own scholarly representations have rendered their relationship, what they have privileged and what they have left invisible, but also sheds new light upon the complex, fissured, ever-evolving phenomenon of nineteenth-century liberalism and its connections to the evolution of Victorian print culture. A relationship that was certainly personal and differences that were felt and expressed with extraordinary animosity were, then, not simply Martineau and Dickens's as individuals, but speak for us to larger patterns of aspiration, resistance and control within early Victorian culture even as they illuminate our own history of disciplinary practice as readers of that culture and ongoing shapers of its meanings.

The Growth of the Press, 1830–1850

The unprecedented expansion of the British press – and indeed that of its American counterpart – in the early Victorian decades is the foundational context for this project. Soon after he established *Household Words*, Dickens used his own weekly magazine to testify to the phenomenon. On 1 June 1850, in the tenth issue of *Household Words*, his sub-editor and business manager, William Henry Wills, presented that growth to the magazine's mass-market readership with his 'The Appetite for News', a popularising account of the subject that had just received more extensive treatment in Frederick Knight Hunt's recently published *The Fourth Estate: Contributions towards a History of Newspapers and of the Liberty of the Press*.[4] Citing the fact that more than sixty-seven million newspaper stamps had been issued in 1848, a figure that represented a more than doubling of press production since the first decade of the century, Wills goes on to describe the nineteen and a half square feet of printed matter that comprised each day's issue of the *Times*.[5] Pointing next to the diversity of material produced by this vastly expanded press, Wills concludes that the 'acres of print sown broad-cast, produce a daily crop to suit every appetite and every taste' and comments that a morning newspaper has become the 'first necessity' to the circadian rituals of much of the British population.[6] Having thus sought to impress upon his readers the extent of this new phenomenon, Wills closes his article with a turn back to Hunt's history of the fourth estate as a way of calling out the role of the press as an essential safeguard of liberty. Citing Hunt's judgement that 'the state is virtually powerless if it attempts to check the press', Wills emphasises how unsuccessful have been government efforts to stem the expansion he has just celebrated and goes on to argue that it is the press, 'more effective than the Magna Charta, because its powers are wielded with more ease', that is the true guardian of the state. Closing by singling out for praise a mixed model of journalism in which 'the dissemination of news takes place side by side with some of the most sound, practical, and ennobling sentiments and precepts', he ends by implicitly defining *Household Words* itself as a distinctively valuable exemplar of that expanded press so essential to the fostering of liberal progress.[7]

As Martin Hewitt has explored in his *The Dawn of the Cheap Press in Victorian Britain*, the expansion of the fourth estate that Wills described was inseparable from the evolution of the nation's political life in the years following the first Reform Act.[8] Building in particular on earlier studies by Lucy Brown and Joel Weiner,[9] Hewitt examines the contest for control of the public sphere that developed during these first decades of the Victorian period and argues that it anticipates a larger movement in the balance of political power in the nation. Waged, on the one hand, by those seeking to expand political discourse in post-Reform Britain and, on the other, by a ruling establishment that, under both Tory and Whig leadership, endeavoured to restrict such growth, this struggle was embodied in the debate over the regime of levies and duties designed to maintain the state's control over the newspaper press. For, as Hewitt's study explores, the early Victorian decades saw a growth in opposition to such control across the political spectrum and the development of an increasingly vocal and increasingly powerful campaign against the 'taxes on knowledge', a campaign that culminated with their final repeal in the mid-1850s. Following that repeal, Hewitt argues, there occurred a 'structural transformation of the press after 1853' that, in turn, posed a major challenge to proponents of Victorian liberalism.[10] Repeal, that is, reduced the sway of the national press centred in London and allowed the creation of a newly powerful provincial popular press, one that eroded 'the self-contained middle-class public sphere on which it was supposed that the rationality of progress was predicated' and so called into question that class's authority and the assumptions of its cultural leadership that were represented most visibly in Matthew Arnold's *Culture and Anarchy*.[11]

In this project, I build from Hewitt's account of the later move towards populist, Gladstonian liberalism and its expression in the development of the post-1850 press. Focusing initially on the decades preceding the repeal of the 'taxes on knowledge' and on Martineau and Dickens's work in and about the press between the mid-1830s and the early 1850s, I argue that these two writers demonstrate the fissures within liberal ideology through their contrasting efforts to sustain a unified, progressive public sphere that could bring together that ideology and a mass-market readership to forestall the very transformation in cultural leadership that Hewitt shows did later occur. That work, as I describe, was founded upon their respective experiences with the print culture that was emerging in the United States. For, while almost every British traveller who visited and wrote about America in this period commented upon the new historical phenomenon of a popular press largely unrestricted by formal state controls, Martineau and Dickens were unusual in the fact that they were practising journalists themselves and, as later chapters will show, were at the time of their visits actively engaged in both examining the relationship between the press and social progress and in exploring the ways in which they could shape their own careers so as to contribute to such progress. Exposed to the kind of mass-market newspaper industry that would not fully develop in Britain until after the repeal of the 'taxes on knowledge', and witnessing how profoundly it was involved in the struggle between pro-slavery forces and the abolitionist movement, Martineau and Dickens experienced at first hand the potential role of the press in forming the social episteme around an issue critical to the future evolution of American society. Their differing responses to that press in the accounts they published after their visits and the different relationships they established for themselves with it in the years that followed thus become a central focus of my argument here.

Transatlantic Liberalism

A second principal focus for this study is the extent to which both the growth of the early Victorian press and Martineau and Dickens's encounters with America took place within the social and political context of the development of nineteenth-century liberalism. Dating back to Locke and taking a wide diversity of forms according to the local conditions under which it evolved, liberalism is, as many of those working on it have noted, a broad, mutating concept that eludes easy definition. Sharing Wendy Brown's sense of it as a 'nonsystematic and porous doctrine subject to historical change and local variation', Kevin Morrison has thus pointed to a recurring tendency whereby 'liberalism has often been defined in ways that fail to capture its bewildering complexity', while Daniel Stout has suggested that the entire 'history of liberalism ... is a history of anxiety about its own capacities'.[12] Despite or perhaps because of its protean nature, liberalism had, as Edmund Fawcett has argued, emerged during the chaotic decades of revolution and warfare following the French Revolution to become the defining political philosophy of industrialising Western civilisation. At its core, as Fawcett describes, liberalism combined a commitment to the essential value of democratic processes with a fundamental belief 'that people have within them an open-ended capacity for betterment and reform: to grow, to improve, to progress, with help or direction from others if need be'.[13] 'Searching for an acceptable political order in a destabilized world of ceaseless change',[14] then, the liberal project sought both to reform society as a whole and to shape the individuals within it, picturing a world in disorder but at the same time confident in the capacity of those individuals and the institutions they constructed to bring order out of that chaos. Within this broad framework, the ways in which liberalism in Britain was differentiated from its forms elsewhere in Europe and then the factors which had led liberalism in the United States to take a different developmental path from the version that evolved in Britain are essential to the case I make here.

For, where Dickens has frequently been folded into the scholarship of liberalism as an exemplar of its development in the middle decades of the nineteenth century and used as an indicator of some of its particular challenges in British Victorian culture, Martineau has received almost no attention in such studies and none at all as a representative of the transatlantic community of liberal progressives. In Elaine Hadley's reading of *Little Dorrit*, for example, Dickens's profound concern over how to reconcile 'utilitarian countability' and its focus upon quantitative analysis and the aggregate mass of the population with the values of liberal individualism results in a text that 'can be read as a fable about the inutility of ethical and fictional character, a depressive rendering of the liberal pursuit of happiness'.[15] Similarly, Emily Steinlight, examining the ways in which 'Victorian fiction charts the instability of the boundaries between the one and the many', explores how Dickens's later novels demonstrate his 'refusal to solve the problem his narratives so spectacularly create: the incapacity of all existing institutions . . . to sustain the quantity of life they produce'.[16] By contrast, Martineau, perhaps because of her standing within our field as a previously marginalised writer whose work is still being recovered but perhaps even more because she has been defined by the critical tradition as essentially an embodiment of 'utilitarian countability', has been almost entirely overlooked in the scholarship of liberalism.

The major exception to this pattern of discussion is Lauren Goodlad's *Victorian Literature and the Victorian State*. In her examination of liberalism and the state, Goodlad not only considers the ways in which Dickens in, for example, *Bleak House* 'persistently undermines the modern agencies that might unsettle pernicious deadlock' but also explores how Martineau's work in the 1830s advocates for an 'ideal of a Christian and civic community overseen by diligent middle-class exemplars' and offers very unDickensian support for the New Poor Law as privileging 'a bourgeois-materialist register of value' and, through the new workhouse system, creating a new and effective approach to addressing the problem of pauperism.[17] Although Goodlad's study touches on Martineau only briefly, the fundamental assumption from which it builds provides a perspective on the complex phenomenon of liberalism that is foundational to my approach in this project. For, as Goodlad argues, British Victorian progressives were widely engaged in an effort both to support and yet also to interrogate 'the substantive individual and social aims on behalf of which power was exercised'.[18] As a result, a defining characteristic of the British version of liberalism was that it operated within a cultural context far more sceptical about the role of the state than was the case on the European continent and privileged instead the role of individual agency. This emphasis upon individual as opposed to state action in turn contributed, as Geoffrey Finlayson has shown, to the rise of the various forms of voluntarism in the economy of social welfare that prevailed in Victorian Britain for much of the nineteenth century and that played an essential role in shaping the industrial state.[19] During the first half of the nineteenth century in particular and thus during the period that is my focus here, British liberalism's version of Foucault's category of 'secularized forms of pastorship [that] sought to strengthen society by maximizing the productive potential of individuals' was, as Goodlad has shown, one that deemphasised the role played by the state elsewhere in Europe and privileged instead the agency of an 'elaborate network of voluntary social practices'.[20]

In emphasising the turn away from reliance upon the state and privileging instead the role of the individual, Goodlad's work points towards a further issue that has passed largely without discussion in the scholarship of liberalism: the extent to which British and American versions of the ideology found common ground. During the first decades of the Victorian period in particular, that is, liberal progressives in both nations were alike in their scepticism over the state's capacity to successfully intervene in social formation and in their privileging instead of individual and local agency. In this regard, modern historians have noted the importance of Tocqueville's observations of and emphasis upon the special role played by voluntary associations in the development of American society. As Mary Kelley has argued, for instance, such associations became 'the key medium for articulation of the citizenry's concern with cultural uplift and moral reform . . . a powerful resource in the making of public opinion'.[21] Helping to shape the public sphere, volunteer groups were, as Kelley's study shows, foundational to the formation of civil society in the United States.

At the same time, however, Kelley has interrogated the masculinist assumptions of Tocqueville's account by exploring the complexities that emerged during the early decades of the nineteenth century as progressive American women increasingly challenged the constraints placed upon them by the roles of republican woman, wife and mother.[22] Resisting their assignment to a primarily domestic function of schooling their families in the virtues deemed essential to the advance of the republic, activist elite white women sought the opportunities to move into public life offered by engaging with voluntary associations and, increasingly, by becoming teachers in the expanding system of national education. Thus, while progressives in

Britain and the United States shared an emphasis upon individual and non-statist collective action, Kelley's work also points towards one of the ways in which the American version of Locke's intellectual legacy had been differentiated from the course of British liberalism. For a social contract that was both more formally and fully democratic than that which prevailed in the Old World had been profoundly complicated by, first, the development of the concept of republican womanhood as a mechanism for regulating women's participation in cultural life and public discourse and, second, by the emergence of resistance to that concept.

In this emphasis, Kelley joins Elizabeth Maddock Dillon, Gillian Brown and other scholars of the early literature and history of the United States in examining how the issue of republican womanhood illustrates the challenges American liberalism encountered as it attempted to reconcile its assumption that the principle of consent was foundational to a democratic society with the reality that women, as well as the vast majority of people of colour, in fact lived under state-sanctioned structures of constraint.[23] Taking the legal forms of, for the one group, married women's subjection to coverture, for the other, of slavery, and for both the lack of access to suffrage, the curtailing of the opportunity to give or withhold consent posed what came increasingly to be seen as a fundamental challenge to the very notion of a democratic society. Culturally, early American democracy reinforced its legal mechanisms through what Dillon has called the 'symbolics of sentimental liberalism', which privileged the role of the republican wife and mother, sequestrating adult women from the worlds of both political life and economic activity and limiting them to enjoying 'the freedom of the liberal subject through affective abundance and nonutilitarianism'.[24] In interrogating earlier critical discussions of republican womanhood that had framed it in terms of the separate spheres in which men and women were assumed to function, Dillon and Brown have thus turned our attention to the ways in which the early nineteenth century sees the emergence in the United States of a 'literary public sphere as a social space that links the public and private and mediates between the two'.[25] In this development, the American experience speaks to a larger division that was in fact characteristic of liberalism not only in the New World but also in the Old. For, at least during the first half of the nineteenth century, liberalism on both sides of the Atlantic largely left unquestioned the belief that its individual subject was male. As Dillon has argued, for example, by 'equating women, and particularly the reproductive capacity of the female body with biological constraint and absence of self-determination', liberalism placed them 'outside of the realm of choice that constitutes the political sphere' and preserved that sphere exclusively for masculine agency.[26] This assumption, which Dickens's work embodies largely uncritically, was one that Martineau worked to resist throughout her career as a professional woman of letters, and it becomes a fundamental point of distinction between the two authors' visions of what constituted a civil society and what was essential to liberal progress.

The fundamental incompatibility between Martineau and Dickens's understandings of the liberal project are further evident in an issue closely tied to these differences over the nature and role of women as liberal subjects: their contrasting representations of slavery and the abolitionist movement. As Anne Boylan and Deborah Gold Hansen have shown, women activists played an essential role in the push towards abolition through their engagement in local voluntary groups such as the Boston Female Anti-Slavery Society and, in turn, that engagement was fundamental to the new constructions of womanhood that emerged in the decades before the Civil War.[27] For Martineau, as Chapter 3 shows, the connection between abolitionism and resistance to the standing liberal assumption of the subject as male was essential to her representation of American society and, in particular, to her account of print media and the press. Dickens, by contrast, as Chapters 4 and 5 explore, represents slavery and the press in exclusively masculine terms and, in both his account of his own travels in America and in the fictional version of the nation developed in *Martin Chuzzlewit*, works to reinforce a more conservative formation of women within the bounds of domestic sequestration, excluded from the public sphere.

Transatlantic Connections

If the work of scholars focused on early American literature has helped point us towards a deeper understanding of the evolution of Lockean liberalism in the United States and its relationship with British liberal traditions, so too studies of transatlantic literary exchange have increasingly revealed the complexities of the history of the interactions between the print cultures of the Anglophone world. Paul Giles, for instance, has explored the 'series of reciprocal attractions and repulsions between opposing national situations' that occurred during the period between the American Revolution and the Civil War and has argued that 'a reverse projection of

Britain manifests itself in the consciousness of American writers, just as the prospect of America produces various forms of disturbance within English texts'.[28] Building from Giles, Joseph Rezek has examined the idea of provinciality as a concept that connects Irish, Scottish and American literary texts in their shared participation in the print world created and maintained by London in its role 'as the cultural capital of the Anglophone Atlantic'.[29] Exploring the ways in which 'the centripetal pull of London created a provincial literary formation that shaped the history of modern aesthetics',[30] Rezek demonstrates the extent to which texts that originated in the provinces were reissued or even initially published in the English capital. Finally, Amanda Claybaugh, Meredith McGill and Jessica DeSpain have all explored the phenomenon of transatlantic reprinting, with Claybaugh emphasising the importance of a single reading public to the development of the literature of reform, McGill focusing upon American reprinting culture as a form of resistance to the imperial reach of Britain, and DeSpain exploring relations between the textual body, the body politic and national identity formation in the United States.[31] Collectively, studies such as these have given us a deeper and richer understanding of transatlantic literary exchange and, in particular, moved us far beyond an earlier focus upon international copyright as the primary defining issue of that exchange.

Martineau and Dickens certainly did campaign for international copyright – indeed, Martineau enlisted Dickens's signature on a petition in its support that she organised and had presented to Congress in 1837[32] – but their engagement in transatlantic exchange went, as this project shows, far beyond that. Martineau, as I discuss in Chapters 2 and 6, not only contributed directly to the American press but also made use of transatlantic reprinting of British publications as a way to infiltrate her work into the hands of American readers whom she wished to influence on the issue of abolition. Dickens, Chapters 3 and 4 show, similarly made use of the recirculation of his work to address American readers, but his texts also both demonstrate those forms of disturbance Giles discusses and explore the relationship between America and Britain, the provincial and the metropolitan, and its role in the formation of national identity on both sides of the Atlantic. For both authors, then, albeit in significantly different ways, responding to the print media of the United States was a distinctive element in their expression of liberal values and a major component of their own professional development and the contribution each made to shaping the British press.

Martineau and Dickens

In examining Martineau and Dickens together in the contexts of Anglo-American liberalism, the dynamics of transatlantic exchange and the development of early Victorian journalism, this project redefines a longstanding scholarly narrative that has controlled our reading of their connection and maintained them in a hierarchical positioning that has obscured the significance of Martineau's role in the development of liberalism and her contributions to both the formation of the press and the emergence of the professional woman author. That is, for almost half a century, the Martineau/Dickens dynamic has been viewed in terms of the forceful narrative established by a single critical essay published in 1970. That study, K. J. Fielding and Anne Smith's '*Hard Times* and the Factory Controversy', examined a bitter quarrel in print that broke out between Dickens and Martineau over the course of a few weeks in December 1855 and January 1856.[33] To their readers at the time, the dispute apparently emerged out of nowhere in mid-December when Martineau published a pamphlet, *The Factory Controversy*, that took aim at *Household Words*'s treatment of the issue of industrial safety.[34] In her text, and despite the fact that she had contributed almost fifty articles to the magazine, Martineau was extraordinarily blunt in criticising Dickens's treatment of industrial safety and his dismissive appraisal of a bill to regulate factory working conditions that was then moving through Parliament. Judging both Dickens and the magazine as a self-styled 'avowed agency of popular instruction and social reform', she dismissed the editor as a 'humanity-monger' and recommended that 'he should not meddle with affairs in which rationality of judgment is required'.[35] A month later, responding with 'Our Wicked Mis-Statements' in the 19 January issue of his magazine, Dickens combined detailed refutation of the statistical data Martineau had used with language clearly intended to put her firmly in her place. Where she had labelled Dickens as wallowing in 'philo-operative cant' and for being a mere 'humanity-monger', for example, he countered by dismissing her text as nothing more than 'weakness in a sick lady whom we esteem', assailing her command of the facts, and closing with a resolve to 'blot her pamphlet out of our remembrance'.[36] Inevitably, this outbreak of hostilities made any further connections between the two combatants impossible and brought to an end their collaborative professional relationship.

Beyond the colourful language that each writer chose to apply to the other in such a public manner, what made this incident so remarkable was that it came after they had known one another for almost twenty years, had long moved in the same progressive circles and had had an extended history of collaboration. As far back as 1836, Martineau was still on her two-year visit to America when Dickens rose to fame with the serialisation of *The Pickwick Papers*, but she included a knowing reference to Sam Weller in one of the books she subsequently wrote out of her travel experiences, while he in turn had his Radical political young gentleman acknowledge the celebrity she had achieved through *Illustrations of Political Economy* and give 'all the young ladies to understand that Miss Martineau is the greatest woman that ever lived'.[37] Nor were their connections merely such textual niceties as these. In 1841, for instance, when Dickens was preparing to visit the United States, she wrote to a mutual friend expressing concern for and practical advice about the travel hardships his wife would face.[38] Throughout the 1840s, her correspondence demonstrates that she read his new works as they appeared, and she clearly kept up with the phenomenon that he became. At the end of the decade and in reviewing the period since Waterloo in her 1849 *History of the Peace*, for example, she celebrated the unique impact he had had upon early Victorian England when she described him as 'greatest among the novelists . . . the Boz who rose up in the midst of us like a jin with his magic glass' and defined him as 'a man of a genius which cannot but mark the time, and accelerate or retard its tendencies.[39] The following year, he returned the compliment by recruiting her as one of the initial contributors to *Household Words* and, between 1850 and 1854, she provided almost fifty articles to his phenomenally successful miscellany.[40] That two progressive Victorian writers, who had risen from modest provincial origins to take their place among the major voices of the age and who clearly had considerable regard for one another, should subsequently fall out so publicly and so bitterly was not simply remarkable, then, but seemed entirely out of keeping with the two-decade history of their relationship.

Fielding and Smith established what would become the presumptive explanation for this rupture with their '*Hard Times* and the Factory Act', an essay that first appeared in *Nineteenth-Century Fiction* and was subsequently collected into the major 1970 commemorative collection, *Dickens Centennial Essays*. Arguing, as its title suggests, that the quarrel originated with *Hard Times* and was, at its heart, a conflict between 'the inhuman school of political economy' Martineau represented and Dickens's 'deep concern both for the individual and for the quality of working-class-life', Fielding and Smith's essay claims that 'differences about political economy must have underlain and caused the whole disagreement'. Reviewing Martineau's pamphlet and the *Household Words* essays it attacks, they find the burden of truth lies with the latter and judge that Martineau's 'grasp of the situation was incompetent'. They go on to appraise the description of her connection with Dickens in the *Autobiography* that she wrote in 1855, when she was mistakenly diagnosed as being terminally ill, and, noting some inconsistencies, judge not simply that 'her account of her relations with Dickens' is 'misleading' but also that she is 'almost inconceivably irresponsible or forgetful about matters of fact'.[41]

For almost half a century, this essay was extraordinarily successful in sustaining Dickens's own injunction to blot Martineau out of remembrance, as it went almost entirely unchallenged by subsequent scholarship and its assumptions were absorbed into the critical episteme.[42] Of particular relevance for my focus here is the fact that it became part of the established narrative of Dickens's work as a journalist and his contributions to the Victorian press. Its conclusions are thus replicated throughout the major studies of this aspect of his life and career, from John Drew's *Dickens the Journalist* to Juliet John's *Dickens and Mass Culture*, Sally Ledger's *Dickens and the Popular Radical Imagination* and Michael Slater's monumental biography, *Charles Dickens*.[43] Although Drew's discussion of the dispute does interrogate Martineau's charges more extensively and sympathetically than the other studies, his account still ends by leaving the narrative established by Fielding and Smith fundamentally in place. While the episode has not drawn as much attention from scholars focused upon Martineau, even those who have commented on it have been unable to refute Fielding and Smith's narrative and call their judgement into question. Instead, from Valerie Pichanik to Deborah Logan, they have deflected the criticism by focusing on another issue: Martineau's claim in the *Autobiography* she wrote in 1855 but that remained unpublished until after her death in 1876 that an anti-Catholic editorial policy at *Household Words* had led Dickens and his sub-editor, W. H. Wills, to reject a story she had offered them in late 1854 for that year's special Christmas number. Taking their author at her word, as in Deborah Logan's comment that 'Martineau found Dickens's anti-Catholic bias offensive enough – as well as inappropriate in a family magazine – to resign her post', Martineau's defenders have also oversimplified the narrative of the quarrel and thus obscured its larger significance, reducing the dispute to the straightforward, if bitter, end of a long-standing professional and personal relationship and identifying it with easily identifiable, narrowly focused specific issues of disagreement.[44]

Fielding and Smith's essay was certainly not unreasonable in founding its reading of the dispute upon the issue of political economy, even if in its unreflective sexism it only too clearly reproduces the cultural norms prevailing at the time of its writing. Indeed, both Martineau and Dickens themselves offer abundant evidence for the extent to which Utilitarian principles and the theories of political economy had become so firmly established a part of the assumed conceptual fabric of the times as to be taken for granted. Despite the fact that she had risen to fame in the early 1830s through her popular series *Illustrations of Political Economy*, for example, even Martineau eventually recognised that political economy had become normalised to the extent that it had lost the freshness of novelty. Writing to a correspondent in 1848 about the tumultuous state of a Europe convulsed by revolution, she noted that 'The Middle Class does not want to be roused to political action by any thing in print; nor to be bored with Politl Economy at such a time' [sic].[45] Still more ironically, it was Dickens himself who actually offered a defense of political economy in defining the focus he had intended for *Hard Times*. Writing to his and Martineau's mutual friend Charles Knight, the publisher of improving material for working-class readers, he thus explained: 'My satire is against those who see figures and averages, and nothing else – the representatives of the wickedest and most enormous vice of this time – the men who, through long years to come, will do more to damage the real useful truths of political economy, than I could do (if I tried) in my whole life.'[46]

The epistemic centrality of political economy in mid-nineteenth-century Britain does not, however, mean that we should see it as a complete and comprehensive lens for understanding the development of liberalism and its relationship with print culture. Indeed, my argument here is that the reading of the quarrel between Martineau and Dickens established by Fielding and Smith has contributed to a narrowing of our understanding not simply of the local event itself but of the wider issues to which it gave expression and, in particular, to fundamental aspects of the ideology of liberalism and its relationship to the development of the Victorian press. As studies of nineteenth-century intellectual history suggest, for example, the Martineau/Dickens quarrel has been subsumed into what Donald Winch has called a large tradition of interpretation of the experience of industrial life in Britain. That tradition, shaped in a post-industrial and post-imperial era and running from F. R. Leavis through Raymond

Williams to E. P. Thompson, represents the Victorian proponents of 'political economy and utilitarianism ... as complicit with the worst aspects of this experience'.[47] Indeed, modern critical thinking has been so completely permeated by this view of Dickens's stance on Utilitarianism that it has prevented our giving Martineau, a public intellectual whose work was founded upon Utilitarian principles but who was also deeply committed to the liberal project, equal shrift in discussions of their relationship and of the era as a whole.

Beyond this reductive narrowing itself, framing the dispute between Martineau and Dickens simply in terms of difference over the conditions of life and work in an industrial society has left unexamined key points of contest that divided both them and progressive liberalism as a whole. Three such points will be recurring areas of attention throughout this study. First, and implicit within the narrower policy issue of industrial safety and its relationship to political economy, is a particular aspect of the relationship between state and individual agency that was, as Goodlad has shown, so central to British liberalism: the role of women in the public sphere and, especially, in promoting progressive causes. Second, and providing the essential locating context for any discussion of social policy and activism, is the development of mass forms of organisation and behaviour located in the new urban spaces that increasingly came to dominate nineteenth-century experience. Finally, and pointing to a fundamental divergence in Martineau and Dickens's understandings of liberalism, is the contest between rival master narratives of historical development that were in play during the early decades of the century. Specifically, the opposition between the post-Enlightenment model of stadial theory to which Martineau remained committed and a more complex, less optimistically teleological reading of historical analogy to which, as Devin Griffiths has argued,[48] Dickens became increasingly drawn, becomes the final defining point of difference between them.

Contested Liberalisms

As Kathryn Gleadle's work on British Unitarianism has shown, the growing emphasis on voluntarism Goodlad has identified as a central component of British liberalism also created new space for women to take on unprecedented public roles, even in the face of opposition from ideological friends no less than opponents. Partly as a result, over the course of the century the importance of female expertise became increasingly normalised and socially acceptable.[49] Unitarianism, with its emphasis upon providing girls access to educational opportunities commensurate with those available to boys, was a crucial agent of this change. While Dickens and Martineau were both, in varying degrees, affiliated with the Unitarian tradition and although they were themselves passionate exemplars of the voluntarism that was so essential to Britain's model of liberal progress, their beliefs on the education of girls and employment for women were fundamentally in opposition.[50] For Martineau, as Linda Peterson has explored, becoming educated and able to professionalise as a woman author provided her with the economic independence that she would advocate throughout her work for all women and also allowed her to model the possibility of an authorial career for the next generation of women writers.[51] Dickens, by contrast, profoundly resistant to female autonomy even among the authors he used for *Household Words* and *All the Year Round*, demonstrates far less interest in female education, had no comparable understanding of the significance of employment for women as an integral component of liberal progress and, indeed, as Lillian Nayder has explored, in both his own life and his writing, largely restricted women to traditional, domestically focused roles.[52] This opposition between the two, which as Brown and Dillon's explorations of the Lockean legacy in early American culture have shown, represents a larger division within liberalism as a whole, becomes one of the fundamental sources of the tension between them and most deeply defines their different embodiments of the liberal tradition. In many ways, that is, the Martineau–Dickens relationship, which reached its nadir with Dickens's concluding hope 'to blot her out of our remembrance', enacts the efforts to erase female agency and the resistance to such attempts that were found alongside one another not only in nineteenth-century social culture as a whole but also even among the advocates of liberal progress.

Over the course of the century, the emergence of new forms of urban concentration as the defining characteristic of modernity further complicated the tensions that existed within liberalism on both sides of the Atlantic. As Richard Dennis has shown, building on Lefebvre's theorising of urban spaces, the first appearances of mass forms of social organisation, consumption and transit that accompanied the growth of the nineteenth-century city also reveal 'the active role of space in stimulating new forms of representation and shaping new identities'.[53] The growth of the reading public Wills described in 'The Appetite for News' and the proliferation of sensationalist material that gave Dickens so much concern in his own manifesto for *Household Words*[54] thus, respectively, both express and react to these new forms of concentration and also point to the broader form of concentration that is my focus here – the development of print media within a rapidly urbanising society and, in particular, the function of the liberal press in addressing the needs of an expanding reading population.

In developing their own responses to those needs and thereby forming both their own journalistic identities and the press they were helping to shape, Martineau and Dickens contrast markedly in their responses to an urbanised society and the new identities it was shaping. Indeed, their own lives embody that contrast: Martineau, who lived in provincial Norwich until her late twenties, had a home in London for a total of less than five years during the 1830s and, in her work, consistently positions herself as a visitor to rather than a dweller in cities. By the mid-1840s she was settled into the house she had designed and built for herself in Ambleside in the Lake District and, as she wrote to the publisher John Saunders in May 1846, 'sitting here in my quiet home, in the quietest of valleys, or crossing the mountains which close it in, I watch the ways and fortunes of the world'.[55] Though she both was well aware of the conditions in which the rural working classes lived and remained in touch with the rhythms of national political life in London, she was, nevertheless, now permanently established in the outsider position from which she wrote for the remainder of her life, a position reinforced by her confinement to her home after the near fatal illness she suffered in 1855. Although Dickens would spend extended periods living outside England and eventually established a rural residence of his own with the purchase of Gad's Hill Place in 1856, in the mid-1840s he still identified as primarily an urban dweller. Later in that same summer Martineau had written to Saunders, he thus wrote from Lausanne to John Forster and agonised over how much living in Switzerland had made him feel 'the absence of streets and numbers of figures. I can't express how much I want these. It seems as if they supplied something to my brain, which it cannot bear, when busy, to lose ... the toil and labour of writing, day after day, without that magic lantern, is IMMENSE!!'.[56]

Beyond the subjective circumstances of their life experiences, however, the differences between Dickens and Martineau's constructions of the phenomenon of city life can be read as, on the one hand, built upon experiential engagement with it and, on the other, founded in a more purely conceptual reading. That is, Dickens's profound participation in the life of the city has long been recognised as one of his most salient characteristics and indeed, as Richard Dennis has noted, the city of the imagination his work constructs became for contemporary readers, and has remained for readers since, more real than actual or historical London.[57] That city, moreover, is essentially the city of imagined experience, written from within by the participating observer whose perspective is very different from that Martineau both advocated and assumed. For, and as she wrote of her visit to Charleston, South Carolina, in early 1835: 'It would be wise in travellers to make it their first business in a foreign city to climb the loftiest point they can reach, so as to have the scene they are to explore laid out as in a living map beneath them.'[58] Whether foreign or domestic, then, the city for Martineau is always more an object of attention and analysis than it is the generator of a distinctive form of human experience – though she comments extensively upon the major American cities she visited, for example, she largely confines herself to critical analysis and offers almost no experiential account of either herself or others as urban subjects. In broad terms, that is, the two authors' views of urban space can be framed as embodying de Certeau's contrast between the perception of the walker moving through the city at ground level and the panoptical view from above associated with cartographers and city planners.[59] Placing Martineau and Dickens's accounts of the nineteenth-century city in dialogue thus not only points to their fundamentally different responses to the movement of history expressed by the emergence of the mass city as the predominant form of human social organization, but also reveals the ways in which they construct those differences throughout their work in the press and in the relationships they create between the forms of journalism and those of fiction.

Finally, examining Martineau and Dickens as a binary dynamic reveals the complications that nineteenth-century experience brought to a fundamental aspect of the intellectual legacy bequeathed by the Scottish Enlightenment: the master narrative of historical progress encoded in stadial theory. Most fully associated with Adam Smith's development of the model, which defined human history as a sequence of progressive phases built around hunting, shepherding, agriculture and commerce respectively, stadial theory became an important assumption within Scottish Enlightenment thinking, although, as Dennis Rasmussen has pointed out, it in fact neither suggests a simple linear forward movement nor assumes that progress is inevitably and uniformly positive.[60] As Ella Dzelzainis's work has shown, moreover, stadial thinking informed both Martineau and Dickens's historical interpretation.[61] On the one hand, that is, it made up a fundamental and enduring component of Martineau's philosophy; on the other, it underlay and yet was also challenged by Dickens's observation of the United States during his 1842 visit. More broadly, however, stadial theory's fundamental assumptions of a generally progressive and unilinear historical structure and its faith in human ability to subordinate the natural world to the forces of economic agency both came under increasing pressure during the middle decades of the century. As Devin Griffiths has argued in his study of 'the decline of totalizing approaches to history and rise of more dynamic and comparative nineteenth-century modes',[62] 'unitary historical narratives' such as those promoted by stadial models were less and less able 'to provide a persuasive account of the uneven past' and, by the 1860s, had given way to new forms of comparative historicism that replaced the older paradigm and its faith in a fundamentally progressive arc to the trajectory of human social development.[63] Although the broad shift Griffith describes coincides precisely with Martineau's own career, my argument here is that it was a change to which she remained essentially resistant. That is, even as she sought to displace the triumphant Whig narrative represented most fully by Thomas Babington Macaulay's account of English history, Martineau remained a faithful proponent of stadial theory's underlying optimistic assumptions. In this, she and Dickens, whose reading of the historical narrative became increasingly sceptical, are finally and most fully divided not simply by differences over a single issue of factory legislation but in their most basic understandings of the potential of the liberal project to shape the future course of human civilisation.

The Formation of the Press

That W. H. Wills should in 'The Appetite for News' have made use of Frederick Knight Hunt's history of the fourth estate and that Dickens should have written to Charles Knight to explain his thinking about political economy points to a final organising focus of this project: the new light it sheds on the densely connected networks that constituted the world of Victorian publishing and the press. Knight, as Chapter 5 will show, was Martineau's essential ally in her attempts to develop journalistic forms to serve working-class readers in the mid-1840s; Hunt would, as Martineau gratefully wrote him, make her 'a gentleman of the press'[64] in 1852, when he invited her to write for that *Daily News* for which Dickens had been the founding editor and so launched her on the most influential phase of her career as a journalist; and Wills himself, as Chapter 6 will show, played a vital part in the events leading up to the quarrel of 1855–6. Examining the development of the Victorian press through the lens of Martineau and Dickens in dialogue thus not only offers us a new appreciation of the relationships between Anglo-American liberalism and the dynamics of transatlantic exchange but also provides us with new understandings of what Laurel Brake has called the 'ghostly dynamic of interlocking structures, referenced but otherwise invisible' that haunts the universe of nineteenth-century journalism. Connecting, for example, individual authors, publishers and printers, political and religious groups, and clusters of readers, these networks, as Brake has shown, formed multiple series of nodes and comprise 'a *structure*, the technic whereby cultural exchange takes place, and they are subject to the historically specific media of transmission at any given period'.[65] Recent work in periodical studies, such as Mary L. Shannon's account of a single London street,[66] has built from Brake's insight and explored the extraordinary compacted density of the world of the Victorian press and the ways in which it was shaped by the many varieties of personal familiarity and relational ties. This project, through illustrating the fissures and tensions within the liberal community, from London-based progressive authors, editors and publishers to members of the Unitarian denomination in both Britain and America and its struggles to remain united over the issue of abolition, seeks to take such work in a new direction and, by paying attention to the Anglo-American nature of the networks that shaped the Victorian press, to expand our understanding of the nature of the transatlantic community of letters in the first half of the nineteenth century.

Chapter Organisation

The transformational effect of Martineau and Dickens's respective experiences of the United States, which she visited from 1834 to 1836 and to which he travelled in the first half of 1842, is the foundation of this study and the focus of its first four chapters. Scholarly accounts of these visits have largely treated them separately, focusing upon a wide range of aspects of the two writers' representations of American culture and society and emphasising in both cases their critique of the failings of democracy in the United States and the deficiencies in the young nation's customs and manners. The single major exception to this individualised treatment and the most substantial comparative study of their travel books, Jerome Meckier's 1990 *Innocent Abroad: Charles Dickens's American Engagements*, voices a judgemental bias similar to that of Fielding and Smith's article on the 1855–6 quarrel. As its title suggests, this account privileges Dickens's depiction of the United States, and Meckier claims Dickens not only had a fuller understanding of the phenomenon that was America than did Martineau but also that his writing about it intentionally served to correct the 'overly confident meliorist's belief' of 'a lady Pangloss like Miss Martineau' convinced that history took the shape of 'a facile linear ascent toward an earthly paradise'.[67] Just has been the case with the Fielding and Smith ranking of the two authors's understanding of the factory safety issue, moreover, so Meckier's reading of their writing on America has had an enduring influence upon later scholarship and the assumptions with which Martineau has been appraised. It resurfaces, for example, explicitly in Juliet John's *Dickens and Mass Culture*, which finds that 'his analysis of Dickens's competitive critique of his predecessors is compelling',[68] and its lingering persistence remains implicitly evident in Ruth Livesey's description of Martineau's representation of American economic development as simply the enthusiasm of a 'radical rationalist'.[69] The assumption that Martineau writes about America in less complex, less valuable ways than Dickens, an assumption that Meckier's reading initiated and that subsequent scholarship has perpetuated, is therefore a particular object of my attention here and one that I seek to interrogate in order to show the full richness of both Martineau and Dickens's positioning within early Victorian transatlantic discourse and the importance of that positioning to their contributions to the formation of the press. Drawing from the work described above on transatlantic liberalism and Anglo-American literary exchange, then, I argue that efforts to gauge whether Martineau or Dickens's representation of America is the more accurate or to judge whether one of them should be subordinated to the other are both misleading and unproductive. Instead, this project argues, we stand to gain a far richer understanding by viewing them in tandem, examining their readings of the United States in terms of larger conversations about what a liberal society could and should be, about the role of print media and, in particular, the press in contributing to the advance of such a society, and then uncovering how the experience of America helped shape their own work in shaping the mass-market journalism that was beginning to take shape in Britain during the 1840s and that would develop rapidly after the repeal of the 'taxes on knowledge' in the 1850s.

To make this case, Chapters 1 through 4 contextualise and explore the two authors' visits to the United States, their writing out of those visits, and their responses to the critical reception with which their texts were met. Chapter 1 works to fill a gap in the critical conversation by connecting Martineau's early writing for and about the press with the intellectual legacy she derived from Enlightenment thought. In particular, it explores her modification of the stadial theory of social progress that she derived from Adam Smith as she blended elements from Smith's work on moral sympathy with Schiller's writing on aesthetics and the formation of a community of taste. After showing how both Smith and Schiller contributed to her understanding of the crucial role of public discourse as an essential agent of social progress, the chapter moves to examine her advocacy for the press in the years immediately before she travelled to America. Martineau's own journalism in the early 1830s, that is, makes a popularised version of the argument that was simultaneously being developed in the elite reviews, emphasising a vital connection between the promotion of universal access to education and the removal of the 'taxes upon knowledge' that inhibited the free circulation of information and ideas. Martineau's distinctive contribution to that argument, however, appears in two articles on Sir Walter Scott that she published shortly after his death in 1833, and the chapter concludes by arguing for a new reading of these essays as a combined statement of the essential need to write women into the narrative of history and a claim for her own authority to undertake such work.

Chapter 2 then considers the American visit itself, the ways in which the three books she wrote out of it depict the role of education and a free press in the formation of American democracy, and the critical reception they received on both sides of the Atlantic. By contrast with the dichotomous readings of a nation divided between North and South along the lines of slave-ownership that have been the norm in studies of her visit, readings that include Meckier's influential account, this chapter argues that the American books offer a more complex and nuanced analysis of a society whose regional variations are most fully understood in terms of the extent to which they either have developed or constrained the development of a free press and a print culture that facilitates the evolution and implementation of liberal ideals. Unlike any previous critical discussion, then, it pays particular attention to Martineau's representation of the western states and, above all, Cincinnati, which she portrays as an exemplar of economic and moral stadial progress and as a counter to Boston, for her the 'city of cant' and an unexpected bastion of resistance to liberal change. Finally, the chapter shows how Martineau returned home committed to finding ways in which her work could participate in and contribute to America's continuing advance and, in particular, focused upon prospective roles for herself in supporting the interwoven causes of abolitionism and of women's ability to become agents of social progress. Her two-year stay in America, in sum, proved decisive in shaping her into a transatlantic journalist.

Turning to Dickens, Chapters 3 and 4, respectively, examine *American Notes* and *Martin Chuzzlewit*. Interrogating John Drew's sense that *American Notes* is largely concerned with 'the invasive power of the press' and Juliet John's claim that it offers a 'dystopian vision of mass culture',[70] these chapters position the American visit in the contexts of both Dickens's ongoing efforts to find a role for himself in the press and his response to the widespread social unrest affecting Britain in the early 1840s. Showing how he arrived in the United States just as a newly established mass-market daily press was becoming ascendant on the East Coast, the chapters explore, first, how *American Notes* responds to the phenomenon of new forms of urban literacy and, second, the ways in which *Martin Chuzzlewit* addresses the relationship between literacy, print media and the experience of modern urbanism. As with Martineau, these chapters also consider the critical reception of Dickens's post-American books and the ways in which he in responded to that reception. Together, the two chapters argue that for Dickens America was far more than what has been generally perceived as an increasingly negative experience that chastened his understanding of the press and of mass culture. Rather, and notwithstanding all his complaints about Americans, tobacco and spit, the encounter with America in fact provided him with a new sense, at once disturbing and alluring, of the potential power of a cheap mass-market press led by entrepreneurial editors operating in a print environment unconstrained by state controls. Moreover, in writing about America, and above all in writing about its newspapers in both *American Notes* and *Martin Chuzzlewit*, Dickens for the first time discovered a methodology for fusing fiction and the press in ways that would be foundational to his most significant contribution to Victorian journalism, *Household Words* and its successor, *All the Year Round*. These chapters thus continue the critical recovery of two of Dickens's least studied texts and, for the first time, make the case that they are connected together as an essential, and vitally constructive, part of his journalistic development.

With Chapter 5, the focus returns to Martineau. Continuing what is the first comprehensive critical discussion of her evolution as a journalist, this chapter connects her contribution to shaping the Victorian press during its extraordinarily rapid evolution in the 1840s to her work for Dickens at *Household Words*. Interrogating Deborah Logan's claim that her career as a journalist only began 'in earnest in 1852 when she became a regular leader writer for the London *Daily News*' and arguing that Ian Haywood's placing her into the 'missionary or monitorial' role performed by 'polite journals of popular progress' diminishes her impact,[71] this chapter shows that her agenda for the press developed earlier and was far more nuanced than has been previously recognised. Establishing herself in the elite intellectual quarterlies, simultaneously working with Charles Knight on *The Penny Magazine* and other projects aimed at mass-market working-class readers, and contributing to Thornton Leigh Hunt and G. H. Lewes's progressive weekly *The Leader* in 1850–1, Martineau developed a remarkably flexible and constantly evolving journalistic presence that, in the 1850s and early 1860s, would allow her to become a consistent force in both mass-market and elite press venues, to appear, simultaneously, in daily, weekly, monthly and quarterly outlets, and to become indeed, as Justin McCarthy and Sir John Robinson would write, 'the most remarkable woman' of the age and the first 'in England who had taken to the regular work of daily journalism'.[72] It was this presence, I argue, that led Dickens in 1850 to invite her to become one of the first group of contributors to *Household Words* and to her going on to appear frequently in the magazine during its early years.

Chapter 6 returns to the dispute that brought an end to all direct connection between Martineau and Dickens and rewrites the established narrative of the quarrel in the context of the previous chapters of this project. It argues for a reading of the dispute that shifts away from the focus on *Hard Times* that had been central to Fielding and Smith and locates it, instead, simultaneously in the local disordered contingencies of the two authors' lives in 1855–6 and, more fundamentally, in their differences over the formation of a modern liberal state and the ways in which print and the press could contribute to its development. Drawing upon scholarship on nineteenth-century intellectual history, correspondence involving Dickens and Martineau that was not visible to Fielding and Smith, and archival research, the chapter also demonstrates how deeply embedded the quarrel was within the networks of mid-century journalism as the two combatants drew into their dispute friends and colleagues both of them had long known and with whom both had worked extensively. Framing this analysis with discussion of Martineau's first and final contributions to *Household Words*, both of which draw upon American subjects, the chapter shows that a bitter dispute that appeared so unlikely at the time it occurred was, in fact, the almost inevitable expression of Martineau and Dickens's fundamentally incompatible versions of liberalism.

Chapter 7 concludes the project by examining the after-life of the 1855–6 dispute with a focus upon Martineau and Dickens's final encounter or, rather, quasi-encounter, an aspect of the dynamic between them that has received no previous critical attention. Focused upon the cultural phenomenon that was Thomas Babington Macaulay, the chapter explores the ways in which Martineau and Dickens's divergent responses to the great exemplar of Whig historical narrative reveal their own evolving concepts of history and their advocacy for those concepts in their late work in the press. On the one hand, Dickens launched *All the Year Round* in April 1859 with the serial publication of *A Tale of Two Cities* and used the opportunity to articulate a remarkably modernist interpretation of comparative historiography that challenged the opposition of Carlylean and Macaulayan models of historical narrative. On the other, continuing her commitment to the stadial model of gradualist progress, in that same month Martineau defined the agenda for her late journalism with the publication of 'Female Industry' in the *Edinburgh Review* as she began to make her final round of arguments for gender equality in education and the expansion of women's access to professional opportunity. Using the occasion of Macaulay's death later that year to unsparingly define the limitations of his work and the historical paradigm it had developed, Martineau found herself embroiled in another dispute with a major canonical figure of Victorian letters in his editorial role. On this occasion, the disagreement was with William Makepeace Thackeray, a longtime friend and intellectual ally of the late historian and founding editor of the newly established *Cornhill Magazine*. Though the argument was less overt than the earlier dispute with Dickens, examining it in the wider context of Martineau's late journalism is no less revealing. For it shows, first, how she intentionally positioned herself against Dickens's new project at *All the Year Round*, and, second, how, through writing extensively and in a variety of venues about the nursing profession and educational opportunities for girls, she evolved her final roles in the press so as to continue her advocacy on behalf of progressive causes and her support for a vision of liberal social development that remained remarkably consistent with the positions she had first advocated in the early 1830s.

Notes

1. Nicholson, 'Transatlantic Connections', p. 166.
2. The *MLA Bibliography*, for instance, lists more than 8,350 entries for Dickens, and 249 for Martineau (last accessed 18 February 2019).
3. The assessment of Dickens was Lord Northcliffe's and is recorded in 'Charles Dickens as an Editor', p. 111; that of Martineau is by A. G. Gardiner, the great early twentieth-century editor of the *Daily News*, and is quoted in Koss, *Fleet Street Radical*, p. 91.
4. Hunt, who himself contributed twenty articles to *Household Words* in its first two years, had also been associated with the *Daily News* since its establishment in 1846 with Dickens as its founding editor. In 1852, then himself editing the paper, he would invite Martineau to join its staff, thereby initiating the most widely influential part of her career in the press. See below, Chapter 6.
5. [Wills], 'The Appetite for News', pp. 238–40.
6. Ibid. p. 239.
7. Ibid. p. 240.
8. Hewitt, *The Dawn of the Cheap Press in Victorian Britain*. Andrew Hobbs's *A Fleet Street in Every Town* appeared as I was completing this project; his account of the transformation of the newspaper world 'from the equivalent of a rowdy radical meeting to a vibrant but unthreatening street market' (p. 19) aligns with Hewitt's discussion and with the evolution I am exploring here through the work of Martineau and Dickens.
9. Brown, *Victorian News and Newspapers*; Wiener, *The War of the Unstamped*.
10. Hewitt, *The Dawn of the Cheap Press*, p. 175.
11. Ibid. p. 178. See also the discussion in Chapter 7 of Martineau and Arnold's differing views on liberal education and the formation of the British ruling classes.
12. Brown, *Walled States, Waning Sovereignty*, p. 141; Morrison, *Victorian Liberalism and Material Culture*, p. 15; Stout, *Corporate Romanticism*, p. 8.
13. Fawcett, *Liberalism: The Life of an Idea*, p. 35.
14. Ibid. p. 4.
15. Hadley, 'Nobody, Somebody, and Everybody', pp. 83, 84.
16. Steinlight, *Populating the Novel*, pp. 21, 30.
17. Goodlad, *Victorian Literature and the Victorian State*, pp. 91, 53, 56.
18. Ibid. p. 8.
19. Finlayson, *Citizen, State, and Social Welfare in Britain*, Chapter 1.
20. Goodlad, *Victorian Literature and the Victorian State*, p. 18.
21. Kelley, *Learning to Stand and Speak*, pp. 7–8.
22. Michael Hill, 'A Methodological Comparison', examines Martineau and Tocqueville's accounts of America from the perspective of sociological methodology, arguing that hers is superior because it drew upon

a far wider range of subjects than his interviews exclusively with elite white males.
23. Brown, *Domestic Individualism*; Brown, *The Consent of the Governed*; Dillon, *The Gender of Freedom*.
24. Dillon, *The Gender of Freedom*, p. 203.
25. Ibid. p. 6.
26. Ibid. p. 15.
27. Boylan, *The Origins of Women's Activism*; Hansen, *Strained Sisterhood*.
28. Giles, *Transatlantic Insurrections*, p. 11.
29. Rezek, *London and the Making of Provincial Literature*, p. 3.
30. Ibid. p. 2.
31. Claybaugh, *The Novel of Purpose*; McGill, *American Literature and the Culture of Reprinting*; DeSpain, *Nineteenth-Century Transatlantic Printing and the Embodied Book*.
32. Martineau, *Letters*, vol. 1, pp. 318–19.
33. Fielding and Smith, 'Hard Times and the Factory Controversy', pp. 22–45.
34. Martineau, *The Factory Controversy*.
35. Ibid. pp. 36, 44.
36. [Dickens and Morley], 'Our Wicked Mis-Statements', pp. 13, 19.
37. Martineau, *Retrospect of Western Travel*, vol. 3, p. 203; Dickens, *Sketches of Young Gentlemen*, p. 109.
38. Martineau, *Letters*, vol. 2, p. 104.
39. *Harriet Martineau's Writing on British History and Military Reform*, vol. 5, p. 309. I discuss this passage more fully below in Chapter 6.
40. For a complete listing see Lohrli, *Household Words*, pp. 357–61.
41. Fielding and Smith, 'Hard Times', pp. 29, 43, 33, 26, 27, 25.
42. The persistence of this understanding of the dispute was evidenced, for example, in a scholarly discussion of Martineau aired on BBC Radio 4's *In Our Time* in December 2016. Available at <http://www.bbc.co.uk/programmes/b084d7b0> (last accessed 12 June 2019).
43. See, in chronological order: Drew, *Dickens the Journalist*, pp. 123–8; Ledger, *Dickens and the Popular Radical Imagination*, pp. 189–91; John, *Dickens and Mass Culture*, p. 78; and Slater, *Charles Dickens*, pp. 309–10.
44. Pichanik, *Harriet Martineau*, pp. 203–4; Logan, *Writings on Slavery and the American Civil War*, p. 196.
45. Martineau, *Letters*, vol. 3, p. 104.
46. Dickens, *Letters*, vol. 7, p. 492.
47. Winch, *Wealth and Life*, p. 369.
48. Griffiths, *The Age of Analogy*.
49. Gleadle, *Borderline Citizens*, pp. 47, 50–2. See also Gleadle, *The Early Feminists*, Chapter 1.
50. Martineau's lifelong connection to Unitarianism has been widely discussed, including in the works by Gleadle cited above and in Ruth Watts's *Gender, Power, and the Unitarians*. With the exception of Walder's *Dickens and Religion* and Helen Aling's unpublished dissertation,

however, there has been surprisingly little extended attention to Dickens's relationship to one of the most important and influential Victorian denominations.
51. Peterson, *Becoming a Woman of Letters*, Chapter 2.
52. Nayder, *The Other Dickens*.
53. Dennis, *Cities in Modernity*, p. 1.
54. [Dickens], 'A Preliminary Word', pp. 1–2.
55. Martineau, *Letters*, vol. 3, p. 59.
56. Dickens, *Letters*, vol. 4, p. 612.
57. Dennis, *Cities in Modernity*, pp. 86–7.
58. Martineau, *Retrospect*, vol. 2, p. 71.
59. De Certeau, 'Practices of Space', pp. 122–45.
60. See Pocock, *Barbarism and Religion*, vol. 2, pp. 309–29, and Rasmussen, 'Adam Smith and Rousseau', p. 70.
61. Dzelzainis, 'Malthus, Women, and Fiction'.
62. Griffiths, *The Age of Analogy*, p. 56.
63. Ibid. p. 12.
64. Martineau, *Letters*, vol. 3, p. 276.
65. Brake, '"Time's Turbulence"', p. 115–16.
66. Shannon, *Dickens, Reynolds, and Mayhew on Wellington Street*.
67. Meckier, *Innocent Abroad*, p. 106.
68. John, *Dickens and Mass Culture*, p. 78.
69. Livesey, *Writing the Stage Coach Nation*, p. 128.
70. Drew, *Dickens the Journalist*, p. 63; John, *Dickens and Mass Culture*, p. 76.
71. Logan, *The Hour and the Woman*, p. 103; Haywood, *The Revolution in Popular Literature*, p. 125.
72. McCarthy and Robinson, *The 'Daily News' Jubilee*, pp. 44, 45.

Chapter 1

'The display of woman's naked mind to the gaze of the world': Harriet Martineau and the Press, 1830–1834

> Fame does not increase the peculiar respect which men pay to female excellence, and there is a delicacy, (even in rude bosoms, where few would think to find it) that perceives, or fancies, a sort of impropriety in the display of woman's naked mind to the gaze of the world, with indications by which its inmost secrets may be searched out.
>
> Nathaniel Hawthorne, 'Mrs Hutchinson'

Hawthorne's 1830 short story takes as its subject the history of Anne Hutchinson, a seventeenth-century midwife and religious leader who was banished from the Massachusetts Bay Colony for the prominent role she took in a 1630s religious schism that threatened to tear the Puritan community apart. For Elizabeth Maddock Dillon, who, as the Introduction showed, 'the antinomies of liberal subjectivity (embodiment/abstraction, private/public, female/male) are proposed in the structure of print', Hawthorne's treatment of Hutchinson's fate exemplifies the way in which antebellum liberalism in the United States 'renders women's authorship both potent and vexed as a public act'.[1] His story, then, speaks to the tensions inherent within a liberalism that both assumed the subject to be masculine and yet found itself confronting female subjects unwilling to be confined to their socially assigned, essentially private roles.

When 'Mrs Hutchinson' appeared in *The Salem Gazette* in December 1830, Harriet Martineau was still living privately in her family home in Norwich, writing frequently for the small-circulation Unitarian *Monthly Repository* but largely unknown to a wider reading public. By 1834, when she left for America on a journey that would last two years, her position had been transformed through the success of *Illustrations of Political Economy*. Published initially as a speculative venture with family members recruited into taking up subscriptions, the series was an almost instant success and was soon selling some 10,000 copies of each monthly number. Drawing readers from across the social classes, among them both Prime Minister Robert Peel and Princess Victoria, the *Illustrations* changed Martineau's life and professional position as decisively as the serialisation of *The Pickwick Papers* would alter Dickens's after its launch in 1836.² Established in London, become a household name on both sides of the Atlantic and subject to critical praise and assault for writing about a field that had previously been regarded as a wholly masculine preserve, Martineau had by the time she left for the United States quickly discovered not only the potential opportunities for a woman to become an actor in the public sphere but also the vexations attendant upon her seizing such agency. Her visit to America between 1834 and 1836, which Chapter 2 explores, would then become a further transformative experience as she encountered the complexities of a republic founded upon liberal principles but in considerable measure defined by the constraints placed upon both white women and all people of colour, constraints in which she discovered the press to be deeply imbricated.

Given the extent to which the *Illustrations* reshaped Martineau's life and professional position, it is hardly surprising that previous studies of this early phase of her career have largely focused upon them. Indeed, with the notable exception of Linda Peterson's *Becoming a Woman of Letters*, almost no attention has been paid to the ways in which her role in the press evolved rapidly during these years. In fact, however, and following immediately upon the first success of her tales of political economy, she sought both to build for herself a more expansive career as a journalist and, in so doing, spoke into a major contemporary debate upon the larger role of the press in a liberal society.³ Following Peterson, my argument here also explores Martineau's development during the early 1830s in terms of her conception of authorship and, in particular, her privileging of 'the ability to convince readers, to move them not just to feel but also to take action'.⁴ But where Peterson concentrates upon how Martineau carved out for herself a position in the London literary marketplace, this chapter focuses upon the ways in which, building upon her own variant of stadial theory, she both developed a case for the periodical press as a proponent of liberal progress and advanced a claim for her own authority to hold a position in that press as an agent of change. In this regard, Martineau's work in the period immediately before her visit to America importantly sets the terms for the ways in which she would experience the New World and was foundational to the role she would take in shaping the British press after her return.

This chapter, then, offers four interwoven perspectives to demonstrate the nature and extent of Martineau's impact upon the press that was developing in Britain during the early 1830s: first, it shows how Martineau formulated her own variant of stadial theory, a variant that built from her reading of Schiller and that placed particular emphasis on the role of public discourse; second, it contextualises Martineau within an ongoing debate in the elite quarterly reviews over the implications of the rapid expansion of the press in Britain that was occurring despite the restrictive efforts of the state to control that growth through the system of stamp duties; third, it demonstrates how Martineau's own contributions to that debate effected her transition from an anonymous contributor to a small, sectarian journal into the named subject, Harriet Martineau, a woman author who claimed her own identifiable voice in far more visible venues; and, finally, the chapter examines the critical reception of her work in this period, the mixture of praise and censure with which it was greeted and the first resistance she encountered to the 'display of woman's naked mind to the gaze of the world' that Hawthorne's story had shown could be seen as so troubling. The chapter closes with a brief discussion of *The Scholars of Arneside*, Martineau's final publication before she left for America and her most developed attack upon the pernicious effects of the 'taxes on knowledge', and, cumulatively, it demonstrates how, during the early 1830s, she laid the groundwork for an argument for women as autonomous liberal subjects taking a full role in the public sphere that would be foundational to her entire career.

Martineau and Stadial Theory

Adam Smith's theory of stadial development, which traces human progress through a sequence of phases built around hunting, shepherding, agriculture and commerce respectively, had become an important assumption within the Scottish Enlightenment and would be foundational to Martineau's thinking throughout her life. Though it was a grand unitary model of history in the way that Devin Griffiths has described, it was also a flexible one and subject to localised reinterpretation. That is, as Dennis Rasmussen has noted, it neither suggests a simple linear forward movement nor assumes that progress is inevitably and uniformly positive. As Rasmussen further points out, moreover, the concept was also useful as a comparative heuristic, a tool to measure different societies against one another.[5] For Martineau, stadial theory served in both these ways, functioning as a model and a methodology. While her version of it certainly does emphasise the broad advance of human progress, she clearly also came to value its comparative function as an analytical tool as well as a means of advocacy for the specific liberal causes that she most wished to support. Above all, and given her own formation within the English Unitarian community with its strong emphasis upon intellectual equality and the importance of female education,[6] Martineau's distinctive contribution to the stadial model would lie in the significance she attached to the advancement of women, a feature of her writing inseparable from her rise to prominence in the early 1830s. Indeed, even the *Illustrations of Political Economy*, as Ella Dzelzainis has shown, are permeated with a sense of the intrinsic connection between progress for society as a whole and women's being given 'equal access to the social and political institutions from which they had so long been unfairly excluded'.[7] Building on this foundational commitment, however, it was the visit to America and what she learned of women's experiences in an ostensibly democratic society that would prove transformational in shaping Martineau's commitment to making use of a transatlantic dialectic of stadial comparison to help advance feminist causes through the press.

If the basic stadial tenets that Smith outlined in *The Wealth of Nations* and, in particular, his *Lectures on Jurisprudence* were central to her own thinking, Martineau also drew heavily upon his *The Theory of Moral Sentiments* and its elaboration of a concept that became an essential component in her version of the stadial model. As Elizabeth Maddock Dillon has noted, in this latter text Smith emphasises sympathy as the basis for mutual understanding and 'shared norms of community behavior'. By modifying a Kantian ideal of freedom and autonomy, that is, sympathy and its extension into sentimentalism 'involves the capacity to bind a community through feeling and through affectively internalized moral codes'.[8] While Martineau's indebtedness to this aspect of Smith's work has been noted in earlier studies, what has not been fully recognised is the extent to which she engaged with Friedrich Schiller to further modify Smith and develop her own variant of the stadial model, a variant that had significant implications for her understanding of the role of the press and her own contributions to it.

For Schiller was an early and enduring influence upon Martineau, and his work played a crucial role in the theory of the press that she developed during this early phase of her career. By the late 1820s she was reading him in the original German and translating passages for the *Monthly Repository*,[9] and in the mid-1840s she freely acknowledged her indebtedness to him in letters to correspondents as diverse as Elizabeth Barrett and Edward Bulwer Lytton – to the latter, indeed, she described him as 'almost the supreme idol' of her youth.[10] Forming a crucial link in the transmission of Enlightenment theory into the age of Reform, Schiller not only played a broad role in the early nineteenth-century propagation of Smith's sense of the nature and role of sympathy into an aesthetic but also, as Dillon shows, connected that aesthetic to the process of social change, advocating its role in securing progress since it 'both enables freedom and constructs social unity and agreement. The aesthetic instructs individuals about their own capacity for freedom while allowing the liberal polis to operate as a community of taste.'[11]

For Martineau, this sense of the liberal polis as a community of taste provided the foundation for the conceptual model of the public sphere that she formulated during the 1830s and to which she gave fullest expression in *How to Observe Morals and Manners*, the methodological text she began en route to America, completed after her return home and published in 1838. Drawing upon Schiller's model, that is, she describes how the cultural observer who is able to transcend 'the complete set of dogmas with which he was perhaps once furnished' can instead learn to appreciate 'the vast effects of a community of sentiment' and come to realise 'that moral power is the force which lifts man to be not only lord of the earth, but scarcely below the angels'.[12] Schiller, then, was for Martineau, an essential catalysing influence upon her conjoined development of Smith's theories of both social history and moral sympathy in the service of liberal progress and, as we shall see, his thought permeates her own vision for the transatlantic press and the role she would take in it.

As she brought Smith and Schiller's theories together into her own variant of stadial theory, moreover, Martineau essentially differentiated herself from Smith in, as Lisa Pace Vetter has shown, the way she moves away from his emphasis upon imaginary shared experience. In its place, Vetter argues, Martineau saw 'discourse' as the essential means by which such sympathy is generated and the vehicle through which a community of taste is constructed, since it is through such discourse that the free exchange of opinion Locke had argued was essential to a liberal society is allowed to develop.[13] The penultimate chapter of *How to Observe Morals and Manners* thus focuses upon the importance of discourse to a full understanding of any society or culture as Martineau decrees that 'the Discourse of individuals is an indispensable commentary upon the classes of national facts which the traveller has observed'; further, she stresses that the open exchange of information and interpretation is vital if the observer is to learn the true state of any society: 'each time that his mind grasps a definite opposition of popular opinion, he has accomplished a stage in his pilgrimage of inquiry into the tendencies of a national mind'.[14] The free expression of that national mind is, moreover, for Martineau an essential indicator of a society's development through the stadial phases and is revealed, she suggests, by the forms taken within a culture by what she calls 'utterance'. In the section of *Society in America* devoted to the discussion of this term (see below, Chapter 2), she defines it as 'the ideas of the people put into language by an individual',[15] ideas most fully expressed by 'popular books' through the evolution of a national literature. While a number of contemporary reviews scoffed at her coinage of the term,[16] it becomes an enduring part of her analytical vocabulary, expressing the need for a free circulation of knowledge and opinion through forms of public discourse that she sees not simply as foundational to her response to the American democratic experiment but, more broadly, as integral to the evolution of a liberal society, the role of the print media, above all the press, and her own agenda for herself as a writer.

Interrogating the Press in the Reform Years

Martineau's innovative expansion of stadial theory to include the relationship between social progress and public discourse developed in the context of an ongoing intellectual debate over the British press that was occurring during the years around the first Reform Act and while her own journalistic career was taking shape. As Martin Hewitt has shown, on the one hand, radicals' frustration at the limitations of the 1832 changes to the political system prompted the 'appearance of several hundred unstamped titles between 1830 and 1836'; on the other, the Whig government responded by both intensifying its efforts to prosecute the printers of such papers even as it sought to appease moderate radicalism with minor adjustments to the stamp duties.[17] Simultaneously, the nature and role of an expanding fourth estate became a recurring topic of discussion in the press itself, most notably within the elite quarterlies that would, over the course of Martineau and Dickens's careers, gradually see their domination of the public sphere eroded by the proliferation of new forms of journalism that spoke to a wider range of readership across the population. As far back as 1824, for example, James Mill had written extensively on the topic of periodical literature in the first two issues of the newly founded *Westminster Review*, focusing upon the need to develop 'a regular and systematic course of criticism' for a form that had taken upon itself the 'task of supplying nourishment to the human mind' upon 'all the most important questions of morals and legislation'.[18] Mill's essays would find frequent successors over the next decade, with contributions ranging from the progressive vision offered by Henry Brougham in the Whig *Edinburgh Review* to the more conservative appraisal offered by Archibald Alison in *Blackwood's Edinburgh Magazine*.[19] As reform changed the nation around them and as the literary marketplace in which they existed evolved so quickly, the extant powers of the press thus pondered on their form's larger role in a period of unprecedented social transformation and, by implication, on their own future standing in the rapidly shifting world of early Victorian print media.

Among these articles, Gibbons Merle's 'Journalism' in the January 1833 issue of the *Westminster Review* is particularly helpful for our understanding of Martineau's positioning within the ongoing debate over the role of the press and, indeed, of her standing within the press itself. For, although the *Westminster* was the progressive journal into which Martineau would be welcomed after her return from America and with which she would enjoy a close, if at times fraught, connection for the next twenty years, in 1833 and at the outset of her career she had not yet gained access to such elite intellectual venues.[20] While Merle's essay does parallel the case for the importance of a free press that Martineau was already making in the journals where she was able to contribute, however, it is silent on the need to expand the press's outreach to working-class readers, a topic about which she was already becoming concerned and which would become, as Chapter 5 shows, central to her work during the decade after her return from America.

Best known for having introduced the word itself to the English language from the French (OED), Merle's 'Journalism' exemplifies Goodlad's argument that nineteenth-century British liberalism was differentiated from its European counterparts by the ways in which it resisted statist constructions and control. To be sure, Merle initially appears to be taking his reader in a quite different direction, as he describes the uncertain social standing of the 'new power' of the press in Britain and the precarious position of 'the unhappy dealer in public instruction'.[21] By contrast, he suggests that in France 'to be a journalist, is to be a person of note; to be an editor, is to be a person of accredited power'.[22] It soon emerges, however, that the prestige enjoyed by French journalists has been gained at a high price, as Merle scornfully goes on to recount how Bonaparte transformed the press into an arm of the state, raising its status while he ensured that it was placed under tight political control, leaving it 'bound hand and foot' even if 'its chains were gilded'.[23]

However, although Britain is, Merle implies, happily free from such intrusive governmental interference, if only because no politician would risk his social standing by writing for the daily press, his argument then transitions to make the liberal case against another form of state intervention – the stamp duties. Plagued by these 'taxes on knowledge', he suggests, the press in Britain has been unable to develop fully, and the consequence of the capital requirements needed to establish and maintain a newspaper has been to create a monopoly in the industry to which 'must be attributed the incongruities, the absurdities, in short the inaptitude, of the daily press'.[24] Remove but this barrier, he claims, and the press is certain to experience change comparable to that which parliamentary reform may only possibly accomplish.[25] That such change is urgently needed, he goes on to argue, derives from the potential of the press as an agent of influence in a mass society and

> arises chiefly from the power of spreading its opinions whatever they are, from its means of rapid communication and perpetual transmission. A sentence though feeble in itself gains a momentum merely by its being sent before ten thousand individuals at the same instant.[26]

Drawing upon a rhetoric that merges economics, education and moral improvement and that also permeates Martineau's prose whenever she writes of the social benefits of literature and press, Merle concludes by imagining a future in which the currently 'unhappy dealer in public instruction' will give way to

> persons possessing peculiar talent or information, who now hold off from the newspaper press or are excluded from it, to come forward in the shape most agreeable to their habits, and throw all the weight of their ability into the general banks of intelligence. The newspaper would become as it is in France, the Exchange of opinion, the political University.[27]

With the reduction of the advertisement duty by 50 per cent later in 1833, a similar cut in the excise duty on paper in 1836 and the reduction of the stamp duty to 1d in 1836, the movement for a free press would soon yield significant results.[28] Even if its victory remained incomplete and the battle for a complete removal of the 'taxes on knowledge' would continue for another two decades, Merle's essay thus coincided with a major shift in the conditions under which Victorian journalism could develop, a shift that would provide the essential context for Martineau's own emergence as a 'dealer in public instruction' who sought to extend her activity and influence by moving beyond the writing on political economy through which she had achieved her initial place in the public sphere to treat an increasingly diverse range of issues in a remarkable range of venues.

'A grand amelioration of the state of humanity': Martineau and the Press, 1832–1834

Even before Merle's article appeared in January 1833, Martineau had taken the opportunity to intimate similar sentiments on the importance of a free press to the advance of liberal society. In so doing, she aligned herself with a progressive middle-class movement to which, as we saw in the Introduction, Dickens would later make his own contributions through his work as the founding editor of the *Daily News* and the creation of *Household Words*. What distinguished Martineau from both Merle in the early 1830s and from Dickens in the mid-1840s and early 1850s, however, was the extent to which she made integral to her advocacy for the free press a conjoined case for the importance of universal education and the explicit emphasis she placed upon education for women and the value of their claiming a place in the public sphere. Through the course of 1832, that is, in both the *Illustrations* and her own journalism, she joins in with the wider debate on the press, advocates for universal access to education, noting its special importance as a means of creating agency for women, and argues for her own authority to contribute to national discourse. Her emerging presence appears most fully in the two essays on Sir Water Scott that she published in *Tait's Edinburgh Magazine* as, barely six months after the first monthly number of the *Illustrations* appeared, she took for her topic the greatest author of the age and, anticipating a strategy she would deploy throughout her career, used the occasion of a writer's death to position him for her readers in terms of a specified narrative of history and to create an alternative rendering she wishes to represent both through her own work and in herself as a writing subject.

Martineau's connecting of liberal progress, education and the press is frequently evident in the articles she wrote for the *Monthly Repository* throughout 1832, the final year in which she was a major contributor to the periodical. Making a characteristic stadial assumption that the movement 'towards the establishment of national or universal education, is . . . decisively prophetic of a grand amelioration of the state of humanity', she also speaks to the political turbulence of the historical moment as she represents such education as a potential source of social stability, since 'the probabilities of internal peace and ministerial leisure are much lessened, the longer the people are left in a state of ignorance under increasing burdens'.[29] In the continuing absence of an actual system of such universal education, however, she notes simultaneously the importance of the press as a vehicle of mass instruction but also the limitations evident in its current state of development. Her 'On the Duty of Studying Political Economy' in the magazine's January issue, for example, thus adroitly endorses her own newly appearing *Illustrations* as she notes that knowledge of the science is confined to a few, that it is not taught in any of the nation's schools, universities or churches and that 'the press alone is open'[30] to the discipline's advocates. A month later, however, she follows up by commenting upon that same press's current lack of efficacy: 'the periodical press is at work upon politics as well as literature; but in what way? – stumbling on amidst a dark accumulation of facts, or finding an uncertain and perilous way by the light of passing events'.[31] Though she does not yet define any general alternative to this unfortunate state of affairs, through combining the diagnosis with the simultaneous appearance of her own first efforts to address it in the *Illustrations* she does implicitly position herself as a 'dealer in public instruction' working through her own form of periodical education to guide her readers through the 'dark accumulation of facts' that besets them.

The optimistic assumptions that underlie her description of the potential of universal education are further complicated during 1832 by her first treatment of a negative exemplar of stadial progress that would become a recurring focus throughout her career: the condition of Ireland under British rule.[32] Having made an extended visit to her brother James at his Unitarian congregation in Dublin the previous summer, Martineau had seen at first hand the effects of a colonial system that imposed taxes upon a Catholic population to support the Protestant Church of Ireland and that, through the legal mechanisms of agrarian tenantry, condemned the rural working class to structural poverty. Both her criticism of British imperialism and her sympathy for the Irish themselves are evident from her forceful comments in the October 1832 essay 'National Education' and, most extensively, in the ninth number of the *Illustrations*, 'Ireland', which appeared the following month. Noting that the national 'eagerness for education is universal' and that parents' 'greatest anxiety is, that their children should have an education', she counters conventional stereotypes about Irish ignorance and, instead, unreservedly criticises British rule for the thwarting of these hopes:

> Nothing can be more complete than the perversion of power, the misapplication of a people's best resources, in the case of Irish education. The intellectual qualities of the people are just so far exhibited as to prove what they might be made; and they are seduced and driven into crime by management and oppression, so as conspicuously to show how mighty an agent education is for evil, if it be not one made for good.[33]

Implicitly connecting her discursive writing for the *Monthly Repository* and her fictionalised instructional texts aimed at a wider reading public, Martineau anticipates the fate of Dora Sullivan, the intelligent young woman at the centre of 'Ireland' who is forced to leave school in order to support her family through spinning, becomes embroiled in her husband's desperate turning to violent crime out after a legal technicality leads to the loss of their tenancy, and who ends transported to the colonies. In her 1832 account of Ireland under imperial rule Martineau thus not only represents the fragility of stadial progress as a whole but also highlights the vulnerability facing women who seek through education to differentiate themselves from the customary norms of their culture. Both points would become central to the far more extensive explorations of liberal republicanism in the United States that she would develop following her visit to America, and are also fundamental to the periodical articles of 1832 that did the most to establish her presence in the liberal press – the two articles she wrote for *Tait's Edinburgh Magazine* analysing, respectively, the genius and the achievements of Sir Walter Scott, who died in September that year.

These essays, which provided Martineau her first opportunity to make strategic use of a genre to which she returned throughout her life – and, indeed, in her own case, beyond it – that of obituary writing, have received considerable attention, and my argument here profits in particular from Ella Dzelzainis's examination of their relationship to the *Illustrations* and Linda Peterson's discussion of the way Martineau used them to launch her career as a woman of letters.[34] My emphasis, however, places the two essays within the detailed context of Martineau's early journalism to show, first, how significant it was that they appeared in the venue that they did and, second, how they blend a core element of her progressive vision – that of resistance to the erasure of women as agents of social progress – with an understanding of Scott's representation of historical narrative that, ultimately, points to an element of intellectual conservatism that was built into her own version of the stadial model.

At the time of Scott's death, Martineau had just become a contributor to the newly founded *Tait's Edinburgh Magazine*, a move that allowed her to expand significantly her role in the periodical press. In June 1832 William Tait recruited her, now widely celebrated for her *Illustrations*, and she had responded with enthusiasm to the opportunity to appear in a periodical that avowed radical sympathies, included contributors such as Mill and Leigh Hunt and that, with Christian Johnstone as a key member of its staff, aligned well with Martineau's own ambitions as a professional woman author.[35] And, importantly, by going against the prevailing practice of anonymous contributions under which she had written for the *Monthly Repository*, *Tait's* provided her first opportunity to appear in the press under her own name and thereby increase her visibility beyond that which she had established as the author of the *Illustrations*.[36] By the September issue, she had provided Tait with two contrasting pieces: the unlikely combination of a Gothic tale of parricide, and a story lamenting the tariff structures impeding trade with China that was a more predictable piece of work from the author of the *Illustrations*. Scott, however, offered a much larger subject and, the month following his death, she wrote to tell her editor that she was writing two articles on him, hoping to show 'how far he has <u>unconsciously</u> opened a way for a new species of literature'.[37] Two weeks later, she sent along the second of these articles, hoping that it, 'as being of a different character from any I have seen, or anticipate on Scott, may interest your readers' and assuring the editor that 'I have done my best to make my argument instructive.'[38]

Indeed, she had, and the space and freedom that Tait provided to treat her subject expansively allowed her both 'to inquire into the discipline of the genius of Scott' and 'to attempt an estimate of the services that genius has rendered to society'.[39] After noting how 'the discipline of natural vicissitude' resulting from his ill health as a child had proved foundational to the formation of his sensibilities, she goes on to praise Scott's purity of character, his authorial modesty and his understanding of 'the importance of his office as an exhibitor of humanity'.[40] His works, she notes in her second essay, have helped advance the ideal of civilisation not only in Scotland but throughout the world wherever they have been read,[41] exposing the dangers of 'priestcraft and fanaticism', 'satirizing eccentricities and follies' and broadly fostering a 'spirit of kindliness'.[42] For all this praise of Scott's character, however, she also calls out two major lacunae in his vision: first, an ignorance of the lower classes of society and the limitations this creates for his ability to perceive the course human history was taking.[43] For all his immense accomplishments, that is, she claims that Scott's 'Toryism prevented his recognizing the ultimate purposes of society' and notes with regret that 'he had not faith in man collectively as he had in individual man, and could not resist the sadness with which political change inspired him'.[44] Second, and far more scathingly, she comments upon his use of the term 'womankind'[45] as an indicator of what, in her assessment, is his greatest deficiency:

> The best argument for Negro Emancipation lies in the vices and subservience of slaves: the best argument for female emancipation lies in the folly and contentedness of women under the present system, – an argument to which Walter Scott has done the fullest justice; for a set of more passionless, frivolous, uninteresting beings was never assembled at morning auction or evening tea-table, than he has presented us with in his novels.[46]

Connecting the representation of women with the abolitionist cause in a way that anticipates her writing about America and listing the four female characters in the entirety of Scott's fiction whose exceptionality affirms the larger pattern, Martineau concludes the article, and her assessment of the then best known and most influential novelist of the nineteenth century, with the scathing verdict that 'he has advocated the rights of woman with a force all the greater for his being unaware of the import and tendency of what he was saying'.[47] Coming perhaps both to praise and bury the hapless late author, Martineau thus presented herself to the respectable middle-class readership of an avowedly progressive magazine founded in the Scottish capital as an unabashed proponent of change who, for the first but by no means the last time in her career, was willing to make use of the passing of a beloved canonical male literary figure to advocate for the causes to which she was most deeply committed and, simultaneously, to establish her own public voice through articulating those causes.

If the essays on Scott thus constitute both a powerful statement of Martineau's boldness as a newly famous professional author and demonstrate the particular emphasis she placed upon women's agency, they also implicitly reveal a characteristic of her work that has not been previously noted and that complicates her form of liberalism: the intellectual conservatism latent in her own adherence to the Enlightenment stadial model. To Martineau, the greatest accomplishment of Scott's career lay in the way in which his novels 'achieved a great moral work of incitement and amelioration' and have collectively 'taught us the power of fiction as an agent of morals and philosophy'.[48] In critiquing his 'Toryism', however, she characterises him as a fundamentally nostalgic figure, defined by 'his perpetual, fond recurrence to the past, his indisposition to change', unable to 'resist the sadness with which political change inspired him'.[49] Martineau's Scott, then, is a magnificent exemplar of stadial progress, a moral teacher who had reshaped the novel in unprecedented ways, and yet, finally, a writer who remains limited by his failure to represent the lives of the working classes and, above all, of women, and thus one whose novels provide 'no long-sighted views respecting the permanent improvement of society – no extensive regards to the interests of an entire nation', and who is bound to the past at a moment in history when 'the serious temper of the times requires a new direction of the genius of the age'.[50]

Recent scholarly understandings of Scott, however, suggest that, in holding him up as such an incomplete proponent of stadial change, Martineau failed to see the fundamental complexities in his representation of historical narrative. Devin Griffiths, in particular, has explored the challenges Scott's fiction poses to the underlying assumptions of the stadial model, arguing that the Waverley novels 'negotiate the relation between history and modernity through moments of transition and contact and, in this way, destabilize confidence in a history composed of isochronous periods'. Substituting 'Enlightenment models of history for complexly graduated relations within and over time', that is, Scott created 'a capacious sociology of the past for which [he] did not yet have a vocabulary', but which his successors would recognise.[51] Working with a model that, even though evolved to incorporate the emphases of her own form of liberalism, still retained its fundamental continuity with Enlightenment stadial theory's basic structure, Martineau thus reveals in these two essays her own commitment to a unitary historical narrative structured into those isochronous periods that Scott's novels in fact called into question and that Dickens, as Chapters 4 and 7 will argue, would increasingly challenge over the course of his career.

If Martineau's two essays on Scott do not, then, entirely capture the complexities of his rendering of the arc of history, they certainly made complete sense in terms of the trajectory of her own budding career in the press. Appearing less than a year after she had come to prominence with the serial publication of *Illustrations of Political Economy*, they consolidated her move away from the secluded venue of the *Monthly Repository*, with its modest readership among Unitarian readers. Indeed, establishing a pattern she would repeat throughout her career, success in new forms of publication foreclosed her connection to those in which much of her work had previously been appearing. By the end of 1832, as the *Illustrations* continued to prosper and the newfound opportunity with *Tait's* opened up, Martineau had effectively moved to give up writing for the *Repository*: of her eighty-two contributions to the magazine between May 1827 and January 1834, sixty-five had appeared before the *Illustrations* began its run and, after a flourish in which she provided sixteen additional pieces during the first great year of her success, she gave it only two last items.[52] Taking Scott as her subject for *Tait's*, then, had been a powerful move towards confirming her own newly achieved standing as a major cultural commentator for the age and establishing herself as an authoritative voice in periodical journalism beyond the more secluded venues of the denominational press.

'The peculiar respect which men pay to female excellence'

In assuming such prominence, however, and as had been the case in Hawthorne's account of the fate of Anne Hutchinson, Martineau would soon discover that fame did not simply 'increase the peculiar respect which men pay to female excellence', as the developing history of the critical reception of the *Illustrations* soon revealed. While the reviews of Martineau's tales have received considerable attention, that is, what has not been previously noted is the extent to which opinion shifted against her after 1832. While *The Examiner* had early evidenced some mixed emotions in both praising the work as 'scarcely to be surpassed in interest, character, and truth', yet also describing it as 'Miss Martineau's *Politico-economical Pap*, only one shilling',[53] in general those reviews that appeared during 1832 were, across the political spectrum, effusively enthusiastic. Christian Johnstone's notice in the progressive *Tait's*, for example, was hardly surprising in its enthusiasm for its new contributor as 'entitled to rank high among those gifted females whose writings have of late so eminently benefited their country'.[54] Far less predictably, though, William Jerdan concluded his eleven columns in the pro-Tory *The Literary Gazette* in similarly gushing terms: 'We know no library in which her works are not worthy to have place; and to the general class of readers their value is incalculable.'[55]

It was only later that the critical reception began to sour and that those reviews that have been highlighted in previous studies of Martineau in fact appeared. What Martineau herself described in the 1850s and with evident residual bitterness as John Wilson Croker's gleeful 'tomahawking Miss Martineau in the Quarterly'[56] was not published until April 1833, for instance, while the most widely discussed of the negative commentaries, William Maginn's image of Martineau in his *Fraser's* 'Gallery of Literary Characters. No. XLII. Miss Harriet Martineau', which has been richly analysed by Ella Dzelzainis, Deborah Logan and Linda Peterson, did not appear until November 1833.[57] This image is certainly foundational to how we have understood Martineau's reception: Peterson, for example, has suggested how the illustration 'admits the disruption' Martineau had created in the literary field and satirises her exchanging a 'place within a family setting for a place in the public realm of literary production', while for Dzelzainis the image reveals a recognition of 'Martineau's prioritization of the reasoning mind over the feeling body' and resistance to this as 'a claim for equality of rights for women'.[58] Although we cannot directly tie the shift in critical reception to her publication of the essays on Scott, my point here is that this shift did indeed occur after their appearance and after she had made use of the death of the dominant canonical male writer of the age both to protest against the erasure of women and implicitly launch her own claim to have a major voice in the public sphere. Coincidental or not, the display of this woman's naked mind to the gaze of the world certainly evoked a remarkably hostile critical response and anticipates a pattern that would recur throughout her career, most notably in her dispute with Dickens in the mid-1850s.

'I do not see that they want news any more than gin'[59]

By the end of 1833, Martineau had thus transformed herself from a provincial writer in Norwich barely known outside the networks of Unitarianism into a professional author moving in London's elite intellectual circles and read throughout the Anglophone world. Building on the overnight sensation of the *Illustrations of Political Economy*, she had taken her first steps into the rapidly expanding press of the Reform years and, as we have seen, both criticised the condition of that press and was critiqued by its established powers. As she began to build her own national presence as a journalist, moreover, she offered her own first comments on the role of the press in advancing her commitment to forms of liberal progress founded upon a stadial theory of historical development that she had long considered and would express most fully in the books she published after her return from the United States. But before she left for America, she also wrote one last piece on the press, *The Scholars of Arneside*, her most extended commentary on the current condition of the press in Britain. Almost unmentioned in previous discussions of her work, this text not only reveals the distinct emphasis she brought to the question of the 'taxes on knowledge' but also prefigures the lens through which she would examine the state of the press in the New World. It becomes, then, foundational to the transatlantic comparison she was to make over the function of the press in Britain and America as an agent of stadial progress in advancing the formation of liberal society.

The Scholars of Arneside was the final instalment in Martineau's *Illustrations of Taxation*, a series that, as its title indicated, was intended to follow up on the success of her series on political economy. Completed on 15 July 1834 'at ten minutes before five o'clock in the afternoon'[60] and less than three weeks before she sailed to America, this closing tale marks her most explicit statement on the condition of the press, the 'taxes on knowledge' and the relation of both to social stability in an industrialising society. On one side, *The Scholars of Arneside* portrays the gentry of a northern mill town, who, as one of its leaders suggests with his contemptuous comment about working-class drinking, reject the very notion that improved access to education, literacy and information could be beneficial to the masses. On the other hand, the narrative centres around Owen Ede, son of an impoverished widow, whose aptitude for learning first secures him advancement in the local paper mill, then leads him into writing for the press and eventually takes him into managing one of those unstamped weekly papers that, by the mid-1830s, were increasingly challenging the legal barriers to an unfettered fourth estate. Ultimately, however, *The Scholars of Arneside* offers no happy account of the working man self-made through the agency of literacy and serving the cause of progress through the press. For the story ends on a much darker note: Owen's less literate, less talented brother is galvanised by reading scraps of newspapers into participating in a primitive form of unionisation, falls afoul of the authorities and ends in prison; a rural mob, agitated by crop failures, illnesses and distress, demonises their mother, the village folk healer, and, assailing her cottage, inflicts 'a night of horrors ... seldom to be heard of, even in the remotest haunts of ignorance' that leads to her death; and Owen himself, surveying the destruction, can only lament the results produced by those 'who take pains, – for any purpose, – to hold men ignorant ... keeping the mind without the light which God has provided for it'.[61]

Melodramatic though this conclusion be, it does make evident the concern Martineau wishes her readers to share over a working class simultaneously both subjected to economic misery and sustained in ignorance through statist obstructions to the free circulation of discourse. Unlike Gibbons Merle, that is, and other elite periodical commentators on the press during this period, Martineau directs her readers' attention to the appalling conditions in which those segments of the population most likely to disrupt social stability and retard progressive development were actually living. Focusing, as she had in 'Ireland' and as she does in 'A Manchester Strike', on those most exposed to the forces of economic change, this didactic narrative speaks to that appetite to participate in the public sphere that Hewitt's work has shown was such a key driver of working-class and radical aspirations during the 1830s. Arguing that 'when newspapers circulate untaxed, and not till then, there will be an approach to general understanding, and to social peace',[62] Martineau's tale offers a dark vision of the future absent such reform, a vision that would soon be even further complicated by her discovery in America of other, more deeply intractable forms of impediment to the circulation of the press and the free formation of opinion. *The Scholars of Arneside*, then, concludes this foundational period for Martineau's contribution to the Victorian press by both anticipating her efforts to advance working-class education through the press and periodical publication that are the focus of Chapter 5, and also looking forward to an aspect of American society that, as Chapter 2 next shows, was fundamental to her appraisal of the liberal republic and its prospects of fulfilling the ideals upon which it was founded.

Notes

1. Dillon, *The Gender of Freedom*, p. 25. See also Hutchins, *Inventing Eden*, pp. 76–8, 103–4.
2. For more detailed accounts of the impact of the series, see Webb, *Harriet Martineau*, pp. 113–14, and Logan's introduction to her edition, *Illustrations of Political Economy*, pp. 34–40.
3. The primary exception to this prevailing focus has been Martineau's two articles on Scott in *Tait's Edinburgh Magazine*. As I argue below, however, these articles have not previously been read in the context of her development as a journalist; so too they have not been seen in relation to her version of stadial history.
4. Peterson, *Becoming a Woman of Letters*, pp. 68–9.
5. Rasmussen, 'Adam Smith and Rousseau', p. 70.
6. See Watts, *Gender, Power, and the Unitarians*.
7. Dzelzainis, 'Feminism, Speculation, and Agency', p. 121.
8. Dillon, 'Sentimental Aesthetics', p. 508.
9. See James Martineau's 1828 comment in *Harriet Martineau: Further Letters*, p. 443. Although the translation her brother mentions was not in fact published, Harriet did contribute a translation of Schiller's 'The Might of Song' to the *Monthly Repository* three years later (5 July 1831, pp. 444–5).
10. Martineau, *Letters*, vol. 2, p. 288. Unlike Dickens, whose library was inventoried in both 1844 (*Letters*, vol. 4, pp. 711–25) and after his death (Stonehouse, *Catalogue*), Martineau left no complete record of the books she owned. While her reading in Schiller, then, can be inferred only through occasional references in her correspondence, those references make clear the significance of his work to her.
11. Dillon, 'Sentimental Aesthetics', p. 503.
12. Martineau, *How to Observe*, p. 229.
13. Vetter, 'Harriet Martineau', pp. 429–30.
14. Martineau, *How to Observe*, pp. 221, 227.
15. Martineau, *Society in America*, vol. 3, p. 205.
16. See below, pp. 43–4.
17. *The Dawn of the Cheap Press*, pp. 4–5.
18. [Mill], 'Periodical Literature', p. 206.
19. [Brougham], 'Progress of the People'; [Alison], 'The Influence of the Press'.
20. [Merle], 'Journalism'. Chapter 6 discusses Martineau's difficulties with John Chapman over publishing *The Factory Controversy* in the

Westminster and her correspondence between April and June 1858 over his mismanagement of the periodical's finances and their resulting final rupture.
21. Merle, 'Journalism', p. 195.
22. Ibid.
23. Ibid. p. 197.
24. Ibid. p. 200.
25. Ibid. p. 203.
26. Ibid. p. 204.
27. Ibid. p. 206.
28. Hewitt, *The Dawn of the Cheap Press*, pp. 5–10.
29. [Martineau], 'National Education', pp. 689, 694.
30. [Martineau], 'On the Duty', p. 25.
31. [Martineau], 'Theology, Politics, and Literature', p. 74.
32. Deborah Logan's account in *Harriet Martineau, Victorian Imperialism, and the Civilizing Mission*, especially Chapter 2, offers the fullest discussion of Martineau's long and extensive interest in Ireland under British rule. By contrast with the focus Logan's title points towards, my emphasis in this study is upon the ways in which Martineau's treatment of Ireland and the Irish together with, as Chapters 3 and 4 show, Dickens's representation of the Irish in America, reveal marked splits within early Victorian British liberalism.
33. [Martineau], 'National Education', p. 691.
34. Dzelzainis, 'Feminism, Speculation, and Agency', and Peterson, *Becoming a Woman of Letters*, p. 74.
35. Martineau, *Letters*, vol. 1, p. 143; for an overview of *Tait's*, see the entry in *Dictionary of Nineteenth-Century Journalism*, pp. 613–14.
36. For a full discussion of *Tait's*, see Alexis Easley's chapters on Martineau and Johnstone in *First-Person Anonymous*.
37. Martineau, *Letters*, vol. 1, p. 152.
38. Ibid. p. 159.
39. Martineau, 'Characteristics of the Genius of Scott', p. 301.
40. Ibid. pp. 306, 303, 311.
41. Martineau, 'The Achievements of the Genius of Scott', p. 446.
42. Ibid. pp. 449, 451.
43. Ibid. pp. 452–3.
44. Martineau, 'Characteristics', p. 313.
45. Martineau, 'Achievements', p. 455.
46. Ibid. p. 456.
47. Ibid. p. 457.
48. Ibid. pp. 452, 458.
49. Martineau, 'Characteristics', p. 313.
50. Martineau, 'Achievements', pp. 454, 458.
51. Griffiths, *The Age of Analogy*, pp. 83, 92.
52. Mineka, *The Dissidence of Dissent*, pp. 414–17.

53. 'The Literary Examiner', pp. 132–3.
54. [Johnstone], 'Miss Martineau's Illustrations', p. 617.
55. 'Illustrations of Political Economy', p. 390.
56. Martineau, *Autobiography*, p. 167; [Croker], 'Miss Martineau's Monthly Novels'.
57. *Fraser's Magazine* 8 (November 1833), pp. 576–8.
58. See Peterson, *Becoming a Woman of Letters*, pp. 90–1, and Dzelzainis, 'Malthus, Women, and Fiction', p. 164.
59. Martineau, *Illustrations of Taxation*, p. 109.
60. Martineau, *Letters*, vol. 1, p. 250.
61. Martineau, *Illustrations of Taxation*, pp. 128, 133–4.
62. Ibid. p. 116.

Chapter 2

Martineau, the Press and Jacksonian America

> This country, which has given to the world the example of physical liberty, owes to it that of moral emancipation also; for as yet it is but nominal with us. The inquisition of public opinion overwhelms, in practice, the freedom asserted by the laws in theory.[1]
>
> Thomas Jefferson

Prefacing 'Civilisation', the chapter that opens the third volume of *Society in America*, with this quotation from Jefferson's 1821 letter to Adams, Martineau pithily sums up her own appraisal of the New World. After a two-year visit that had taken her on a journey of 10,000 miles and to twenty-two of the twenty-six states,[2] her reading of the United States echoes Jefferson in its rich sense of the expansive potential of the young continental nation, deep anxiety over the corruption of the ideals on which the republic had been founded and diagnosis that, at the heart of that corruption, was the suppression of public discourse and consequent distortion of those freely formed opinions upon which a liberal society depended. Such a judgement might appear to align with the representations of the United States offered by Martineau's predecessor British travellers, including Frances Trollope and Basil Hall, as well as her successors from Frederick Marryat to James Silk Buckingham and, most central to this study, Charles Dickens. Uniformly, that is, albeit in different forms and to varying degrees, the British visitors described an arc of gathering disillusion following their initial hopeful encounters with America. Martineau, however, is distinguished from her contemporaries in three ways that are central to my argument here: first, despite the young democracy's evident failings, she continues to represent the American project as a potential if still partially realised exemplar of liberal progress; second, by examining samples of the periodical press from across the nation, she not only builds the case for journalism's essential role in forwarding that project but also illustrates its vulnerability to appropriation by illiberal forces; and third, she evidences a resolve to do more than simply offer a dismissive damning criticism of the American press as had her fellow British writers. Instead, she begins the process of seeking out an ongoing role for herself in shaping the advance of liberalism across the Anglophone world through her own transatlantic engagement, a process that first becomes evident while she was still in America and then emerges more fully in the writing that resulted from it once she had returned to Britain.

The period between *The Scholars of Arneside*, which she completed in July 1834 immediately before she sailed to the United States, and the appearance of *Society in America* in May 1837 was, then, fundamental both to her own formation as a journalist and to the contribution she would make to shaping the early Victorian press. By December 1838, *Society in America* would be followed by two further books – *Retrospect of Western Travel* and *How to Observe Morals and Manners* – and two major articles in the *Westminster Review*, on the novels of Catharine Sedgwick and on the abolitionist movement, respectively. Collectively, these texts form a unified body of work that treats extensively with the relationship between historical progress, liberalism and the press and that also makes it evident that Martineau had used the sabbatical period of travel and research to deepen her sense of the dynamic relationship between public discourse and the formation of communities of sympathy that, as Chapter 1 explored, was central to her model of social progress. Moreover, through the encounter with the New World and, in particular, through her experiences of a society and economy that was dependent upon slavery, in which women occupied a constrained position within the culture of republican motherhood, and where the free formation of opinion through public discourse in the press was substantially compromised, she developed a far richer understanding of the complex contradictions within American liberalism. Deploying the quotation from Jefferson, who combined the stature of one of the nation's founders with a private life that so manifestly embodied these contradictions, thus not only prefaces her individual chapter on civilisation in the United States but stands more comprehensively as a summary diagnosis of the condition of the republic as a whole and points toward her developing understanding of the role of the press in shaping its future.

In focusing upon these imbricated complexities and highlighting Martineau's examination of the American press, this chapter reads her visit from a perspective that differs markedly from the dominant focus of previous studies. For those accounts, beginning with R. K. Webb's foundational *Harriet Martineau: A Radical Victorian* and continuing through the work of, most notably, Deborah Logan and Caroline Roberts, have placed Martineau's response to slavery at the centre of their narratives of her engagement with America.[3] Given the depth of her commitment to the abolitionist cause, such a focus has been understandable, and her role in the movement and support for it on both sides of the Atlantic is unquestionably a fundamental and enduring concern throughout her life and work. At the same time, however, the intense focus upon slavery in these earlier studies has had the unintended consequence of representing the American visit as a largely discrete episode, disconnecting it from her earlier work, downplaying its vital formative effect upon her evolution as a journalist and thereby deemphasising the depth of its role in her contribution to the shaping of the early Victorian press. Her development and that work were, as Chapter 1 has demonstrated, well under way before she left for the New World and, as both this chapter and Chapter 5 will show, continued after her return and were directly influenced by her experience in America. Even more broadly and significantly, however, although previous scholarship has discussed the ways in which Martineau joined with the abolitionist movement in linking the argument against slavery with that for women's full social agency, it has largely overlooked the ways in which her time in America allowed her to explore the nature of stadial development in a partially democratised society and her growing understanding of the role of the press in enabling that progress. By contrast with earlier studies, my argument here is that Martineau's concern with slavery can be most fully understood when it is set in the context of her larger narrative of historical development and connected to her overarching focus upon the stadial advance of liberal civilisation. While the abolition of slavery is indeed an essential issue in that advance, then, her discussion of it is inseparable from her examination of the ways in which the free circulation of discourse in the press is essential to the interplay of opinion that contributes to the formation of those communities of sympathy upon which depends the progress of liberal society as a whole.

To make that case, this chapter builds through three sections, drawing upon each of Martineau's American books as well as the two *Westminster* articles. First, it examines the ways in which

Martineau represents the United States as a complex exemplar of stadial development, one in which potential, accomplishment and regression contend with one another and in which the position of women most fully exemplifies America's distorted construction of the liberal subject. Demonstrating how the American continent itself embodies that stadial potential, this section also considers Martineau's representation of the cities that were being created in the New World and explores how her first depictions of urban life establish a pattern of distanced analytical reading that will continue throughout her career and that is a key point of differentiation between her and Dickens. Second, the chapter shows how, more extensively and thoroughly than any other contemporary visiting writer, Martineau examines the development of education in American society, particularly in relation to issues of race and gender. Through describing how a wide range of educational practices and institutions were contributing to social formation, she demonstrates the relationship between the ways in which education was developing across America and the nation's complex and uneven stadial progression. Third, and most extensively, the chapter focuses upon Martineau's exploration of the press in the United States. Highlighting examples of American periodicals, journals and editors from across the nation, she shows her readers a fourth estate that was expanding rapidly in parallel with the growth of the nation itself, that operated in an ostensibly free marketplace without the constraints imposed in Britain through the 'taxes on knowledge', and yet that was also becoming subject to increasingly systematised forms of suppression. Countering that suppression, she positions the abolitionist press as a vital form of resistance and an essential agent of the free circulation of public discourse that she argues is essential to social progress. In conclusion, noting Martineau's first attempts to find ways in which she could support the efforts of the abolitionists, the chapter discusses her first efforts to find a role for herself in the world of American print and so anticipates what would become her lifelong commitment to taking a transatlantic role in the press in the years after her return from America.

Stadial America and Republican Women

'With its boundary . . . ever shifting westwards . . . and inexhaustible wealth in the soil, ready for the hand which shall have enterprise to work for it', America for Martineau 'was meant to be everything'.[4] In a striking contrast with her travelling British contemporaries, whose texts established images of the wilderness state of the American continent and the miseries of travelling across it as standard tropes of their writing, Martineau represents America as literally a new world that is taking shape before her eyes and focuses her readers' attention upon the ways in which human agency is developing the potential latent in that world. Moreover, unlike both Frances Trollope, who visited before her, and Frederick Marryat and Charles Dickens, who followed, she for the most part decentres her own subjective experience and instead inscribes an image of the New World as an embodiment of stadial change and progression into her description of the continent itself. This representation of America as an exemplar of the potential assumed by the stadial model is especially evident in her accounts of two features routinely included in British travel narratives – Niagara Falls and the Mississippi River – which Martineau links into a conjoined image of the nation's abundance and irresistible forward progress.

By the time she visited Niagara in the mid-1830s, the Falls had already become a standard element in the tourist itinerary, and rapturous accounts of their effect upon the observer were a stock feature of contemporary travel writing. In the account she offers, however, Martineau quickly moves beyond the established pattern of response as, in a rare exception to her usual minimalist narratorial self-referentiality, she describes how she learned 'the secrets of the cataract' by daring to stand precariously on a bridge 'projected over the precipice' suspended above the 'dizzying whirl' of the water'.[5] Having positioned herself as an unconventional female observer simultaneously embracing physical danger for its own affective sake and in order to gain access to new knowledge, she then makes another unexpected move as she connects the Falls with the Mississippi, linking together disparate phenomena that most foreign visitors typically placed in opposition to one another. Uniting the two into a single vision of progressive change as she describes the process of 'world-making', she reflects upon them as complementary representations of the progressive and continuous nature of change. On the one hand, standing behind the Falls and seeing in the crumbling rock face tangible evidence of geological evolution, she recognises that 'Niagara itself is but one of the shifting scenes of life, like all of the outward that we hold most permanent' and that 'the spot on which I stood shall be the centre of a wide sea, a new region of life'.[6] On the other, in describing the Mississippi she stresses its role in the processes of change that are essential to the world-making that underlies the stadial evolution of history:

> So it was on the Mississippi, when a sort of scum on the waters betokened the birth-place of new land. All things help in this creation. The cliffs of the upper Missouri detach their soil, and send it thousands of miles down the stream. The river brings it, and deposits it, in continual increase, till a barrier is raised against the rushing waters themselves. The air brings seeds, and drops them where they sprout and strike downwards, so that their roots bind the soft soil, and enable it to bear the weight of new accretions.[7]

Using her description of two of America's iconic natural features, Martineau thus constructs and connects a representation of herself as an observer both daring and authoritative and an optimistic image of a continent that is, in the free circulation of the very materials that comprise its physical fabric, the embodiment of unlimited potential and progressive stadial change.

Building upon this foundational view of the continent itself, Martineau also makes use of the Mississippi to direct her readers' attention to the role of human agency in shaping America's potential into an emerging civilisation. Her 'Mississippi Voyage' chapter of *Retrospect of Western Travel* thus stands in stark contrast with both Frances Trollope's opening to *Domestic Manners of the Americans*, where the river is described as if it were the gates of Hades with nothing more than 'the fragment of a world in ruins' along its banks,[8] and later with Dickens's *American Notes*, where the father of waters is simply an 'enormous ditch, sometimes two or three miles wide, running liquid mud'.[9] For Martineau directs the reader towards a very different interpretation through the two epigraphs with which she prefigures the chapter – one from a *Quarterly Review* account of the wilderness explored by Lewis and Clark; the other from Virgil's ninth eclogue and combining images of natural fertility with a sense of the transformative capacity of human endeavour. As Thomas Ruys Smith has noted, Martineau uses the quotations to anticipate the reversal she wishes her readers to embrace – that a river seen by other travellers as merely unpicturesque and unsublime was in fact an embodiment of the New World's creativity and bounty.[10] Beyond underwriting a stadial vision of the continent itself, moreover, the quotations also continue to construct Martineau's own authorial stature: quoting

Virgil in the original and citing from the *Quarterly*, which had published Croker's savage review of the *Illustrations* in 1833, she not only claims the intellectual authority of a classical education normally reserved for male writers but also demonstrates her willingness to put the pages of one her most inveterate critics to work in support of her own text's goals. In the body of the chapter and when she moves into recounting the actual journey Martineau does acknowledge an almost inconceivable solitude in the undeveloped wilderness, but she also notes the 'grandeur' of the river itself and points to the ways in which it serves social development through connecting the isolated settlements along its banks to a 'busy world' beyond themselves and establishing the threads of ongoing development.[11] Furthering her point, she repeatedly, and uniquely in her American books, names the vessel on which she is travelling: calling attention to its being dubbed the *Henry Clay*, Martineau references the statesman best known for his support of the Gallatin Plan to develop a transportation infrastructure that would enable national economic development,[12] a man whom she had earlier met and admired during her stay in Washington and whose Kentucky home she would soon visit as she continued her exploration of the American interior. Though the Mississippi may still represent a largely undeveloped western frontier, then, even as she describes travelling on it north from New Orleans Martineau calls back to the forces of human economic activity that, as the American books frequently document, are rapidly moving the recently undeveloped continent through the phases of stadial progress.

Martineau thus differentiates her representation of the New World from those of other visiting British writers through both affirming the natural potential of the continent itself and highlighting human economic energies as a positive, productive force impelling American society onwards. At the same time, however, she is also distinctive in the particular attention she gives to critiquing the possibilities American cultural practices made available to women. Building on the case she had developed before travelling to the New World, especially in her essays on Scott, Martineau argues in *How to Observe* that the standing of women is the most revealing indicator of a society: not only is 'the degree of the degradation of woman . . . as good a test as the moralist can adopt for ascertaining the state of domestic morals in any country', she posits, but 'where moral force is recognized as the moving power of society, it seems to follow that the condition of Women must be elevated'.[13]

In America, however, as discussed above in the Introduction, liberal democracy had constructed the role of republican wife and mother as an essential strategy for containing women's claim to be recognised as autonomous subjects. Excluding women from the worlds of politics and economic activity that were driving the nation's stadial advance and reinforcing its legal constraints upon them through, in Elizabeth Maddock Dillon's term, the 'symbolics of sentimental liberalism', the culture of republican motherhood had, as Gillian Brown has argued, confined them into a form of domesticity that 'signifies a feminization of selfhood in service to an individualism mostly available to (white) men'.[14] By examining the position of women within this culture, then, Martineau puts America to that test of 'the degree of the degradation of women' through which she ascertains 'the state of domestic morals in any country'.[15] The results she reports significantly complicate the stadial optimism she had recorded about the continent itself and the economic advances being created through capitalist expansion.

For, as she further comments in *How to Observe*, the core of her diagnosis of the position of women in the New World lies in the contradiction she observes in the way that 'the Americans unite some of the low qualities of feudalism with some of the highest of a more equal social organization'.[16] Using 'feudalism' as she had in her second essay on Scott, where she had associated it with his lack of 'long-sighted views respecting the permanent improvement of society',[17] she goes on to argue that

> the old feudal notions about the sex flourish. . . and these notions, in reality, regulate the condition of women. American women generally are treated in no degrees as equals, but with a kind of superstitious outward observance, which, as they have done nothing to earn it, is false and hurtful.[18]

Anticipating the analyses of female sequestration developed in modern scholarship through the work of Brown, Dillon and others, Martineau portrays women in America as 'shut out of the world of reality, and compelled by usage to endure the corrosion of unoccupied thought, and the decay of unemployed powers'.[19] This insight, together with the actual experience of witnessing 'the vacuity of mind under wh women suffer in their state of depression',[20] led her, as she wrote to the New York Unitarian pastor William Ware, to include descriptions of cases of female alcoholism in *Society in America*, rupturing propriety by even mentioning the illness as she made visible the debilitating effects upon women of their feudalised marginalisation.

Nowhere in her account of America is the denial of female identity and agency as liberal subjects more visible than in the South, as Martineau places the commodification of enslaved women and the practice of miscegenation at the centre of her representation of Southern culture. In connecting the anti-slavery argument with her diagnosis of the position of white women within the culture of republican motherhood she was, as Caroline Roberts has shown, mirroring a standard trope in abolitionist rhetoric.[21] What makes Martineau's account distinctive and evidently especially shocking to contemporaries, however, was the way in which she made explicit use of her own positionality as a welcomed guest within Southern homes to place her readers in the uncomfortable role of witnessing vicariously how the domestic ideal actually operated. Having emphasised in the Introduction to *Society in America* that she had been 'received into the bosom of many families, not as a stranger, but as a daughter or a sister',[22] she takes advantage of this vantage point to describe Southern life from within in a way entirely unlike any other travelling writer from Britain. For she shares her hosts' accounts of the everyday commodification of enslaved women and the ways in which 'every white lady believes that her husband has been an exception to the rule of seduction'.[23] It soon emerges, however, that her hosts are frequently aware that their husbands are not in fact exceptions to the general rule, and this then leads to 'an end to all wholesome confidence and sympathy', destroys the trust of marriage, and 'woman sinks to be the ornament of her husband's home, the domestic manager of his establishment, instead of being his all-sufficient friend'.[24] The combination of slavery itself and the culture of miscegenation thus not only eliminates free agency and consent for the enslaved but also, by corrupting the marriage relation and the ideal of republican motherhood to which it is tied, erodes the ties of sympathy essential to the formation of a moral community. While Martineau certainly does describe both the physical barbarism associated with slavery and the emotional devastation created by the selling apart of family members, it is miscegenation and its consequences that are central to her account in the 'Morals of Slavery' section of *Society in America* as she defines 'the licentiousness of the masters' as 'the proximate cause of society in the south and south-west being in such a state that nothing else is to be looked for than its being dissolved into its elements'.[25] That this section is immediately followed by 'Civilisation' and the prefacing quotation from Jefferson that stands as the epigraph to this chapter only further emphasises the deep contradictions Martineau exposes within American liberalism as she makes the binary chattelising of both enslaved and white women through Southern male miscegenation her primary signifier of 'the degree of the degradation of women' in America in the mid-1830s.

Martineau and the American City

If Martineau explicitly adopted an insider role within Southern families to describe for her readers the ways in which patterns of sexual appropriation denied female agency and called into question the culture of republican motherhood upon which the ideology of American liberalism depended, she chose a quite different positionality from which to represent the American city. Advising travellers 'to make it their first business in a foreign city to climb the loftiest point they can reach, so as to have the scene they are to explore laid out as in a living map beneath them',[26] she emphasises the desirability of a degree of separation between the observer and the object of scrutiny. This sense of the city as informative text, providing documentation to the detached observer, emerges too as she imagines the value of 'a faithful register of births, marriages, and deaths' in furnishing the 'enlightened philanthropist' with 'all the materials he requires, as completely as if he were hovering over the kingdom, comprehending all its districts in one view'.[27] Reading the city, in de Certeau's sense, as a place, something to be examined through a panoptic view from above,[28] Martineau thus establishes an ideological perspective that will become fundamental to the difference in the ways in which she and Dickens engage the phenomenon of urban life and its implications for the development of liberal societies. Where he had already begun his career in the early 1830s writing from and of the streets of London, immersed in the living space of the metropolis, it was not until she travelled to America that Martineau wrote explicitly about any city at all. Moreover, when she did so both her choice of location and mode of representation reveal not an engagement in the experiential quality of urban life and its meaning for those formed within it but, rather, a focus upon the role of specific features of selected locations as exemplars of the condition of American society as a whole and as indicators of its stadial evolution towards the fulfilment of the liberal values upon which the United States had been established.

The length of her stay and extent of her travels meant that Martineau actually visited more American cities than any other contemporary British writer. However, while her texts do reference this wide range of locations – Philadelphia, Washington, Charlottesville, Charleston, New Orleans and Cleveland all appear, for example – Martineau treats none of these cities in significant detail. Perhaps even more strikingly, New York is essentially absent from her texts and, by contrast with the centrality of its role in Dickens's rendering of America, remains invisible to Martineau's readers. Instead, she focuses most extensively on two cities and the regions for which they metonymically stand: contrasting the European-inflected culture and slavery-dependent trading economy of Boston with the westward-oriented 'Queen City' of Cincinnati as an embodiment of more nearly realised American potential, Martineau makes their opposition fundamental to her reading of the United States. Calling out Cincinnati in this way, an aspect of Martineau's writing which has gone largely undiscussed in previous studies of the American visit, was unusual among contemporary travel writers, and Martineau's account marks itself explicitly as a corrective to Frances Trollope's. Privileging the young American city over its venerable eastern counter, moreover, was deeply provocative and prompted, as Chapter 5's discussion of the critical reception to the American books indicates, a considerable backlash to which Martineau in turn would respond as she advanced her position in the British press during the late 1830s.

If Martineau's readers had expected a sympathetic account of Boston, given her and her family's prominence in Unitarian circles, the city's role as both the centre of New England Unitarianism and the intellectual hub of the young nation and the amount of time she spent in Massachusetts over the course of her visit, *Society in America* and *Retrospect of Western Travel* would certainly have come as a surprise. Though she offers a brief description of the natural beauty of Massachusetts Bay and a more extended account of the rigours and pleasures of a New England winter, the city itself is largely invisible and, with one important exception, its population is absent from her pages. Instead, her focus is on appraising Boston as a centre of progressive thought and intellectual leadership in America. In that regard, uncompromisingly labelling it as 'the headquarters of Cant',[29] Martineau portrays Boston as a damning indictment of the American leadership class. The 'Allegiance to Law' chapter of *Society in America* thus emphasises the ties between the city's merchants and the custom and practice of Southern slave culture and demonstrates the connections between that culture and ostensibly progressive New England. In so doing, the chapter makes Boston its central example of the threat posed to progress throughout America by the forces of chaos embodied in the mob. Moreover, rather than some spontaneous outburst of proletarian rage, the Boston mob she describes is 'wholly composed of gentlemen',[30] members of the professional classes determined to maintain the economic basis of their wealth and the terms of their trade with the South. Quoting an 'eminent lawyer' who tells her that their intent is to tar and feather William Lloyd Garrison in defense of that trade and to 'show that they would not have such a person live among them',[31] Martineau makes use of these gentlemen's own words to indicate how they have aligned themselves with both the ideology and even the tactics of their Southern counterparts.

If Martineau's criticism of Boston and her engagement in the abolitionist movement in Boston have been a staple in critical discussions of her visit to America and need only a brief recapitulation here, the role she assigns to Cincinnati has gone almost entirely unremarked. And yet it is to Ohio that she turns for an exemplar of an American community that more nearly models an ideal of republican civilisation and stadial progress. Arguing that the west is where the traveller should go 'when he desires to see universal freedom of manners' and where he will encounter 'the freest people I saw in America'[32] and consistent with the stadial vision of the continent she had represented in its physical fabric, she portrays the western states, and, above all, Cincinnati as the fullest development of an authentically American civilisation. Describing her visit to 'the great City of the West' in June 1835,[33] Martineau thus emphasises the essential connection between its advanced state of social development and the level of intellectual, artistic and print culture that it has created. Although she actually arrived in Cincinnati from the east, coming down the Ohio after her visit to Henry Clay's home in Kentucky, her description of the city in *Retrospect of Western Travel* is positioned immediately after a chapter on Missouri, a state to which she did not in fact travel, and thereby heightens a contrast with the latter as 'a nest of vagabond slave-dealers, rapacious slave-drivers, and ferocious rioters'.[34] The narration of the Cincinnati chapter itself is then built around the figure of her local guide, Dr Daniel Drake, making him an exemplar of western progress, while Martineau also takes the opportunity to comment on Frances Trollope's bazaar, 'the great deformity of the city'[35] so as to define her account of the city as a corrective to that of her vituperative Tory predecessor, for whom it had been barely more than an 'uninteresting mass of buildings'.[36]

Describing an outbreak of cholera as a prelude to arriving in the city and meditating on the 'horror of such a paroxysm of society' to which such epidemics can lead,[37] Martineau anticipates the introduction of Dr Drake as her metonymic representative of western progress. Born in 1785 in New Jersey, Drake had migrated to Ohio with his family while he was still an infant and, after early thoughts of a career in business, had followed his father's advice and returned east to train as a physician at the University of Pennsylvania. As Henry Shapiro and Zane Miller describe, in Philadelphia Drake came under the influence of, first, Benjamin Rush, whose 'intellectual achievement was in many ways the capstone of the American enlightenment', and second, Benjamin Barton, professor of medicine, natural history and botany, who modelled 'the need for careful and systematic observation as the first step in understanding a knowable universe'.[38] Trained by Rush and Barton to become as Baconian in his scientific methodology as Martineau herself, Drake returned to the west and became not just one of the pioneers of medicine in Ohio but also an important figure in the development of knowledge in botany, geology and meteorology. A supporter of Henry Clay and a critic of Andrew Jackson, he 'saw in the construction of institutions of social control the essential mechanism for the fulfillment of America's promise as heir to Enlightenment liberalism'[39] and was thus available to Martineau as a pattern model of American stadial leadership.

Indeed, for Martineau, a man such as Drake, 'a complete and favourable specimen of a Westerner',[40] offered an ideal representative of America's best potential to become an exemplary liberal society. Describing how at the time of his arrival in Ohio 'there were not above a hundred white persons in the state, and they all French' and noting how the riverbanks were just 'one expanse of canebrake, infested by buffalo',[41] she contrasts this with the thriving city Drake shows her party during their visit in the summer of 1835. Emphasising particularly new schools, banking-houses and the church of St Paul, Drake points to forms of the institutional infrastructure that was beginning to take shape far from the established cities of the east coast. He then takes Martineau to visit the Western Museum, the site of Joseph Dorfeuille's sensationalist exhibit of scientific curiosities that Frances Trollope had both helped develop and then praised in *Domestic Manners of the Americans* as a 'pandemonium' and 'one of the most amusing exhibitions imaginable'.[42] Again contrasting her account with that of her conservative predecessor,

Martineau criticises the display as mere 'trumpery'. Praising instead the museum's comprehensive collection of US currency and voicing a hope that Cincinnati merchants will continue to use the opportunities their trade provides to expand it, she emphasises the city's significance as a representative of stadial progression into the age of commerce and directly connects its commercial strength to the educational and cultural value of its nascent institutions.[43] Finally, Drake serves to point out how much print media have contributed to the emergence of an evolved public sphere as he shows Martineau and her party the thriving bookstore of one Mr Flash and 'the improved and improving literary taste of the place' as well as 'the periodicals, – the respectable monthlies, and the four daily, and six weekly papers of the city'.[44] A far cry from frontier Kentucky, in which he had lived as a child and where he recollected that newspapers were as scarce 'as Sibylline leaves',[45] the Cincinnati that Drake depicts and himself embodies thus stands as a model of what civic progress can achieve in America and a marked contrast with Boston and the eastern leaders Martineau had excoriated.

To confirm Drake's importance as an architect of social amelioration, emphasising the significance of constructing institutions that will support such progress, and simultaneously reinforcing the model of stadial change she had previously developed in her description of the continent itself, Martineau concludes her account by quoting extensively from his 1833 'Remarks on the Importance of Promoting Literary and Social Concert in the Valley of the Mississippi'. This address, which Drake gave to the Literary Convention of Kentucky held at Transylvania University, the first college to be established west of the Allegheny Mountains, closely echoes her own eulogy to the 'world-making' powers of the Mississippi discussed above. For Drake describes the literal building of the lower states by the river's sedimentary action, its role as 'an exhaustless power of union',[46] and, going on to define the West and 'the great valley' as a distinct region with immense potential, finally offers an idealised vision of the future that can result from the social elites providing cultural leadership to society:

> Communities, like forests, grow rigid by time. To be properly trained, they must be moulded while young. Our duty, then, is quite obvious. All who have moral power should exert it in concert. The germs of harmony must be nourished, and the roots of present contrariety or future discord torn up and cast into the fire. Measures should be taken to mould a uniform system of manners and customs, out of the diversified elements

which are scattered over the West. Literary meetings should be held ... to bring into friendly consultation our enlightened and zealous teachers, professors, lawyers, physicians, divines, and men of letters. ... Plans of education, adapted to the natural, commercial, and social condition of the interior, should be invented. ... In short, we should foster Western genius, encourage Western writers, patronize Western publishers, augment the number of Western readers, and create a Western heart.[47]

In Martineau's vision of America, then, it is here that she finds the most advanced example of the nation's stadial development, a vision that she shared with the unknown artist who painted the cultivated Ohio Valley (Fig. 2.1) in 1840, between her and Dickens's visits to Cincinnati and their very different representations of the west.[48] The city, Drake's pastoral leadership and his vision of a progressive Western civilisation thus comprise Martineau's most complete response to the deficiencies identified by Jefferson and offer a model of stadial American development that fundamentally differentiates her understanding of the New World from those developed by her British contemporaries, including, as Chapters 3 and 4 will explore, liberal allies such as Dickens.

Education in America

One of the major early supporters of Transylvania University where Drake spoke was Henry Clay, who was appointed Professor of Law in 1805 and served as a Trustee from 1807 until his death in 1852. Indirectly referencing an institution so closely associated with Western progressive leadership by quoting Drake's remarks, and once again evoking Clay in her account of the American interior, Martineau points to another distinctive feature of her representation of the United States. For throughout her travels she examines the ways in which education operates to support, or retard, liberal progress in the New World. Indeed, more than any of her fellow British travel writers and to an extent that has not been previously noted, she records both institutional and domestic forms of instruction and learning and comments extensively on the ways in which the nation was shaping its future through the forms of education that it was developing for its population. She mentions brief visits to newly established institutions such as Allegheny College in Pennsylvania[49] and the Franklin Institute in Montgomery, Alabama,[50] while she also frequently remarks on the conditions of domestic culture that she encounters in her visits to ordinary American homes. She notes, for

Figure 2.1 *On the Ohio River*. Unknown artist, 1840. Smithsonian American Art Museum: museum purchase.

example, that she found herself 'less than three weeks in the country ... in a state of something like awe at the prevalence of, not only external competence, but intellectual ability'.[51] Later, in singling out such details as the 'excellent small collection of books' belonging to the daughter of the house she visits in an isolated homestead out on the Illinois prairie or in telling the story of an Ohio wagon driver and 'his hopes from his girl of fourteen, who writes poetry, which he keeps a secret, lest she should be spoiled', she builds on these early impressions and again suggests that America was most fully coming into its own identity as it pushed the frontier west and as it made educational opportunities available to women.[52] In emphasising such details as these she also makes visible to her readers the fact that, as Robert Gross has described, high levels of literacy and extensive reading were, and had been even before independence, a distinguishing feature of American society.[53] When she turns to her fullest accounts of specific educational institutions, however, her representation evidences the regional differences in literacy that Gross has also described.[54] Even more central to her examination of the liberal project in America, however, is her extended description of two of its elite universities, Virginia and Harvard. For she demonstrates how these two institutions, one Southern, one Northern, both embody the deficiencies of what she labels the regressive aristocratic culture that she associates with the older, more European-oriented parts of the nation and that is being propagated through educational practices deeply imbricated in the economy of slavery.

Martineau visited Charlottesville and the University of Virginia in early 1835 and then, after her travels through the South and midwest, attended Harvard's commencement later that same year, and she drew upon these two experiences to represent both the qualities and the limitations of elite education in America in ways that align with the obstacles to stadial progress that she defines through her accounts of slavery, the position of women and the condition of the press. While Jefferson's university, for example, is distinguished by the liberal structure of its curriculum, including its freedom from doctrinal constraint and the quality of both students and faculty,[55] it is also defined by its fealty to John C. Calhoun of South Carolina, Jackson's vice-president: 'the political attachments of this once democratic institution are to the leader who, in order to uphold slavery, would ... establish a Lacedemonian government throughout the South; making every white man a soldier, in order to preserve a false idea of honour, and to obviate danger from the oppressed servile class'.[56] Representing a peculiarly Southern version of liberalism that combined concern for the protecting the minority rights of the region against the democratic majority of the North with efforts to maintain legal protections for the white planter class,[57] Calhoun is one more exemplification of the connection Martineau makes between slavery and the exclusion of women from access to the social structures that confer power. For, reinforcing the masculinism of the university's culture and its ties to the honour code that sustains white Southern society, and contrasting with the simple domestic pride in female learning she had noted in the midwest, she goes on to include a brief passage describing how a member of her party asked a special favour:

> One of the ladies took an opportunity of asking me privately to request leave to attend a lecture with the Natural Philosophy class, in the morning. Ladies are excluded by rule: but she thought that the rule might for once be infringed without injury in the case of foreign ladies. The Professor kindly made no difficulty; and my prompter highly enjoyed her single opportunity.[58]

Implacably ironic in both its negatives and the questions it implies, this incidental commentary and scathing understatement testify to the ways in which Martineau's interpretation of American liberalism not only emphasises the connection between slavery and the erasure of white women as autonomous subjects but also points to the ongoing replication of that connection through the culture and practice of elite educational institutions.

A subsequent visit to Amherst College, where Martineau ironically notes that 'the admission of girls to such lectures as they could understand (this was on Geology) was a practice of some years' standing; and that no evil had been found to result from it',[59] might briefly appear to suggest that Northern society offers a more progressive alternative. However, her most extensive account of educational practice in Massachusetts – a description of the commencement she attended in Cambridge some months after the visit to Charlottesville – only builds upon and reinforces her critique of the elite institutions, and reinforces her larger account of the failure of Boston's Unitarian elite to provide the leadership of which the nation was in such need. For Harvard, though not directly tainted by association with slavery as was Virginia, has perhaps an even more fatal flaw: 'falling behind the age', locked into its role as 'the aristocratic college of the United

States', and unable to keep up with newer, more innovative institutions, it is portrayed as in danger of becoming simply irrelevant:

> More and more new colleges are rising up, and are filled as fast as they rise, whose principles and practices are better suited to the wants of the time. In them living is cheaper; and the professors are therefore richer with the same or smaller salaries; the sons of the yeomanry and mechanic classes resort to them; and, where it is the practice of the tutors to work with their pupils, as well as lecture to them, a proficiency is made which shames the attainments of the Harvard students.[60]

Though her report of Harvard's demise proved to be somewhat premature, Martineau's version of these two elite campuses deconstructs the conventional binary opposition of North and South, linking the two universities as bastions of masculinist social elitism and defining them as institutional expressions of the class leadership that had become an impediment to progressive change in America and an obstacle to the development of a healthy public sphere.

Set against these depictions of elite university education, however, and anticipating the arguments she would go on to make throughout the remainder of her career for the value of women's access to employment beyond the home, Martineau does offer a brief description in *Society in America* of the ways in which manufacturing industries in New England have created new forms of circulation that disrupt the larger narrative of cultural constraints placed upon American women. For, as the young men of the region have migrated to the west in search of the kind of new opportunities Cincinnati represents, the ensuing shortage of labour has created 'a most welcome resource' to the thousands of women thus able to take factory jobs.[61] While these women do continue to fulfil conventional social obligations by supporting their families, they are now also independent actors, able to establish the terms of their employment and, in the new mill towns, for the first time gaining access to institutional distributors of knowledge – the lyceum, the library and the lecture series.[62] Although the American books focus primarily upon the social construction of elite women in the New World, this brief vignette of the industrial working class thus offers a line of prospective evolution out of the chivalric episteme. For, and as Martineau argues in *How to Observe*, the stadial progression of the liberal state is intrinsically bound up in the development of an industrial society:

an artisan population is a prophecy of the future, and the beginning of the fulfilment. The ideas of equal rights, of representation of person as well as property, and all other democratic notions, originate in towns, and chiefly in manufacturing towns.[63]

She touches only briefly in the American books on this issue of the ways in which the combination of paid employment and educational opportunities were a vital mechanism in the formation of working-class women as autonomous subjects in a liberal society. However, it was to become a central theme of her periodical writing during the 1840s and 1850s and, as the following chapters will show, a fundamental point of difference between her and Dickens's understandings of the nature of social progress, a difference that becomes most visible in their very different readings of one particular industrial setting: the planned community that was developed in Lowell, Massachusetts and that will be discussed in Chapters 3, 5 and 7.

Opinion and the Press in Jacksonian America

In her representation of the American continent itself, then, and in her explorations of the nation that was being created upon it through economic development, the role and cultural practices of both slavery and republican motherhood, and the function of educational institutions in both maintaining and challenging the conventional episteme, Martineau offered her readers a complex appraisal of the New World's potential and the contradictory liberal society that was taking shape across the Atlantic. Fundamental to that appraisal was an issue that preoccupied not only other visiting British writers but Americans themselves: the role of opinion in shaping a democracy. As Gillian Brown has shown, for example, the debate over Locke's understanding of 'opinion itself as an ongoing negotiation between individuals and the customs of their countries' was at the core of the formation of the American public sphere.[64] Sharing with British liberalism an assumptive resistance to statism and governmentality, the democratic impulses of the American project placed an even greater emphasis upon the formation of individual opinion and civic engagement, albeit only for the free white males defined as authentic liberal subjects. Martineau, as Lauren Goodlad has commented,[65] was particularly alert to the limitations of legal structures in developing an ideology and noted that 'laws and customs cannot be creative of virtue: they may encourage and help to preserve it; but they cannot originate it'.[66] In her reading of America, then, the issue of opinion becomes fundamental and not only speaks to her emphasis upon the role of education as an agent of social formation but also leads to the extensive exploration her books and articles offer of the role of print and the development of the press.

Negative commentary upon the deference of individual opinion to the force of public opinion became a stock-in-trade of early Victorian British travel writers from Frances Trollope to Charles Dickens. Although at first glance it might appear that Martineau apparently shared in this easy dismissal of the 'restraint of perpetual caution',[67] she in fact offers a more nuanced reading of the phenomenon, as is evidenced by her treatment of an apparently unrelated but in fact profoundly indicative standard feature of contemporary travel writing: its commentary upon the propensity of the American male for armed combat. For where her fellow travellers made glancing references to duelling as an American oddity perpetuating a practice that had all but died out in Britain, Martineau treats it far more seriously and far more extensively. Indeed, she represents it as a fundamental signifier of the honour code that regulates masculine behaviour in the United States and as an expression of the lack of defined structure to political life during the early years of the republic. In this, her account anticipates modern scholarly discussions. Kenneth Greenberg, for instance, has described duelling as a corporeal manifestation of a culture that universally placed particular emphasis upon 'the parts of a man that were visible to the public',[68] while Joanne Freeman has explored the ways in which the 'culture of honor was a crucial proving ground for the elite' on the uncertain terrain of the young nation where public opinion of a man's reputation was fundamental to his political success.[69]

Though duelling occurred most widely in the South, Martineau accordingly emphasises its importance as representative of the nation as a whole. On the one hand, that is, she notes that the practice is to be found in its most extreme form in New Orleans, where 'the spirit of caste, and the fear of imputation, rage in that abode of heathen licentiousness' and where she records that, in 1834, more duels were fought than there were days in the year.[70] Driven by 'the meanness of the fear which lies at the bottom', the young men who are the predominant actors in this ritual performance of masculinity are, she comments, paying 'the wages of slavery to a false idea of honour'.[71] On the other hand, she also suggests that the code is an inescapable characteristic of American masculinity as she makes a passing reference to the historic duel between Aaron Burr and Alexander Hamilton and notes that 'it was pretty generally agreed that [Hamilton] could not help fighting'.[72] In *Retrospect of Western Travel* she builds upon this brief remark by deploying a short narrative that reinforces a more abstract claim made in her earlier book. Arguing that Burr had manipulated Hamilton into the duel out of fear of 'the imputation of want of courage' should he refuse to fight,[73] she then recounts how he had practised his marksmanship to increase the chances of killing his opponent, and, in his eventual success in doing so, achieved a goal he had been unable to accomplish through the political process. Evidencing her assumption that 'laws and customs cannot be creative of virtue' and exploiting a legal system that refuses to intervene, Burr becomes the embodiment of a cultural code based upon an assumed right to inflict deadly force as a form of legitimate political action, and ritual masculine violence is thus rendered normative. Though the duel between Burr and Hamilton was a generation into the past at the time she wrote, that the practice it exemplified is still so alive when she visits New Orleans in 1835 becomes another marker of America's feudalism – its difficulty in liberating itself from a more primitive past and its continuing challenges in cultivating the free formation of opinion upon which a democracy and liberal progress depend. Duelling, then, in Martineau's analysis of America is not simply an eccentric practice to be mocked from an outsider position but, rather, an all too concrete exemplification of a cultural crisis of which Americans themselves are well aware, as she makes evident by quoting the Unitarian pastor Henry Ware and his *Sober Thoughts on the State of the Times*:

> Public opinion, – a tyrant, sitting in the dark, wrapt up in mystification and vague terrors of obscurity; deriving power no one knows from whom; like an Asian monarch, unapproachable, unimpeachable, undethronable, perhaps illegitimate, – but irresistible in its power to quell thought, to repress action, to silence conviction, – and bringing the timid perpetually under an unworthy bondage of mean fear.[74]

Set against the constitutional framework of republican democracy in its majesty and immunity from impeachment, the Orientalised figure of public opinion Ware imagines not only underwrites the continuing inability of American society to free itself from outdated practices such as duelling but becomes a larger, essential force in Martineau's representation of the role of the press in the development of the new society.

For, as John Nerone has noted, early American print culture gave a special place to the newspaper press in the formation of a republican ethos. Seeing no inevitable dichotomy between newspaper and book, commentators 'cited the growth of newspapers as evidence of the increasing intelligence and literacy of the population, assuming the newspaper to be the necessary vanguard of print culture'.[75] For British observers, however, such an unfettered, expanding newspaper press offered a vision of what might emerge back at home given the campaign against the 'taxes on knowledge' in the aftermath of the Reform Act and as Chartism gave expression to the increasing appetite for news emerging among the radical working classes. As they had chastised American conformism, then, travelling writers not only routinely commented upon this distinctively republican form of print media but also largely tended to hold it up as a dystopian model of what might be in Britain's future. Martineau's predecessors, such as Frances Trollope, as well as those who visited America after her, including J. S. Buckingham, Frederick Marryat and Charles Dickens, thus routinely condemned the American press.[76] Trollope, for instance, deplored 'the mass of slip-slop poured forth by the daily and weekly press',[77] while Dickens's reactions are examined more fully in Chapters 3 and 4. At first glance, Martineau appears to be following this same line of attack in commenting on 'the baseness of the newspapers, whose revilings of all persons in turn who fill a public station are so disgusting'.[78] However, and as her emphasis on the attacks on those in 'a public station' suggests, her analysis of the role of the press in the New World is, in fact, more complex and nuanced than those of her compatriots, is inseparable from her broader discussion of the role of print culture and education in the ongoing formation of the nation, and, ultimately, argues for the essential role of the press as an agent of progress.

Martineau and Dickens visited America at a pivotal moment in the history of the press and, crucially, did so on different sides of a tipping point in its growth. At the time of Martineau's visit in the mid-1830s the nation was in the throes of transitioning to a society in which print culture and a modern mass-market press were about to emerge to rival and eventually dominate over oral forms of public discourse. The mechanics of printing and paper production, the invention of stereotyping, the improvement in transportation networks and a postal policy that favoured the distribution of newspapers had all established the essential infrastructure.[79] Even at the start of the 1830s, with around 900 newspapers appearing, the United States already had more than twice as many as Great

Britain. That number would grow to over 1600 by 1840 and to more than 2,500 by 1850, with most of the increase occurring in the daily press.[80] Americans themselves were fully aware of the newly achieved importance of the press, as Margaret Fuller would record: 'The most important part of our literature ... lies in the journals, which monthly, weekly, daily, send their messages to every corner of this great land, and form, as present, the only efficient instrument for the general education of the people'.[81] Significantly, however, and differentiating her from Dickens's experience just a few years later, Martineau primarily encountered the American press before its transition to a mass-market medium was far advanced. That is, although she had arrived in New York a year after Benjamin Day's launching of the *Sun*, 'the first successful popular newspaper in America',[82] she was neither in the country long enough to see the full flourishing of the penny press nor was her attention focused upon the mass-market press and its impact upon national culture. Indeed, as David Henkin has shown,[83] the shift to such a press fully took place during the two decades after her visit and, as Chapters 3 and 4 discuss, was a phenomenon to which Dickens was more fully able to respond and, indeed, one to which he was perhaps more responsive. Moreover, though she clearly was familiar with newspapers produced in the major urban centres and their editors – for example, with the *New York Evening Post*, which she praised privately,[84] and with its editor, William Cullen Bryant, whom she would later defend against Dickens's representation and with whom she had an enduring connection[85] – she does not discuss them in the American books.

Nevertheless, and unlike any other of the British travel writers who essentially represented the American press as a static object for attack, Martineau emphasises the transition towards a print-centred culture, suggesting both the inevitability of such a change and its role in the stadial evolution of American society. On the one hand, she critiques the pernicious effects she often finds in American public speech:

> The grievance lies in the prostitution of moral sentiment, the clap-trap of praise and pathos, which is thus criminally adventured. This is one great evil. Another, as great, is the mis-estimate of the people. No insolence and meanness can surpass those of the man of sense and taste who talks beneath himself to the people because he thinks it suits them.[86]

On the other, recognising that the public sphere is in the midst of a fundamental shift, she suggests that the replacement of that earlier, more oral culture by the new forces of print marks a step away from the nation's founding era and into a less certain future:

> I suspect that there is a stronger association in American minds than the times will justify between republicanism and oratory; and that they overlook the facts of the vast change introduced by the press, – a revolution which has altered men's tastes and habits of thought, as well as varied the methods of reaching minds.[87]

Echoing both her own 1832 essays and Merle's 1833 *Westminster* article on the rise of a mass culture, Martineau thus speaks to the potential role of the press in forming not simply public opinion but the very 'habits of thought' of the populace, shaping the public sphere in a way that had been unimaginable when discourse relied upon speech more than print. Not surprisingly, then, she makes the status of the press one of her essential criteria for gauging the larger health of a society, arguing in *How to Observe* that 'not by individual newspapers must the traveller form his judgment, but by the freedom of discussion he may find to be permitted' and, though her critique of individual American papers stands, she qualifies it with an expression of faith in the standing of the nation's press as a whole:

> The very existence of the newspapers he sees testifies to the prevalence of a wide habit of reading, and consequently of education – to the wide diffusion of political power – and to the probable safety and permanence of a government which is founded on so broad a basis, and can afford to indulge so large a licence.[88]

Moreover, if she was not in America quite in time to see the full emergence of the mass-market urban daily press, she did witness a press in a stage of development that she could compare to that of other forms of print media, above all the belles lettres. Five months after the publication of *Society in America*, making her debut in one of the elite British quarterlies, Martineau's *Westminster Review* article, 'Miss Sedgwick's Works', uses her friend's career to exemplify the stadial progress of the national literature. As she surveys Sedgwick's oeuvre from its beginnings in 1822 through to her most recently published *The Poor Rich Man, and the Rich Poor Man*, Martineau examines the condition of a recently formed national literature and both reinforces the argument she had made in *Society in America* that 'popular books are the ideas of the people put into language by an individual' and anticipates the corollary point she would express in *How to Observe* the following year that 'the popular fictions of a people ... must be a mirror of their moral sentiments and convictions, and of their social habits and manners'.[89] Drawing again upon what David Lloyd and Paul Thomas have defined as Schiller's seminal framing of an essential connection between the individual and the stadial progress of society as a whole – 'the function of culture is to cultivate the identity between the ideal or ethical Man in every subject and the state which is its representative'[90] – Martineau outlines a three-stage development from fiction 'which imitates itself' to that which is 'a transcript of actual life' to an ideal form that can 'be new to every mind, and in absolute harmony with all'.[91] Within this template, she suggests, the striking 'progression' evident in Sedgwick's writings has carried her firmly into the second phase and, offering 'the first true insight into American life', marks 'the first complete specimens of a higher kind of literature', 'the first distinct utterance of a fresh national mind'.[92] Sedgwick herself had been offended by Martineau's more robust appraisal of her earlier work in *Society in America*[93] and their friendship was irreversibly damaged as a result. This second review, nevertheless, serves both to confirm the fundamentally affirmative vision of the American project evident throughout Martineau's writing from her visit even as it also suggests that the nation's belletristic literature had as yet less weight in shaping public discourse than the press had already come to assume.

Accordingly, throughout the American books and articles Martineau focuses the reader's attention upon the press and, rather than on the still forming urban press, upon the workings of newspapers within the smaller, more localised communities that she visited. In doing so, she demonstrates how provincial American periodical publications acted as forms of record and helped build localised forms of the public sphere for the individual communities of a nation that remained strongly regionalised and was still largely lacking a unifying infrastructure. What she looks for in the newspapers she finds is, moreover, revealing about both her methodology and the ways in which she conceptualises the press as a whole. In discussing her visit to Charleston, South Carolina, for example, she follows a general directive with an account of the explicit value she found in the local paper: 'Another care of the traveller should be to glance at the local newspapers. This first morning I found a short newspaper article which told volumes. It was an Ordinance for raising ways and means for the city.'[94] Taking an interest in something so thoroughly mundane as municipal sources of revenue and offering this pragmatic focus on the kind of everyday functionalities upon which any community depends, Martineau represents American newspapers to her readers in a way entirely different from the sweeping, moralising judgements that dominated the accounts of her fellow British travel writers. Moreover, and consistent with her emphasis upon the western states as most fully representing the nation's stadial potential, it is there that she finds her most favourable examples of the press. Having commented on how closely newspapers follow on the heels of the expansion westward, for example, she jokes about Milwaukee's having 'a printing-press and newspaper, before the settlers had had time to get wives'.[95] Travelling in Michigan, she identifies this pace of development as unique to the young democracy: 'it could happen nowhere out of America, that so raw a settlement as that at Ann Arbor, where there is difficulty in procuring decent accommodations, should have a newspaper'.[96] Though this particular example is 'poorly printed', in praising the quality of its content Martineau expresses a recurring judgement. While she offers her readers no account at all of northern Ohio's principal city, for example, she makes a point of singling out 'a single number of the Cleveland Whig' as 'the very best newspaper that I saw in the United States',[97] exemplifying the ways in which her commentary on the newspapers she came across in the western states aligns the role of the provincial press in social formation with her metonymic depiction of Cincinnati as an American civic exemplar.

A darker consequence of this role, however, is evident as she shows how, especially in the South, that provincial press worked to suppress forms of discourse that diverged from normative patterns of culture and practice and created those very constraints upon opinion that were so problematic to the healthy formation of a liberal society. For, in addition to pointing to how legal sanctions support the erasure of slavery from Southern newspapers, with 'laws against the press ... as peremptory as in the most despotic countries of Europe', she notes how few papers there are in the region – seventy-nine in Georgia, Louisiana and South Carolina combined, as opposed to 595 in Massachusetts, New York and Pennsylvania – as well as how 'poor and empty' so many of them are. The combination of the coercive force of these laws and the impoverishment of the public sphere, she suggests, has debilitating effects upon 'the gentry of the south' themselves. Out of touch with the wider world and embedded in 'delusions on their own affairs', they remain unable to imagine alternative possible futures for their society, 'fettered by their own presses'.[98]

Moreover, at the heart of her account of the South is a bizarre, even grotesque mixture of suppression and propagation of information around the forms of violence associated with slavery. In New

Orleans, for example, she encounters a curious dichotomy between what she sees all around her and what she can read in the press:

> I never could get out of the way of the horrors of slavery in this region. Under one form or another, they met me in every house, in every street, – everywhere but in the intelligence pages of newspapers, where I might read on in perfect security of exemption from the subject. In the advertizing columns, there were offers of rewards for runaways, restored dead or alive; and notices of the capture of a fugitive with so many brands on his limbs and shoulders, and so many scars on his back. But from the other half of the newspaper, the existence of slavery could be discovered only by inference.[99]

Given her references to the widespread prohibitions against slaves learning to read and write,[100] the target audience for such accounts as did make their way into the press can only have been white readers. Reinforcing normative expectations of the treatment of runaways, the actual news columns maintained the status quo of slavery through the 'perfect security of exemption' that allowed their silence, a phrasing that captures the universality of prevailing practice yet does so with an irony that suggests its fragility. That fragility, moreover, is made palpable in the measured report Martineau gives of an exceptionally barbaric lynching in Alabama:

> Just before I reached Mobile, two men were burned alive there, in a slow fire, in the open air, in the presence of the gentlemen of the city generally. No word was breathed of the transaction in the newspapers: and this is the special reason why I cite it as a sign of the times; of the suppression of fact and repression of opinion which, from the impossibility of their being long maintained, are found immediately to precede the changes they are meant to obviate.[101]

In its slow deliberation, its unusual rhetorical punctuation controlling the pace of the prose, and its use of 'transaction' to render the lynching as a form of commerce this is one of Martineau's most powerful statements about the horrors intrinsic to slavery. At the same time, the narrator's closing assumption that even the worst forms of communal violence cannot long sustain the suppression of public discourse points again to the connection between social progress and the unrestricted circulation of ideas, thereby linking this account of Southern slavery back to the social unrest of Britain in the late 1830s and the movement to free the press from the 'taxes on knowledge' that she had described in *The Scholars of Arneside*.

In her extensive recording of the condition of the American provincial press and capturing of the ways in which it was both emerging as a form of mass media while continuing to function as an agent of constraint within local societies, Martineau offered a far richer analysis than any other contemporary visitor. Even more significantly, however, she provided her readers with an unparalleled account of the innovative practice of an American who could not only imagine but also showed himself fully able to manipulate the future. For her discussion of the ways in which Andrew Jackson, the seventh president of the United States, made use of the press becomes an expression of her profound concern over the threats posed to liberal progress through the harnessing of its power to serve a specific political agenda. Jackson, Martineau suggests, echoes another authoritarian leader who had appropriated a liberal revolutionary movement to his own ends as she depicts him, like the Napoleon in Gibbons Merle's *Westminster* article, as a head of state who has learned to use the press as an instrument of political policy.

When Martineau arrived in the United States in the late summer of 1834, Jackson was coming to the end of his second term as president. Having been defeated in the 1824 election, he had run successfully against Adams in 1828 and then seen off the challenge of Henry Clay in 1832. While Martineau might have sympathised with Jackson's efforts to expand democracy and his position during the Nullification Crisis in the early 1830s, she was, as we have seen, both a supporter of Henry Clay and his efforts to develop the nation's infrastructure and a vocal opponent of Jackson's attempt to undermine a national banking system.[102] As her American books reveal, moreover, she was also deeply opposed to his innovative use of the press to secure and sustain political power. For, as Andie Tucker has shown, Jackson had learned from his election defeat in 1824 and, for the 1828 campaign, intentionally dismantled the separation between political office and the press: 'editors were also campaign officials, political advisors were also editors, and public printing contracts were granted for political jobs well done'.[103] Following his electoral victory, Jackson rewarded many of these journalists with public office, making them among the first beneficiaries of the spoils system of patronage with which his presidency is associated. For Martineau, who would within a few years turn down a Civil List pension precisely because of her concern over its implications for her journalistic independence,[104] such a system was anathema and a profound threat to the free circulation of ideas that alone could ensure the healthy progressive development of a nation.

Rather than attack Jackson himself, however, she focused upon the architect of his system of control – Amos Kendall, who served as US Postmaster General and who, through this office, became the primary orchestrator of Jackson's efforts to manipulate the press to his own political ends. As Patrick Joyce has noted, the United States was well ahead of European countries in having intentionally developed the postal system as an instrument of forging national community,[105] and Kendall is, in Martineau's account, 'the moving spring of the whole administration; the thinker, planner and doer; but it is all in the dark'.[106] Intervening in the postal system so as to ensure speedier delivery of pro-Jackson newspapers from the west, he thus buttressed Southern support for the president by sanctioning the efforts of postal officials to prevent the distribution of abolitionist materials.[107] Appalling though she clearly finds Kendall's actions – she describes his staying in office as 'one of the deepest wounds which has been inflicted on the liberties of the nation'[108] – Martineau also expresses a sense of awe at the power he has succeeded in generating:

> Documents are issued of an excellence which prevents their being attributed to persons who take the responsibility of them; a correspondence is kept up all over the country for which no one seems to be answerable; work is done, of goblin extent and with goblin speed, which makes men look about them with a superstitious wonder; and the invisible Amos Kendall has the credit of it all.[109]

Doing far more than simply obstructing the free circulation of knowledge, that is, Kendall has achieved an unprecedented degree of control over public discourse and one that Martineau can only label 'goblin', an adjective wholly uncharacteristic of her generally rationalist prose and that speaks to her sense of the alarming potency of the hold he has established over, and through, the press.

Martineau was not alone in commenting on the hold Jackson had developed over the press. Even Frances Trollope, with whom she had so little in common, noted how, through requiring reports on newspaper distribution from local postal officials and thereby 'knowing the political character of every newspaper', the Secretary of State ensured that he was 'enabled to feel the pulse of every limb of the monster mob'.[110] By calling out Kendall's role, however, and placing both him and the master he served in the broader context of her extended account of print media in America, Martineau suggests that Jackson's influence was larger and more nefarious than even that of the pro-slavery Southern press and thus indicates the broader significance of the threat he posed to the progress of liberal society in the nation as a whole.

Martineau's exploration of America's stadial development, her emphasis upon the importance of pastoral leadership to form a public sphere that would support liberal progress and her analysis of both the importance and vulnerability of the emerging press to political manipulation all come together in her account of one particular episode during her visit. This episode – her brief stay in Charleston, South Carolina, and encounter with a local Unitarian publication – has gone almost entirely unnoticed in previous scholarship. However, it, and its long-lived aftermath, are profoundly indicative of what the two years in America contributed to her understanding of the role of the press, her ambitions for herself in it and her discovery of the unanticipated challenges of transatlantic exchange even among the network of liberal progressives.

In April 1835, six months into her visit, Martineau travelled into the deep South and to Charleston. There, she was the guest of Samuel Gilman, the local Unitarian pastor, and his wife Caroline, editor of a weekly miscellany that went through a number of titles but is best known as *The Southern Rose*. The Gilmans were Northern transplants who had met when Samuel was a student at the Harvard Martineau would observe so critically later that same year and had moved to the South after their marriage and his ordination. The visit appears to have gone well, and during her stay Martineau had two evidently pleasing opportunities to experience at first hand the ways in which print culture circulated across the Atlantic through the press: first, she recorded visiting the public library with her travelling companion, Louisa Jeffrey, and noted how 'we amused ourselves with files of newspapers, which have survived all disasters, – old London Gazettes and colonial newspapers extending as far back as 1678'.[111] Second, and as Samuel Gilman described in a glowing letter about his guest to her mother back in England:

> One peculiar bond of interest between us was that all her early attempts at publication . . . were issued in the "Monthly Repository", just about the time when I used to contribute to the periodical a series of papers . . . We passed several hours in looking over those volumes.[112]

Though her *Illustrations of Political Economy* were widely known through unlicensed reprinting, that Martineau's earlier, unheralded work in the modest Unitarian journal should have travelled to America as part of a shared transatlantic community of print offered palpable evidence of the opportunities for exchange and the role that the press might play in advancing progressive causes.

Nine months later, however, having completed her tour through the Southern and western states and settled in Boston for the winter, Martineau wrote to remonstrate with Caroline Gilman in very different terms. Her complaint was over the reprinting of two more recent *Monthly Repository* pieces in *The Southern Rose*, and the terms of her concern are revealing:

> Since that time, circumstances have changed, on your part, not on mine. Your paper, the Rose, has become a decided Pro-Slavery paper. The four last Nos that I have seen are all strongly so; & it is no news to you, dear friend, that my principles will not allow me to support in any way a pro slavery publication. In the last No, I find an <u>old</u> article of your own on the religious opportunities of slaves, republished <u>after</u> the voluntary relinquishment of the schools for coloured people by the clergy of Charleston; &, next to this, two parables of mine, <u>with</u> my name, & <u>without</u> the date, of their prior publication, – looking exactly as if I had just written them for your paper.[113]

Unhappy at the impression of 'double-dealing' she feels this will create, Martineau asks Gilman to print nothing more from her 'as long as your publication countenances Slavery', and then closes out her letter by describing her life in Massachusetts and sending affectionate remembrances to her Southern friends. Perhaps for the first time in her career, but certainly not for the last, Martineau thus acts to defend her authorial position from what she sees as misrepresentation and places considerable strain upon an established friendship through her willingness to express peremptorily the vehemence of an ideological disagreement.

In the single critical comment on this episode,[114] Deborah Logan has noted that Martineau's letter was written a week after a meeting of the Boston Female Anti-Slavery Society at which she reluctantly accepted an invitation to speak and thus made public her support for the abolitionist cause. In her biography, Logan reads this meeting itself as 'the pivotal event' of the visit and argues that it changed Martineau's entire public position and had lifelong consequences for her relationship with America.[115] Clearly, it was an important moment, and Martineau certainly presents it as such. However, as Dallas Liddle and Linda Peterson have shown,[116] and as Chapter 6 will further explore, the ways in which Martineau narrates epiphanic episodes in her life are frequently complex and often serve purposes other than those their overt design would simply suggest. Here, my argument is that the heroic self-fashioning Martineau offered twenty years after the event when she composed her *Autobiography* is only a part of the story and that the letter to Gilman the week following the meeting points to a meaning that is most fully understood within the context of her examination of the barriers to stadial progress that she had increasingly come to understand and her growing insight into the role of the press in sustaining the culture of slavery and, more broadly, creating resistance to the development of a fully liberal society.

At first glance, however, Martineau's letter does seem entirely at odds with her initially cordial relationship with the Gilmans and their shared commitment to educative work through the press. As John Allen Macaulay has shown, with only seven churches across the states of the future Confederacy, Southern Unitarians were a marginalised group and had none of the stature their New England counterparts enjoyed. In this context, their work of advocating moderate progress depended heavily on print publication, and Samuel Gilman had been especially successful in establishing a book and tract society in Charleston.[117] Given the tenor of Martineau's visit to Charleston, then, it seems only natural that she would have lent her support to Caroline's magazine by giving permission to reprint her work. Indeed, before the appearance of the issue to which Martineau took such exception, Gilman had previously made much of her friend in the pages of the periodical: she highlighted Martineau's visit to Charleston as it occurred and not only continued the connection with the *Monthly Repository* by reprinting parts of 'Some Autobiographical Particulars' but also included the more recent 'A Letter to the Deaf', which had first appeared in *Tait's Edinburgh Magazine*. Finally, the two items that she reprinted on 14 November and that were the occasion of Martineau's protest would appear to be entirely unexceptionable minor pieces: 'The Solitary: A Parable' and 'A Parable', both of which had originally appeared in the 1830 *Monthly Repository* and are short accounts of lives devoted to religious faith.[118] Collectively, this body of recirculated material testifies to the warmth of the personal ties between Martineau and the Gilmans in early 1835 as well as to their shared participation in a transatlantic network of progressive Unitarian writers and publishers, seeking to use the educative power of periodical literature to advance that 'grand amelioration of the state of humanity' for which Martineau had earlier argued in the *Monthly Repository* itself (see above, p. 38).

If Martineau's abrupt insistence that Gilman stop reprinting her texts is at odds with their prior history, moreover, her charge that the *Rose* has abruptly turned into 'a Pro-Slavery paper' at first seems unreasonable and excessive. For 'the four last Nos' of which she complains in no way manifest any change in the magazine's established patterns of practice. Thus, in addition to an episode of Gilman's ongoing serialisation of her own *Recollections of a Southern Matron*, the 14 November issue (Fig. 2.2) includes two chapters translated from an obscure German novel, various pieces of verse which may have been by Gilman,[119] as well as the essay 'Religious Privileges of the Negroes in Charleston'. It is this latter text of which Martineau specifically complains in her letter, although to dub it 'Pro-slavery' might appear harshly damning in much the same way as her labelling Dickens twenty years later a mere 'humanity-monger' in the course of their precipitous falling-out. Given what we have seen of the forcefulness of Martineau's attacks upon the overtly racist slavery-supporting Southern press in the work she published after returning to England, moreover, her reaction to Gilman does indeed seem out of keeping with their prior personal connection and shared participation in the reformist Unitarian press.

The change in Martineau's feelings about appearing in *The Southern Rose* and the vehemence of her critique to Gilman may be explained, however, not by any shift in the periodical itself but, rather, in the ways Martineau herself had deepened both her understanding of American culture and society as well as her perception of the role of the press in the months between April and December 1835. Although it is almost unknown now, Gilman's magazine was both highly successful and widely influential during the 1830s: together with its predecessors, *The Rose Bud* and *The Southern Rose Bud*, it comprised, as Jan Bakker has shown, the first publication 'for young people ever published on a regular basis in the United States'. After a year running it as a magazine directed towards juvenile readers, Gilman had rebranded it for an adult audience in 1833 and secured enough subscribers to order print runs of 1,000 copies. With readers from Maine to St Louis and even Cuba, it made the editor, in Bakker's words, 'the best known female author of the South in the first half of the nineteenth century'.[120] But in achieving that standing, it appears, Gilman had taken on a role that Martineau evidently came to find increasingly problematic as she grew to know Southern life and culture more deeply in the months after she travelled on from Charleston through Georgia and Alabama towards New Orleans.

The Southern Rose.

FLOWERS OF ALL HUE, AND WITHOUT THORN THE ROSE.—MILTON.

VOL. 4.]   CHARLESTON, S. C. SATURDAY, NOVEMBER 14, 1835.   [No. 6.

ORIGINAL SKETCHES.
RECOLLECTIONS OF A SOUTHERN MATRON.
CHAP. XI.
JACQUE'S FUNERAL.

The earliest summon'd, and the longest spared,
Are here deposited, with tribute paid
Various; but unto each *some* tribute paid.
— WORDSWORTH'S EXCURSION.

Let me pause to bestow a parting notice on one, who is still associated with the happiest and tenderest scenes of my youth. Jacque's labors, as is customary with aged slaves, had been gradually suspended. He still performed a few voluntary duties, and might be seen on sunshiny days propping a failing fence, clearing an encumbered hedge, drying nets, making baskets of rushes or oak, attending to his pigs and poultry, or with a characteristic eye to his master's interests tottering to the fields, and shaking his head if he detected any symptom of waste. Still retaining a feeling of authority, he was angered by idleness; even the young slaves whose greatest toil was to turn summersets, and dance to their own whistling, tried to look busy or grave when his eye was on them, long after his corporeal and mental powers had ceased their activity.* But the time drew near when old Jacque must die. It was in vain that mamma gave him her personal attendance, sent him daily luxuries, and anticipated his wants with almost filial tenderness; the golden cord of his life was loosened, and we were told one morning that he had died, breathing a prayer for his master's family.

Mamma had asked him many years before if there was any thing she could do for his comfort.

Tank you much, my missis, he answered, Jacque hab every ting him want in dis world, cept he shroud, praise God.

Mamma gave him money, and he expended it on grave-clothes. He had taken them out and aired them from year to year; now they were indeed to enfold his venerable remains; and we were a mourning family; true, we were not clad in weeds, but a tender tie had been riven, and it was riven with tears. None but those who live under our peculiar institutions can imagine the strong bond existing between faithful slaves and the families with whom they are connected.

I was informed by maum Nanny, Jacque's

* There is a salutary law that owners shall provide for infirm slaves; this with the attachment of their own kindred on plantations as well as that of their owners, tends to secure the South from pauperism. There is but one street beggar in Charleston, and it is hinted that he is growing rich on his profession.

wife, that he had left something for me in the *sill* of his chest, as his dying bequest. An old pocket-book was found there which I opened, and discovered several bills of continental money carefully wrapt in paper.*

Slaves on plantations prefer to bury their dead at night or before sunrise. Neighboring plantations are notified, and all who can obtain tickets from overseers attend. A spot of ground is allotted for their burial place, and simple monuments of affection may usually be found in them. The ceremony of interment is commonly performed by a class-leader, a pious colored man, who is the spiritual teacher of the neighborhood, and prepares his brethren by an examination into their belief, and a watch over their conduct and feelings, for communion.

The 'pomp and circumstance' of the burial, for it is not less among slaves, in proportion, than in palaces, delayed the funeral until midnight. As the visiters assembled, they crowded the hut of the deceased, and when that was full, stood around the entrance near the coffin. At short intervals some among the group commenced a hymn in which all joined; refreshments were then decorously distributed.†

The death of Jacque was particularly affecting to me, for I had been his especial favorite. I went with the boys to see him after his decease, and though I did not feel the faintness which came over me at witnessing the remains of grandmamma, yet I had that dizzy sensation which youth often experiences at the immense difference between a bright intellectual glance, and the glazed eye or moveless lid, between the warm touch of affection, and the stiff, cold hand that returns no pressure.

The night of his interment was mild, and I sat at my window by the star-light, watching the approach of the negroes as they crossed the fields or came through the avenue. Torches were seen glowing in the range of white-washed huts, and a bush-light‡ was flaming near Jacque's habitation, which was so brilliant, that I perceived the coffin, and the groups gathering round it; while occasionally strains of their hymn came floating with a

* It may scarcely be necessary to mention that this incident and others in the Southern Matron like those in the Northern Housekeeper are founded in truth.

† This solemnity is usually styled by the negroes 'a setting up.' When a funeral occurs at too great a distance from the city to procure tea, coffee, &c. or the owners do not provide them, the body is interred, and the friends afterward celebrate what is called a 'false burying,' where religious services are performed, and refreshments provided.

‡ A fire of lightwood kindled on a small mound of earth.

softened cadence on the breeze. The procession was formed; six women dressed in white preceded the coffin, and the pall-bearers bearing torches were on each side. Their path lay near the house, and nothing was to be heard but an occasional ejaculation, 'Lord Jesus'! 'He knows!' 'God have mercy!' 'His will be done!'

The burial place was near the river, and a huge oak threw its arms over it as if protecting the dwelling of the dead. I could see them as they wound down the slope and stood in a circle round the grave, distance still softening their sacred song. It was one which I had heard from infancy in their devotional exercises, but never had it touched my feelings as now when it rose over poor Jacque's last dwelling place. The leader spoke; at first his voice was low, then rising to that declamatory shout, which often carries the feelings captive, it reached me where I sat. He described the tomb of Lazarus, and said that Jesus wept, and that they might weep, for a good brother was gone, and there was no Jesus by his grave to bring him back; he dwelt on the character of Jacque, and on their duty in imitating his example, told them to be grateful for their religious blessings, for while the heathen were in darkness a great light had shone upon them; dwelt long on their sinfulness and God's anger, and taxed his imagination to paint the torments of hell unless they repented and accepted the gospel.

Familiarity with his dialect prevented with me all that might have been ludicrous to a stranger. He prayed for his master and mistress, that God might reward them for all their goodness to brother Jacque. Oh Lord Jesus, he cried, bless my young maussas. Gie em good counsel, and let em drink of de water of life, and bless my young missis, may she know de Lord dat bought her, and may she bring her alabaster box of ointment and pour it out for the love of her maussa, Christ.

As these words reached me, I could not restrain my tears, I laid my head on the window-sill and sobbed aloud. Another hymn was sung. The words of Watts, the sweet singer of the Christian Israel, whose tender notes fall like gentle dew on the heart of monarch and slave, rose in the quiet midnight under that starry heaven.

"Why do we mourn departed friends,
Or shake at death's alarms?
'Tis but the voice that Jesus sends
To call them to his arms."

As they ceased, the waving lights passed away. I was again alone with night in her silent beauty. I threw myself on my bed, the sounds still vibrating on my memory, and as my eyes closed in sleep, a vision of the mansion whither the spirit of Jacque had risen

Figure 2.2 *The Southern Rose*, 14 November 1835. The University of Alabama Libraries Special Collections.

Seen from this perspective, Gilman's essay, which describes the slave-owning whites of Charleston as benevolent in their practices and suggests that 'it must be delightful to those who are interested in the religion of this interesting class of people to perceive that not a narrow ray of light but the full glow of gospel radiance is thus poured upon them',[121] is certainly an accommodationist expression of white privilege. As Stephanie Jones-Rogers has noted, moreover, the *Southern Rose* inculcated 'the daily practice of slave ownership' into the minds of its target audience of young readers,[122] and it was evidently Martineau's growing awareness of this function that shifted her perception of the periodical during the months following her visit to Charleston. In this regard, the lead-off piece for the 14 November issue is even more revealing than the essay of which she explicitly complained. For the place of honour that week was held by the eleventh chapter of Gilman's long-running *Recollections of a Southern Matron*. Together with its predecessor, *Recollections of a Housekeeper*, this novel became a diptych of American domestic life, each text seeking to explain women's lives and roles in one major region of the nation to readers in the other. As they did so, however, the novels remained fundamentally committed to idealising Southern culture and so participated in a larger defining pattern of Southern domestic fiction. As Elizabeth Moss has commented, such novels, including Gilman's, affirmed an 'unyielding faith in the redemptive potential of southern women', yet also reflected 'the fundamental conservatism of its readers and writers and their shared belief in the moral superiority of their region'.[123] Given all that Martineau had learned in the months following her visit to Charleston about the republican ideology of womanhood, the conditions of slavery and the role of the press across the nation, what her letter to Gilman appears to express is a judgement that her friend has gone native, assimilated to Southern culture, participating in its work of maintaining slavery and becoming, in effect, a collaborator.[124] In this sense, *The Southern Rose*'s accomodationist ideology stands in tacit alliance with the forces obstructing progress in the nation, and Martineau's complaint about being reprinted in it, then, is not simply a piece of personal vituperation but, just as her accounts of her role at the meeting of the Boston Female Anti-Slavery Society a week earlier, profoundly reveals the understanding of America she had developed over the course of the first half of her visit.

The depth and significance of this increased understanding and the importance Martineau attached to differentiating herself from Gilman and *The Southern Rose* becomes further apparent in the increasing negativity of the ways in which she treated her quondam friend in her published texts. For although the letter itself was of course a private communication, in the public record Martineau offered a series of ever more explicit critical references to Gilman. First, the appendices to *Society in America* turn the tables of recirculation on Gilman and include a reprinting from *The Southern Rose* of Chapter 6 of *Recollections of a Southern Matron*. Focused upon the domestic life of a planter family, the chapter describes its hapless efforts to home-school its children and the culture of infantilised dependency in which the enslaved people on the estate are maintained. Cited without the context of Gilman's larger text and positioned within the penumbra of Martineau's overarching narrative of the United States, the chapter serves to evidence a representation of Southern life that parallels her critical account and provides none of the redemptive justification Gilman's novel as a whole had offered. Moreover, although Martineau offers the reader no framing language to account for the chapter's inclusion in the appendices, she follows it with an appendix that provides statistical data 'respecting the public Educational provision in the United States'.[125] Separated into sections on the Free and Slave states, the appendix lists four Southern states with no schools at all and implies that the deficiencies described in Gilman's chapter are structural and systemic rather than a merely picturesque account of a single plantation. Second, following up on this implicit critique, *Retrospect of Western Travel* includes, though it does not name, Gilman herself in its excoriating description of the Charleston slave market:

> A lady chose this moment to turn to me and say, with a cheerful air of complacency; – 'You know my theory, – that one race must be subservient to the other. I do not care which: and if the blacks should ever have the upper hand, I should not mind standing on that table, and being sold with two of my children.' Who could help saying within himself, 'Would you were! So that that mother were released'![126]

Although Gilman's identity would have been recognisable to only a few here, her reduction to a single moment and, indeed, a single sentence aligns her with the most brutal accounts of slavery in Martineau's texts and erases entirely any other consideration of her life and work. Finally, twenty years later as she wrote what she thought would be her final book and as the United States was moving ever closer to civil war, Martineau not only reproduces this passage almost verbatim in the *Autobiography* but now identifies Gilman by name, describing her as 'a northern wife, who had rushed into that admiration of Slavery which the native ladies do not entertain'.[127] Just as she would later that same year throw over her longstanding relationship with Dickens in the course of insisting upon her version of the industrial safety dispute, so, too, Martineau shows in this last reference to Gilman her willingness to regard erstwhile friends and liberal allies as collateral damage in her argument for social progress.[128]

If Martineau's encounter with the Gilmans and *The Southern Rose* and the extent of her critical representation of Caroline certainly prefigure the arc of her relationship with Dickens, just as in that later case, then, the episode reveals far more than simply personal diatribe. For Gilman and her weekly periodical become a proxy representative for what Martineau evidently sees as a profoundly dangerous form of print media: an ostensibly progressive miscellany that was, in fact, working to render normative the practices of a culture based upon slavery, and thereby implicate activist women writers in that normalisation. In this regard, the timing of the letter to Gilman does have an essential if previously unappreciated tie to the Boston abolitionist meeting that preceded it. For Martineau represents that meeting, the efforts of the Boston Female Anti-Slavery Society (BFASS) and William Lloyd Garrison's work to make *The Liberator* the vanguard of American progressivism as collectively constituting America's best hope of fulfilling its potential and completing its stadial advance. In this context, Gilman, an elite Northern woman who had allied herself with the South and whose work in both the press and her fiction rationalised an economy based upon slavery, not only becomes as complicit as the mainstream Boston leadership class Martineau had judged so definitively in her accounts of the mob and of Harvard, but takes on her full significance as a foil to the heroic efforts of the women abolitionists and of Garrison, united in their resistance and in their commitment to using print and the press to remake the public sphere.

Martineau's choice of the BFASS as her exemplar of the progressive movement and the emergence of what became her lifelong friendship with Garrison have certainly been more fully recognised than her connections with Gilman and *The Southern Rose*. What has not been examined so closely in previous studies, however, is the significance of these particular Boston ties within the larger case she makes about the role of print and the press as essential agents of progress. For, and as Anne Boylan has commented, while the BFASS was one of many early nineteenth-century women's organisations that played an essential role in new constructions of womanhood,[129] it was distinctive in the way in which it employed 'the power of the printed collective utterance' as a strategy that both advanced is specific causes and furthered the larger claim for women's engagement in political action.[130] Martineau herself notes how its opponents had used print and the press to stigmatise the women by describing their activism as transgressively exceeding the constraints of the culturally normative:

> Bills were posted about the city on this occasion, denouncing these women as casting off the refinement and delicacy of their sex: the newspapers, which laud the exertions of ladies in all other charities for the prosecution of which they are wont to meet and speak, teemed with the most disgusting reproaches and insinuations: and the pamphlets which related to the question all presumed to censure the act of duty which the women had performed in deciding upon their duty for themselves.[131]

She then goes on to describe how, in the response to this effort to exclude women from public discourse, the BFASS petitioned the Massachusetts legislature directly and was able to win its case.[132] Moreover, the Society's strategic significance to Martineau's analysis of the role of the press in America went well beyond this single petition and lay most importantly with its alliance with the Garrisonian wing of the abolitionist movement. For, as Debra Gold Hansen has shown, not only was the Society leadership unusual in the challenges it offered to conventional understandings of what was appropriate behaviour for women but, by the late 1830s, it was also becoming profoundly divided by a schism between supporters of Garrison and those who, more closely tied to the evangelical churches and alarmed by the racist riots in the city in 1834, were reluctant to challenge clerical authority and resisted Garrison's more assertive leadership.[133] As Martineau wrote to the British Quaker abolitionist Elizabeth Pease, she was well aware of these divisions and the painfulness of 'the exposure of the enmities of those whose first friendship sprang up in the field of benevolent labors'.[134] However, as had been the case with Gilman and as would later appear in her dispute with Dickens, awareness and pain become subordinated to the larger argument that she wishes to make to her readers. Martineau would make strategic use of these divisions within the abolitionist movement to advance her cause in the second of two articles on America that she wrote for the *Westminster Review*, 'The Martyr Age of the United States', which appeared in December 1838 (three years after she had remonstrated with Gilman) and which is discussed below in Chapter 5.

'I much desire to occupy, when I go away, some position in your periodical literature'

Within weeks of the Boston meeting and the letter to Gilman, Martineau attempted to find a way to participate in shaping America's future both by entering its public sphere directly and by exerting control over the circulation of her work. First, she wrote to John Gorham Palfrey, Unitarian minister and then editor of the *North American Review*, to outline a vision of what she hoped to achieve:

> I have much to ask, & something to say about putting the literary intercourse, & intellectual exchanges of our respective countries upon a better footing. For my own part, I much desire to occupy, when I go away, some position in your periodical literature which may enable me, possibly, to make some of our European experience useful to your new world. I believe that such a literary companionship between some of you & us might prevent <u>you</u> from innocently copying some of our legislative & philosophical errors, refresh <u>us</u> with some of the healthy influences which arise from your youth & freedom.[135]

Perhaps not surprisingly, given the verdict on Boston's leadership she would go on to publish, nothing came of this offer. Indeed, Palfrey was to run one of the more dismissively gendered appraisals of her visit as his magazine's review of *Society in America* commented that 'Her Progress through the country was a Visitation and Inspection'.[136] Second, however, Martineau took steps to manage the representation of her texts for American readers. In January 1836, just two months after the altercation with Gilman, she published *Miscellanies*, a two-volume collection largely comprised of pieces she had written for the *Monthly Repository*, with Hilliard, Gray Company of Boston. In making her selection for these reprints, however, both the ordering of the items and the inclusion of two articles that had not originally appeared in the Unitarian magazine are revealing. For *Miscellanies* opens with the essays on Scott from *Tait's Edinburgh Magazine* that, as we have seen, had been such a significant statement of her own authorial intent. Gavin Budge has suggested that in republishing these two texts Martineau had in mind an audience of Southern readers of Scott and his appeal to their idealisation of the feudal past, and that she was indirectly critiquing their pro-slavery culture.[137] While that appeal was certainly real, and understanding Martineau's editorial choice in this way would align with her response to Gilman, we may also read the selection in two additional ways. First, the essays for *Tait's* had portrayed Scott's transformation from the individual shaped by private experience into a commodified object of public attention and fame; foregrounding them in the collection suggests the heightened sensitivity to the effects of such a shift Martineau had herself gained from her own experiences in America. Second, while Scott was indeed widely embraced in the South, as Budge suggests, it is important to note that, as Anne Stapleton has shown, he enjoyed enormous popularity across the entire nation.[138] Martineau's highlighting him with pride of place in the collection may, then, have had a twofold implication. While it pointed to how much she herself had learned about celebrity and the costs it levied, it also reinforced her diagnosis of the feudalism lurking in America at large, not just in the South, and her assessment of the extent to which fealty to elite European cultural models served to impede the new nation's stadial progress and complete realisation of the ideals upon which it had been founded. With the publication of these volumes, then, and even before she left for home, Martineau began the work of establishing herself as an enduring presence in American letters and the press – work that, as Chapters 5 and 7 will show, she continued throughout the 1840s and on through the early years of the Civil War.

Notes

1. Harriet Martineau, *Society in America*, vol. 3, p. 1.
2. Ibid. vol. 1, pp. x–xiv.
3. See Webb, *Harriet Martineau*, Chapter 5; Logan, *Writings on Slavery*; Roberts, *The Woman and the Hour*, Chapter 2.
4. Martineau, *How to Observe*, p. 112; *Society in America*, vol. 2, p. 222.
5. Martineau, *Retrospect*, vol. 1, p. 172.
6. Martineau, *Society in America*, vol. 1, pp. 210–11.
7. Ibid.
8. Trollope, *Domestic Manners of the Americans*, pp. 1, 2.
9. Dickens, *American Notes*, pp. 190–1.
10. Smith, *River of Dreams*, pp. 92–3.
11. Martineau, *Retrospect*, vol. 2, pp. 172, 193.
12. Howe, *What God Hath Wrought*, pp. 87–9.
13. Martineau, *How to Observe*, pp. 174, 37.
14. Dillon, *The Gender of Freedom*, p. 203; Brown, *Domestic Individualism*, p. 7.
15. Martineau, *How to Observe*, p. 174.

16. Ibid. p. 117.
17. Martineau, 'The Achievements of the Genius of Scott', p. 454.
18. Martineau, *How to Observe*, pp. 176–7.
19. Martineau, *Society in America*, vol. 2, p. 296.
20. Martineau, *Letters*, vol. 2, p. 6.
21. Roberts, *The Woman and the Hour*, pp. 42–9.
22. Martineau, *Society in America*, vol. 1, p. xv.
23. Ibid. vol. 2, p. 327.
24. Ibid. vol. 2, p. 338.
25. Ibid. vol. 2, p. 330.
26. Martineau, *Retrospect*, vol. 2, p. 71.
27. Martineau, *How to Observe*, pp. 163–4.
28. De Certeau, *The Practice of Everyday Life*, pp. 91–3, 117–22.
29. Martineau, *Society in America*, vol. 3, p. 31.
30. Ibid. vol. 1, p. 163.
31. Ibid. vol. 1, p. 174.
32. Ibid. vol. 3, p. 21.
33. Martineau, *Retrospect*, vol. 2, p. 215.
34. Ibid. vol. 2, pp. 213–14.
35. Ibid. vol. 2, p. 249.
36. Trollope, *Domestic Manners of the Americans*, p. 33.
37. Martineau, *Retrospect*, vol. 2, p. 217.
38. Shapiro and Miller, *Physician to the West*, pp. xiii, xiv.
39. Ibid. p. xxi.
40. Martineau, *Retrospect*, vol. 2, p. 223.
41. Ibid. vol. 2, p. 223.
42. Trollope, *Domestic Manners of the Americans*, p. 53.
43. Martineau, *Retrospect*, vol. 2, p. 235. My attention was first drawn to this aspect of Martineau's representation of Cincinnati by Emily Pazar, then a student in the University of Delaware's Winterthur Program in American Material Culture, through her seminar paper, 'Ideas on Display: Spectacle and Education in Museums, According to Frances Trollope and Harriet Martineau'.
44. Martineau, *Retrospect*, vol. 2, pp. 235, 223.
45. Drake, *Pioneer Life in Kentucky*, quoted in Tucher, 'Newspapers and Periodicals', p. 395.
46. Martineau, *Retrospect*, vol. 2, p. 226.
47. Ibid. vol. 2, pp. 229–30.
48. This painting, about which little is known, is reminiscent of Thomas Cole's 1834–6 *The Course of Empire*, especially the second work in the series, *The Pastoral or Arcadian State*, but with the inclusion of the steamboat aligns the artist with Martineau's affirming emphasis upon the effects of technology-driven economic development. See Stoll, *Ramp Hollow*, pp. 38–9 for a discussion of Cole in terms of stadial theory. My thanks to Adam Grimes for pointing out the connection with Cole.

49. Martineau, *Harriet Martineau's Autobiography with Memorials*, vol. 3, p. 118.
50. Martineau, *Society in America*, vol. 1, pp. 302–3.
51. Ibid. vol. 1, p. 27.
52. Ibid. vol. 1, pp. 18, 357.
53. Gross, 'Reading for an Extensive Republic'.
54. Ibid. pp. 516–18, 525.
55. Martineau, *Retrospect*, vol. 2, pp. 21–4.
56. Ibid. vol. 2, p. 30.
57. Button, 'American Liberalism from Colonialism to the Civil War and Beyond', pp. 21–41, 35.
58. Martineau, *Retrospect*, vol. 2, pp. 33–4.
59. Ibid. vol. 3, p. 13.
60. Ibid. vol. 3, pp. 30–1.
61. Martineau, *Society in America*, vol. 2, p. 243.
62. Ibid. vol. 2, p. 248.
63. Martineau, *How to Observe*, p. 145.
64. Brown, *The Consent of the Governed*, p. 7.
65. Goodlad, *Victorian Literature and the Victorian State*, p. 15.
66. Martineau, *Society in America*, vol. 3, p. 130.
67. Ibid. vol. 3, p. 14.
68. Greenberg, *Honor & Slavery*, p. 15.
69. Freeman, *Affairs of Honor*, pp. xv, 168.
70. Martineau, *Society in America*, vol. 3, p. 56.
71. Ibid. vol. 3, pp. 56, 58.
72. Ibid. vol. 3, p. 57.
73. Martineau, *Retrospect*, vol. 2, p. 282.
74. Martineau, *Society in America*, vol. 3, pp. 69–70.
75. Nerone, 'Newspapers and the Public Sphere', p. 231.
76. Buckingham, *America: Historical, Statistic, and Descriptive*; Marryat, *Diary in America*.
77. Trollope, *Domestic Manners of the Americans*, p. 268.
78. Martineau, *Retrospect*, vol. 1, p. 50.
79. Howe, *What God Hath Wrought*, p. 227.
80. Nord, *Communities of Journalism*, p. 94.
81. Fuller, *Papers on Literature and Art*, quoted in Price and Smith, *Periodical Literature in Nineteenth-Century America*, p. 6.
82. Tucher, 'Newspapers and Periodicals', p. 405.
83. Henkin, 'City Streets and the Urban World of Print'.
84. Martineau, *Letters*, vol. 1, pp. 315, 321.
85. Ibid. vol. 2, p. 148; vol. 3, pp. 19, 309.
86. Martineau, *Society in America*, vol. 1, p. 134.
87. Martineau, *Retrospect*, vol. 2, p. 247.
88. Martineau, *How to Observe*, pp. 197, 198.
89. Martineau, *Society in America*, vol. 3, p. 205; *How to Observe*, p. 142.

90. Lloyd and Thomas, *Culture and the State*, p. 48.
91. 'Miss Sedgwick's Works', pp. 43, 44.
92. Ibid. pp. 46, 59, 64, 65.
93. Martineau, *Society in America*, vol. 3, p. 213.
94. Martineau, *Retrospect*, vol. 2, p. 71.
95. Martineau, *Society in America*, vol. 2, pp. 5–6.
96. Ibid. vol. 1, p. 319.
97. Ibid. vol. 1, p. 153.
98. Ibid. vol. 2, pp. 344, 345, 352.
99. Martineau, *Retrospect*, vol. 2, pp. 143–4.
100. Martineau, *Society in America*, vol. 2, pp. 345–6.
101. Ibid. vol. 2, p. 141.
102. Ibid. vol. 2, pp. 284–8.
103. Tucher, 'Newspapers and Periodicals', p. 399.
104. Martineau, *Letters*, vol. 2, p. 72.
105. Joyce, *The State of Freedom*, p. 55.
106. Martineau, *Retrospect*, vol. 1, p. 257.
107. Howe, *What God Hath Wrought*, pp. 428–30.
108. Martineau, *Society in America*, vol. 1, p. 61.
109. Martineau, *Retrospect*, vol. 1, p. 257.
110. Trollope, *Domestic Manners of the Americans*, p. 263.
111. Martineau, *Retrospect*, vol. 2, p. 74.
112. Martineau, *Harriet Martineau's Autobiography*, vol. 3, p. 110.
113. Martineau, *Letters*, vol. 1, pp. 280–1.
114. Ibid. p. 281, n. 2.
115. Logan, *The Hour and the Woman*, pp. 85–6.
116. Liddle, *The Dynamics of Genre*, pp. 48–53; Peterson, *Becoming a Woman of Letters*, Chapter 2.
117. Macaulay, *Unitarianism in the Antebellum South*, pp. 3, 67.
118. Following up on earlier reports of Martineau's arrival in the US and of her imminent arrival in Charleston, Gilman's account of Martineau's visit and 'A Letter to the Deaf' both appeared in the 4 April 1835 issue, pp. 121–7; 'Some Autobiographical Particulars' was reprinted in the 27 June 1835 issue, pp. 172–3.
119. Saucier, 'The Rose Bud', p. 293.
120. Bakker, 'Caroline Gilman and the Issue of Slavery', p. 273.
121. *The Southern Rose*, 14 November 1835, p. 42.
122. Jones-Rogers, *They Were Her Property*, p. 13.
123. Moss, *Domestic Novelists in the Old South*, pp. 41, 14.
124. Jones-Rogers, *They Were Her Property*, pp. 14–15 points out that Gilman had also published a critical op-ed in the 31 October issue 1835 of the *Southern Rose* – one of those 'four last Nos' Martineau referred to her letter – attacking Catharine Sedgwick's representation of slavery in *The Linwoods* and argues that she did so as a means of 'providing her young readers with a ready response to abolitionist attacks on southern slavery'.

125. Martineau, *Society in America*, vol. 3, p. 333.
126. Martineau, *Retrospect*, vol. 2, p. 85.
127. Martineau, *Autobiography*, p. 343.
128. Although this last rendering of the incident would not appear until after Martineau's death in 1876, Gilman was still alive to read it, having moved back to Rhode Island after her husband's death. Denying ever having visited the slave market, she described Martineau's request to reprint the letter to her mother quoted above and how, 'entirely ignorant of the serpent slander that lay coiled in her manuscripts', she had acceded. 'Miss Martineau's Attack on Miss Caroline Gilman', p. 1.
129. Boylan, *The Origins of Women's Activism*, p. 6.
130. Ibid. p. 159.
131. Martineau, *Society in America*, vol. 3, p. 111.
132. Martineau, *Retrospect*, vol. 3, pp. 160–2.
133. Hansen, *Strained Sisterhood*, p. 141. See also her extended discussion of the abolitionist movement in Boston, pp. 93–123.
134. Martineau, *Further Letters*, p. 51.
135. Martineau, *Letters*, vol. 1, pp. 282–3.
136. 'Miss Martineau's *Society in America*', p. 423.
137. Budge, *Romanticism, Medicine, and the Natural Supernatural*, p. 138.
138. Stapleton, 'MORE Matter'.

Chapter 3

American Notes and the 'frightful engine' of the Press

Writing a little over six years after Martineau had returned home, Dickens concluded the account he published of his own visit to America by identifying the nation's newspapers as the 'tangled root' of the nation's 'foul growth'. In his rendering of the new civilisation, these newspapers are the 'frightful engine' that has become 'the standard literature of an enormous class, who must find their reading in a newspaper, or they will not read at all', creating a 'monster of depravity' and forming a 'licentious Press' that is the greatest single impediment to the advance of the republic.[1] More vehement in his condemnation than any previous British visiting writer, Dickens joined his compatriots in identifying the tyranny of 'public opinion' in the United States as the underlying condition that had allowed such a press to develop,[2] and he aligned himself with Martineau in describing such tyranny as the reason for the suffocation of all dissent against the culture of slavery. Despite these passing similarities, however, closer attention to both *American Notes* and *Martin Chuzzlewit* indicates that Dickens and Martineau in fact offer fundamentally incompatible interpretations of America, interpretations that both rest upon and reveal their differing visions of liberalism, narratives of the historical arc and understandings of the role of the press as an agent of progress. Where Martineau continued to affirm the viability of the American project, notwithstanding both the conjoined issues of slavery and the 'feudal' categorisation of women as well as the constraints she described facing the press, Dickens returned home disillusioned with the young democracy, scathing in his assessment of its prospects and deeply ambivalent about its newspapers, even as he evidently endorsed its ideology of republican motherhood and the exclusion of women from the public sphere. If he differed so essentially from Martineau in his appraisal of the New World, however, Dickens's encounter with America was no less significant for his own career than Martineau's had been. Indeed, his representation of the nation in *American Notes*, the critical response to the book in the press on both sides of the Atlantic and his reaction to that response collectively form a crucial phase in the development of his understanding of the popular press and his own potential role in it.

In examining the American visit as a formative phase of his career, this chapter enters into a conversation in Dickens studies that has been developed most notably by John Drew and Juliet John. For Drew, despite the difficulties *American Notes* creates for the reader through its uncertainty as to what audience it wants to address, the book is clearly about 'the invasive power of the press'.[3] For John, Dickens's experience of culture shock during his American visit is manifested primarily in his development of a dystopian vision of what mass culture could mean and a new awareness of its potential dangers.[4] Invaluable though these studies are, both read *American Notes* through a lens that focuses from Britain to the United States, a feature of much of the critical conversation around the text since its initial publication. That perspective assumes America's cultural subordination to England as a given, placing the New World into a merely subaltern relationship to the Old and consequently focusing largely upon the deficiencies and limitations of a society so distant from the metropole.

As noted above in the Introduction, however, new understandings of transatlanticism offered by scholars of early American literature have suggested a more complex history for the interactions between the print cultures of the Anglophone world and moved the critical conversation on beyond a narrower concentration upon the issues related to international copyright. Building on the body of scholarship on transatlantic exchange represented by the work of Amanda Claybaugh, Paul Giles, Meredith McGill, Joseph Rezek and Jessica DeSpain, this chapter and the one that follows revise the line of interpretation established by Drew and John so as to move the emphasis away from the qualities for which Dickens lambasted the United States and towards creating a fuller recognition of the ways in which his encounter with North America played an essential role in his formation as both journalist and novelist. While Dickens appeared to follow Trollope, Marryat and Hall in simply excoriating the excesses of the American press, then, I argue here that *American Notes* also reveals, in Giles's phrase, the ways in which 'the prospect of America produces various forms of disturbance' in his response to the New World and the literary and journalistic culture evolving across the Atlantic.[5] By focusing upon the particular forms of disturbance

American Notes registers, we can understand more fully the conflicting pulls within the text itself and, most importantly for my case here, illuminate the role played by America in shaping Dickens's own contribution to the Victorian press. This chapter and the following will thus argue that *American Notes* and *Martin Chuzzlewit* show Dickens in the process of developing a foundational vision for massmarket popular journalism, a vision that would be such an essential part of his work throughout the 1850s and 1860s and that articulates a version of liberal ideology that is both more conservative and more Anglocentric than Martineau's.

To make this case, the chapter is organised into four sections. First, it shows that Dickens, as had been the case with Martineau, travelled to America at a point in his career when he was keenly engaged in exploring the role of the press in managing processes of social change and conflict. In this regard, *Barnaby Rudge*, the novel he completed just weeks before sailing, prefigures his engagement with America in ways that have not previously been recognised. The chapter next moves to consider *American Notes* and the visit it describes along lines that parallel Chapter 2's discussion of Martineau. For, second, it revisits the established narrative of Dickens's account of his travel to and through America, focusing away from the familiar images of disgust over manners and customs that have preoccupied critical discussions. Instead, it emphasises the ways in which *American Notes* both argues against the stadial model of progressive history that was so fundamental to Martineau and simultaneously asserts a sense of normative value in British culture and institutions that is intensified for Dickens by his separation from them. In this respect, the text's Canadian sections, which have been almost entirely overlooked in the critical conversation, become an essential counter to *American Notes*'s representation of the United States. At the same time, the chapter argues that his account of New York can be seen as the first instance of what would become a defining characteristic of his mature work. Offering a vision of a new world of unrestricted print and textual production, Dickens's New York markedly contrasts with Martineau's representation of a range of American cities as exemplars of America's uneven positioning along the arc of stadial progress. Instead, Dickens's New York, a vibrant living space where the prospect of a mass-market press unfettered by state controls is represented as simultaneously fascinating and deeply disturbing, stands as an avatar of the future world of urban print and mass literacy to which both his later fiction and journalism so extensively respond. Third, building from this image of New York, the chapter examines how *American Notes* renders educational institutions, literacy and print media as a set of both signifiers and agents of social progress among different subsets of the American population. By contrast with Martineau's representation, I argue that, rather than making the attempt to produce a comprehensive assessment of the New World itself, Dickens's account remains intrinsically Anglocentric, seeing aspects of America largely as variants upon British ideologies assumed as normative. Most notably, for example, in its highly conventional images of femininity, *American Notes* shares none of the interest that had been central to Martineau's focus upon interrogating the ways in which local forms of cultural production and women's opportunities to take leadership roles in the abolitionist movement disrupted the still persistent culture of republican motherhood and contributed to the advance of a liberal democracy. Finally, in the chapter's fourth section I offer a new reading of the initial, transatlantic reception of *American Notes*. Although it is clear that Dickens had anticipated a negative reaction from American readers, he was evidently taken aback by the breadth of that response, the terms in which even his British ideological allies attacked the book and, for the first time in his career, the almost universal disregard with which a new work of his was greeted. Examining the terms in which he was criticised in the reviews that appeared over the winter of 1842–3 as he discovered that the transatlantic press could indeed be a 'frightful engine' directed against himself, we can thus discern a previously unrecognised framework for understanding Dickens's representation of print and the press in the new work he had already begun as the reviews of *American Notes* were continuing to appear: *Martin Chuzzlewit*, which is the subject of Chapter 4.

'Great Britain drenched in gore': *Barnaby Rudge*, Dickens and the Press

As noted in Chapter 2, Martineau's participation in the wider discussion that developed over the role of a free press and the debate over its political influence that occurred around Parliament's 1836 move to reduce the stamp tax by 75 per cent[6] was made evident immediately before her visit to America in *The Scholars of Arneside*. Though less overtly self-conscious and self-reflective, Dickens was clearly no less engaged in the same debate as Martineau and no less interested in exploring the question of what his own role in the press might become. Only weeks before sailing from Liverpool, for instance, he had wrapped up *Barnaby Rudge* and, with it, the unsuccessful experiment of *Master Humphrey's Clock*. Together with another abandoned editorial venture – his two-year stint running *Bentley's Miscellany* – the *Clock* points to his evolving interest in the editorial function within popular periodicals and the opportunities it might afford him. In particular, as John Drew has noted, by contrast with the largely behind-the-scenes role of the editor in Bentley's magazine, Master Humphrey himself anticipates the vantage points of Dickens's later journalistic career and, in particular, the recurring interest in trying 'to envisage and comprehend the cryptic city' that is so characteristic of Dickens's urban journalism of the 1850s and 1860s.[7] That interest, as the second section of this chapter will show, emerges more fully in the New York chapter of *American Notes* and, as Chapter 4 will explore, first becomes an essential element of his representation of London in *Martin Chuzzlewit*.

Barnaby Rudge has long been the subject of less critical attention than any other of Dickens's novels and, with the major exception of important studies by Robert Patten and John Bowen, has in recent years been discussed largely in isolation and without any extended consideration of its place in his unfolding career.[8] Indeed, for an exploration of its connection to his American visit we have to look back as far as Myron Magnet's 1985 *Dickens and the Social Order*, a study that focused upon the need for a society 'to fulfill its duty of civilizing and humanizing its citizens' without which 'whole classes of them will remain brutes'.[9] What has not been observed in previous critical discussions of the novel, however, is the way in which it reveals how the American visit took place just as Dickens was beginning to use his fiction to explore the relationship between the press and the rapidly evolving phenomenon of modern urban life in the context of the threat of political violence endemic during the latter half of the 1830s. But *Barnaby* does in fact show how Dickens regarded the dangers latent in a mass population concentrated in the city and driven by the combination of ignorance and political manipulation as even more urgent than the unrest Martineau had depicted in her tale's account of the village mob in Arneside.

For, unprecedented in their depiction of the urban savagery unleashed by the Gordon riots, the novel's often noted descriptions of mob violence include an account of the press that points to what Drew has noted would become a central focus for Dickens: his emphasis upon the need to decipher the cryptic urban environments that were becoming the dominant element in modern society and that were increasingly being rendered into meaning through the proliferation of mass print culture. In *Barnaby*, even if the rioting mob appears to be 'a creature of very mysterious presence, particularly in a large city',[10] it is actually an agent of large-scale violence that is at least in part orchestrated by crude, early forms of mass media. Beginning with the mysterious distribution of unnamed handbills invoking generalised anti-Catholic hatred among the populace,[11] the novel then moves on to show how the rioters are stirred into specific action through the directives of The Thunderer, the title of an actual item in the historical record of the Gordon Riots. Intended for publication on 8 June 1780, The Thunderer apparently never existed other than in the form of 'England in Blood', a handbill advertising it in advance for which its originator was convicted of seditious libel at the Old Bailey in December 1781.[12] Owning a copy of Thomas Holcroft's *Plain and Succinct Narrative of the Late Riots* in which this handbill was reprinted (Fig. 3.1), Dickens folds the historical artefact seamlessly into his own text as if it were indeed the never realised broadsheet it anticipates and amplifies its influence among the London populace.[13] Taking the language of the handbill from Holcroft, with its railing against 'the infernal Designs of the Ministry, to overturn the religious and civil liberties of this country in order to introduce Popery and Slavery', Dickens turns it into an avatar of the radical press of the 1830s as he describes how The Thunderer 'was always in request; and whether read aloud, to an eager knot of listeners, or by some solitary man, was certain to be followed by stormy talking and excited looks'.[14] Its readership, moreover, becomes pervasive, spreading beyond the rioters themselves and even infiltrating the household of Gabriel Varden himself, locksmith and metonymic embodiment of social order. For Gabriel is no more able to restrain his wife's servant from absorbing the pamphlet's pernicious effects than he is to prevent the rioters breaking down the gates of Newgate: 'indeed the peace of mind she had derived from the perusal of that paper generally, but especially of one article of the very last week as ever was, entitled "Great Britain drenched in gore", exceeded all belief'.[15]

If this primitive early form of the press is thus shown to have a critical shaping effect upon the mob and its plunging civil society into chaos, an important aspect of that chaos emerges in a particular detail of the destruction wrought by the mob. For, having destroyed Newgate, the rioters move on to Bloomsbury Square and the house of Lord Mansfield, the Lord Chief Justice whose ruling in Somersett's Case had removed the legal justification for slavery in England and Wales. Burning down the house, the mob destroys 'the great Law Library, on almost every page of which were notes in the Judge's own hand, of inestimable value'[16] and thereby creates a complex moment

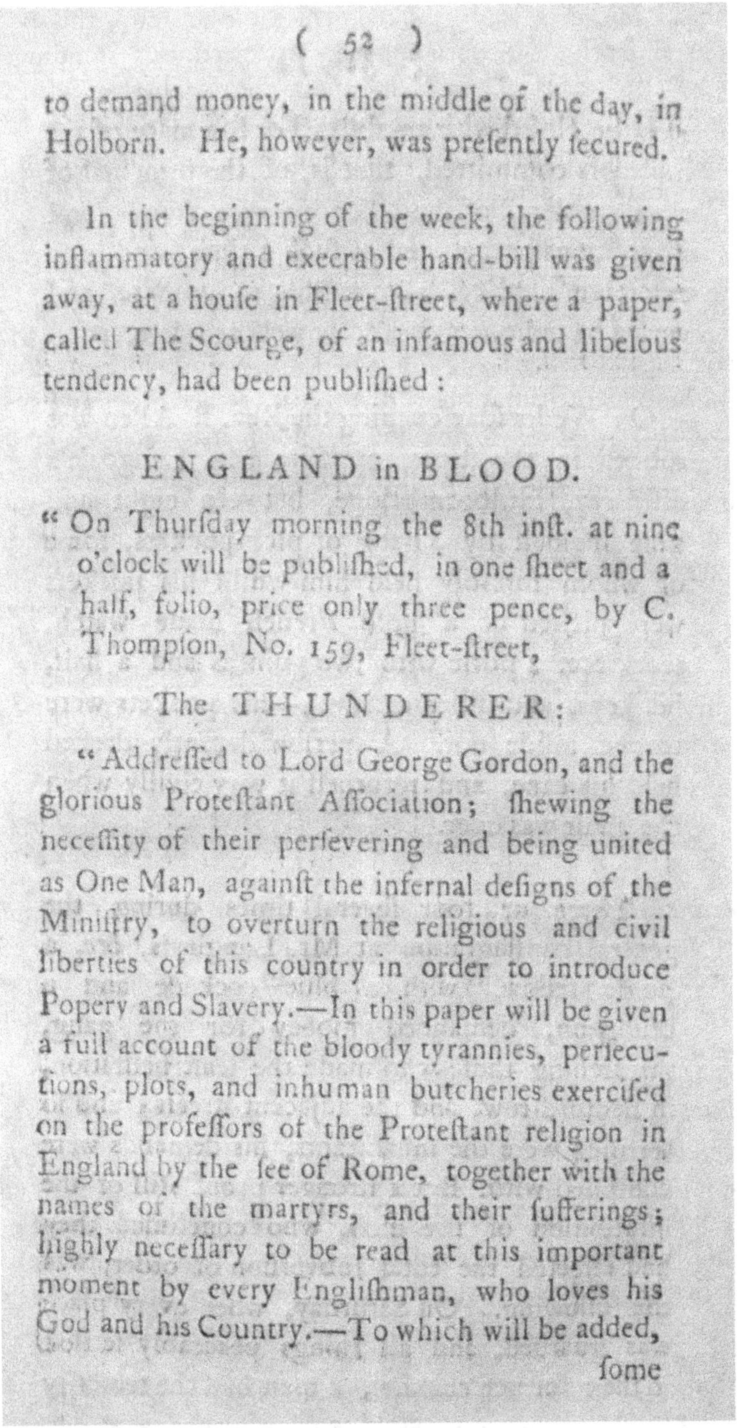

(52)

to demand money, in the middle of the day, in Holborn. He, however, was presently secured.

In the beginning of the week, the following inflammatory and execrable hand-bill was given away, at a house in Fleet-street, where a paper, called The Scourge, of an infamous and libelous tendency, had been published:

ENGLAND in BLOOD.

"On Thursday morning the 8th inst. at nine o'clock will be published, in one sheet and a half, folio, price only three pence, by C. Thompson, No. 159, Fleet-street,

The THUNDERER:

"Addressed to Lord George Gordon, and the glorious Protestant Association; shewing the necessity of their persevering and being united as One Man, against the infernal designs of the Ministry, to overturn the religious and civil liberties of this country in order to introduce Popery and Slavery.—In this paper will be given a full account of the bloody tyrannies, persecutions, plots, and inhuman butcheries exercised on the professors of the Protestant religion in England by the see of Rome, together with the names of the martyrs, and their sufferings; highly necessary to be read at this important moment by every Englishman, who loves his God and his Country.—To which will be added,
some

Figure 3.1 *The Thunderer.*

that has been largely overlooked. On the one hand, this body of written and printed texts is a form of synecdoche, standing for a legal system and its role in maintaining the social order with which *Barnaby Rudge* ultimately aligns itself, the passages of extraordinary empathy with the mob notwithstanding. On the other, and as those passages make evident, the action of the mob in 1788 references the devastating level of potential threat to British social stability posed through the political unrest of the working classes in Britain. Finally, in the context of news coverage of pro-slavery rioting in the United States, including Martineau's December 1838 publication of 'The Martyr Age', Dickens's alluding to Lord Mansfield both connects transatlantic representations of the threat to civic order and suggests the capacity of the British state to reform itself and foster liberal progress.[17] Although Lord Mansfield's library, handbills and the Thunderer play no further part in the text, these brief appearances of rudimentary forms of print media and references to the relationship of textual knowledge to social progress just months before his departure for America stand as Dickens's first reference in his fiction to the broad capacity of the press to shape public discourse, and reveal that his concern over its potential to undermine the foundations of social stability clearly predates his encounter with the New World and its newspapers.

'Forms of disturbance': Dickens and America

Dickens's deeply fascinated, deeply troubled reaction in *Barnaby* to the spectacle of the urban riots and his first treatment of the role of the press in shaping major social phenomena provide the context in which this section reads his experience of the New World itself and his writing about it in *American Notes*. That experience clearly was, as Juliet John has argued, shaped by a degree of culture shock inevitable for someone who had previously travelled so little out of his native country.[18] The deeper forms of disturbance America evokes, however, emerge through the combination of Dickens's response to a continent that itself seems to embody a regressive historical narrative and his reactions to a newly developing nation that simultaneously draws deeply upon its British origins even as it modifies them and rejects large parts of the inherited cultural model. For Dickens, that is, what appears most disturbing of all is the way in which this new world resists his interpretive efforts and asserts a linguistic and textual identity of its own. The dissonance that this combination of phenomena creates for him resonates throughout the text: it first becomes apparent during the transatlantic voyage itself before he even lands in Boston, and it is subsequently magnified and reinforced by his travel into the American interior and his encounters with its topography. Ultimately, however, it is in his exploration of urban America, above all New York and the textual landscape this particular city creates, that he discovers most fully what it is that both repels and intrigues him in the New World.

In her study of uncolonisable spaces in the nineteenth-century British imaginary, Siobhan Carroll has described the sea as 'a dangerous atopia, a space antithetical to civilization, and the antipode of the stable, ordered space of the nation'.[19] Standing simultaneously as the venue for global transportation and the 'international space to which Britain must expose its imperial agents', the ocean, she continues, articulates both British claims of imperial power and the disorder that threatens such aspirations. Carroll thus provides a valuable model for reading a part of *American Notes* that has received surprisingly little attention: Dickens's transatlantic passage and the ways in which the account of the voyage anticipates his reaction to the dynamic energies of American society. For the journey proves to be one that begins in confident expectation but then quickly dissolves to discomfort, disorientation and terror, qualities evident even in the moment of departure. As he is leaving Liverpool on the newly established Cunard steamer service to Boston, that is, Dickens represents the steamship *Britannia* both as playing into its eponymous role as an emblem of national pride, a 'noble ship' that 'breaks proudly through the lashed and foaming water', and yet simultaneously as something far less reassuring, the first of the text's 'frightful engines'. For, and in terms reminiscent of Frankenstein's creature, he notes that the ship itself 'throbs like a strong giant that has just received the breath of life', all too like the new nation for which it is bound.[20] Once out on the atopic ocean, in the void between the two continents, both the *Britannia* itself and Dickens's own epistemological foundations become threatened by utter dissolution, as he feels

> as though the ship were filled with fire in hiding, ready to burst through any outlet, wild with its resistless power of death and ruin. At first, too, and even when the hour, and all the objects it exalts, have come to be familiar, it is difficult, alone and thoughtful, to hold them to their proper shapes and forms. They change with the wandering fancy; assume the semblance of things left far away; put on the well-remembered aspect of favourite places dearly loved; and even people them with shadows.[21]

Helpless before a winter storm, the ship 'darts onward like a monster goaded into madness, to be beaten down, and battered, and crushed', in a frenzy that leaves even Dickens beyond the power of language to describe: 'To say that all is grand, and all appalling and horrible in the last degree, is nothing. Words cannot express it. Thoughts cannot convey it. Only a dream can call it up again, in all its fury, rage, and passion.'[22] The 'small snug chamber of the imagination'[23] that he had fondly imagined when picturing his stateroom before coming on board has given way to this state of abjection, with not even language itself able to preserve him from the prospect of utter oblivion. The storm passes, the voyage ends safely and Dickens replaces the accounts of its terror with successive heroic images of, first, his celebrity arrival in Halifax and, then, his unsteady rolling ashore in Boston in 'involuntary imitation of the gait of Mr T. P. Cooke, in a new nautical melo-drama'.[24] Even so, neither the ceremonial greeting nor his comic self-fashioning in terms of a hero of the London stage can efface the abiding sense of atopic vulnerability that had been the most powerful impression from his passage across the Atlantic and that provides a first and striking contrast between his and Martineau's apprehensions of the world beyond Britain.

Those differences, moreover, are reinforced by *American Notes*'s account of Dickens's immersion in what he presents as the increasingly primitive regions of the nation's interior. As has long been recognised, his growing disgust with both American society and the very fabric of the continent itself builds almost uninterruptedly the further west he goes. Less fully observed, however, has been the extent to which, as with the transatlantic voyage, Dickens's description of his method of travel itself becomes inseparable from the response he has to the topography through which he passes and embedded in his growing sense of disorder. For paralleling his descriptions of the *Britannia* are accounts of American means of steam transportation that, like the ship, bring with their own frightful engines the threat of explosive destruction into an environment that itself threatens slower forms of violence and dissolution. On the one hand, he successively endures a series of railroads from, first, the 'thirsty monster' that carries him from Boston to Lowell through a landscape 'in every possible stage of decay, decomposition, and neglect', to, second, the ride across the 'startling contrivances' that pass for bridges in Maryland, and, finally, the laboured journey on a track whose construction is 'indifferent' across 'wet and marshy' northern Ohio towards 'sluggish' Sandusky.[25] On the other hand, even more threatening are the riverboats of the Ohio and Mississippi, floating bombs with a great body of fire . . . that rages and roars beneath the frail pile of painted wood: the machinery, not warded off or guarded in any way, but doing its work in the midst of the crowd of idlers and emigrants and children[26]

imminently threatening all on board with destruction. The climactic peak of Dickens's account of his travel then becomes, as has often been noted, his vision of the river to which these railroads and river boats lead him, the Mississippi which he sees as 'a slimy monster hideous to behold'[27] and the nadir of the continent's inexorable loss of its very form:

An enormous ditch, sometimes two or three miles wide, running liquid mud, six miles an hour: its strong and frothy current choked and obstructed everywhere by huge logs and whole forest trees: now twining themselves together in great rafts, from the interstices of which a sedgy lazy foam works up, to float upon the water's top; now rolling past like monstrous bodies, their tangled roots showing like matted hair; now glancing singly by like giant leeches; and now writhing round and round in the vortex of some small whirlpool, like wounded snakes.[28]

Combining an ever-darkening description of the continent itself with recurring accounts of the explosively destructive power of the mechanisms by which humanity is imposing itself upon it, Dickens's rendering of America inverts Martineau's representation of a deeply fertile natural environment being forged into shape through, literally, those same mechanisms of human agency she had observed from the deck of that aptly named river steamer, the *Henry Clay*.

Focusing on the Mississippi as Dickens's heart of darkness, both Myron Magnet and Ella Dzelzainis have identified the profoundly anti-stadial character that emerges in Dickens's reading of the United States. Moreover, in exploring the degenerative emphasis in his rendering of the American continent, both have connected it to the theories of French naturalist the Comte de Buffon.[29] De Buffon's eight-volume *Histoire Naturelle* (1749–88), a set of which Dickens owned at the time of his visit,[30] described America as having emerged from the Flood after the rest of the world, with deleterious effects upon its climate, flora, fauna and population. For Dzelzainis, de Buffon's work provided Dickens with an explanation of why America failed to follow another Enlightenment paradigm, that of the 'stadial conception of civilized progress that connected social manners and political institutions',[31] a conception that had underwritten the great expectations with which he had travelled to explore the new democracy and which, as we have seen, was fundamental to Martineau's reading of

America and of the Mississippi. However, although her discussions and Magnet's certainly offer a persuasive way to understand Dickens's response to the United States, they also follow a long pattern in the critical conversation of erasing another part of North America, one that prompts in him a very different reaction, and one that complicates the notion of unidirectional continental degeneration.

For, as enthusiastically as it teaches its readers to despise the United States, so *American Notes* quietly celebrates Canada for the ways in which it sustains, and indeed advances, an essentially British identity in the New World. In this, Dickens's text contrasts markedly with Martineau's American books, which had limited their account of Canada to a single statement of regret that 'that poor country should belong to us, its poverty and hopeless inactivity contrasting, so much to our disgrace, with the prosperous activity of the opposite shore',[32] a comment that both implicitly argues for republican democracy as the vehicle of liberal progress and questions the value of British colonial practice. Dickens's interpretation could hardly be more different, beginning with his making landfall in Halifax on the day of the opening of the Legislative Council and General Assembly and using the occasion to remark on the ways in which the satellite bodies copy the opening of Parliament so closely in their small form 'that it was like looking at Westminster through the wrong end of a telescope'.[33] Though the simile emphasises how distant are the originary forms of British statehood, it also genially suggests the continuing ties across the Atlantic and a sense of connection that is rapidly effaced by his subsequent experience of those United States that await him just a short distance away across the Bay of Fundy.

Four months later, with that experience almost complete, Dickens returns to Canada, and the descending narrative trajectory of the journey across the United States abruptly gives way to the raptures of his description of Niagara and the glowing account of Ontario and Quebec that follows. By contrast with his revulsion over the Mississippi and all that American liquid slime for which it metonymically stands, the Falls have an immediate purifying impact upon him:

> Still do those waters roll and leap, and roar and tumble, all day long; still are the rainbows spanning them, a hundred feet below. Still, when the sun is on them, do they shine and glow like molten gold. Still, when the day is gloomy, do they fall like snow, or seem to crumble away like the front of a great chalk cliff, or roll adown the rock like dense white smoke. But always does the mighty stream appear to die as it comes down, and always from its unfathomable grave arises that tremendous ghost of spray and mist which is never laid . . . [34]

As Natalie McKnight has argued, in this response to Niagara Dickens aligned himself with a well-established tradition of British travellers to North America, as diverse as Martineau and Marryat, who consistently drew upon the language of the Romantic sublime to express the sentiment the Falls evoked.[35] However, if, on the one hand, his language here might be seen as little more than touristic cliché, it takes on a larger significance for the text as a whole, given his earlier representations of the atopic Atlantic and then the miasmic landscape of the United States. Beyond the chaste purity ascribed to the falling water, whether as liquid or vapour, is an acceptance of, even a celebration of, a process of sublime dissolution that has an entirely different valence from the sense of displacement into oblivion that permeates the text's anxiety over either potential shipwreck on the Atlantic or explosion on the Ohio. In gazing upon Niagara, that is, Dickens is able to create a sense of calm, tranquil stability within the very motion of the Falls that contrasts markedly with both the sensory overload that he records throughout the previous weeks of travel across America and with Martineau's enthusiastic embrace of her precarious perch above the cataract and rendering of its geological work as an emblem of the very continent's stadial formation. Moreover, as Dickens's subsequent account of his stay in Canada reveals, that sense of stability is fundamentally tied into his representation of this part of North America as having remained essentially European and, above all, English.

Even more revealing than his language itself is the vantage point he takes on the Falls, since, once having crossed the border, he 'never stirred in all that time from the Canadian side',[36] and he thus begins a celebration of Canada that frames the colony as possessing all the virtues he had found lacking in the United States. From Toronto, with its orderly streets, fine houses and excellent shops, to 'the exquisite expanse of country, rich in field and forest' that he travels across on the way to Quebec,[37] Canada offers Dickens an almost entirely affirming experience and one that is essentially linked to having retained many of its English cultural qualities even as it is fulfilling the stadial ideal and evolving into a progressive society in its own right:

> Few Englishmen are prepared to find it what it is. Advancing quietly; old differences settling down, and being fast forgotten; public feeling and private enterprise alike in a sound and wholesome state; nothing of flush or fever in its system, but health and vigour throbbing in its steady pulse; it is full of hope and promise. To me – who had been accustomed to think of it as something left behind in the strides of advancing society, as

something neglected and forgotten, slumbering and wasting in its sleep – the demand for labour and wages; the busy quays of Montreal . . . the commerce, roads, and public works, all made *to last*, the respectability and character of the public journals . . . were very great surprises.[38]

In the fullest exception to the general erasure of Canada from the critical conversation around *American Notes*, Goldie Morgentaler has noted that the country at the time was in fact a much more restless society and, in particular, much more torn in its response to the United States than readings such as this would suggest.[39] Nevertheless, for Dickens, Canada, even French Canada, presents as a model of social evolution and, with 'nothing of flush or fever in its system', stands in marked contrast to the over-heated, sickly cauldron that is the democratic society to its south, the riot-torn London of *Barnaby Rudge* and, by extension, a contemporary Britain gripped by the threat of social tumult. Although Dickens devotes less than a complete chapter to the four weeks he spent in Canada and provides his readers with a far less detailed account of his travels than he had given of the United States, his very muteness is a testimony to the degree of familiarity and comfort he feels once he returns to a society still vitally connected to Great Britain and far more defined by that connection than is the insurgently evolving nation below the forty-ninth parallel.

Following the Canadian interlude and immediately before his departure for England, Dickens describes one final American site in the account of an unsatisfactory visit to a Shaker village in Lebanon, New York. In doing so he closes out the text's representation of women in the New World, a representation that consistently iterates his own normative conceptions and that stands in marked contrast to Martineau's exploration of the challenges posed to the liberal project by female aspirations to be recognised as autonomous subjects fully participating in civic life. At Lebanon, for example, having dismissed the sect's prayer dancing as 'infinitely grotesque', he localises its failings into the person of its female leader, a woman kept 'in strict seclusion . . . never shown to profane eyes', marked, he imagines, by the bizarre ugliness that characterises the community as a whole, and with whose sequestration he is in 'perfect concurrence'.[40] As coarsely patriarchal as this is, however, it both extends the representation of cloistered femininity that his work had already established as a normative ideological pattern before he crossed the Atlantic and also offers what is effectively only a harsher version of the pattern already laid out in *American Notes* itself.

For consistently and throughout the text, Dickens represents American women as primarily the passive objects of male protection and thus excluded from full liberal subjectivity. His first extended account of a female subject, that of Laura Bridgman, the deaf, dumb and blind resident of the Perkins Institute for the Blind, establishes the pattern. 'This gentle, tender, guileless, grateful hearted being'[41] is depicted as a model product of benign, paternalistic treatment, and the reader is left to imagine her as eternally quiescent, safe within the walls of the protecting institution. Although Dickens does describe how she was taught to read and write and so differentiates her from the other individual women the text describes through being defined in relation to literacy,[42] by sentimentalising her presentation, as Karen Bourrier has argued, he moves the reader away from a consideration of the larger implications of female literacy and towards perceiving Bridgman primarily as a singular individual overcoming almost insuperable difficulties.[43] Following this account and a passing reference to the female inmates of the Eastern Penitentiary, whom he implausibly suggests that the prison experience 'humanizes and refines' even as it proves so destructive to its male inmates,[44] Dickens makes almost no further reference to women in America until he arrives at the single positive detail he offers about his voyage up the Mississippi. There, in what he portrayed to Forster as 'a pretty little scene',[45] he describes a 'little woman so full of hope, and tenderness, and love, and anxiety'[46] travelling home to St Louis after giving birth in her mother's home in New York and taking her newborn baby to his father. Reinforcing his sentimentalised definition of female lives as framed by their domestic roles and contained within familial structures, this passage stands in complete opposition to Martineau's reading of republican motherhood's cultural limitations as a form of constraint and as indicative of the larger failings of American liberalism.

From the visit to the Shaker community, Dickens moves rapidly to 'The Passage Home', his idyllic account of the voyage back across the Atlantic. Eschewing further encounters with the ambivalent power of steam and travelling under sail on the *George Washington*, a vessel named for one of the few American public figures to retain his respect, Dickens celebrates the re-creation of an English community on board – 'as cheerful and as snug a party, with an honest manly-hearted captain at our head, as ever came to the resolution of being mutually agreeable, on land or water'.[47] And, as he feels again secured in a sense of familiar community, the narrative voice moves from the sour recording of large parts of the text in America and claims a renewed sense of agency in condemning the exploitation of poor migrants and calling for government intervention to regulate their conditions of passage.[48] The Dickens whose rise to fame had been driven in part through his extraordinary power of rendering individual suffering here recovers a voice that had been largely muted throughout his time in the United States. Above all, and even more intensely than during the Canadian interlude, as he moves back towards a familiar culture, his outbound anxiety over the atopic ocean gives way to a renewed sense of home that had been lost during those months in the United States. Thus, with the ship approaching Europe again, he gazes over the calm sea at night off the coast of Ireland and reminisces:

> I recollect when I was a very young child having a fancy that the reflection of the moon in water was a path to Heaven, trodden by the spirits of good people on their way to God; and this old feeling often came over me again, when I watched it on a tranquil night at sea.[49]

Returning to England's 'luxuriant garden', with feelings 'no tongue can tell, or pen of mine describe',[50] he is rendered mute again not by the threat of the dissolving ocean as on the passage out, nor by the destructive threats with which America and its frightful engines had assailed him, but, rather, by being reunited with the comforting familiar that needs no language to be described and that he invites his readers to join him in simply recognising as a given.

Urban Space and Literacy for the Masses

Complicating the descending arc of a narrative that takes Dickens into the heart of the American darkness and then, via a restorative sojourn in British Canada, safely restores him home, is his account of urban space in the New World. For, if the American continent itself proved to be an increasingly overwhelming experience of degeneration and an inversion of the progressive stadial narrative, the new cities appearing upon it challenge Dickens's capacity to make sense of a culture defined by its insistent immediacy and apparent lack of historicity. Once the initial exhilaration of landing in the New World had dissipated, during the six weeks he spent on the Eastern seaboard he was to find himself constantly disconcerted by his encounters with America's cities, struggling to decipher the newly built world and the culture emerging there, unable to see in them the models of progress Martineau had discerned, even as he was able to experience them as startling but distinctly living urban spaces in ways she does not register. Among the various cities he encountered, one stands out. By contrast with Martineau, for whom, as Chapter 2 argued, Boston and Cincinnati stood as contrasting exemplars of America's continuing ties to the Old World and its successful shaping of the New, to Dickens it is New York that most fully shapes his representation of urban life across the Atlantic. For, more closely resembling London than any other American city, New York provides him with an image of an emerging modern city, shaped by textual experience, driven forward by an emergent mass-market press.

In this respect, New York is differentiated from all the other cities he encounters, each of which finds its distinctive way of eluding his interpretive grasp. Even in the first days after his arrival, for example, even in Boston where he would develop his closest American ties, America appears naggingly unreal to him: overwhelmed by the intensity of the painted New England exteriors, for example, Dickens finds the city 'all so slight and unsubstantial in appearance'.[51] Just as he had turned to the English stage at the moment of landing to anchor his cultural displacement within the known, so here again he renders the cityscape legible by transforming it into a familiar English theatrical genre with the comment 'that every thoroughfare in the city looked exactly like a scene in a pantomime'.[52] His subsequent day trip out to the industrial town of Lowell generates a similar sense of unreality, as he appears disoriented by the lack of history manifested by the sheer newness of urban construction, from the 'new wooden church which . . . looked like an enormous packing-case without any direction upon it' to the hotel that 'had exactly the appearance of being built with cards'.[53] And his sense of fragility in this environment is evident even as he straddles a thin line between comic and potentially tragic visioning of the scene: 'I was careful not to draw my breath as we passed, and trembled when I saw a workman come out upon the roof, lest with one thoughtless stamp of his foot he should crush the structure beneath him, and bring it rattling down.'[54] As further acquaintance with the cities of the east coast confirms this sense of unreality, Dickens finds his observations increasingly less amenable to being stabilised into a comedic vision. In Philadelphia, where the 'distractingly regular' grid pattern drives him to feel that he 'would have given the world for a crooked street',[55] he is still able to transmute the oppressive sense the city instils, albeit at the cost of transforming himself into something that better matches the built city and its culture:

> The collar of my coat appeared to stiffen, and the brim of my hat to expand, beneath its quakerly influence. My hair shrunk into a sleek short crop, my hands folded themselves upon my breast of their own calm accord, and thoughts of taking lodgings in Mark Lane over against Market Place, and of making a large fortune by speculations in corn, came over me involuntarily.[56]

Days later, however, having moved on to Washington, DC with its incompletely realised design, the American city has become for him 'a monument raised to a deceased project, with not even a legible inscription to record its departed greatness',[57] and even the possibility of a comic response such as that he had been able to generate in Philadelphia evaporates. As his travels then take him into the nation's interior, the accounts of its cities become still more perfunctory: Pittsburgh, the Cincinnati Martineau had rendered as the ideal exemplar of American stadial advancement and Louisville thus receive little more than passing mentions. Only in St Louis, where 'the old French portion of the town' provides something of that irregularity he had so craved in Philadelphia, is the arc of Dickens's increasing disengagement with urban America momentarily interrupted as he delights in discovering an architecture that draws its charm from being both rooted in historic time and in the Old World:

> these ancient habitations, with high garret gable-windows perking into the roofs, have a kind of French shrug about them; and being lop-sided with age, appear to hold their heads askew, besides, as if they were grimacing in astonishment at the American improvements.[58]

Standing apart from this pattern of representation, however, is New York, the one American city that does prove legible to Dickens and evidently does so because it most closely corresponds to the known urban space of London. That is, New York is the only city in America that the text presents as a fully realised urban environment, and also one that crucially is exceptional in the ways in which it is both built upon and itself builds multiple forms of textual production and consumption. Offering neither Boston's intensely vivid cleanliness, Lowell's combination of innovation and industrial order, Philadelphia's insistent regularity nor Washington's incomplete empty spaces, Dickens's New York is fecundly abundant in the diversity of its forms of life and energy, a fully realised space through which he walks as if he were at home. The range and variety of Manhattan's urban architecture, the plethora of humanity in the streets, the abundance of commercial life manifested in the financial district and in the docks along the river – from Broadway to the Bowery, New York pulsates for Dickens and generates an insistent particularity in the language of observation and energy in the rhythm of his prose that occur nowhere else in his account of America:

> The pavement stones are polished with the tread of feet until they shine again; the red bricks of the houses might be yet in the dry, hot kilns; and the roofs of those omnibuses look as though, if water were poured on them, they would hiss and smoke, and smell like half-quenched fires. No stint of omnibuses here! Half a dozen have gone by within as many minutes. Plenty of hackney cabs and coaches, too; gigs, phaetons, large-wheeled tilburies, and private carriages . . . . Negro coachmen and white; in straw hats, black hats, white hats, glazed caps, fur caps; in coats of drab, black, brown, green, blue, nankeen, striped jean and linen; and there, in that one instance (look while it passes, or it will be too late) in suits of livery.[59]

Here, for the first and only time in America, Dickens encounters an urban streetscape that aligns with his expectations and desires, and he is thus able to render the cryptic city as knowable and intelligible, a spectacular space in which he is able to remain an observing subject, preserved from a fear of being subsumed by the alien other that is so often voiced during his American travels.

This differentiation between Dickens's experience of New York and his engagement with other American urban spaces rests above all on the ways in which the city played, as David Henkin has argued, a distinctive role in the creation of a new public that was 'firmly situated in public space' and 'around shared reading practices'.[60] Henkin's discussion of the 'emerging circuits of communication and navigation within the growing city' and of the development of public spaces as communal sites of reading emphasises New York's special function in antebellum American society and the unparalleled contribution it made to the formation of public discourse.[61] It is to this feature of the city that Dickens most fully reacts and that leads him to distinguish it from other American urban environments. For city reading, to borrow Henkin's valuable term, permeates Dickens's New York and differentiates it from every other location *American Notes* describes. From the ubiquitous flag-staffs 'with something like Liberty's head-dress' atop them to signs 'in shape like river buoys, or small balloons, hoisted by cords to poles' tempting the poor to eat the oysters they advertise,⁶² the streets are a continuous field of text. Tavern houses, less insistent than the flagpoles on unilateral national identity and acknowledging transatlantic cultural exchanges that *American Notes* otherwise erases, regularly adorn their walls with 'coloured prints of Washington, and Queen Victoria of England, and the American Eagle', along with

> portraits of William, of the ballad, and his Black-Eyed Susan; of Will Watch, the bold Smuggler; of Paul Jones the Pirate, and the like, on which the painted eyes of Queen Victoria, and of Washington to boot, rest in as strange companionship, as on most of the scenes that are enacted in their wondering presence.⁶³

And even the wretched tenements through which Dickens wanders reveal 'walls bedecked with rough designs of ships, and forts, and flags, and American Eagles out of number'.⁶⁴

If Dickens's perception of New York thus positions it as the American exemplar of modern urbanism and a space in which textual interpretation has become an integral part of engagement in the public sphere, the full significance of that positioning becomes evident if we set it in the context of *American Notes*'s wider representation of issues associated with literacy and education. To Martineau, as Chapter 2 has argued, these aspects of national life served to illustrate both the major impediments to stadial advance that American culture had constructed and the ways in which those impediments could themselves be offset by progressive activism. In her reading of the United States it is education, literacy and print that can drive America's evolution towards a liberal society in which the governed are finally able to give their consent. Over the course of his visit, by contrast, Dickens, increasingly disturbed by the experience of America, became far less confident in the nation's stadial progress, and his responses to it express that growing ambivalence. Specifically, in using the issues of education, literacy and print to implicitly compare one of the major immigrant populations that was flooding into America at the time of his visit with the sampling of indigenous inhabitants he comes across during his travels and then contrasting both with an exemplary model of working-class cultural literacy, *American Notes* offers a version of civilisation that defines fundamental distinctions between Martineau and Dickens's understandings of the liberal project.

By contrast with Martineau, for whom, as Chapter 2 argues, the development of education in America was an essential indicator of its stadial progress towards realising the ideal of a liberal society, Dickens offers only one comment on the topic. Taking the form of a single paragraph about Harvard, this passage includes praise for its faculty, who 'shed a grace upon, and do honour to, any society in the civilised world', and for the ways in which the institution exemplifies a larger national virtue of American universities, which

> disseminate no prejudices; rear no bigots; dig up the buried ashes of no old superstitions; never interpose between the people and their improvement; exclude no man because of his religious opinions; above all, in their whole course of study and instruction, recognise a world, and a broad one too, lying beyond the college walls.[65]

For Juliet John this paragraph shows Dickens expressing a sense that intellectual life in America, and specifically in Cambridge, offers an alternative to the predations of the mass culture and indicates how much he valued the social circle he developed among the Harvard academics because it 'represented culture, in particular a learned culture that saw itself serving needs beyond the commercial'.[66] While it certainly speaks to Dickens's fondness for his Cambridge friends, however, the paragraph provides no evidence to support its larger claims about the Harvard faculty, let alone its assertions about the quality of American higher education as a whole – Dickens, writing on the basis of his brief time in Boston, assuming that educational access is simply a matter affecting males, and neither then nor later visiting any other school or college, quite literally does not know what he is talking about. Despite the limitations of this passage, and even though it was the combination of generalising on this scale and lack of substantiating knowledge in support of his claims that laid *American Notes* open to attack by reviewers on both sides of the Atlantic, the superficiality of his appraisal of the formal structures of education in the New World does not prevent Dickens's offering a significant reading of the role of literacy amongst its people.

For while, like Martineau's texts, *American Notes* is largely oblivious to many of the demographic groups that were forming the new society, it does pay particular attention to two specific populations who stand, respectively, as indicators of the nation's future and its past. On the one hand are the immigrant Irish who at the time of Dickens's visit formed such a large proportion of all new arrivals in the United States; on the other are the Native American tribes whom the Irish, along with other newcomers, were rapidly displacing. In his account of both groups Dickens emphasises the importance of engagement in the emerging forms of print culture: for the Irish, literacy is essential to success and to participation in the formation of a new civil society; by contrast, the Native Americans, who live largely outside of Western forms of literacy, are condemned to ever-increasing marginalisation and eventual oblivion.

Spread across the length of its text, *American Notes* includes three short narratives depicting the immigrant Irish, each of which both emphasises the importance of literacy to successful integration yet also simultaneously reinforces racial stereotypes of the Irish themselves. Collectively, moreover, these vignettes invoke the larger subject of Ireland and of the issues that led to these Dickensian subjects having emigrated from there, and they anticipate a treatment of the politics of Irish nationalism and its representation in the press in *Martin Chuzzlewit* that will be discussed in Chapter 4. The first of these accounts occurs in that New York where an ability to read the cityscape is, as we have seen, becoming defined as increasingly essential for participating in modern life. Sitting in the Carlton Hotel, Dickens recognises two Irish working men as still new to America 'by their long-tailed blue coats and bright buttons, and their drab trousers'. Struggling to decipher the city, one of the two 'carries in his hand a crumpled scrap of paper from which he tries to spell out a hard name, while the other looks about for it on all the doors and windows'.[67] Coming to their rescue, Dickens inscribes the social values he wants to privilege as he, first, makes sense of an address that 'might have been scrawled with the blunt handle of the spade the writer better knows the use of, than a pen' and, second, goes on to recount for his readers the Irishmen's story of honest toil, family devotion and unbroken ties to their old home across the ocean.[68] Normalised as exemplars of working-class virtue and domestic faithfulness, defined as deficient in an essential skill for success in an increasingly text-defined world, this pair thus both demonstrates the importance of patriarchal intervention in their reading matter and establishes the standard against which Dickens's subsequent descriptions of other Irish immigrants will be measured. Five chapters after this encounter with the two working men in New York, he describes, and enthusiastically endorses, an Irish temperance society march in Cincinnati. In his most affirmative image of the city Martineau had made her American exemplar, Dickens describes the marchers' commitment to the cause in the visual rhetoric of the 'well-painted banners' they carry:

> There was the smiting of the rock, and the gushing forth of the waters; and there was a temperate man with 'considerable of a hatchet' (as the standard-bearer would probably have said), aiming a deadly blow at a serpent which was apparently about to spring upon him from the top of a barrel of spirits. But the chief feature of this part of the show was

a huge allegorical device, borne among the ship-carpenters, on one side whereof the steamboat Alcohol was represented bursting her boiler and exploding with a great crash, while upon the other, the good ship Temperance sailed away with a fair wind, to the heart's content of the captain, crew, and passengers.[69]

Managing to combine taming those violent engines of American locomotion that elsewhere so trouble Dickens's text through creating forms of popular entertainment that enact the virtue of restraint, this group simultaneously provides an image of social integration and integrity to which the two New York immigrants can aspire and acts as a reminder of the dangers to which the Irish are especially assumed to be vulnerable. For, finally, reinforcing the text's sense of the fragility of the achievement of civilisation by the Irish and standing in marked contrast to the more optimistic version of the immigrant future, is the last of these three episodes – an encounter with an Irish camp near the Shaker village at Lebanon, New York that Dickens comes across at the very end of his time in America:

> With means at hand of building decent cabins, it was wonderful to see how clumsy, rough, and wretched its hovels were. The best were poor protection from the weather; the worst let in the wind and rain through wide breaches in the roofs of sodden grass, and in the walls of mud; some had neither door nor window; some had nearly fallen down, and were imperfectly propped up by stakes and poles; all were ruinous and filthy. Hideously ugly old women and very buxom young ones, pigs, dogs, men, children, babies, pots, kettles, dunghills, vile refuse, rank straw, and standing water, all wallowing together in an inseparable heap, composed the furniture of every dark and dirty hut.[70]

Dissolving into the wet ooze that has, by the end of the book, become metonymic for Dickens's disgust with America, this immigrant group wallows in the mud, like the pigs that have dotted his American landscape, appears entirely devoid of language and has only failure and oblivion before it.

If these three glimpses of Irish newcomers both span the range of possibility for immigrants to the New World and define their prospects of success in terms of the ability to develop normative social virtues and a capacity to participate in the discourse of public literacy, Dickens's representation of Native American culture highlights the fate of populations who remain outside such discourse. By contrast with Martineau, who almost entirely erases Native Americans and their history from her optimistic stadial vision of the new nation's historical potential,[71] Dickens describes the impact the arrival of the

Europeans has had upon indigenous cultures. First, and inverting the fate of the Irishmen in New York and Cincinnati, Dickens records how Native Americans' inability to understand the language presented to them has been the instrument of their exclusion from the newly forming society. During a brief stop in Harrisburg, he has the opportunity to examine several treaties between Native American tribes and the Commonwealth of Pennsylvania. Although he sentimentalises the 'poor Indians' as 'simple warriors' taught by 'white men how to break their faith', he also notes how they used in place of signatures 'rough drawings of the creatures or weapons they were called after' and how they were misled into putting their marks to 'treaties which were falsely read' to them.[72] Second, as he moves further into the nation's interior his accounts intensify the impression of the Native Americans' increasing marginalisation. Travelling down the Ohio, for example, he anthropomorphises the river itself running past a burial mound on its banks as he includes it in the idealised rendering of aboriginal life: 'it shared one's feeling of compassion for the extinct tribes who lived so pleasantly here'.[73] Returning to Ohio from St Louis, Dickens resumes the note of idealistic yearning in describing a group of Wyandots who are being displaced from their ancestral lands near Upper Sandusky, reluctantly abandoning 'the familiar scenes of their infancy, and in particular . . . the burial-places of their kindred'.[74] The ambivalence of Dickens's entire response to America is evident even as this iterative nostalgic tonality entices the reader into a sympathetic response. For such stereotypes of the Native Americans and, no less, the Irish had, as Joseph Rezek has noted, their 'roots in stadial theories of history and racial difference' and were 'part of cultural nationalism's ideological weapons'.[75] For all that Dickens resisted seeing and representing the New World as the model of stadial progress Martineau celebrated, he joined her in endorsing the underlying theory that pushed Native Americans beyond the pale of civilised society, as is evident from *American Notes*'s final and most extended account of Native American culture.[76]

Shortly after his projection of nostalgic melancholy on to the riverside burial mound, Dickens narrates his meeting on the boat to Louisville with Peter Pitchlynn, a Choctaw chief. Pitchlynn, who was of both Choctaw and Anglo-American ancestry, is also a significantly hybridised figure in terms of literacy. Introducing himself to Dickens by sending in his card, he proves able to converse about both British and American authors, discussing how Fenimore Cooper 'had painted the Red Man well', Scott's poetry and 'the opening of The Lady of the Lake, and the great battle scene in Marmion, in which, no doubt, from the congeniality of the subjects to his own pursuits and tastes, he had great interest and delight'.[77] Referencing Scott with none of the diagnostic instrumentality Martineau had deployed to comment upon the 'feudalism' of American culture, Dickens positions Pitchlynn between the evolving world of print that white America is rapidly making a dominant social force and the diminishing, fading era of the Native American tribes as they vanish mutely into oblivion and frames him as little more than an object of poignant regret. That Dickens was oblivious to his own assumptions here is evidently confirmed in a letter later describing the meeting where he records his 'great shock' that Pitchlynn's card had been printed rather than inscribed with a Native American symbol, as if he found that somehow culturally inauthentic without fully recognising why he did so.[78]

'Gorging with coined lies the most voracious maw': Dickens and the Press in America

Dickens's account of the American continent, the contrast he draws between the United States and British Canada, the spectacle of textual modernism he uncovers in New York City and the extent to which he defines two marginalised populations in terms of their access to literacy and print all contextualise and complicate his response to the American press. The critical conversation that has previously been primarily focused upon his final assault upon the corrosive 'frightful engine', however, has obscured two essential aspects of his engagement with American periodicals. First, it has overlooked the extent to which, like Martineau, he examined the American press as a predictor of what the future might hold in store for British journalism and, second, it has downplayed the significance of the contrast between those newspapers attacked in the context of *American Notes*'s penultimate chapter on slavery and the very different representation of *The Lowell Offering* he gives much earlier in the text.

Dickens's correspondence from America makes evident the extent to which he took the opportunity to examine the phenomenon of the American press during his visit. From soon after his arrival, for example, like many a travelling Victorian specimen collector, he gathered samples of American newspapers to send home to England, particularly to John Forster.[79] Then, on reaching New York, he sought out William Cullen Bryant, editor and part-owner of the *New York Evening Post*, 'the leading serious paper of the nation', to whom he had written that he was, apart from Irving, the person he most wanted to see.⁸⁰ Moreover, although he expressed a more emphatic sense of exasperation over the ways in which the press treated him for raising the international copyright issue, he nevertheless acknowledged the strengths of American newspapers in a way that is entirely absent from either *American Notes* or *Martin Chuzzlewit*. As he wrote to Forster on 24 February 1842:

> The *New York Herald*, which you will receive with this, is the *Satirist* of America; but having a great circulation (on account of its commercial intelligence and early news) it can afford to secure the best reporters. . . . My speech is done, upon the whole, with remarkable accuracy.⁸¹

Although comparing it to the scurrilous *Satirist* was hardly a compliment, Dickens's 'but' here also acknowledges that, unlike the London paper, the *Herald* combined both the financial success that resulted from its mass-market sales with high-quality reporting, creating something that had as yet no counterpart in the British press.

For, like Martineau, Dickens visited America after the material, economic and political conditions necessary for the creation of a mass-market press in the United States had come into being. Indeed, in arriving just over five years after Martineau had returned home, Dickens was even more able than she had been to experience a fourth estate that was more fully developed and more deeply a part of the national political discourse than was the case back home in Britain. In 1842, though still less than a decade old, that mass circulation press was beginning to replace its subscription-driven predecessor with the appearance, first, of the *Sun* in 1833 and, most tellingly, with James Gordon Bennett's establishment of the *New York Herald* in 1835, the newspaper with which Dickens would become most fully engaged and which in turn would take a leading role in the American response to *American Notes*. Even at this early stage of their development, moreover, the *Herald* and its peers had led to the creation of a press very different from its British counterpart: blending substantive discourse with popular entertainment, using each to drive the other and relying upon both to create a market for the advertising through which they generated much of their revenue, these new mass-market papers claimed a far wider influence over their society than the daily press in Britain could yet aspire to. Nowhere perhaps was this more apparent to Dickens than in the coverage his own visit received, with the *New York Herald* publishing a special number devoted to him and his works on 15 February 1842 (Fig. 3.2). Moreover, leading that popular press were figures also without parallel in Britain – entrepreneurial

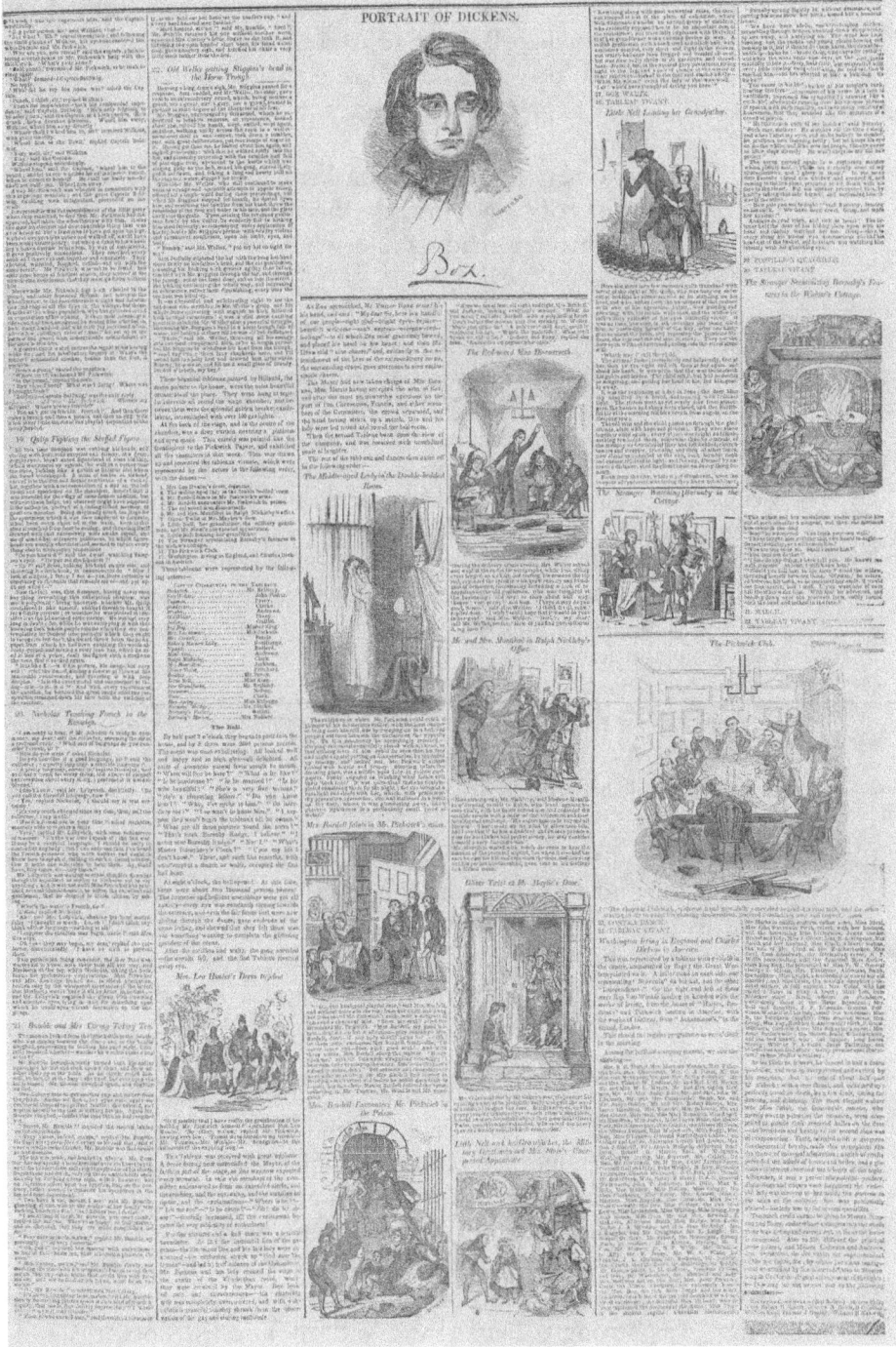

Figure 3.2 *The Extra Boz Herald*. Victoria and Albert Museum, London.

editor-proprietors free to establish start-up newspapers, unhindered by the 'taxes on knowledge' that had so cramped the evolution of the British press, able to play an essential role in the formation of public opinion, and, as Chapter 4 will suggest, avatars of Dickens's own editorial ambitions.[82]

This new phenomenon of a mass-market daily press is everywhere visible on the streets of New York, the city where modern urban life is given meaning through reading and where the cries of the newsboys resound:

> What are the fifty newspapers, which those precocious urchins are bawling down the street . . . what are they but amusements? Not vapid waterish amusements, but good strong stuff; dealing in round abuse and blackguard names; pulling off the roofs of private houses, as the Halting Devil did in Spain; pimping and pandering for all degrees of vicious taste, and gorging with coined lies the most voracious maw; imputing to every man in public life the coarsest and vilest motives; scaring away from the stabbed and prostrate body-politic, every Samaritan of clear conscience and good deeds; and setting on, with yell and whistle and the clapping of foul hands, the vilest vermin and worst birds of prey – No amusements![83]

The negativity of the judgement loaded into Dickens's extended comparison of the American press with various forms of vice is palpable and, for Juliet John, the hostility is a significant part of his broader 'antipathy to a debased mass culture'.[84] If, though, we turn back to David Henkin's discussion of the city growing into a space shaped by public reading and his calling out the newsboys as figures standing at the transition point between the orality of street criers and the new age of mass-market print distribution,[85] their presence can be seen as speaking to Dickens's experience of America in a different way. That is, they point to the opportunity his visit gave him to see at first hand a modern urban society where, by precise contrast with the increasingly restrictive conditions to which newspapers were subject in Britain in the 1830s,[86] the press was free to operate without legal constraints in a free-market economy. Unlike Martineau, who had made the contrast between the provincial and abolition press central to her reading of America, for Dickens that emerging urban society and the populist press serving it are the focus of attention. As a result, his personal enthusiasm for Bryant and for a *New York Evening Post* that was strongly Democratic and abolitionist notwithstanding, the two exemplars of American periodical culture he includes in *American Notes* speak to both the dangers and potential he finds in the mass-market press of the New World. The slavery chapter, comprised largely of extracts from American newspapers, together with its successor and Dickens's parting shot at the 'frightful engine', that is, bookend with his description of the visit to Lowell (discussed below) and his praise for the millworkers' periodical miscellany as an exemplar of populist journalism.

American Notes's treatment of slavery brings another important form of disturbance to the text, complicating and destabilising it in a variety of ways. To be sure, Dickens does claim moral authority over the issue itself and even uses it to generate a response to the vexatious reprinting of his writings. As Meredith McGill has noted, while he is actually engaged in his brief trip to Richmond, for example, Dickens's 'moral certainty' of slavery's 'depravity helps stabilize his narrative perspective',[87] enabling him to read the barren Virginia landscape as an allegorical representation of the corruption sustaining the economy. Moreover, by drawing so extensively on Theodore Weld's *American Slavery As It Is* for the substance of the slavery chapter itself, he may, as Amanda Claybaugh has argued, succeed in completing a transatlantic circuit that 'returns the slave owners' words back to the southern states, but only after passing them through the defamiliarising perspective of a quite different public, the non-slave-owning public of the northern states and of Great Britain'.[88] Finally, in constructing this circuit, Dickens was able to reverse the polarity of reprinting he had lamented in a letter he wrote home from Baltimore to Lord Brougham:

> Any wretched halfpenny newspaper can print [a writer] at its pleasure – place him side by side with productions which disgust his common sense – and by means of the companionship in which it constantly shews him, engenders a feeling of association in the minds of a large class of readers, from which he would revolt, and to avoid which he would pay almost any price.[89]

However, although in making this point Dickens might seem to echo Martineau's complaint to Gilman at the way she was reprinted in *The Southern Rose*, the two cases are significantly distinct. On the one hand, Dickens's complaint is a general one, not a specific defense against the way his own work had been treated in a particular American publication. On the other hand, and as McGill also notes, Dickens's own recycling comes at the cost of untethering the horrific accounts from Weld's anchoring context and, threatening 'to float free of reference, slipping from moral condemnation into voyeurism'.⁹⁰ In this, Dickens's positioning of the American press in the context of slavery thus contrasts markedly with what Martineau achieved in her extensive writing on the relationship between the two. Unable to call upon the extensive travel through the South that Martineau had made an explicit part of her own claim to authority upon the subject, and making no reference to the work of the abolitionist and anti-slavery movements anywhere in the book, Dickens both lacks the authority of personal experience and runs the risk of over-determining the slavery chapter by relying so entirely on texts that are not his own. Moreover, in appropriating Weld without attribution, Dickens erases the work being done by the abolitionist movement and the contributions of such key leaders of the cause as Weld and his wife, the former Angelina Grimké, whom Martineau had singled out for special praise as heroic exemplars. Above all, he leaves invisible the contribution being made by the abolitionist press that Martineau had made central to her reading of America and to which, by 1842, she was regularly contributing.

The instability thus created within the text by Dickens's assault upon the pro-slavery newspapers and the mass-market press for which they stand as proxy can, however, be more fully understood if we position it against the praise he lavishes on the only American periodical that he calls out by name, *The Lowell Offering*. Even though Dickens had recorded a sense of his own unease at the newly built world that Lowell offers, he is wholly enthusiastic about the living conditions the model industrial society is providing for its workers, a population he represents as universally female and whose lives he renders in entirely domestic terms. Compliant and unassuming, these young women are 'healthy in appearance', 'well-dressed, but not to my thinking above their condition', unaffected, hard-working and thrifty.⁹¹ For Dickens, that is, this is a population that has evidently adapted to the opportunities of industrial society without developing any troubling aspirations to new forms of cultural and political power. Moreover, what he singles out for particular praise is the mill workers' construction of an active cultural life that is intrinsically domestic in focus: he emphasises that they play the 'joint-stock piano' in their boarding houses, notes that they subscribe to circulating libraries and, above all, praises their production of the only American periodical for which he has anything positive to say, the modestly titled *Lowell Offering*. Asserting the women's right to create such a 'means of mutual instruction, improvement, and rational entertainment',⁹² he moves on to define its virtues, noting that 'it will compare advantageously with a great many English Annuals', and presenting it in terms that diametrically oppose it to his later judgement upon America's newspapers:

> It is pleasant to find that many of its Tales are of the Mills and of those who work in them; that they inculcate habits of self-denial and contentment, and teach good doctrines of enlarged benevolence. A strong feeling for the beauties of nature, as displayed in the solitudes the writers have left at home, breathes through its pages like wholesome village air; and though a circulating library is a favourable school for the study of such topics, it has very scant allusion to fine clothes, fine marriages, fine houses, or fine life.[93]

Praising a version of American life entirely at odds with what becomes his own representation of the continent and the nation, Dickens thus renders the *Offering* as a model working-class publication. Moreover, in describing these women and the magazine they publish, he privileges models of femininity and cultural production that contrast strikingly with Martineau's resistant representation of American women as liberal subjects largely effaced from public life and assigned to the role of republican wife and mother. For, in their modest decorum, social conformity and promulgation of 'self-denial and contentment' and 'enlarged benevolence', the Lowell workers and their *Offering* represent a vision of women and their compliance with a subordinate social role, one that is both consistent with Dickens's rendering of women throughout *American Notes*, that places them in marked contrast with the rampantly masculinised qualities he defines as the new society's greatest failings and that he associates with its newly emerging mass-market press. As such, in its description of an idealised working-class periodical *American Notes* aligns itself with what Ian Haywood has described as the ideology of pacification that middle-class British authors and periodical editors developed during the 1840s in response to the rise of a radical working-class press[94] and to which Dickens would make his greatest contribution with the establishment of *Household Words* in 1851 and its successor *All the Year Round* at the end of the decade.

The Transatlantic Reception of *American Notes*

> Dickens's book is on the way to me. Meantime, I have seen large portions of it in the papers, & rejoice to find how far more moderate his tone is therein than in his speeches & conversation, & letters. It is absurd

enough to pretend to an impression before having read the book: but I <u>have</u> an impression that it is humane, good-tempered, faithful, as far as it goes, – but superficial, rather affected & fine in parts, likely to occupy the whole world for a month or two, & then be absolutely forgotten in the superior merits of his fictions. Is this a good guess?[95]

Martineau's private comments to Henry Crabb Robinson in her letter of 29 October 1842 reveal rather more than just her own willingness to come to a summary judgement about Dickens and a book she had not actually read that perhaps suggests their later falling out was not entirely unpredictable. For, in describing the author as immoderate and his text as 'superficial' she anticipated the general thrust of the initial critical reception *American Notes* received, a reception that, as her appraisal also anticipates, further assumed that Dickens had misjudged his own abilities in attempting to be something other than a novelist. And indeed, on both sides of the Atlantic and as has been long recognised, Dickens's first major venture outside fiction was judged with almost universal severity. Even before the book appeared, Dickens had himself provoked an adverse response in the United States through his collaboration sub rosa with John Forster to produce an article on the American press that both anticipated and fuelled hostile reactions to the text from across the Atlantic. What he evidently did not expect, however, was the uniform negativity of the British reviewers, who largely followed Martineau in dismissing *American Notes* as unworthy of the creator of *Pickwick*, *Nickleby* and the other early novels that had so endeared Boz to the reading public. If the general negativity of *American Notes*'s critical reception has been a familiar part of the critical conversation, however,[96] what has not been previously brought to light is the extent to which that reception evolved into a transatlantic debate over contrasting visions of the press, the relationship between British and American print culture and Dickens's own role and standing as a journalist. Reading the paratextual significance of Dickens and Forster's 'The Newspaper Literature of America' through this lens, then, together with the body of critical reviews of *American Notes* itself, thus concludes this chapter and points to *Martin Chuzzlewit*'s importance as the next phase in Dickens's formulation of the role of print and the press in shaping modern culture and his definition of the role he aspired to play in that process.

Even before his travelogue was published in London on 19 October 1842, Dickens had previewed the final terms of his judgement on that 'frightful engine' taking form across the Atlantic by collaborating covertly with Forster on an article for the *Foreign Quarterly*

Review, which his friend also edited.[97] Closely prefiguring *American Notes* itself, Forster's article aligns the state of the press with the wider condition of society and literature in the United States as it attributes the failings of American journalism to three main causes: first, the role of editors such as Colonel Webb of the *New York Courier and Enquirer* – whom even the *Herald* terms 'a frank, manly blackguard';[98] second, the lack of 'some moderating and regulating power' to shape social progress;[99] and finally, the vacuum produced by America's having no national literature to give it cultural definition. Lamenting that even the very physical form of the press was debased, with its 'miserable whity-brown paper; its dingy, uncomfortable print',[100] Forster called upon 'the literary talent of the country to intervene' and create a journalism worthy of the new society.[101] In all this, his article set the table for the final chapter of *American Notes*, and the similarities were clearly not accidental. Indeed, Dickens went out of his way to point out the connections by inserting a puffing footnote into his own text as he encouraged his readers to 'refer to an able, and perfectly truthful article, in *The Foreign Quarterly Review*, published in the present month of October; to which my attention has been attracted, since these sheets have been passing through the press'.[102] The thinly veiled coincidence, however, is belied by the manuscript of *American Notes* in the Forster Collection at the National Art Library, which clearly shows that the footnote was written as part of the original text and not, as Dickens claims, added at the proofs stage of the printing process.[103]

If the evident collusion between Dickens and Forster here and the extent and range of their attacks suggest that the two men saw the American press as an enemy to be taken seriously, the nature of their assault is itself revealing. First, despite Dickens's having amassed those samples of American newspapers and despite the fact that he had written home to Forster from America praising papers such as the *New York Herald* for the accuracy of its reporting, neither he nor Forster made any attempt to offer a balanced appraisal. For all the readers of either the *Foreign Quarterly* article or *American Notes* could know, every paper in America was despicably corrupt, while the existence of a serious press as represented by Bryant's *New York Evening Post* is simply erased. Second, the decision to select the *Herald* as the primary focus of the *Foreign Quarterly* article was unlikely to have been a casual one. For not only was the *Herald* the leading force in the newly dominant daily press but its editor, J. Gordon Bennett, well known for his Anglophobic and pro-slavery views,[104] was an easy target, unlikely to receive any sympathy from a British audience and positioned by the article to fall directly in line with the attack upon the American press that *American Notes* itself would soon reveal. Finally, in making their call for the nation's literary elite to step forward and assume leadership of the press, Dickens and Forster revealed that they were not particularly concerned with fostering their readers' understanding of the actual nature of contemporary American letters. Instead, what their critique demonstrates is an attachment to a vision of an author-centred national culture in which journalism served as an extension of the larger literary life. Such a vision scarcely applied to the American literary marketplace gripped by Jacksonian decentralised democracy and which, as Meredith McGill's work has shown, was still based upon the recirculation and wholesale dissemination of texts that would otherwise have been unavailable to a mass readership.[105] It did, however, apply far more precisely to conditions in Britain, where the rapidly changing conditions in which the press operated and an expanding national readership were creating unprecedented opportunities for growth, and where Dickens was eager to find a role for himself.[106]

The *New World*, however, was not content simply to be put to use in the service of any Dickensian agenda for the press and, back across the Atlantic, both the *Foreign Quarterly* article and *American Notes* itself prompted reactions against the Old World's attempts at hegemony that asserted the very national cultural autonomy Forster and Dickens had denied. Their primary target, the *New York Herald*, led the way and began its campaign with comments on the first proof sheets of *American Notes* on 21 October 1842, just two days after the book's publication in London. The *Herald* went on to run a series of articles right up until the entire text was published in New York in early November. Building up its readers' appetite for the extended extracts the paper ran on 8 and 9 November, these articles were also an opportunity for it to dismiss the *Foreign Quarterly Review* article as 'the first gun in the long war that has at last broken out between the literature of America and that of Europe, for the empire over the human mind in both hemispheres'.[107] And in that war the paper claimed for itself the role of revolutionary leader against the worn-out press of the Old World, choosing an especially provocative avatar to target a British audience:

> We are beyond the possibility of a doubt, the Napoleon of the press in both hemispheres. The New York Herald is unquestionably the greatest and mightiest intellectual institution of civilized society in the present century. Look at the excitement, the ferment, the fuss, and the fury

which its existence, progress, power, circulation and influence cause in both the old and the new world – in London and in New York – in the grave quarterly reviews and in the newspaper press of both continents.[108]

Invoking the spirit of Napoleon in very different terms from those in which Gibbons Merle had described the shaping spirit of modern French journalism, the *Herald* here is certainly a much more evolved creature than that mere 'monster of depravity' presented in Forster and Dickens's descriptions. Indeed, as it continues its exploration of the larger social role of the press, the *Herald* goes on to invoke 'a master spirit to wield the energies of the press' and 'call humanity back to honor, to principle, to morals, to religion and to intelligence'.[109] Resolutely dismissive of Dickens's assault upon American society and its print media, then, the *Herald* concludes its case by arguing for the growing centrality of newspapers in public discourse and stakes its claim that 'the newspaper literature of New York can compare with any other capital in the world',[110] a claim that *American Notes* had already implicitly acknowledged in its account of the new American journalism. Finally, when it printed extended extracts from *American Notes* Bennett asserted his control over Dickens's text by, as Jessica DeSpain has noted, selecting passages that would especially incense the *Herald*'s readers and giving them titles of his own to further intensify the response.[111]

If such an energetic American response to Forster and Dickens's attacks was perhaps unsurprising, much less predictable was the extent to which Dickens's assault on American journalism prompted a discussion of the role of the press back home in Britain. And yet such a discussion is precisely what emerged in the reviews of *American Notes* that appeared over the fall and winter of 1842–3. All of the major heavyweight quarterlies carried articles on *American Notes* and, without exception, they elided assessment of Dickens and his travel book into that ongoing debate over the role of mass-market journalism and its relationship to the evolution of democratic civil societies that, as discussed in Chapter 1, had developed since the 1820s. Ironically, in these reviews, Dickens himself, or, rather, Boz, becomes a metonymic figure, a problematic representative of the self-assertiveness of the increasingly literate lower social orders seeking to claim a role for themselves in shaping public discourse – almost, as it were, an American.

Invariably, that is, the heavyweight reviewers began their appraisals not with the actual text of *American Notes* but by speculating on the phenomenon of Boz himself and applying to him judgements remarkably similar to those he himself had rendered upon the American press. What, they wondered, was to be made of the celebrated popular entertainer's attempt to claim for himself a new role as substantive analyst of another society and its culture? *Fraser's Magazine* led the way in November 1842 with its judgement that 'every thing is made to wear Boz's peculiar colours, and is stamped with his idiosyncrasy'.[112] And the *Quarterly* followed suit, wondering 'whether the powers – or perhaps we should say the habits of his mind – are equal to any sustained exertion' and commenting dismissively, 'his best things, to our taste, are some short tales published under the absurd pseudonyme of Boz'.[113] As Morris Golden has suggested, such a line of attack was to be expected from the more conservative quarterlies, for which political difference from and class bias against Dickens underwrote the hostility,[114] and Dickens thus encountered his own version of the cultural policing to which Martineau had been subjected largely on account of her gender and gender politics. What was less to be anticipated, however, was the fact that the most authoritative of the progressive major reviews took a similarly regulatory approach to his text, just as its editor had endeavoured to restrain Martineau from writing about the position of women in America.[115]

For the critique that most antagonised Dickens was James Spedding's in the *Edinburgh Review*, which came out in January 1843.[116] Critical discussion of this article has long focused upon the amount of energy Dickens expended in seeking a retraction of Spedding's claim that he had gone to America merely as 'a kind of missionary' in the cause of international copyright.[117] More revealing here, however, is what the article says about 'Boz' and how dismissive it is of the mass-market press as a whole. Like the other quarterly writers, that is, Spedding begins with patronising assumptions about 'Boz' himself:

> We all know 'Boz', though we may not have seen his face. We know what he thinks about affairs at home, with which we are all conversant. . . . We know, therefore, what to infer from his pictures of society abroad; what weight to attribute to his representations; with what caution and allowance to entertain them.[118]

Then, having lamented Boz's lack of formal training and his haphazard education 'among the odd characters in the odd corners of London',[119] Spedding suggests that 'though Mr Dickens *knows* better, it is too much to expect of him that he should have always acted upon his better knowledge; especially when we consider that he had his character as an amusing writer to keep up'.[120] Galling as this surely was, however, an even deeper critique of Dickens's ambitions was implied as Spedding moved on to a wholesale assault upon the very idea of mass-market journalism, something epitomised in America, with a daily press unrestrained and 'turned loose in a land of cheap printing and no stamp duties – where every body could read, and every body took a part in politics'.[121] With its searing questions about Dickens's social standing and scepticism over the very value of daily journalism, Spedding's critique understandably sparked its target's wrath, as is palpable in his letters on the issue.[122] Matters were surely exacerbated by the fact that, of all the quarterlies, it was the *Edinburgh* with which Dickens had the closest ties – he was friendly with its current editor, Napier McVey, and its founding editor, Francis Jeffrey, was his closest mentor[123] – and Spedding's notice appeared even as Dickens was engaged on a long-running correspondence with McVey about the possibility of his contributing to the magazine. The ferocity of his response, then, is understandable, even as both the critique and his reaction to it only testify to the larger point that the great quarterlies were a segment of the fourth estate in which he was unable to make a place for himself.

Back across the Atlantic, one major American magazine, that *North American Review* to which Martineau had offered her services in vain, bucked the almost universal trend and did carry a positive account of *American Notes*.[124] Ironically, however, even this article echoed Spedding's appraisal of both Dickens himself and the daily press. For, although it opened with an extended glowing account of Boz the man and the combination of entertainment and moral beauty in his fiction, the article mirrored Spedding's classist critique as it commented on the 'cockneyism' of his language and, noting that 'Dickens has never been much of a traveller', dismissed his insights into American society.[125] Most damningly of all, it set at naught his appraisal of the daily press: 'We look upon the boundless power Dickens ascribes to the worst part of the American newspaper press with as much incredulity as we should upon the asserted wonders of any necromantic agency'.[126] Making matters even more complicated was the fact that this review was written by Cornelius C. Felton, the Harvard Professor of Greek, and one of Dickens's closest Boston friends. As Chapter 4 will show, Dickens – who was never one to forget a slight, especially a public slight – would soon build a wickedly comic response to Felton into *Martin Chuzzlewit*, appropriating a fictionalised version of his friend into his larger treatment of the American press and using him to express his own views of its standing.

The range and intensity of the reaction over the winter of 1842–3 to the *Foreign Quarterly Review* article and the chapter on the press in *American Notes* made a further response from Forster and

Dickens entirely predictable. Forster thus ran a follow-up article in *Foreign Quarterly Review* in April 1843, attacking his critics on both sides of the Atlantic.[127] Celebrating the 'discussion of the nuisance which it has exposed', he argued that his original essay had been misinterpreted as badly by the *Westminster Review* as by the American press – 'scarcely a day has passed in which it has not furnished a leading topic of outrageous abuse to the "Herald" and its associates throughout the country'.[128] Deeply concerned that the 'tyranny of the majority' threatens to turn American democracy into little more than mob rule, Forster goes on to suggest that the clear class divisions within British society actually provide an essential stability. While he acknowledges that the domestic press certainly has its deficiencies, he claims that it 'represents not unworthily the civilization and intelligence of England. A great people finds free utterance in it for every difference of thought and opinion, and a respectable community has no call to be ashamed by it'.[129] Unlike his first article, which had prompted such a storm of response, this one passed largely unremarked and, with it, the transatlantic conversation apparently came to an end. By this time, however, Dickens himself was well under way with the serialisation of *Martin Chuzzlewit*, the first number of which had appeared three months earlier in January 1843, coinciding with Spedding's *Edinburgh Review* attack on *American Notes*. As the next chapter will argue, in taking the novel to America only three instalments later, Dickens may well, as has long been assumed, have been looking to boost its flagging sales, but he was also clearly not finished with the reverberations from those forms of disturbance his transatlantic journey and its textual consequences had produced. In *Martin Chuzzlewit*, then, he builds upon *American Notes* and the reception it had received, continuing both his own exploration of the role of the press and print culture in a rapidly evolving society and furthering his argument against those who had dismissed his capacity to interrogate the modern world.

Notes

1. Dickens, *American Notes*, pp. 268–70.
2. Ibid. p. 252.
3. Drew, *Dickens the Journalist*, p. 63.
4. John, *Dickens and Mass Culture*, p. 76.
5. Giles, *Transatlantic Insurrections*, p. 11.
6. Jones, *Powers of the Press*, p. 21.

7. Drew, *Dickens the Journalist*, p. 52.
8. Bowen, *Other Dickens*, Chapter 6; Patten, *Charles Dickens and 'Boz'*, Chapter 7.
9. Magnet, *Dickens and the Social Order*, p. 171.
10. Dickens, *Barnaby Rudge*, p. 429.
11. Ibid. p. 334.
12. See <https://www.oldbaileyonline.org/browse.jsp?id=t17811205-56-defend644&div=t17811205-56#highlight> (last accessed 12 June 2019).
13. For details on Dickens's ownership of Holcroft's pamphlet, see Rice, *Barnaby Rudge: An Annotated Bibliography*, pp. 86–7. My thanks to Professors Ian Haywood and Steve Poole for their help in tracking down the source of Dickens's access to the handbill.
14. Holcroft, *A Plain and Succinct Narrative*, p. 52; Dickens, *Barnaby Rudge*, p. 326.
15. Dickens, *Barnaby Rudge*, p. 342.
16. Ibid. p. 551.
17. Gabriel Varden's rescue from the mob by Joe Willett, who has returned home having lost an arm serving in the British army at Savannah, Georgia, furthers the transatlantic association between forces of social unrest and, while it may evoke the anti-slavery riots to which Martineau refers, also works implicitly to criticise the American project as a whole.
18. John, *Dickens and Mass Culture*, p. 76.
19. Carroll, *An Empire of Air and Water*, p. 73.
20. Dickens, *American Notes*, p. 17.
21. Ibid. p. 19.
22. Ibid. p. 24.
23. Ibid. p. 9.
24. Ibid. p. 32.
25. Ibid. pp. 75, 74, 127, 217.
26. Ibid. p. 175.
27. Ibid. p. 190.
28. Ibid. p. 191.
29. Dzelzainis, 'Dickens, Democracy, and Spit'; Magnet, *Dickens and the Social Order*, pp. 217–19.
30. Dickens, *Letters*, vol. 4, p. 711.
31. Dzelzainis, 'Dickens, Democracy, and Spit', p. 40.
32. Martineau, *Retrospect*, vol. 1, p. 142.
33. Dickens, *American Notes*, p. 30.
34. Ibid. p. 221.
35. McKnight, 'Dickens, Niagara Falls and the Watery Sublime', pp. 69–70.
36. Dickens, *American Notes*, p. 221.
37. Ibid. pp. 226, 230.
38. Ibid. p. 233.

39. Morgentaler, 'Dickens in Canada', p. 154.
40. Dickens, *American Notes*, p. 237.
41. Ibid. p. 40.
42. Ibid. pp. 44–6.
43. Bourrier, 'Reading Laura Bridgman', pp. 56–7.
44. Dickens, *American Notes*, p. 121.
45. Dickens, *Letters*, vol. 3, p. 198.
46. Dickens, *American Notes*, p. 192.
47. Ibid. pp. 241–2.
48. Ibid. pp. 244–6.
49. Ibid. p. 247.
50. Ibid. pp. 248–9.
51. Ibid. p. 34.
52. Ibid.
53. Ibid. p.75.
54. Ibid.
55. Ibid. p. 110.
56. Ibid.
57. Ibid. p. 130.
58. Ibid. p. 194.
59. Ibid. pp. 90–1.
60. Henkin, *City Reading*, p. 10.
61. Ibid. p. 103.
62. Dickens, *American Notes*, p. 93.
63. Ibid. pp. 99, 100.
64. Ibid. p. 101.
65. Ibid. p. 35.
66. John, *Dickens and Mass Culture*, p. 86.
67. Dickens, *American Notes*, p. 91.
68. Ibid. p. 92.
69. Ibid. p. 181.
70. Ibid. p. 235.
71. Martineau's most extensive account of Native American interaction with white civilisation consists of a brief account of the capture and treatment of a group of settlers from Deerfield, Massachusetts, in the late seventeenth century: *Retrospect*, vol. 3, pp. 4–10. Given the way in which she represented Andrew Jackson's role in manipulating the press to advance a pro-slavery agenda (as discussed in Chapter 2), the parallels with his efforts to remove indigenous populations from ancestral lands is striking. As Steven Stoll has described, however, stadial theory consistently marginalised the agrarian peasantry (*Ramp Hollow*, pp. 36–49) in favour of the division of labour and formation of capital, a marginalising that may explain why – with the exception of Ireland – Martineau almost universally privileges later phases of stadial development and erases populations based exclusively on the land.

72. Dickens, *American Notes*, p. 160.
73. Ibid. p. 178.
74. Ibid. p. 216.
75. Rezek, *London and the Making of Provincial Literature*, p. 21.
76. Both Dickens's treatment and Martineau's erasure of Native American subjects from her accounts of America can be contrasted with her friend Anna Jameson, whose *Winter Studies and Summer Rambles in Canada* offers a much more engaged and empathetic account.
77. Dickens, *American Notes*, pp. 185, 184.
78. Dickens, *Letters*, vol. 3, p. 400.
79. A number of the cuttings Dickens mailed back to England have been preserved in the Forster collection at the National Art Library. See MSL/1876/Forster/176.
80. Webb, 'Charles Dickens in America', p. 62. Dickens's comment is in *Letters*, vol. 3, pp. 58–9.
81. Dickens, *Letters*, vol. 3, p. 84.
82. Daly, *Covering America*, pp. 56–71, provides an overview of this period of dynamic growth; Seitz, *The James Gordon Bennetts*, Chapter 2, discusses the founding of the *Herald* and Gordon's political influence.
83. Dickens, *American Notes*, pp. 98–9.
84. John, *Dickens and Mass Culture*, p. 101.
85. Henkin, *City Reading*, p. 111.
86. Hewitt, *The Dawn of the Cheap Press in Victorian Britain*, pp. 5–10.
87. McGill, *American Literature and the Culture of Reprinting*, p. 126.
88. Claybaugh, *The Novel of Purpose*, p. 79.
89. Dickens, *Letters*, vol. 3, p. 145.
90. McGill, *American Literature and the Culture of Reprinting*, p. 129.
91. Dickens, *American Notes*, pp. 76, 78.
92. Ibid. p. 79.
93. Ibid.
94. Haywood, *The Revolution in Popular Literature*, p. 123.
95. Martineau, *Letters*, vol. 2, p. 135.
96. Fielding's '*American Notes* and Some English Reviewers' provides the most extensive reading of the critical response and has largely framed subsequent discussions.
97. [Forster], 'The Newspaper Literature of America'.
98. Ibid. p. 204.
99. Ibid. p. 214.
100. Ibid. p. 200.
101. Ibid. p. 215.
102. Dickens, *American Notes*, p. 270.
103. See *American Notes*, Manuscript, National Art Library, MSL/1876/Forster/156.
104. Crouthamel, *Bennett's* New York Herald, pp. 56–8, 69–71.

105. McGill, *American Literature and the Culture of Reprinting*, pp. 102–8.
106. Drew, *Dickens the Journalist*, pp. 67–8, discusses Dickens's two letters to Lady Holland in July 1842, seeking her support to become editor of the recently defunct London *Courier*, and notes Dickens's comparison of his experience with a newspaper to that of an engineer with a steam engine.
107. 'Dickens' First Words on America', p. 2.
108. 'The New York Herald – Its Position, Prosperity, Circulation, and Prospects in Two Hemispheres', p. 2.
109. Ibid.
110. 'The Newspaper Writers of New York', *New York Herald*, 9 November 1842, p. 2.
111. DeSpain, *Nineteenth-Century Transatlantic Printing and the Embodied Book*, pp. 40–1.
112. 'Dickens's American Notes', p. 621.
113. 'American Notes, for General Circulation', p. 504.
114. Golden, 'Politics, Class, and *Martin Chuzzlewit*'.
115. Martineau, *Letters*, vol. 1, pp. 339–40.
116. 'American Notes for General Circulation'.
117. Ibid. p. 500.
118. Ibid. p. 498.
119. Ibid. p. 499.
120. Ibid. p. 500.
121. Ibid. p. 519.
122. *Letters*, vol. 3, pp. 422–4, 431–2.
123. I have explored Dickens's relationship with Jeffrey more fully in '"Faithful Sympathy": Dickens, the *Edinburgh Review*, and *Household Words*', *Victorian Periodicals Review* 44 (2011), pp. 42–68.
124. 'American Notes for General Circulation. By Charles Dickens'.
125. Ibid. pp. 224, 229.
126. Ibid. p. 230.
127. [Forster], 'The Answer of the American Press'.
128. Ibid. pp. 250, 267.
129. Ibid. p. 255.

Chapter 4

'Yield to the mighty mind of the Popular Instructor': Print and the Press in *Martin Chuzzlewit*

If *American Notes* manifests the forms of disturbance evident in Dickens's response to the New World and the literary and journalistic culture evolving across the Atlantic, its successor builds upon and elaborates that first reaction. For *Martin Chuzzlewit*, which Dickens began writing within weeks of his travelogue's publication, both works through the aftershocks of his own initial reaction to America and, in a variety of ways, pushes back against the almost uniformly dismissive critical reception with which its predecessor had been greeted. On the one hand, that is, the novel, and in particular its representation of the United States, can be read as a response to not only the predictable hostility with which the American press had greeted *American Notes* but also to the unexpectedly wide-ranging dismissal by British critics of the book itself and of the ways in which they had dismissed Dickens's attempt to move beyond his established cultural position as the most popular comic novelist of the day. On the other, *Chuzzlewit* extends *American Notes*'s examination of the relationship between literacy and urban space, its exploration of the role of an emergent mass-market press in the formation of a public sphere essential to the stadial advance of civil society, its regulation of women through the ideology of republican motherhood and the resulting suppression of their potential agency as autonomous liberal subjects.

In examining these interwoven issues, moreover, while *Martin Chuzzlewit* certainly builds upon *American Notes*, it also calls back to the concern articulated in *Barnaby Rudge* over the prospect of social upheaval fuelled by the concomitant development of an activist radical popular press, a prospect that became all the more immediate during the early months of the novel's serialisation. For its first numbers, including those set in America, coincided with a wave of Irish nationalist agitation against British rule led by Daniel

O'Connell that both gripped domestic public life throughout 1843 and found widespread support in the United States. As a result, the novel's timing afforded Dickens the opportunity to make transatlantic connections among his representations of literacy, the press, the nature of liberal society and the sustaining of orderly historical progress in a rapidly modernising society. In the ways that the novel makes these connections, moreover, he developed a response to both British and American critics of his authorial ambition as he incorporated journalism into fiction and fiction into journalism, demonstrating an unprecedented fusion of the genres that would, a decade later, become foundational to his own most important contribution to the Victorian press – the hybrid weekly miscellanies *Household Words* and *All the Year Round*.

Although *Martin Chuzzlewit* has long been one of Dickens's less studied works, the novel has also become the subject of a critical conversation that has increasingly recognised its pivotal role in the development of his career. Gerhard Joseph has commented, for example that, even as it continues 'the newspaper virtues of Dickens' early years' in its energy and variety, *Chuzzlewit* also 'shares with all of Dickens' mature work a combination of expansiveness and compactness'.[1] Developing this insight, John Bowen argues that in its concern with commodification, surveillance and the role of language and rhetoric, *Chuzzlewit* is 'one of the most important of all nineteenth-century novels' and 'a key harbinger of modernism',[2] while Ruth Livesey defines it as 'a novel preoccupied with time and mobility . . . a cross-roads in Dickens's career'.[3] This chapter's reading of the novel as no less an essential precursor to Dickens's later work in the press than to his development as a novelist brings a new perspective to that critical conversation. Rather than seeing the 'newspaper qualities' Joseph notes as an indicator of Dickens's immaturity, my argument here builds upon Bowen's focus upon the novel's exploration of the importance of language and Livesey's account of its place in the historical moment to make the case for a new reading of *Chuzzlewit* that emphasises the extent to which it both develops a sense of modern society in which forms of reading and writing have an essential role in the shaping of the public sphere and prefigures a vision of the mass-market press and the editorial function Dickens would put into place in the early 1850s.

In arguing for the novel's pivotal place in Dickens's development of his vision for the press and his own role within it, this chapter also responds specifically to the work of Jonathan Arac, Meredith McGill, Juliet John and Matthew Schneider. First, it engages McGill's suggestion that, in writing about the American press, Dickens, supported by John Forster, was attempting to create a 'strategy of containment', a strategy that rested upon the claim that 'the difference between English and American print cultures lies not in the products of the press but in a social order that enforces a distinction between legitimate and illegitimate representation'.[4] Second, it extends Juliet John's insight that an important outcome of the experience of *American Notes* proved to be the way in which an author who had established himself 'by declaring his right to write ... in the face of established cultural hierarchies by whose standards he was disadvantaged, starts in America to champion some of the hierarchies that his very success had undermined'.[5] Third, it draws from Arac's discussion of Dickens's part in a wider early Victorian project of producing 'knowledge from the observation of disorder and disruption'[6] so as to develop an alternative to Utilitarian models of social organisation. Finally, notwithstanding the strength of these desires both to contain the unruly force that is America, to champion British culture as hierarchically normative and to construct a new ideology of social order, the chapter also expands upon Matthew Schneider's description of the ways in which the text is constantly drawn towards 'transgression of the structuring boundaries upon which systems of signification depend'[7] and constantly threatens to undermine the very systems of order it seeks to construct. Despite having drawn far less attention than much of Dickens's fiction, collectively this body of critical work has thus done much to develop a recognition that *Martin Chuzzlewit* not only plays an essential role in the development of his career and in the evolution of the Victorian novel itself, but also that it is a deeply complex text riven by contradictory and disruptive energies.

In seeking to advance a critical conversation that has brought such new understandings of the novel's significance within the scope of my project here, the central claim of this chapter, then, is that while the novel may appear to desire to quarantine the upstart Americans through its parodic representations, it more fully presents them as part of a shared transatlantic world in which print and the press are taking on unprecedented importance in shaping the public sphere. That world, as Bowen has described, is unprecedentedly proto-modernist in its emphasis upon the role of language in creating meaning and shaping the historical narrative. Rather than being merely an abrupt shift in the plotting, then, moving the narrative to America in the fifth monthly number evidences that 'steadier eye upon the general purpose and design'[8] that Dickens claimed as his intent in the first preface to the novel, since it allows him to construct two versions of the modern world that are simultaneously connected and contrasted with one another. In this context I argue that, in ways that have not previously been fully recognised, these two versions are differentiated by their representations of modern urban-based life and of the role that writing, print culture and the press play in making that world intelligible both to its fictional inhabitants and to the novel's readers. Examining these two versions of modernity further reveals that, even while acknowledging the new global power being created by the emergence of the United States, the novel grows into asserting the London metropole as the centre of the Anglophone world. As a result, by contrast with Martineau, who had embraced a continuing engagement in the abolitionist cause and saw the cause of liberal progress as inextricably transatlantic, Dickens turns away from a republican America that had failed to live up to his imagined expectations. Instead, he moves back towards Britain and, for all his subsequent criticism of specific British institutions and governmental practices, lays the foundation of a position of support for state-maintained political order that he would maintain throughout the remainder of his career.[9] That support, which had been anticipated in the ways in which *Barnaby Rudge* champions the state's response to the threat posed by the Gordon Riots, becomes evident in *Chuzzlewit* through the text's treatment of one of the most visible threats to Anglocentric political order in the early 1840s – Irish nationalism and the support it received from the immigrant population of the United States. Through its representation of Catholicism and of the Irish nationalist cause in the press on both sides of the Atlantic, *Chuzzlewit* works, to borrow Schneider's phrasing, simultaneously both towards reestablishing the structuring boundaries that are essential to the preservation of social order even while suggesting their fragility and vulnerability. Despite the extent to which the novel continues *American Notes*'s privileging of English national identity and its affirmation of England as the leading force of global civilisation, however, it also reveals how Dickens was irresistibly drawn to the ways in which American individualistic capitalism was manifested through the nation's press. For, finally, I interrogate Arac's reading of the novel as one that expresses Dickens's aspiration to create 'a vision of people's specific interdependence, a sociology to replace the atomism and laissez-faire of Utilitarian psychology and political economy'.[10] Countering this reading of Utilitarianism, which parallels Fielding and Smith's interpretation of the later dispute between Dickens and Martineau over factory safety and the relationship between the state and personal agency in a liberal society, I argue that *Martin Chuzzlewit* is as much fascinated as it is repelled by America's freedom from the state-sanctioned constraints under which journalism operated in Britain and the opportunities this combination offered to an entrepreneurial man of the press. In this regard, rather than simply the 'frightful engine' he had labelled it in *American Notes*, the American press also becomes an unlikely model for the potential power of an editor to bend and shape an unruly world to his own will and a precursor of the editorial function Dickens would create for himself in the early 1850s.

To make this case, the chapter is organised into four sections. First, beginning with Forster and Dickens's April 1843 follow-up to their earlier article on the American press in the October 1842 *Foreign Quarterly Review*, it positions *Martin Chuzzlewit* in the context of the ongoing critical response to *American Notes*. It then connects the article to the novel's representation of print, literature and the press in the United States, emphasising how, by contrast with the version of the young nation that *American Notes* had offered just months before, *Chuzzlewit* both presents an America that is largely devoid of any redeeming attributes and is even more systematically critical of American literary and press culture than its predecessor. Second, the chapter examines the complex ways in which the novel represents literacy, print and the press in England. On the one hand, that is, it constructs a nostalgic version of England that is everything its America is not – a society anchored in deep connectedness to both place and time and where print culture, especially book culture, is the palpable manifestation of that sense of connection. On the other, it depicts a public sphere, most notably in London, where the emerging forms of modern urban life are creating far more ambivalent kinds of space in which, as in the New York David Henkin describes, circuits of communication are created through public acts of writing and reading. In its third section, the chapter argues that its American and British versions of this modernist world where reading and writing, literature and the press are shaping the public sphere come together most fully during an episode that has previously gone almost without critical comment: Chapter 21's account of the Watertoast Association of United Sympathizers, a group that supports the Irish nationalist cause and promulgates its views through the *Watertoast Gazette*. Reading this episode in the context of press coverage of Ireland on both sides of the Atlantic and placing it against the representation of Catholicism in *Barnaby Rudge*, this section reveals Dickens unprecedentedly blending the forms of journalism and fiction to comment upon the potential latent in the combination of the two to shape public discourse. As he effects this fusion, moreover, he also demonstrates to all those who had criticised his ambitions in moving beyond popular fiction writing just how profoundly innovative a force he indeed could be. Finally, the chapter closes by turning to another part of the text that has been largely understudied: its depiction of Hannibal Chollop, the newspaper editor encountered in the mud and mire of Eden, and suggests that, rather than simply an object of satire, Chollop is in fact the figure who most fully represents the potential for his own future role in the British press that Dickens found in America.

'The Burden whereof, is Hail Columbia!': *Martin Chuzzlewit's* America

'The civilization and intelligence of England'

Writing his biography of Dickens thirty years after *Martin Chuzzlewit* was first published, John Forster claimed that the origins of the novel's American sections lay in the way in which Dickens was 'moved to reopen' his appraisal of the United States by the hostile reception his travel book had received and that he was particularly inspired by 'the challenge to make good his *Notes* which every mail had been bringing him from unsparing assailants across the Atlantic'.[11] Pointing only briefly to the *Edinburgh Review*'s acknowledgement of its error in saying that 'Dickens had gone to America as a kind of missionary in the cause of international copyright',[12] Forster makes no mention of the overwhelmingly negative reviews *American Notes* had received in Britain itself and, instead, concentrates upon the wounded hostility of its readers in the United States. As the previous chapter has shown, however, the assailants in the heavyweight British quarterlies were no less unsparing than the American reviewers and, with no injured national pride to defend, had directed their focus upon failings they attributed to Dickens's class origins, the limits of his education and his temerity in breaking out of the role of ebulliently comic and sentimental novelist through which he had come to fame. Since these reviews appeared late in 1842 and during the early months of 1843, both the genesis of the novel and Dickens's decision to move the plot to America thus occurred in the context of the almost universally hostile reception his travel book was encountering on both sides of the Atlantic. Rather than the explanation that has been frequently offered – that this was an abrupt response to lower sales of the monthly Numbers – my argument here, then, is that Dickens's choice to make America an essential part of the novel can be seen as an extension of the conversations he had already prompted about the relationship between the New World and the Old, the role of print journalism constructing the public sphere and his own standing and authority as a writer.

That this is indeed the case is evident from a second article on the American press Forster wrote for his *Foreign Quarterly Review*. 'The Answer of the American Press' was published in April 1843 even as Dickens was writing the novel's fifth number in which Martin announces his decision to go to America. Like its predecessor the previous October, the article closely prefigures issues that Dickens would address in his own text as Forster re-engages with the transatlantic debate about the nature and social role of the press that Dickens's travel book had provoked. Citing and specifically responding to not only the *New York Herald*'s comments and Felton's *North American Review* article but also to the *Edinburgh*, the *Westminster* and *The Times*, he restates the opinions of his first article and defends both Dickens and, more broadly, the superiority of the press in Britain. Quoting extensively from the series of leaders the *Herald* had published around the publication of *American Notes*, he is unrepentant in his attack upon the American press – 'founded on the junction of literary incompetency and moral indecency'[13] – and critical of those journals, particularly the *Westminster*, that stand up for it. In this view, the newspapers of America are precisely the inverse of the leader of progressive change that the *Herald* had claimed to be in its response to *American Notes*:

> They level, to an undistinguishable mass, the educated, the ignorant, and the base. They drive into one bad direction all the forces of society, which, if personal liberty is to be preserved, or the rights of individual thought and opinion respected, ought to be engaged in counteracting each other. Democracy is little understood, if this is supposed to be democracy. It is a state of equal and universal slavery: the tyranny to which all are subject, being that of a press the most infamous on earth.[14]

By contrast, he suggests,

> English journalism, whatever its defects may be, represents not unworthily the civilization and intelligence of England. A great people finds utterance in it for every possible difference of thought and opinion, and a respectable community has no cause to be ashamed of it.[15]

Moreover, although there is indeed a gutter press in England, Forster regards it as much less of a concern than is the case in America, since its 'most evil and influential element dashes itself against the general structure of society in vain'.[16] Affecting shock that the *New York Courier* should 'denounce licence, vulgarity and libel', he then draws upon the classical tradition to emphasise his condemnation as he reminds the reader that 'With what face the Gracchi could complain of sedition, has been for a number of years a matter of considerable wonder.'[17] Forster's allusion to the Roman brothers who rose from the people to serve as tribunes and who were both assassinated as a result of their efforts to implement populist reforms reinforces his branding of the New World as a society in which there is 'no effort to check the influences which are running riot'[18] and, indeed, in which the press contributes to the forces of disorder. Making the point that the New York press was an agent of the very social disorder of which it complained through its scandal-mongering and consequent degradation of public taste, he implies that, if it should be brought down by that same public taste, it would have no better grounds for complaint than had the Roman brothers for the final outcome of their populist initiatives. While there is no explicit manuscript evidence to demonstrate the collusion here between Dickens and Forster as overtly as there had been with the earlier *Foreign Quarterly* article and *American Notes*,[19] the allusion to the Gracchi implicitly provides similar corroboration. For, as we shall see below in discussing Mrs Hominy's significance in the novel, the Gracchi and the role they come to play in *Martin Chuzzlewit* amply testify that this second article was again a closely orchestrated joint endeavour intended both to anticipate and underwrite a case Dickens was about to make in his own text.

'A state of vacancy'

If Forster's second article prefaces the novel's treatment of America in a parallel manner to which his first had served *American Notes*, Dickens also repeats his travel book's anticipation of the New World through the way in which he represents the transatlantic voyage towards it. For the atopic ocean that had been the precursor to his own more closely personalised experience of America reappears in the novel as Martin and Mark similarly venture through the 'whirling madness' of a storm at sea.[20] But, where the Dickensian narrator of *American Notes* had been overwhelmed by the dissolving power of the ocean in tumult and had almost lost the capacity of language to render experience into meaning,[21] Mark Tapley is far more in control of the novel's narrative perspective and articulates a much more assertive appraisal that prefigures the America towards which they are sailing:

> the sea is as nonsensical a thing as anything going. It never knows what to do with itself. It hasn't got no employment for its mind, and is always in a state of vacancy. Like them Polar bears in the wild-beast-shows as is constantly a nodding their heads from side to side, it never *can* be quiet. Which is entirely owing to its uncommon stupidity.[22]

In this dismissive judgement, Mark predicts precisely what will become the foundation of the novel's representation of the United States: its 'state of vacancy', physical, spiritual, intellectual, and the resulting cultural void that leaves its population unable to resist the aggressive agency of the mass-circulation press that rushes in to fill the vacuum left for it.

Once Martin and Mark actually land in the New World, the foundation for that vacancy is suggested in the way in which the novel presents the built world of American civilisation as a much diminished version of the one that had been represented in *American Notes*. To be sure, taking up only eight of the novel's fifty-four chapters and needing to enact the plotting of Martin's mortification and renewal in Eden, the American portion of the text was bound to offer a more compact and restricted account of the nation than would have been appropriate to the travel book that preceded it. But in *Chuzzlewit* that very absence of detail becomes the essential point. Where *American Notes* had begun its account of the United States with Dickens's enthusiastic response to Boston, Lowell and his journey through New England, the novel's version plunges immediately into New York and the world according to Colonel Diver, editor of the *New York Rowdy Journal*. But even New York, which Chapter 6 of *American Notes* had celebrated in terms of its commercial abundance, cultural complexity and diverse populace, is shrunk into a single sentence that merely describes Martin and Mark 'seeing it from the best points of view, and pausing in the principal streets, and before the best public buildings'.[23] Gone entirely is the rich life of the cityscape that had so caught Dickens's eye in *American Notes*, gone is the dense textuality David Henkin has described as embodying New York's vitality and sense of dynamic growth and, gone with them, is the earlier book's sense of an emerging new nation and the ladder of opportunity that literacy and endeavour could offer to at least some of its marginalised populations. Moreover, beyond this first point of contact in New York and unlike *American Notes*, where the reader had accompanied Dickens through a wide range of explicitly named and described travel experiences and locales, the novel provides almost no distinctive sense of place anywhere this side of an Eden that is itself no more than 'a marsh on which the good growth of the earth seemed to have been wrecked and cast away'[24] – not just the Atlantic Ocean, but the entire nation of America itself becomes atopic in the rendering Dickens offers in *Chuzzlewit*.

Just as the new nation appears to be a physical 'state of vacancy', a society without any grounding sense of space, or, indeed, barely even of solid ground, so too Dickens represents it as devoid of any temporal order. A world of the utterly immediate, with none of the measured progressions that accompanied the stadial vision of human history and its sense of a gradualist social evolution, America intentionally separates itself from the past, functions wholly in the present and has no evident vision of the future towards which it is impelling itself. As Ruth Livesey has commented, it is a 'frighteningly undifferentiated place: a flat land lacking social, cultural, and aesthetic distinctions', with Eden, the settlement that exists solely on paper, its archetypal 'un-narratable site'.[25] By contrast with *American Notes*, where Dickens's accounts of Canada had infused a balancing sense of normative stadial progress occurring at least somewhere on the North American continent, the confinement of *Chuzzlewit*'s narrative to Martin and Mark's experiences in New York and then to an atopically unspecific account of their journey into and back from Eden reinforces an unrelenting representation of a United States unaware of its historical origins, oblivious to its future potential, mired in its unsavoury present.

'The Popular Instructor'

As the novel renders the United States in this markedly diminished way from the treatment given even in its predecessor, however, it simultaneously expands its representation of the role of print culture in the New World. Where *American Notes* had made its attack upon the 'frightful engine' of the press from the external vantage point of the Dickensian narrator safely back in England, *Martin Chuzzlewit* depicts an American population that itself embodies Mark Tapley's description of the atopic ocean that 'hasn't got no employment for its mind, and is always in a state of vacancy'. Living entirely in the immediate moment, the Americans are, as Martin is told by a steam boat captain, 'a busy people . . . and have no time for reading mere notions. We don't mind 'em if they come to us in newspapers along with almighty strong stuff of another sort, but darn your books.'[26] Building on Dickens's own description in *American Notes* of the 'good strong stuff' filling the New York mass-market papers,[27] the captain's summative appraisal epitomises a society that subsists on, even revels in, an intellectual diet of exclusively fast print. As a result, and having no use for the longer historical perspectives associated with book culture and a tradition of literary production, transmission of knowledge and cultural formation, the Americans are, as Major Pawkins briskly testifies, ever ready to shrug off the burden of the past and eternally begin anew, textually as much as historically: 'the one article of his creed, in reference to all public obligations involving the good faith and integrity of his country, was, "to run a moist pen slick through everything, and start fresh"'.[28]

Given such a version of the nation's intellectual disposition and attitude towards literacy, it is not surprising that the novel finds no place for any exemplar of the periodical press such as that which *The Lowell Offering* had provided in *American Notes*. Instead, *Chuzzlewit* offers two representatives of American print culture who collectively bear witness to the qualities identified by the steam boat captain and the major. Appearing in the text immediately upon its arrival in the New World, these two examplars focus upon the mass-circulation metropolitan press Dickens had already attacked both in *American Notes* and via Forster's two *Foreign Quarterly Review* articles and, through their placement at the start of the American portion of the narrative, set the terms for the novel's entire reading of the New World.

Indeed, even before Martin and Mark reach land, their first encounter of America is with the 'legion' of news-boys who clamber on to the ship:

> 'Here's this morning's New York Sewer!' cried one. 'Here's this morning's New York Stabber! Here's the New York Family Spy! Here's the New York Private Listener! Here's the New York Peeper! Here's the New York Plunderer! Here's the New York Keyhole Reporter! Here's the New York Rowdy Journal! Here's all the New York papers!'[29]

Far more aggressive than the 'precocious urchins' on the New York streets of *American Notes*,[30] these news-boys anticipate the novel's first example of the editorial subject, Colonel Diver of the *New York Rowdy Journal*, Dickens's fictitious rendering of Bennett, Webb and the other leaders of the new urban newspapers that were emerging as the most significant development in American journalism. For Diver introduces Martin and the reader not only to New York and America but also to an editorial power without parallel back in the Old World, as he asserts himself as the defender of 'the Palladium of rational Liberty', guardian of 'the well of Truth, whose waters are black from being composed of printer's ink', and self-appointed protector of those masses who will willingly 'yield to the mighty mind of the Popular Instructor'.[31] Redolent of the editorial language with which the *New York Herald* had asserted its role as a champion of American leadership in advancing the cause of liberal civilisation, the hyperbole of Diver's claims marks him as Dickens's first extension into his own text of the critique Forster had offered in the *Foreign Quarterly Review* essay just three months before.

If, however, Diver is overtly a response to the American press's attacks on Dickens and *American Notes*, he can also be seen as a less direct counter to the ways in which British reviewers had criticised Dickens himself. For the narrator describes Diver's appearance to an extent that is all the more striking for being as detailed as the novel's account of the city whose opinions he shapes is sparse:

> a sallow gentleman, with sunken cheeks, black hair, small twinkling eyes, and a singular expression hovering about that region of his face, which was not a frown, nor a leer, and yet might have been mistaken at the first glance for either. Indeed it would have been difficult on a much closer acquaintance, to describe it in any more satisfactory terms than as a mixed expression of vulgar cunning and conceit. This gentleman wore a rather broad-brimmed hat for the greater wisdom of his appearance; and had his arms folded for the greater impressiveness of his attitude. He was somewhat shabbily dressed in a blue surtout reaching nearly to his ankles, short loose trousers of the same colour, and a faded buff waistcoat, through which a discoloured shirt-frill struggled to force itself into notice, as asserting an equality of civil rights with the other portions of his dress, and maintaining a declaration of Independence on its own account.[32]

Pictured with greater material specificity than any other of the novel's American characters, Diver's squalid and shifting identity smoothly aligns him with an urban press defined by the list of newspaper titles that had greeted the travellers upon their arrival. But, while this description of the déclassé journalist does provide support for Meredith McGill's argument that one of the novel's fundamental strategies is to find ways in which to contain the American press, Dickens may be doing even more here with his framing of Diver. For, having had his own standing as a social commentator so sharply questioned in terms of social class by the British reviewers of *American Notes*, he turns the same tactic against his metonymic representative of the New York press: Diver, with his slovenly dress and a face that renders no constant meaning is at once the most completely rendered American body in the novel and an incarnation of the failings and untrustworthiness of the nation's entire print culture. By contrast, Martin himself, who until this point in the narrative has presented as little more than a callow narcissist, is now tacitly allowed to assume the part of gentlemanly representative of English superiority to the United States and all its vulgarity (Fig. 4.1). Connecting Diver and the newspapers through which 'the bubbling passions' of his country 'find a vent' with the novel's rendering of the as yet unformed nature of the continent itself,[33] Dickens thus achieves three distinct effects. First, he makes use of the hapless editor to reinforce the claims he and Forster had been making about the appalling quality of the American press. In so doing, he plays into the well-established stereotype that earlier British writers had developed and that, as we have seen, even Martineau drew upon as the starting point for her ultimately much more nuanced exploration of the press in the United States. Second, Diver and the mass-market, politically engaged journalism he represents voice again the concern Dickens had first expressed over the role of such a press in *Barnaby Rudge* and that he would again articulate during the early 1850s as the pressure mounted to reduce the last of the 'taxes on knowledge'. Finally, the combination of Diver's representation as so palpably déclassé, so much a product of the New York streets, enables Dickens to turn against the New York press the very critique that had been made of him by elite British reviewers, thereby both intensifying his attack on the former and, through the narrator's implied differentiation from the target of his language, defending himself against the charges of the latter.

If Dickens uses Diver's socially amphibian positioning to frame the novel's first encounter with the American press, its second takes place at a much more assured point in the class structure but, ultimately, turns out to be no less complex in its workings. For the

150 Contested Liberalisms

Figure 4.1 Mr Jefferson Brick proposes an appropriate sentiment.

same Chapter 16 that introduces Diver also brings into the narrative Mr Bevan, the gentleman from Massachusetts with 'something very engaging and honest in the expression of his features' who has helpfully profited sufficiently from foreign travel to perceive his nation's limitations.[34] However, despite his plot function as the Good Samaritan who enables Martin and Mark to escape from Eden and notwithstanding the established critical assumption that he is simply a genial homage to Cornelius C. Felton, the Harvard professor of Greek who became one of the closest friends Dickens made during his visit,[35] Bevan's role in the novel's representation of the press turns out to be more intricate than has been previously recognised. For it turns upon the way in which he alludes to Benjamin Franklin's essay, 'Account of the highest Court of Judicature in Pensylvania, viz. The Court of the Press', as a way to condemn Diver:

> 'He is one of a class of men, in whom our own Franklin, so long as ten years before the close of the last century, foresaw our danger and disgrace. Perhaps you don't know that Franklin, in very severe terms, published his opinion that those who were slandered by such fellows as this colonel, having no sufficient remedy in the administration of this country's laws or in the decent and right-minded feeling of its people, were justified in retorting on such public nuisances by means of a stout cudgel?'[36]

Dickens, as the 1845 inventory of his library in Devonshire Terrace shows, owned a collection of Franklin's complete works that included this essay;[37] his appropriation of it into his own text, however, is anything but innocent. First, Franklin's original is a thoroughly satirical piece, mocking the excesses of the American press in terms that went far beyond the bounds of propriety within which Dickens and his contemporaries could make their own attacks:

> But any man who can procure pen, ink, and paper, with a press, a few types, and a huge pair of blacking balls, may commissionate himself, and his court is immediately established in the plenary possession and exercise of its rights. For if you make the least complaint of the judge's conduct, he daubs his blacking balls in your face wherever he meets you; and besides tearing your private character to splinters, marks you out for the odium of the public, as an enemy to the liberty of the press.[38]

But, as he transposes Franklin's text into Bevan's mouth, Dickens represents the sentiment of the original quite literally, depriving the father of American journalism of all of his corrective satiric irony, reinforcing the novel's larger representation of Americans as unable to reflect upon their own culture and aligning him with its Anglocentric attack upon the nation's press. Second, in addition to thus being made to appropriate Franklin for Dickensian purposes, Bevan also serves to undermine his originating model, C. C. Felton. For, in the one major positive review of *American Notes* that had appeared, Felton, as we saw in Chapter 3, had, if only in passing, joined in the wider chorus of criticism with his comment that 'We look upon the boundless power Dickens ascribes to the worst part of the American newspaper press with as much incredulity as we should upon the asserted wonders of any necromantic agency.'[39] By retracting that judgement and acknowledging that 'If another Juvenal or Swift could rise up among us to-morrow, he would be hunted down',[40] Bevan, and indirectly Felton himself, are made to accede to Dickens's description of the nation's cultural deficiency and his allegation that not only the daily press but American letters as a whole are incapable of maintaining order in a society desperately in need of such forms of control. While Felton may have provided the inspiration for an ostensibly model American, then, he is also made to pay a price for having criticised his friend in print and, indeed, through his fictional counterpart is involuntarily enlisted to serve as an important agent of Dickens's response to the attacks upon *American Notes* and his own authorial standing.

'The Mother of the Modern Gracchi'

Where Diver and Bevan function in these ways as localised attacks upon America's journalism and press, albeit attacks that are more complex than has been previously recognised, the novel's third representation of the nation's print culture and literary life makes a broader comment and one that is deeply indicative of Dickens and Martineau's differing understandings of liberalism. For, as the American chapters progress, they merge their consistent lament over the dearth of any life of the mind in the New World into a sustained assault upon the intellectual independence of women. The first indicator of this occurs in New York, where the women Martin encounters are represented as abandoning their natural sphere, from the young Miss Norris who 'was distinguished by a talent for metaphysics, the laws of hydraulic pressure, and the rights of human kind' to the lecture-attending ladies about whom the ostensibly reliable Bevan testifies that 'domestic drudgery was far beneath the exalted range of these Philosophers' and that 'They go to these places of resort, as an escape from monotony; look at each other's clothes; and come home again.'[41] Suggesting that American women's attempts to develop autonomous intellectual lives correlate to their neglect of domestic responsibilities and values, the novel implies that this neglect in turn contributes to those 'bubbling passions' that underlie the new nation's cultural instability.

That suggestion, moreover, is affirmed most explicitly once Martin leaves New York and through the two encounters he has on his journeys to and from Eden with Mrs Hominy, 'The Mother of the Modern Gracchi',[42] the novel's most developed representative of American letters and an even more conservative vision of republican motherhood than Dickens had offered in his descriptions of women in *American Notes*. For, as he depicts the American interior and by contrast with Martineau's highlighting Cincinnati and the significance of the contribution that an authentically American literary culture emerging in the west was making to stadial progress, Dickens fuses a dismissive account of the nation's letters with parodic representation of any and all efforts by American women to enter the public sphere as autonomous liberal subjects.

Mrs Hominy, who is entirely supernumerary to the novel's plotting, encapsulates everything that the text suggests is lacking in American cultural values. Introduced by the anonymous gentleman who imposes her upon Martin's protection as the spouse of 'one of our chicest spirits',[43] she is travelling to visit her family in the settlement of New Thermopylae established on the banks of the Ohio. Despite the settlement's classically heroic name, however, the barbarians here clearly lie within, and the narrator soon requires no intermediary character through whom to render the text's judgement. For Mrs Hominy, he suggests, is a 'woman of masculine and towering intellect' and both a product and producer of the

> cant of a class, and a large class, of her fellow-countrymen, who, in their every word, avow themselves to be as senseless to the high principles on which America sprang, a nation, into life, as any Orson in her legislative halls.[44]

Aligning her claims to intellectual authority with a broadly generalised diagnosis of the nation's failure to live up to its founding principles, the narrator thus reinforces the novel's larger representation of women in America. For, where the few women described in *American Notes* had offered some corrective to the social failings of the nation, those who appear in *Chuzzlewit* are made consistent with the novel's satiric vision, with Mrs Hominy as its fullest representative of an America that is moving backwards, declining from the promise of its founding, sliding into the ooze of its primeval landscape, deluding itself with grandiose claims of cultural value.

By contrast with Mr Bevan, moreover, whose American identity is represented as having been leavened through contact with the superior nations of Europe, Mrs Hominy's experience of other cultures is made to align with the failings of her own, linking together her travel, her defining maternal soubriquet and her habit of collapsing the separation between private and public life that is consistently a negative indicator throughout the novel's American sections:

> But Mrs Hominy was a traveller. Mrs Hominy was a writer of reviews and analytical disquisitions. Mrs Hominy had had her letters from abroad, beginning 'My ever dearest blank,' and signed 'The Mother of the Modern Gracchi' (meaning the married Miss Hominy), regularly printed in a public journal, with all the indignation in capitals, and all the sarcasm in italics.[45]

Moreover, her framing herself in terms of the Roman brothers who had made an appearance in Forster's *Foreign Quarterly Review* article just a few months earlier adds a layer of significance to Mrs Hominy's presence in the text that has gone unremarked in critical discussions of the novel and that connects her to Dickens's larger concern with the role of the press in social formation. First, that is, by subsequently insisting upon the iterative act of self-definition as that Mother of the Roman consuls, Mrs Hominy follows a precedent established by Colonel Diver almost in the first moments that Martin and Mark are in America. For, in a world that lacks those 'structuring boundaries upon which systems of signification depend' Matthew Schneider has described, she becomes just one more instance of the endlessly recurring American characters who inscribe themselves into presumptive roles that take the place of any stable identity. Second, and following a precedent that Dickens himself had set through his deployment of classical allusion in *American Notes*, Mrs Hominy's self-fashioning follows the novel's wider pattern of using such references to indicate the failings of the new democracy – from Bevan's comments on the nation's hostility to Juvenalian satire to the slave, Cicero, whom Mark Tapley meets in New York and whose body, with its story of the savage brutality that has been inflicted upon him, points, as Larisa Castillo has argued, to the ways in which Americans assume that their own natural rights include the abrogation of the freedom of others.[46] Finally, through styling herself in a way that parallels her American male counterparts' assumption of military titles, Dickens renders Mrs Hominy into a profoundly debased version of the classical original. For Cornelia, daughter of the general who had defeated Hannibal, was, as David Stockton has described, 'a woman of exceptional character, intelligence, culture, and energy who exerted a powerful formative influence over two remarkable sons left in her sole care from their early childhood'.[47] In depicting Mrs Hominy as the buffoonish successor to her Roman model, however, Dickens simultaneously aligns her with the anti-stadial degenerative vision of the United States that pervades *American Notes* and *Martin Chuzzlewit* and reinforces his attacks upon both American women's agency outside the home and the failure of the nation's masculine elite to exert leadership over their culture and give it direction.

Not for nothing, then, is the text's final image of Mrs Hominy one of her collaborating with the two literary ladies and in the process bolstering Dickens's most comically dismissive representation of American literature:

> 'Mind and matter', said the lady in the wig, 'glide swiftly into the vortex of immensity. Howls the sublime, and softly sleeps the calm Ideal, in the whispering chambers of Imagination. To hear it, sweet it is. But then, outlaughs the stern philosopher, and saith to the Grotesque, "What ho! arrest me for that Agency. Go, bring it here!" And so the vision fadeth.'[48]

To be sure, the comic splendour of the language here suggests Dickens's delighted fascination with those points at which structuring boundaries collapse into chaos, and the literary ladies in this respect can be seen as transatlantic kin to the novel's nonpareil of linguistic self-fashioning, Mrs Gamp. Ultimately, however, and in a way that is wholly consistent with the text's entire account of the New World's version of the modern world, this last glimpse of American literary life, Mrs Hominy, the literary ladies and their vortex of immensity not only confirms that 'state of vacancy' Mark Tapley had anticipated at the empty core of the nation's identity but insinuates that misguided forms of femininity play a significant role in the creation of that emptiness. Not surprisingly, then, Martineau, for whom female leadership in the abolitionist movement in Boston had symbolised the possibility of stadial progress for America and who had passed over *American Notes* as merely superficial, despaired over the novel that followed it: 'Never was I pulled down into such a slough as Chuzzlewit... I feared many things for Boz, but not this. He must redeem himself soon, or it will be too late.'[49]

'An atmosphere of unaccountable fascination': *Martin Chuzzlewit*'s England

Arriving back from their unhappy sojourn in America, Martin and Mark Tapley find refuge and refreshment in a cheap dockside tavern that in its very construction of space marks their return to the Old World:

> It had more corners in it than the brain of an obstinate man; was full of mad closets, into which nothing could be put that was not specially invented and made for that purpose; had mysterious shelvings and bulkheads, and indications of staircases in the ceiling; and was elaborately provided with a bell that rung in the room itself, about two feet from the handle, and had no connexion whatever with any other part of the establishment.[50]

Not since the opening paragraphs of *American Notes* and his description of the 'profoundly preposterous box' that was his state-room on the SS *Britannia* and where his portmanteaus could no more be accommodated than 'a giraffe could be persuaded or forced into a flower-pot'[51] had Dickens written with such affectionate delight about the absurd eccentricities of a constrained space. Indeed, this single-sentence description of a location that vanishes from the text almost as quickly as it appears points to a fundamental contrast within the novel between atopic America and an England that, rooted in time as much as place, apparently possesses the stability that is wholly lacking in the 'state of vacancy' across the Atlantic. For, constantly portraying English life in terms of rich historicity and the slow accretion of the past upon the present, *Martin Chuzzlewit* invokes a version of England that stands in opposition to the dystopian United States and the degenerating continent on which they are founded. In both its early rural sections, which deploy the pastoral more extensively and instrumentally than any other Dickensian text, and in its creation of London and its 'unaccountable fascination'[52] as the prototype of the contemporary city, *Chuzzlewit* thus privileges a construction of the nation that combines a nostalgic sense of the continuing infusion of the past into the present with a more complex set of responses to the modern society that was coming into being.

While plot structures that move between specific rural settings and the irresistible draw of London recur throughout Dickens's career, *Chuzzlewit* is unique for the ways in which the English countryside is rendered in terms that not only pair it with the nation's capital but also place it in opposition to the topographic presentation of the American interior. By contrast with *American Notes*, where Dickens's account of the New World is preceded and framed by his extended description of the transatlantic voyage, the slow descent of Martin and Mark's journey into the febrile slime and decay of the continent and ultimately towards Eden takes much of its force from the contrast with the emotional resonance of the English rural world created in the novel's early chapters. For these establish an image redolent in the robust and glowing terms of autumnal ripeness and brisk wintry vigour: the 'noiseless passage of the plough as it turned up the rich brown earth', trees with 'autumn berries hung like clusters of coral beads', and the last rays of the sun striking 'out paths of deeper gold' all develop a form of English pastoral unusual in Dickens but one that becomes essential to the novel's transatlantic oppositions.[53] Where America will be marked by its disconnection from its own past, moreover, this rural world is instilled with layers of old time, layers embodied briefly in that setting sun which acted 'like a sudden flash of memory or spirit kindling up the mind of an old man' and even more fully in the village church that appeared to be 'the hoarding-place of twenty summers, and all their ruddiness and warmth were stored within'.[54] By contrast with Dickens's version of America, moreover, a nation as devoid of religious life as it is of ecclesiastical architecture, Wiltshire's churches form an essential part of the imagined rural community that the novel constructs. For both in the village and in nearby Salisbury they contain the organs upon which Tom Pinch plays, connecting those who hear his music and providing Tom himself with a sense of integrated wholeness that proves elusive in his actual everyday life:

> Great thoughts and hopes came crowding in his mind as the rich music rolled upon the air, and yet among them – something more grave and solemn in their purpose, but the same – were all the images of that day, down to its very lightest recollection of childhood. The feeling that the sounds awakened, in the moment of their existence, seemed to include his whole life and being.[55]

If the church thus serves as both repository of and catalyst to Tom's individual memories, embedding both him and the village in the continuity of long historical time, so the village's only other specified location, the Blue Dragon, performs cultural identity in a different yet complementary way. For it provides the space in which Mark Tapley enacts the kind of sociable community through play and popular entertainment that is signally lacking among the Americans: 'Lord, there's no dulness at the Dragon! Skittles, cricket, quoits, nine-pins, comic songs, choruses, company round the chimney-corner every winter's evening – any man would be jolly at the Dragon.'[56] Whether it be in this cozy idealised present, then, or in the ways in which it gathers its inhabitants into the nurturing richness of its pastoral idyll, the Wiltshire village expresses a sense of rootedness in place and time that is wholly absent from the novel's version of America.[57]

Despite this foregrounding of the village as a bucolic sheltered idyll infused with the nostalgic tones of eighteenth-century pastoral poetry, however, rural Wiltshire is not entirely insulated from either the darker elements of the novel or its acknowledgement of the historical immediacies of its creation. On the one hand, that is, for all the endless hyperbole and threatening language of the Americans, the plot's one actual moment of violence occurs in this avowedly pastoral English setting when Jonas Chuzzlewit beats Tigg to death in a wood as the sun goes down. On the other, and somewhat discordantly with the prevailing tone of the country scenes, the narratorial voice at one point slips into a tone of high moral outrage over the failings of the English political classes as it makes reference to a decade of unrest among the agricultural working class that had come to a peak in 1843:[58] 'Oh magistrate, so rare a country gentleman and brave a squire, hadst thou no duty to society, before ricks were blazing and the mob were mad; or did it spring up armed and booted from the earth, a corps of yeomanry, full-grown!'[59] Suggesting, if only in passing, the potential for working-class violence in terms that recollect the description of the Gordon Riots in *Barnaby Rudge*, the text is thus unable to sustain completely its displacement of rural England into some imagined bucolic past and in this it both looks forward to the novel's representation of London and, as the third part of this chapter shows, anticipates the ways in which Dickens brings Britain and America together over the issue of insurgent Irish nationalism.

By contrast with America, whose cities are largely erased from the narrative, *Martin Chuzzlewit*'s London, as Dorothy van Ghent first so influentially showed, is synonymous with a sense of the animated urban labyrinth that has come to be seen as a fundamental element of the Dickensian universe.[60] Like its characters, the novel is irresistibly drawn towards an 'unaccountable fascination' with the city, the essential elements of which are summarised during Tom Pinch's daily walk to his workplace in the Temple. Descending from Islington into the 'ghostly air' and 'strange charm', he becomes 'enveloped' in the city before turning into the 'quiet court-yards' where his own echoing footsteps

> sounded to him like a voice from the old walls and pavements, wanting language to relate the histories of the dim, dismal rooms; to tell him what lost documents were decaying in forgotten corners of the shut-up cellars, from whose lattices such mouldy sighs came breathing forth as he went past.[61]

As much as it is defined by points of observation from above such as the view from the roof of Todgers's or the Monument, London is no less fully realised by the combination of hidden depths and elusive texts. In this, the city is the polar opposite of an Eden that never becomes more than the map in Scadder's office, a two-dimensional fictitious schema.[62] By contrast, resisting any easy narrating of itself into a readily legible place, London's underground spaces and the secret lives they both preserve and withhold from view constitute the essential element of the built city: from Guy Fawkes, whose activity 'beneath the vaults of the Parliament House at Westminster' opens the novel to the

> wine-merchants and wholesale dealers in grocery-ware [who] had perfect little towns of their own; and, deep among the very foundations of these buildings, the ground was undermined and burrowed out into stables, where cart-horses, troubled by rats, might be heard on a quiet Sunday, rattling their halters, as disturbed spirits in tales of haunted houses are said to clank their chains.[63]

Palpable yet barely visible, present yet almost absent, London's mysterious depths and hidden spaces form its identity and establish it as a built world entirely different from the blank that New York becomes in the novel – indeed, a world entirely different from the novel's whole sense of America, where the absence of interior built spaces images the dearth of any interior life among the population.

What this London does recall, however, is the New York of *American Notes*, with the surface energy of its stress, alluring subterranean fascination of Five Points and the rich visual textuality of its cityscape. By contrast with its predecessor, *Chuzzlewit* distinguishes England from America in its contrast between the eviscerated 'state of vacancy' that defines the culture of the New World and the profoundly historicised social environment of the Old, one that is simultaneously more thoroughly known and yet more elusively unknowable and that, through this combination, becomes both more alluring and more uncanny, more endearing and more disturbing. Then, unlike the American sections of the novel and their focus on, first, the press as a primary indicator of the limitations of national culture and, second, Mrs Hominy as a negative exemplar of both its literature and aspirations towards female autonomy, *Chuzzlewit* imagines an England where books, print and writing simultaneously evoke the nostalgic past and anticipate new forms of modern urban life in which those circuits of public communication *American Notes* had captured in New York are beginning to take shape. Significantly, however, but consistent with the ways in which both the travel book and the novel had recorded the rise of an American urban mass-market press that had as yet no parallel in Britain, *Chuzzlewit* represents English newspapers, whether rural or metropolitan, as still marginal to the public sphere, still on the periphery of print culture.

'That whiff of russia leather'

In its depiction of print, the novel's nostalgic impulses are most fully developed around Tom Pinch and his abiding animation by, even dependence upon, the material culture of the book:

> But what were even gold and silver, precious stones and clockwork to the bookshops, whence a pleasant smell of paper freshly pressed came issuing forth, awakening instant recollections of some new grammar had at school, long time ago, with 'Master Pinch, Grove House Academy', inscribed in faultless writing on the fly-leaf! That whiff of russia leather, too, and all those rows on rows of volumes, neatly ranged within – what happiness did they suggest! And in the window were the spick-and-span new works from London, with the title-pages, and sometimes even the first page of the first chapter, laid wide open: tempting unwary men to begin to read the book, and then in the impossibility of turning over, to rush blindly in, and buy it! Here too were the dainty frontispiece and trim vignette, pointing like hand-posts on the outskirts of great cities to the rich stock of incident beyond.[64]

Defining Tom even before he is shown playing the church organ, this passage on the Salisbury book shops and their wares both connects him with the novel's early idealised rendering of pastoral by calling out his attendance at 'Grove Academy' and, through the very materiality of the new books, articulates a set of associative values that will later distinguish them from American print culture. The rich smell of their paper and binding in 'russia leather', for instance, suggests how far removed they are from the 'miserable whity-brown paper' of the American newsprint Forster had excoriated in the *New York Herald* and its 'dingy uncomfortable print'.[65] Moreover, the 'dainty frontispiece and trim vignette pointing like hand-posts' not only reinforces this sense of high-quality material production but, as Ruth Livesey has shown, connect Tom's books with the novel's frontispiece and the iconic, recurring finger post of the text, its emblem of the need for stability and order in a world threatened by 'the accelerating rush of unmoored transatlantic futurity'.[66] 'Spick-and-span' though they may be, these books are clearly expressions of a culture that is slower and more deeply stable than the world of American print. At the same time, however, and suggesting that the novel's versions of the transatlantic world are less dichotomous than they might appear, for the serial reader of 1843 the books are also the products of an England that exists at its own different historical point from the one imagined in the text. That is, in their slow stability, they and their imagined recollections of a happy childhood stand in contrast with a Dickensian form of serial publication that, barely half a dozen years old, written under the pressures of monthly deadlines and issued in an ephemeral form that more resembles those transatlantic newspapers than the books the text yearns over here, is truly the product of the modern world of fast print that the novel both critiques and embodies. It seems almost inevitable, then, that after his move to London Tom should be gifted an asylum from a city that he is manifestly unequipped to negotiate in the form of his job 'as a kind of secretary and librarian'[67] and the opportunity to restore textual harmony, even if only for himself:

> He had got the books into perfect order now, and had mended the torn leaves, and pasted up the broken backs, and substituted neat labels for the worn-out letterings. It looked a different place, it was so orderly and neat: Tom felt some pride in contemplating the change he had wrought, though there was no one to approve or disapprove of it.[68]

Repaired, catalogued and arranged, the books of Tom's library balance against those on which he had gazed in the Salisbury book-shop window early in the novel. Here, his action in the plot essentially concluded, he is transposed from looking in on the world of books to becoming one with it, defined by images of a narrowly achieved order that is framed in terms of adjectives the novel typically assigns to feminine domesticity, and serving as the guardian of repositories of imagined worlds in which he can only participate vicariously. In this way, and as Gerhard Joseph has shown, Tom thus finds 'compensatory comfort' in books for the limitations of his life and, in the library he is given to manage, takes refuge from modern life and a city whose labyrinthine qualities overwhelm him.[69]

If, however, Tom's delight in the material object of the book and the escape the plot grants him thus communicate the novel's affection for, to adapt Elizabeth Miller's term, slow print and its associated values,[70] other areas of the novel render a less easily nostalgic, more modern world in which forms of writing and print function in more complex ways. Though this will appear most fully in London, it is prefigured in rural Wiltshire, which becomes deeply textualised in ways that will come to suggest forces of disruption, change and instability within even the ostensibly stable pastoral setting. To be sure, the significance of such moments often remains latent, their potential hidden from the reader. The crow that skims across the snowy winter fields, 'a blot of ink upon the landscape' that marks yet does not give meaning to the scene, is one such moment, while the Blue Dragon on his sign outside his eponymous inn, 'waxing, with every month that passed, so much more dim and shapeless, that as you gazed at him on one side of the sign-board it seemed as if he must be gradually melting through it, and coming out upon the other' is another.[71] But that blot left by the crow anticipates a later form of inscription upon the landscape and the 'dark, dark stain that dyed' the wood where Jonas murders Tigg. And the Blue Dragon will disappear and be supplanted by Mark Tapley, for whom the inn is renamed after his marriage to Mrs Lupin. Though Mark's elevation may be 'wery new, conwivial, and expressive!'[72] and certainly not as violent as that Jonas effects, it is also a shift that marks Mrs Lupin's erasure as the inn's owner and aligns with a marginalising of female agency that is no less evident in the novel's England than it had been in its American episodes.

Most notably, of course, Wiltshire houses Pecksniff, the profoundest, and funniest, embodiment of the indeterminate and unreliable nature of text in the novel. Constructing himself in terms of forms of print culture that establish him as Tom Pinch's polar opposite, he stages his self-presentation for Martin's arrival, for example:

Mr Pecksniff had clearly not expected them for hours to come: for he was surrounded by open books, and was glancing from volume to volume, with a black-lead pencil in his mouth, and a pair of compasses in his hand, at a vast number of mathematical diagrams, of such extraordinary shapes that they looked like designs for fireworks.[73]

Later, he will continue the contrast with Tom as he corrupts the pastoral village's associations with long time by conflating material and spiritual standing with his claim of 'a considerable balance in my favor at present standing in the books beyond the sky'.[74] Pecksniff's framing throughout the novel in terms of references to *Paradise Lost* and *Tartuffe* has been widely commented upon, most notably by Alexander Welsh,[75] as has the appearance of these texts in the illustration that accompanies his unmasking.[76] And, in a novel where letter-writing is both such an important functional device and deeply complex form of communication, Carol Hanbery MacKay has noted how appropriate it is that Pecksniff's final appearance should be as 'a drunken, begging, squalid-letter-writing man'.[77] For all their celebration of a richly English pastoral that is unique in Dickens, then, and that certainly does stand in contrast to the miasmic horrors of the American interior, the Wiltshire scenes also anticipate the novel's complex rendering of forms of writing and print that are most fully developed in its representation of London and the mysterious figure of Nadgett.

If Tom is the creature of the hidden space, old books and stabilised order, Nadgett is utterly at home in the city, someone who hides in plain sight, constantly generates new text and thrives in all the flux of urban life. In the very uncertainty of his appearance he even recalls the novel's other urban writer, Colonel Diver of the *Rowdy Journal*:

> He was mildewed, threadbare, shabby; always had flue upon his legs and back; and kept his linen so secret by buttoning up and wrapping over, that he might have had none – perhaps he hadn't. He carried one stained beaver glove, which he dangled before him by the forefinger as he walked or sat; but even its fellow was a secret . . . he belonged to a class; a race peculiar to the city; who are secrets as profound to one another, as they are to the rest of mankind.[78]

Though he may be as shabby and socially unplaced as was Diver, however, Nadgett is far more professionally and textually elusive than the American, carrying 'contradictory cards' that identify him as anything from a coal-merchant to an accountant, avoiding anything that might fix his definition and, indeed, 'as if he really didn't know the secret himself'.[79] Like Diver, he circulates through his city, observing and recording, but never engaging. Making 'nothing of emptying a capacious leaden inkstand in two sittings',[80] he is constantly in search of material about which to write and, equally constantly, does so without any visible purpose. Finally, where Diver is a creature of print and lives for the public consumption of his texts, Nadgett's whole goal is to remain private, mysterious, the man who 'wrote letters to himself about him constantly' and who 'don't like word of mouth . . . We never know who's listening.'[81] Epitomising simultaneously the surveillance John Bowen has noted as lying at the core of modern urban life and a London that, as Julian Wolfreys has commented, 'is where the knowable is constantly displaced',[82] Nadgett may or may not be the mysterious man 'mending a pen at an upper window' across from Todger's,[83] but perhaps the still more intriguing possibility is that, in a city whose population live largely unknown to one another, he easily could be. For, in his ubiquitous presence across the London sections of the plot, Nadgett points darkly to what Adam Grener has described as the way the novel uses coincidences to 'continually draw our attention to a discrepancy between an individual's sense of self-sufficiency and concrete webs of social connection'.[84] *Martin Chuzzlewit*'s modern London, with its subterranean cellarage, labyrinthine surface and proliferation of private texts is simultaneously hidden and visible, known and irresistibly mysterious, Nadgett the epitome of its uncanny fascination, its fusion of the familiar and the profoundly alienated, the visible and the anonymous. And, through Nadgett more than any other figure in the text, London becomes the embodiment of a society that is ultimately far more deeply mysterious and far more potentially disturbing than the callow dystopia Dickens finds in America – the avatar of a modernity that perhaps lay beyond Martineau's ken and that resisted her liberal faith in both post-Enlightenment stadial progress and the role of print culture in helping shape that progress and maintaining its structuring boundaries.

Curiously, although Nadgett thus out-Divers Colonel Diver as a representative figure of the modern city and the potential power of language and writing to shape meaning within it, the novel does not use him to initiate any examination of the English press equivalent to its depiction of the new mass-market urban press of America and such editors as that of the *New York Rowdy Journal*.

Indeed, the English press portrayed in the novel appears to belong to the nostalgic version of England first established through the pastoral rendition of rural Wiltshire and epitomised, as Ruth Livesey has noted, in the stagecoach journey.[85] Both Mercy Pecksniff's description as '"a gushing thing" (as a young gentleman had observed in verse in the Poet's-corner of a provincial newspaper)' and the London undertaker Mr Mould's relish in the prospect of seeing his wife's domestic joke in print – 'Hollow elm tree, eh? Ha ha! Very good indeed. I've seen worse than that in the Sunday papers, my love'[86] – contribute to the sense of the press as an ahistorical construct removed from the vigorous debate over its role that, as we have seen, was in fact occurring on both sides of the Atlantic at the time the novel was written. Tom Pinch's description of a London paper only furthers this sense of a press less invasive than its American counterpart, less active a participant in shaping the public sphere:

> 'I have been looking over the advertising sheet, thinking there might be something in it, which would be likely to suit me. But, as I often think, the strange thing seems to be that nobody is suited. Here are all kinds of employers wanting all sorts of servants, and all sorts of servants wanting all kinds of employers, and they never seem to come together . . . Even those letters of the alphabet, who are always running away from their friends and being entreated at the tops of columns to come back, never *do* come back, if we may judge from the number of times they are asked to do it, and don't.'[87]

As indecipherable to Tom as the city in which he finds himself, the classified newspaper advertisements remain entirely opaque to him and, though he describes them with an uncharacteristic degree of wit, they also serve to reinforce his allegiance to the stable world of the codex in which, as we have seen, he finds forms of meaning and stability that elude him in his actual engagement beyond the self. However, if *Martin Chuzzlewit* thus does not overtly address the nature of the contemporary English press, its role in shaping the public sphere and the part Dickens might seek to play in that shaping, it does, as the next section of this chapter argues, find a way to do all these things in a section of the novel that has gone almost entirely overlooked: Chapter 21's account of the Watertoast Association, its publication, the *Watertoast Gazette*, and the role of the two in supporting the Irish nationalist cause.

'Popular enquiry and information': *Martin Chuzzlewit* and the Dickensian Press

Soon after *American Notes* had appeared and during the first months of *Martin Chuzzlewit*'s serialisation, the subject of Ireland had come to the forefront of political life on both sides of the Atlantic. Under the leadership of Daniel O'Connell, the movement to repeal the Act of Union burst into activity. Throughout the spring and summer of 1843, it staged a series of what *The Times* would anxiously term 'monster meetings', mass rallies throughout Ireland, and solicited aid from the Repeal Associations that had sprung up in the cities of the eastern seaboard of the United States that were home to large influxes of Irish emigrants. Responding enthusiastically, these Associations raised considerable amounts of funding to be sent back across the Atlantic. In reaction, the British government deployed troops to Ireland to maintain order and, late in 1843, tried and convicted O'Connell himself for sedition. Although the conviction would subsequently be overturned on appeal, it effectively defused the movement and brought the immediate crisis to a close, even as it certainly provided no resolution to the larger underlying issues.[88]

The unrest that accompanied the movement, and indeed the potential for violent conflict it posed, connect the nationalists with both the rioters of *Barnaby Rudge* and with the focus upon the potentially centripetal relationship between individual selfhood and the stability of the social order that, as Myron Magnet has shown, was a central concern for Dickens in the early 1840s.[89] Indeed, this concern is pervasive throughout *Chuzzlewit* from its opening chapter and what John Bowen has called the 'unsettling, almost nihilistic, energy'[90] that threatens, literally, to undermine society with its evocation of the Guy Fawkes conspiracy.[91] Throughout the novel, moreover, that destructive energy is intermittently tied to Catholicism which, as had been the case in *Barnaby Rudge*, may not be attacked as itself the cause of social disruption but is certainly associated with it and, by implication, with the cause of Irish nationalism. From the Guy Fawkes plot to the narrator's comparison of Nadgett's monitoring Jonas to 'the daily inspection of a whole order of Jesuits',[92] the novel's references to Catholicism invoke stereotypes of plotting and conspiracy. As Jeremy Tambling has noted, moreover, this tone continues into its use of the Monument as a focal point of the London cityscape. For, as Dickens's overt allusion to a couplet from Pope's *Moral Essays* reveals, an inscription blaming Catholics for starting the Great Fire had been attached to the plinth of the Monument until 1831,[93] writing historical prejudice into popular memory and associating Catholicism with threats to the stability of the nation.

Just as the novel represents Catholicism through stereotypical terms that render it politically subversive, moreover, so too it turns away from *American Notes*'s predominantly optimistic rendering of Irish immigrants to the United States. In their place, it offers two brief and stereotyping vignettes of Irish servants in New York: first, the serving girl at the Pawkins boarding house who is framed by her contiguity to the ubiquitous pigs and her unreflective assumption of subordination to her 'master'; and, second, the servant who opens the door at the Norrises

> with such a thoroughly Irish face, that it seemed as if he ought, as a matter of right and principle, to be in rags, and could have no sort of business to be looking cheerfully at anybody out of a whole suit of clothes.[94]

Passing though these two instances may be, they not only replace the larger accounts of the Irish immigrants that had been such an important feature of *American Notes* but also encode a racialised stereotyping that dehumanises the Irish and places them in limbo within the text: no longer British and certainly not fully American, left, as it were, in another of the novel's states of vacancy.

Five years after completing *Chuzzlewit*, Dickens revealed just how intentionally he had incorporated the Irish issue into the novel's serialisation. Late in 1849, three years after his brief tenure as founding editor of the *Daily News*, and in the midst of planning the launch of *Household Words*, he wrote a second preface for the forthcoming Cheap Edition. Rather than insisting upon his efforts to achieve greater consistency in the design of a serial plot as he had in the first preface, in writing for the Cheap Edition he focused defensively on charges of exaggeration in his rendering of America:

> I wish to record the fact that all that portion of Martin Chuzzlewit's American experience is a literal paraphrase of some reports of public proceedings in the United States (especially of the proceedings of a certain Brandywine Association), which were printed in the Times Newspaper in June and July 1843 – at about the time when I was writing those parts of the book. There was at that period, on the part of a frothy Young American party, demonstrations making of 'sympathy' towards Ireland and hostility towards England, in which such outrageous absurdities ran rampant, that, having the occasion ready to my hand, I ridiculed them.[95]

This 'portion of Martin Chuzzlewit's American experience' occurs in Chapter 21, which was part of the novel's ninth monthly number and first appeared in September 1843 as, bound for Eden, he and Mark Tapley encounter General Cyrus Choke, Mr Lafayette Kettle and the Watertoast Association of United Sympathizers. The latter organisation, together with its newspaper, the *Watertoast Gazette*, exists to support the Irish nationalist cause in its efforts to repeal the Act of Union, and, confident in their transatlantic sway, its members revel in the prospect of the effects their publication must be having upon the young Queen in England:

> 'there ain't a ĕn-gīne with its biler bust, in God A'mighty's free U-nited States, so fixed, and nipped, and frizzled to a most e-tarnal smash, as that young critter, in her luxurious lo-cation in the Tower of London, will be, when she reads the next double-extra Watertoast Gazette.'[96]

Delighting in liberty's freedom from the constraints imposed upon the press by the British authorities, the Americans repudiate 'British Institutions and their tendency to suppress that popular enquiry and information which air so widely diffused even in the trackless forests of this vast Continent of the Western Ocean' and celebrate how their own superiority means 'that the knowledge of Britishers themselves on such points is not to be compared with that possessed by our locomotive and intelligent citizens'.[97] In the limited critical attention it has received, this episode has been seen as a piece of Dickensian fun, taking his earlier criticism of the New York press in a lighter direction and merely incidental to the larger direction of the novel. But whenever Dickens goes out of his way to defend a specific aspect of his fictional, or indeed his editorial, practice, his doing so typically indicates that the issue in question is one of unusual concern to him. Such is certainly the case with his revisiting here what was by the time he wrote this preface a six-year-old news item.

In the only extended critical discussion of this episode, Lowell Blaisdell has identified and discussed the relevant articles in *The Times* that Dickens mentions.[98] The paper published a number of pieces on Ireland and the nationalist movement during the spring and summer of 1843, and the two articles most relevant to the Watertoast episode appeared on 7 and 8 July 1843, respectively. In the first of these, the paper had included an American letter to Daniel O'Connell sent to accompany a donation to the nationalist cause he was leading:

FROM THE BRANDYWINE EMMETT REPEAL ASSOCIATION OF DELAWARE, ADDRESSED TO MR DANIEL O'CONNELL

'Sir, – we beg leave to address you in the name of the Emmett Repeal Association of Brandywine, and to transmit to your order a bill of exchange for 7£, in union with our sister association at Wilmington, payable at sight. The amount of our contribution is but small, yet it will afford a great consolation to us to be admitted at the eleventh hour to a participation in aiding to rend the chains of oppression that bind your long misgoverned green isle.'[99]

The next day, *The Times* parodied this letter and the segments of American society that had produced it in a follow-up leader, expressing a condescending assumption of national superiority:

The character of the letters is consoling: they wholly relieve us from the pain of supposing that the talent, education, or respectability of America is in any way mixed up with these furious and uncivilized attempts to foster revolt and disorder in the bosom of an allied country.[100]

Noting that Dickens wrote his own chapter no more than four weeks after the appearance of these two articles, Blaisdell suggests that they likely offered useful filler material for a novelist writing under the pressure of his monthly deadlines and that they are primarily significant for the ways in which Dickens advanced 'the quality of the ridicule to the scale of superb satiric farce'.[101]

My contention here, however, is that Dickens's Preface, written three years after the failed venture into editing the *Daily News* and just three months before what would become the extraordinary success of *Household Words*, speaks directly to the vital role *Martin Chuzzlewit* played in Dickens's formation as a journalist. For this apparent plot tangent, just like details ranging from Tom Pinch's gazing into the bookshop windows in Salisbury to the relentless mockery of Mrs Hominy, is part of the novel's whole extensive exploration of the role of writing, print and the press in a modern society. Indeed, by introducing an episode from contemporary British political life into the novel and exploring it within an American section of the text, it breaks down the chronological contrast between the British and American sections of the plot, bringing them together in a shared transatlantic culture and demonstrating their interconnectedness. Rather than a digressive comic interlude, then, this particular episode is in fact central to the novel's exploration of print and the press and marks, almost, Dickens's final word in the conversation about his own authorial standing that had begun a year earlier with the responses to *American Notes* from both sides of the Atlantic.

For the whole framing of the Watertoast episode is insistently transatlantic, bringing together the Old and New Worlds around an issue that, for the novel's first readers, was quite literally snatched from the headlines and bending it to Dickens's own purposes:

> 'Here!' said the young Columbian, in a wrestling attitude, 'upon this sacred altar. Here!' cried the young Columbian, idealizing the dining-table, 'upon ancestral ashes, cemented with the glorious blood poured out like water on our native plains of Chickabiddy Lick! Bring forth that Lion!' said the young Columbian. 'Alone, I dare him! I taunt that Lion. I tell that Lion, that Freedom's hand once twisted in his mane, he rolls a corse before me, and the Eagles of the Great Republic laugh "Ha Ha"!'[102]

As his contemporaries would have recognised when the number appeared in September 1843, Dickens's real-life target in describing this young man and his hyperbolic rhetoric was American support for the cause of Irish independence from the United Kingdom, support that he goes on to undermine by placing the Americans' sympathy with O'Connell in undifferentiated proximity with their prejudice against the Irish themselves:

> the Watertoast Association sympathized with a certain Public Man in Ireland, who held a contest upon certain points with England: and that they did so, because they didn't love England at all – not by any means because they loved Ireland much: being indeed horribly jealous and distrustful of its people always, and only tolerating them because of their working hard, which made them very useful; labour being held in greater indignity in the simple republic than in any other country upon earth.[103]

Continuing the Watertoasters' delight in their own rhetorical enthusiasm, General Choke goes on to read out a letter clearly modelled on that published in *The Times* on 7 July:

> 'SIR,
> I address you on behalf of the Watertoast Association of United Sympathizers. It is founded, sir, in the great republic of America; and now holds its breath, and swells the blue veins in its forehead nigh to bursting, as it watches, sir, with feverish intensity and sympathetic ardour, your noble efforts in the cause of Freedom.'[104]

Having reached these heights, however, the Association is immediately plunged into bathetic defeat. For, taking advantage of both the new pace of transatlantic exchange that steam shipping had enabled in the few years since Martineau's visit and the inevitable lag between public events and his serialisation, Dickens then deflates the Watertoasters by working into the text a version of a news story that had already appeared in the press on both sides of the Atlantic. In July 1843, that is, and after the publication of the two articles in *The Times*, news of O'Connell's having earlier spoken in favour of Negro emancipation had reached America and led to his widespread condemnation in the press.[105] Drawing upon this chain of actual events, in the fictional world the Watertoasters react to news of O'Connell's speech by destroying the writing which has brought it and then abandoning language itself in a response that becomes almost sub-human: 'They tore the letter, cast the fragments in the air, trod down the pieces as they fell; and yelled, and groaned, and hissed, till they could cry no longer.'[106] Their idol shattered, the members of the Association resolve forthwith to disband and liquidate their remaining funds to buy a piece of plate for an anti-Abolitionist judge.[107] Dickens thus ends the episode by aligning American support for the Irish with pro-slavery ideology, thereby undermining the two causes and using the American press to condemn itself by its active participation in both.

In the context of the novel's broader representations of Catholicism and the Irish with whom it was routinely associated, Dickens's creation of the Watertoast Association and its *Gazette* can, then, be seen as much more than the 'superb satiric farce' Blaisdell has suggested. Moreover, if the historical moment is read from below, those elements within the issue of repeal that Dickens excludes from his representation become more visible. As they do, they reveal more about his own developing ideological position, more about his agenda as a shaper of public opinion, and, finally, more about the way in which, through writing *Martin Chuzzlewit*, he became newly aware of the overlap between his roles in and power over the worlds of both fiction and journalism.

The Times itself points to this in the way in which it treated the repeal issue very differently from Dickens in its coverage throughout the summer of 1843. For, while the paper was as fully supportive of the British authorities as the American press claimed, it nevertheless offered its readers a more nuanced reading of the complexities of the situation in Ireland than anything we find in Dickens. That same 7 July article which provided the basis of the Watertoast episode through its reprinting of the letter from the Brandywine Association, for example, went on to run to some 6,400 words. In its course, the article included details of the British military response to unrest in Ireland, letters from repeal associations in other American cities and an extended report on O'Connell's speech to the meeting at the Dublin Corn Exchange. O'Connell's rights-based claim that the Reform Act had not provided the same degree of access to the franchise as it had for other parts of the United Kingdom was thus given voice, as was his argument that the position of the Irish was analogous to that of slaves in America. Following this extensive reporting, the next day's issue did indeed include that leading article quoted above that satirised the letter from the Brandywine Association, but it also preceded that piece with a leader on the debate in the House of Commons which included details about the role of the dysfunctional Church of Ireland in the national crisis as well as a discussion of how the pattern of absentee land ownership combined with extortionate rents had undermined the very structure of the Irish economy. Even though no one would have accused *The Times* of being a bastion of liberalism and even as the paper makes its own support of British authority quite clear, that is, its coverage also acknowledges the enormous complexity of the Irish problem and makes visible the concerns and beliefs of its opponents.

Of all this, however, there is nothing in *Martin Chuzzlewit*. Rather, following and magnifying to considerable comic effect the methodology of *The Times*'s 8 July satirical leader, Dickens focuses not on the underlying substantive issues but, as Blaisdell argued, on the parodic opportunities their expression made available to him. The effect of this focus, however, is more than just static comedy, for it becomes actively rhetorical in shaping the reader's response: by making his mockery of the Brandywine Association's letter to O'Connell the centrepiece of his fictional version of the episode, Dickens concentrates the reaction of his readers upon a comic representation of the repealers' language and so enables them to avoid engaging with the actual substance of the concerns of the Irish and their American supporters. Taking an authentic letter supporting the Irish nationalist cause, adapting it from its reprinting in the London *Times* and inserting it into a 'reprinted' imaginary American paper he creates for the purposes of the novel, Dickens performs his own act of brilliant recirculation, appropriating the ideas and language of his opponents, turning them back upon their originators and revealing how fiction and journalism could combine to stunning effect.

That O'Connell should have been part of the collateral damage in this Dickensian act of revisioning is both deeply ironic and revealing.

Ironic, that is, because in his fictionalised reproduction of material from American newspapers, Dickens was building on the very strategy he had used in the slavery chapter of *American Notes*. And, uniquely among contemporary critics, O'Connell had recognised the rhetorical forcefulness of the move:

> I am greatly pleased with his 'American Notes'. They give me, I think, a clearer idea of every-day life in America than I ever entertained before. And his chapter containing the advertisement concerning slavery is more calculated to augment the fixed detestation of slavery than the most brilliant declamation or the most splendid eloquence. That chapter shews out the hideous features of the system far better than any dissertation on its evil could possibly produce them, odious and disgusting to the public eye.[108]

If there is rich irony in Dickens having absorbed the author of this insight into *Chuzzlewit*'s adoption of a similar strategy for its own ends, the move is also profoundly indicative of how Dickens emerged from his experience in America with a more Anglocentric view of the world and one that, as Juliet John has noted, privileges those hierarchies he had earlier worked to call into question. For, having known O'Connell's powers since his days reporting for the *Morning Chronicle*, Dickens was well aware of the 'Liberator's' ability to arouse the sentiment of the masses and his potential to cause social disruption.[109] His own willingness to use the strategy of recirculation here, then, to merge the Irish nationalist supporters with rabid pro-slavery advocates and to abandon *American Notes*'s complexly sympathetic treatment of Irish immigrants thus reveals just how far Dickens has moved from the transatlantic forms of liberalism to which Martineau had become all the more deeply attached through her encounter with the New World. At the same time, as the richly imaginative, delightfully manipulative Watertoast episode confirms, it is through writing *Martin Chuzzlewit* that Dickens most fully expresses the lessons he has learned from America itself and from the critical reactions to his first account of the New World, most fully discovers his abilities as an author as immersed in journalism as he is in fiction and most fully comes to appreciate the power he could achieve through combining the two forms. Hitting back again at the mass-market American press that had vilified *American Notes*, responding to the elite British quarterlies and their charge that 'Boz' was incapable of more than popular entertainment and putting the 'Liberator' in his place, Dickens has restored order on his terms, bent both his readers and his critics to his will, and, taking Colonel Diver at his word, made all of them 'yield to the mighty mind of the Popular Instructor'.

'A true-born child of this free hemisphere'

As this chapter and its predecessor have argued, then, Dickens's recordings of his encounter with American newspapers tell us less about the United States itself than they reveal the sense he had of his own standing within the British press, the extent of his response to criticism directed at him on both sides of the Atlantic and the opportunities that he was coming to realise were available to him through his unique ability to blend the forms of fiction with those of journalism. Two years after finishing *Martin Chuzzlewit* Dickens was to have a short-lived and unsuccessful stint as editor of the newly founded *Daily News*. Though that experiment failed, four years further on he would find his most triumphant role in Victorian journalism – owning and editing first *Household Words* from 1850, and then *All the Year Round* during the 1860s. Given the journalistic course he would embark upon so shortly after completing *Martin Chuzzlewit*, one last element can be discerned as part of his legacy from the American visit – the way in which he in fact drew upon Colonel Diver and his ilk, those swaggering, assertive leaders of the emerging urban mass-market press, commanding their terrain in the United States, as models of the potential power of the entrepreneurial editor. Anything but patterns of English gentility, J. Gordon Bennett, Colonel Webb and their like were much closer forerunners of Dickens's future editorial self than that William Cullen Bryant he had claimed to admire so much but for whom he had found no place in his writing about the American press. By contrast with Bryant and his polite, responsible journalism, the robber barons of the popular urban dailies with their innovative drive, unbounded energy and reshaping of the very landscape of the press demonstrated a brash editorial leadership for which Dickens evidently felt no less real an attraction than the repulsion from America his texts overtly insist upon. For *Martin Chuzzlewit* offers us one last encounter with the American press, deep in its dark heart, deep in the swampy banks of the Mississippi. Though Eden itself barely exists beyond the sketch in Scadder's office and though 'the Eden Stinger, a daily journal' is as yet unrealised, the proprietor and editor of the paper is the magnificently tangible Hannibal Chollop, 'a splendid sample of our na-tive raw material' marauding beyond the pale of civilisation, free from all constraint.[110] Despised in every respect by the gentlemanly Martin, Chollop outdoes Mrs Hominy herself in seizing control of classical allusion as he gleefully asserts his robust path towards taking over the press: '"I shot him down sir," pursued Chollop, "for asserting in the Spartan Portico, a tri-weekly journal, that the ancient Athenians went ahead of the present Locofoco Ticket."'[111] Unconstrained by either the received values of classical civilisation or the European traditions for which they stand as proxy, Chollop is to his compatriots the most American of Americans, the incarnation of a new Adam:

> 'Our fellow-countryman is a model of a man, quite fresh from Natur's mould!' said Pogram, with enthusiasm. 'He is a true-born child of this free hemisphere ... a child of Natur, and a child of Freedom; and his boastful answer to the Despot and the Tyrant is, that his bright home is in the Settin Sun.'[112]

Inviting the reader to participate in the satire, Dickens's language might appear to simply contain Chollop, placing him as a disturbing if comic version of all that the novel has argued is wrong with the press in America, restoring the structuring boundaries for which the novel so often yearns and which it yet so often overturns. But, in that same language, in his uncertain social origins, in his lack of refinement, in the creative destruction of his path and in his resolute determination to create himself and to shape the press to his purposes, Hannibal Chollop is one more of the novel's many curious doublings, one more of Dickens's surrogates:

> Mr Chollop was a man of a roving disposition; and in any less advanced community, might have been mistaken for a violent vagabond. But his fine qualities being perfectly understood and appreciated in those regions where his lot was cast, and where he had many kindred spirits to consort with, he may be regarded as having been born under a fortunate star, which is not always the case with a man so much before the age in which he lives ... he was in the habit of emigrating from place to place, and establishing in each some business – usually a newspaper – which he presently sold: for the most part closing the bargain by challenging, stabbing, pistolling, or gouging, the new editor, before he had quite taken possession of the property.[113]

Over the course of Dickens's career, his various publishers might also have been forgiven for more than once feeling that they had been challenged and stabbed, gouged and pistol-whipped by someone willing to ride roughshod over those who crossed him. But on the muddy banks of the Mississippi, mired in the pestilential swamp that is Eden, he conjures up this vision of the self-made, self-remaking rampant editor. In Hannibal Chollop his dark avatar, a rough beast slouching out of the American west, eagerly anticipating the journalistic kingdom for which he was born, Dickens thus prefigures both his own future and the future of the British popular press he would so dominate during the final twenty years of his life.

Notes

1. Joseph, 'The Labyrinth and the Library', pp. 3, 4.
2. Bowen, *Other Dickens*, pp. 183, 184–5.
3. Livesey, *Writing the Stage Coach Nation*, p. 122.
4. McGill, *American Literature and the Culture of Reprinting*, pp. 132, 133.
5. John, *Dickens and Mass Culture*, p. 84.
6. Arac, *Commissioned Spirits*, p. 17.
7. Schneider, 'Spitting At/As Abjection', p. 220.
8. Dickens, *Martin Chuzzlewit*, p. lxix.
9. Although beyond the scope of my argument here, Dickens's growing support for British imperial order is evident, for example, in his 1848 'The Niger Expedition' review for *The Examiner* (see Drew, *Dickens the Journalist*, pp. 98–100) and his later defense of Governor Eyre's brutal suppression of the Morant Bay rebellion (see *Letters*, vol. 11, pp. 115–16). Martineau, by contrast, was outraged by Eyre's actions and those of his defenders (*Letters*, vol. 5, pp. 125, 149, and *Letters to Wedgwood*, p. 273).
10. Arac, *Commissioned Spirits*, p. 69.
11. Forster, *The Life of Charles Dickens*, vol. 1, pp. 277, 285.
12. Ibid. vol. 1, p. 277.
13. [Forster], 'The Answer of the American Press', p. 250.
14. Ibid. p. 251.
15. Ibid. p. 255.
16. Ibid. p. 265.
17. Ibid. p. 275.
18. Ibid. p. 252.
19. See above, pp. 126–7.
20. Dickens, *Martin Chuzzlewit*, p. 246.
21. Dickens, *American Notes*, p. 24.
22. Dickens, *Martin Chuzzlewit*, p. 248.
23. Ibid. p. 285.
24. Ibid. p. 375.
25. Livesey, *Writing the Stage Coach Nation*, pp. 127, 140.

26. Dickens, *Martin Chuzzlewit*, p. 274.
27. Dickens, *American Notes*, p. 98.
28. Dickens, *Martin Chuzzlewit*, p. 268.
29. Ibid. p. 255.
30. Dickens, *American Notes*, p. 98.
31. Dickens, *Martin Chuzzlewit*, pp. 257, 262, 265. The printer's ink image, and the underlying hostility it expresses to forms of the press he resisted, proved to have enduring appeal to Dickens: in early 1850, shortly before the launching of *Household Words*, he wrote declining to support a petition on removing the stamp duty from newspapers and gave as his reason his concern that, if the tax were removed, 'we might be deluged with a flood of piratical, ignorant, and blackguard papers, something like that black deluge of Printer's Ink which blights America' (*Letters*, vol. 6, p. 36). See also the discussion below in Chapter 6, p. 256.
32. Ibid. p. 256.
33. Ibid.
34. Ibid. pp. 275, 278.
35. Metz, *The Companion to* Martin Chuzzlewit, p. 241.
36. Dickens, *Martin Chuzzlewit*, p. 276.
37. Dickens, *Letters*, vol. 4, p. 716.
38. Franklin, *The Complete Works*, vol. 2, p. 465.
39. [Felton], 'American Notes for General Circulation. By Charles Dickens', p. 230.
40. Dickens, *Martin Chuzzlewit*, p. 276.
41. Ibid. pp. 289, 294.
42. Ibid. p. 369.
43. Ibid. p. 367.
44. Ibid. p. 369.
45. Ibid.
46. Ibid. pp. 276, 280; Castillo, 'Natural Authority in Charles Dickens's *Martin Chuzzlewit*', p. 446.
47. Stockton, *The Gracchi*, p. 26.
48. Dickens, *Martin Chuzzlewit*, p. 541.
49. Martineau, *Letters*, vol. 2, p. 217.
50. Dickens, *Martin Chuzzlewit*, p. 547.
51. Dickens, *American Notes*, p. 9.
52. Dickens, *Martin Chuzzlewit*, p. 618.
53. Ibid. p. 7. Nancy Metz, *The Companion to* Martin Chuzzlewit, p. 41, points out the degree to which Dickens here is overtly invoking the tradition of eighteenth-century pastoral poetry and notes the bathetic contrast as the passage ends with Pecksniff's pratfall at the foot of his own steps. It is a mark of the novel's complexity, however, that this conclusion does not reduce the entire description to parody or lessen its affective contrast with Dickens's descriptions of the miasmatic American landscape.

54. Dickens, *Martin Chuzzlewit*, pp. 6, 7.
55. Ibid. p. 71.
56. Ibid. p. 67.
57. Ruth Livesey notes how *Martin Chuzzlewit* marks the first appearance of what becomes a recurring feature of Dickens's fiction and the ways in which 'place is given increasingly material specificity to endure through time and resist a flattened and foreshortened national future' (*Writing the Stage Coach Nation*, p. 130).
58. Metz, *The Companion to* Martin Chuzzlewit, p. 381.
59. Dickens, *Martin Chuzzlewit*, p. 495.
60. Van Ghent, 'The Dickens World: A View from Todgers's'.
61. Dickens, *Martin Chuzzlewit*, p. 618.
62. Ibid. p. 355.
63. Ibid. pp. 2, 130.
64. Ibid. p. 70. See also Chapter 6, pp. 256–8, for a discussion of Dickens's *Household Words* article 'A Paper-Mill' and its similarly nostalgic representation of material culture and the printing process.
65. [Forster], 'The Newspaper Press of America', p. 200.
66. Livesey, *Writing the Stage Coach Nation*, p. 152.
67. Dickens, *Martin Chuzzlewit*, p. 606.
68. Ibid. p. 766.
69. Joseph, 'The Labyrinth and the Library', pp. 12–13.
70. Miller, *Slow Print*.
71. Dickens, *Martin Chuzzlewit*, pp. 197, 24.
72. Ibid. p. 806.
73. Ibid. p. 79.
74. Ibid. p. 136.
75. Welsh, *From Copyright to Copperfield*, Chapter 5.
76. Dickens, *Martin Chuzzlewit*, p. 798.
77. MacKay, 'The Letter-Writer and the Text', p. 754; Dickens, *Martin Chuzzlewit*, p. 832.
78. Dickens, *Martin Chuzzlewit*, pp. 446–7.
79. Ibid. p. 446.
80. Ibid. pp. 587–8.
81. Ibid. pp. 586, 589.
82. Bowen, *Other Dickens*, pp. 191–2; Wolfreys, *Writing London*, p. 143.
83. Dickens, *Martin Chuzzlewit*, p. 132.
84. Grener, 'Coincidence as Realist Technique', pp. 324–5.
85. Livesey, *Writing the Stage Coach Nation*, pp. 130–5.
86. Dickens, *Martin Chuzzlewit*, pp. 11, 402.
87. Ibid. pp. 567–8.
88. Bew, *Ireland: The Politics of Enmity*, pp. 153–66.
89. Magnet, *Dickens and the Social Order*.
90. Bowen, *Other Dickens*, p. 185.
91. Dickens, *Martin Chuzzlewit*, p. 3.
92. Ibid. p. 587.

93. Ibid. p. 577. Tambling, '*Martin Chuzzlewit*: Dickens and Architecture', p. 164. See also Metz, *The Companion to* Martin Chuzzlewit, p. 422.
94. Dickens, *Martin Chuzzlewit*, pp. 266, 286.
95. Ibid. p. 847.
96. Ibid. p. 345.
97. Ibid. pp. 346–7.
98. Blaisdell, 'The Origins of the Satire', p. 101, n. 4.
99. 'Ireland', p. 3.
100. 'London, Saturday, July 8, 1843', p. 5.
101. Blaisdell, 'The Origins of the Satire', p. 96.
102. Dickens, *Martin Chuzzlewit*, p. 359.
103. Ibid. p. 360.
104. Ibid.
105. Blaisdell, 'The Origins of the Satire', p. 93.
106. Dickens, *Martin Chuzzlewit*, p. 361.
107. Ibid. p. 362.
108. O'Connell, *Correspondence*, vol. 2, p. 297.
109. Litvack, 'The Politics of Perception', p. 39.
110. Dickens, *Martin Chuzzlewit*, pp. 355, 354, 520.
111. Ibid. p. 521.
112. Ibid. p. 533.
113. Ibid. p. 520.

Chapter 5

'Called hither by the commotion of the times': Martineau and the Press, 1837–1850

When Martineau arrived home from America in the summer of 1836, she had, as would be the case for Dickens six years later, developed a host of personal connections, some of which would become lifelong friendships, and a newly deepened awareness of the ties between the Old World and the New. However, while Dickens would return largely disillusioned with the young republic, Martineau brought back with her a new sense of engagement in a transatlantic progressive community, one in which she was determined to remain actively engaged. During her two-year stay in the United States and as she had learned more about both the abolitionist movement and the ways in which American culture deployed the concept of republican motherhood to create an episteme that imposed such wide-ranging constraints upon the nation's women, she had become increasingly committed to finding a role for herself in the work of forwarding liberal progress in America as well as at home in Britain. As Chapter 2 argued, moreover, her experience of the United States expanded both her understanding of the American press's role in the formation of a modern society and her insight into the ways in which a rapidly evolving medium unfettered by formal political controls could work in support of progressive causes and yet, despite its ostensible freedom, still also be used as an instrument of obstruction, constraint and political manipulation. The commitment to the role of the press as an essential agent of liberalism that she had articulated in her work before leaving for America was thus extended and broadened by her two years of travel there and would be further intensified after her return home during a period when the British press was itself developing at an unprecedented pace and under conditions of heightened social tension.

For, and as Martin Hewitt has shown, in the late 1830s and throughout the 1840s political unrest, increasing pressure for a complete repeal of the 'taxes on knowledge' and the transformation in distribution practices enabled by the new railway networks laid a foundation for the age of cheap print that would enable a massive expansion of the press during the second half of the century.[1] Deeply concerned by that unrest, positioned by her own changing life circumstances to appreciate fully the impact and importance of evolving methods of the distribution of print media and long committed, as Chapter 1 showed, to the abolition of state-imposed tariffs impeding the free circulation of discourse through the press, Martineau experimented during the 1840s with a wide range of initiatives that, collectively, positioned her at the heart of early Victorian journalism. As a result, by the time Dickens invited her to become a contributor to *Household Words* in 1850, she was a major acquisition for his new project: an author of unquestioned intellectual authority, an established presence across many of the forms into which the periodical press had evolved and a woman journalist whose stature in both Britain and America had no equal among the writers whom he recruited to help launch the magazine.[2]

Previous critical readings of Martineau's work during the 1840s, however, have positioned her simply in terms of a broader reading of the liberal response to the perceived threat of the radical press that Dickens's founding of *Household Words* is seen to exemplify. As Ian Haywood has argued, for example, in creating his new weekly Dickens was just one more instance of efforts by middle-class editors and publishers to counter the unstamped radical press, the 'material agency of radical and popular print, its tangible and iconic power, its conspicuous presence as an expression of public opinion and popular taste, circulating with speed through the nation'.[3] In these efforts during the 1840s and 1850s, Haywood and others have shown, Dickens, along with figures such as Charles Knight and Henry Brougham and organisations such as the Society for the Diffusion of Useful Knowledge, sought to counter the influence of Edward Lloyd, G. W. M. Reynolds and other radical writers and editors whose work was routinely mystified and demonised by middle-class liberals.[4] By seeing Martineau primarily in this context, however, interpretations such as these have collapsed the first two decades of her career into an undifferentiated monolith, limiting it to little more than a continuing effort to shape popular culture in ways simply 'missionary or monitorial'.[5] In this view of her work, the exemplary text becomes the *Illustrations of Political Economy*, which Haywood sums up as the embodiment of an ideology that is 'grimly deterministic, reductive and fatalistic'.[6] While acknowledging the force of this analysis of Martineau's early career and recognising the degree to which she did indeed find her milieu among what Haywood has called 'the polite journals of "popular progress"',[7] this chapter's contention is that, just as her later quarrel with Dickens has been reductively over-determined, so too her agenda for and role in the press during the 1840s was far more nuanced than has been previously recognised and that her work in this period laid the foundation for her to become one of the nation's most influential journalists from the early 1850s through the mid 1860s.

Indeed, my argument here directly counters the wider understanding of Martineau's career in journalism to which even scholars focused specifically on her work have given voice. Deborah Logan, for instance, has suggested that Martineau's later influential career in the press was 'unanticipated yet inevitable' and that it only began 'in earnest in 1852 when she became a regular leader writer for the *Daily News*'.[8] In countering such views, I contend here that Martineau followed a highly intentional course of developing her position as a professional journalist during the period following her visit to America as she engaged in a series of projects that allowed her to experiment with her own role in the press precisely at a time when that press itself was beginning a period of unprecedented expansion. Continuing her dedication to building those communities of sympathy that would support the stadial progress to which she was so fundamentally committed and influenced by her transatlantic engagement with feminist and abolitionist causes, Martineau's work during the 1840s thus offers a more complex understanding than has been previously recognised of the dynamic between middle-class liberalism and the agency of the working classes, and reveals her continuous efforts to find a role in the press through which she could most fully contribute to shaping the public sphere.

To demonstrate this progression and explore the intentionality with which Martineau developed her unrivalled position in early Victorian journalism, this chapter is organised into four parts. First, drawing extensively upon her correspondence, it defines the threats to liberal progress that she perceived arising from increasing working-class unrest and the rise of Irish nationalism, threats to which she responded with an almost evangelical sense of purpose. As she wrote to Lidian Emerson in April 1848, for example, with Europe convulsed by another wave of revolutions, 'I am called hither by the commotion of the times: – summoned <u>to work</u> – which we shd all be thankful to be permitted to do in such times.'[9] Even as she articulated these concerns and this dedication, however, Martineau also found cause for optimism in an aspect of the nineteenth-century capitalist economy that she had noted in her accounts of America: the potential for women to achieve autonomy and agency through access to education and paid employment in an increasingly industrialised society. Moving on from this analysis of Martineau's sense of the threats to and opportunities for liberal progress, the next two sections of the chapter examine how, during the late 1830s and early 1840s, Martineau worked to establish herself as a major voice across a wide range of journalistic venues. Her *Westminster Review* articles of the late 1830s thus collectively not only constitute an extension of the case she had argued for liberal progress in her American books but also mark her claim for a kind of authoritative role in the elite intellectual quarterlies that, as Chapter 3 demonstrated, Dickens was never able to achieve. Then, and simultaneously as she was working with the *Westminster* to position herself in the most prestigious sector of the progressive British press, Martineau also partnered with Charles Knight at the opposite end of the spectrum of periodical publication, as the third section of the chapter examines. Initially at Knight's *The Penny Magazine* and on through the *Weekly Volume* series that she launched with him in 1844, Martineau sought to counter the growing influence of the radical press by providing 'improving' reading for working-class readers. While this set of efforts does indeed have a missionary, monitorial character, it was also, in two particular ways, much more important to her career than this narrower bent would suggest. First, it becomes evident that, through the experience of these projects, Martineau grew increasingly aware of the limits of her own ability to speak to the working classes that were her ostensible target; second, even as she focused overtly on this group of readers, she also sought to influence a variety of other audiences in both Britain and America. The combination of a growing understanding of her own range of capability and an increasing ambition to address a wide and diverse readership would in turn contribute to the frustrations she encountered in two further collaborations: her work in the second half of the decade with the Howitts at the *People's Journal* and with Thornton Leigh Hunt and G. H. Lewes at *The Leader*. Both of these ventures, as the chapter's closing fourth section shows, failed to match the goals she had set for herself and the press.

These frustrations also explain why, as Chapter 6 will examine in greater detail, the invitation to join the first group of contributors to Dickens's new journal was both timely and apposite. Given the position she had achieved and the efforts she had been undertaking in the press ever since returning from America, Dickens's recruiting her made perfect sense in light of his own agenda for *Household Words* to promote cross-class cultural community and to 'bring the greater and the lesser in degree, together, upon that wide field, and mutually dispose them to a better acquaintance and a kinder understanding'.[10] Martineau's retroactive suggestion in the *Autobiography* that 'Magazine writing [was] quite out of my way' and that she only agreed reluctantly to write for such a weekly magazine as *Household Words*[11] has, then contributed to the ways in which the established scholarly narrative of her relationship with Dickens has occluded a full understanding of her role in the development of the early Victorian press. For both her suggestion and that occluding narrative belie the trajectory of a journalistic career that was built upon her development of a consistent presence in both mass-market and elite venues and that would culminate, by the late 1850s, with her simultaneous appearance in daily, weekly, monthly and quarterly outlets and in periodicals on both sides of the Atlantic. In establishing herself during the 1840s as uniquely able to write for the heavyweight reviews and their readership amongst the intellectual elite but also for mass-market periodicals directed towards the working and middle classes, Martineau thus created for herself a distinctively influential position in mid-Victorian journalism, one that was unprecedented for a professional woman author, that would only be reinforced by the addition of her role as a leader writer for the *Daily News* from 1852 onwards, and that, as Chapter 7 will explore, contributed to her formative influence upon a rising generation of aspiring professional women authors.

'Nobody brings the stomach pumps': The 1840s and the Crisis of Liberalism

In describing the 'commotion of the times' to Lidian Emerson, Martineau was specifically referencing the immediate, widespread political disturbances of 1848, but, as her work and correspondence throughout the decade evidence, the comment also summarises her sense of the factors influencing liberal progress that had shaped her work since returning from America. Three particular issues stand out in her framing of not only the major challenges facing British society during the 1840s but also of the opportunities available to liberalism to foster continuing stadial progress. First, building upon a concern for the condition of the working classes that had been apparent in her writing before she left England in 1834, her anxiety was further intensified by the spread of unrest during the early 1840s and by the rise of a radical press that articulated and, she believed, fomented that unrest. Second, extending this anxiety about the nation's precarious stability was the intensification of an issue with which Martineau had directly been concerned since the early 1830s: Ireland, and the increasing political tensions that resulted from the combination of longstanding efforts to repeal the Act of Union with the heightened suffering created by the Famine. In this context, the rise of Daniel O'Connell to the peak of his influence and his sway over the Anglo-American public sphere was for Martineau, as it was for Dickens, a critically problematic phenomenon. Third, and contrasting with both these two disruptive forces and with Dickens's reading of the forces created by industrial society, Martineau builds from her experience of the constraints placed upon women in America and focuses repeatedly upon the opportunities the new economy was creating for women's employment beyond the home, the agency such employment provided and ways in which it enabled women to become fully realised liberal subjects. In this emphasis upon the significance of female employment, Martineau not only anticipates the new discourse of work that would develop in Britain during the 1850s but herself becomes an exemplary subject.[12] For, as this chapter will show, in constructing her identity as a professional author, engaging fully in the networks of early Victorian publishing and increasingly controlling the venues to which she gained access and the topics on which she wrote, the trajectory of her own career epitomised the potential for a woman to contribute to shaping a liberal society and advancing its stadial progress.

In common with many other middle-class liberal social commentators of the time, Martineau's single greatest source of anxiety about the future of the nation was the condition of the British working classes and their vulnerability to radical influences. Writing to Richard Monckton Milnes in 1843, for instance, she shared her impassioned vision of 'an innumerable multitude of human beings at hand, animal in all but their human capacity for vice & misery ... herding together in brutal gregariousness, now struggling & flying at each others' throats in untamed anger, or, if at peace, united by no higher affection than instinct'.[13] Her perception had evidently been exacerbated by the visit to America, since her experience there had brought her to the realisation that, notwithstanding Britain's transformation through the emergence of an industrial society, 'we have a population in our manufacturing towns almost as oppressed, and in our secluded rural districts, almost as ignorant, as your negroes'.¹⁴ Writing this in 1838 to Massachusetts abolitionist Abby Kelley and expressing a sense of congruity between enslaved people and the industrial working classes, Martineau thus complicates her own foundational belief in stadial progress and so incidentally complicates critical readings that cast her as committed to simply teleological models of Utilitarian political economy. For, linking republican America with ostensibly democratising Britain, this sense of a transatlantic community in suffering implies both that for the United States the act of emancipation would be only a beginning, as Martineau's letter indeed goes on to acknowledge, and also that the challenges facing British society are even more intractable than she had been able to perceive before her encounter with social conditions in the United States.

In referring in her letter to Kelley to the 'secluded rural districts', moreover, Martineau points to a distinctive quality in her diagnosis of the condition of the working classes. While much contemporary concern during the 1840s focused upon the new phenomenon of the rapidly growing industrial cities – a focus that has often been replicated in modern critical scholarship of the period – Martineau's work expresses a deepened understanding of provincial and rural society. This understanding, one that was surely a consequence of her move out of London following the onset of her first major illness, distinguishes her from many other commentators of the period, including, as Chapter 4 examined, Dickens, who at the same period was increasingly coming to see urban space as the defining condition of modern life. The foundation of Martineau's insight into the nature of rural society is, however, evident in her work long before she settled in Ambleside in 1845. Both the 1834 tale *The Scholars of Arneside* discussed in Chapter 1 and her 1839 novel *Deerbrook* make the darker characteristics of a rural population cut off from wider cultural influences central to their representations of British provincial life. In each text, moreover, the narrative pivots around a mob's violent attack upon a household that represents the efforts of enlightened intellectuals to foster the development of a community of sympathy through the dissemination of knowledge and inculcation of the habit of learning into rural society.¹⁵ Martineau's perception of the nature of working-class life beyond the great cities developed most fully from 1845 on, when, having recovered from her first major illness and moved from Tynemouth to the Lake District and the newly built house that would be her home for the remaining three decades of her life, she found herself actually living in an ostensibly idyllic community that turned out to be not at all what it might have seemed from without – or indeed to some observers within. As she wrote to Elizabeth Barrett the following year, 'dear good old Wordsworth for ever talking of rural innocence, & deprecating any intercourse with towns, lest the purity of his neighbours shd be corrupted',[16] simply had no understanding that, as she would later tell Fanny Wedgwood, 'there is no hoggish sensuality, no devilish malice, no low trickery, no reckless crime of any kind that you may not find in this small hamlet, where poor Wordsworth would have concluded all sorts of innocence to abound'.[17] Exacerbating her newly proximate awareness of rural proletarian depravity was the realisation that, lacking any countering influence, the village was devoid of that Schillerian community of sentiment she had theorised in *How to Observe* as foundational to social progress. Writing to Lord Howick, she thus voiced her concern for the population 'not only on account of their dreadful depression & ignorance, but from the absence of all association among them, by which the superior minds might aid & direct the others'.[18] Moreover, just as she saw no ameliorating influences reaching the lowest social classes from above, so too she lamented that those in the more privileged ranks, even those in the progressive Whig elite, remained largely oblivious to the state of the masses around them. As she wrote to Lady Grey in 1848, 'I could not have conceived of any thing like the blank unconsciousness I found among the upper classes in London of the workings of society in the heart of the country'.[19] Though the fear of social violence that she articulated early in the decade was alleviated with the decline of Chartist radicalism and the receding of the prospect of actual revolution, Martineau remained convinced, then, as she graphically expressed the parlous condition of the body politic to William Johnson Fox in 1849, that 'We are going down into a political death, & nobody brings the stomach pumps.'[20]

Adding to this ongoing sense of the threat posed to liberal progress by the conditions in which the English rural proletariat lived was Martineau's fully sharing in a widely voiced and growing concern that emerged during the early 1840s over Ireland and the issue of Repeal. Dickens, for example, although not actually visiting Ireland itself until the late 1850s or even writing explicitly about the political question there, did, as Chapters 3 and 4 have shown, address it obliquely but extensively through his accounts of Irish emigrants in *American Notes* and his transmutation of their support for the Repeal movement in the Watertoast episode of *Martin Chuzzlewit*. Martineau herself had, following her visit to her brother and his Unitarian congregation in Dublin in 1831, made Ireland the eponymous subject of one of her earliest *Illustrations of Political Economy*,[21] and her continuing concern with Irish issues is manifest throughout her correspondence of the 1840s. Although she would not find a larger venue that allowed her to return to the Irish question until she took on the project of completing Charles Knight's *History of the Peace* in 1849, her evolving opinion of Daniel O'Connell in the years leading up to that project indicates the degree of significance she attached to Ireland throughout the decade.

For central to her 1840s commentary on Ireland is her growing sense of alarm over O'Connell, particularly of his ability to influence transatlantic discourse. In this, Martineau is at one with Dickens's 1843 representation of the phenomenon of the 'Liberator' in *Martin Chuzzlewit* and the concern he would express over the prospect of a demotic voice that positioned itself beyond the pale of British liberal discourse. While Martineau in 1838 had been sufficiently optimistic that O'Connell could be reined in that she could write to Lydia Maria Child that she had 'got at' him on the issue of abolition and hoped 'to see an alteration in his tone',[22] by 1844 and during his trial for sedition she was asking Fanny Wedgwood rhetorically 'Is there in History a worse man, – I mean, a worse member of society?'[23] What particularly troubled her appears to have been, as she had written to Milnes three months before the trial, the extent to which O'Connell had shaped the perception of Repeal among Americans, who 'want information terribly'[24] and were, as Dickens had mockingly suggested a year earlier in the Watertoast episode, susceptible to the representations that reached them from across the ocean. Indeed, having achieved precisely the kind of transatlantic influence in the press that she had hopefully imagined for herself even before she left America, O'Connell's sway left Martineau uncertain of the success of her own efforts 'to give some idea to the Amerns of the real state of the Repeal question'.[25] As Dickens would similarly discover when he incurred Martineau's wrath some years later, however, once she did have an appropriate publishing opportunity, she made ample use of it. For the by then late O'Connell, that occasion presented itself late in the decade when she took on the project of completing the *History of the Peace* for Charles Knight. Making O'Connell the villain of the piece in her extended discussion of the Irish issue, she went on to skewer his 'utter unworthiness of all trust'[26] and then celebrated having done so as she wrote to William Johnson Fox that O'Connell 'is now universally despised in Ireland, & believed by all but the priests to have set back Ireland half a century'.[27] Demonstrating how completely she had come to regard the Irish nationalist leader as an entirely regressive force, this final comment on O'Connell in her letters of the 1840s aligns her and Dickens in their disparaging assessment of his influence, looks forward to the pro-Union emphases of the articles on Ireland that she would write for both the *Daily News* and *Household Words* in 1852 and, again, points to the ways in which her later charges that the magazine was tainted with anti-Catholic bias fail to account for the complexity of the differences that ultimately underlay the convulsive ending of her connection with Dickens.

Of those differences none was more revealing for both their later individual dispute and the larger divisions within liberalism than the third major component in Martineau's diagnosis of the state of the nation during the 1840s: her understanding of the new opportunities an industrial economy was creating for women. Throughout her writing during the decade, Martineau both calls out and validates the shifting balance between women's roles in, on the one hand, maintaining the traditional domestic sphere and the values associated with it and, on the other, the emergence of new possibilities through increased access to education and employment beyond the home. By contrast with Dickens, who, as Chapters 3 and 4 argued, had extended and deepened in *Martin Chuzzlewit* the marginalising of female agency that he had privileged in *American Notes*, throughout the 1840s Martineau reaffirms a commitment to women's autonomy and access to education. In doing so, as Deborah Logan has noted, she was building from her earliest work in the press. Writing in the *Monthly Repository* as far back as 1822, that is, Martineau had insisted that a woman who is barred from higher education 'is confined to low pursuits, her aspirings after knowledge are subdued, she is taught to believe that solid information is unbecoming her sex ... and thus before she is sensible of her powers, they are checked in their growth'.[28] As Chapter 2 has shown, moreover, that foundational commitment, which Martineau drew from her formation within Unitarianism and its strong traditions of opportunity for women, had been given a new focus by her observation of women's lives in America. Following her return home, her belief was sharpened during the 1840s by a sense that a fundamental shift in the social position of women was beginning to occur in Britain. For, as she wrote to Lord Howick in 1844, despite the enormity of the problems the nation was facing, the age was nevertheless one in which 'the rapid improvement in the cultivation & standing of Women'[29] was clearly under way. In this regard, Martineau went on to argue, Britain was increasingly differentiating itself from the United States where, as she had shown in the American books, female dependency was, to borrow Elizabeth Maddock Dillon's words, the fundamental mechanism for women's being 'banished from the production of meaning and power within liberalism'.[30] Driven in her own life by what she described to Elizabeth Barrett as the 'desire to keep up that union of practical domestic with literary labour wh has been such a blessing to me ever since I held the pen'[31] and enacting what she later described to Eliza Meteyard as 'the vocation of a single life for women',[32] Martineau laid out for Howick a vision of a progressing nation that united elements of traditional domestic values with systemic structural change to social life beyond the home: 'middle class women are, by hundreds of thousands, the conservators of purity of morals, while they are finding themselves possessed of new powers, & are opening up a new & higher destiny to those who follow them'.[33] In the vanguard of social progress, then, it is these women, she argues, who will be far more effectual agents of change than the Ten Hour Bill to reform factory labour conditions that is the presumptive subject of her letter. By simultaneously emphasising the collective agency of these hundreds of thousands of middle-class women and questioning the efficacy of state-mandated legislative solutions, Martineau merges her advocacy for women with what we have seen to be British liberalism's fundamental privileging of individual endeavour over the activism of governmental structures. This combination of faith in the progressive leadership of middle-class women and scepticism over the ability of the state to intervene effectively in the workings of the economy thus manifested in Martineau's correspondence in the mid-1840s was, then, not only a consistent characteristic of her thought but also illustrates the potential fissures within progressive British liberalism and anticipates the divisions that would so dramatically split her and Dickens apart in the mid-1850s.

'The vehicle of my entire moral philosophy': Martineau and the *Westminster Review*

During the early 1830s, as Chapter 2 showed, Martineau had taken her first steps out of the close-knit world of denominational journalism by transitioning from the *Monthly Repository* to writing for *Tait's Edinburgh Magazine*. Having used *Tait's* as a venue in which to announce her first claims of authorial authority through the two essays on Scott, however, she published in it no further and, on her return from America, once again repositioned herself in the British press. Paralleling the ways in which Dickens would, as his market value grew, assert increasing control over his own work through repeatedly pushing his publishers into renegotiating contracts, so Martineau's less assertive but no less determined readiness to relocate the venues in which her work appeared became a defining aspect of her career. Where for Dickens the major concern was often to maximise his income, however, Martineau, who developed a presence in a far wider range of the press than he and who was not subject to the economic pressures of having to support a large family that he faced, appears to have privileged finding access to venues that would best allow her to advance the liberal ideologies to which she was committed. In the case of *Tait's*, Christian Johnstone's dismissive account of *Society in America* during the summer of 1837 would hardly have been conducive to a continuing relationship with the magazine but, even by the time Johnstone's review appeared, Martineau was already in the process of establishing herself within other journalistic networks that better enabled her to achieve her goals. The steps she took to reposition herself in the period immediately following her return from America thus marked the foundation of a career centred in London rather than Edinburgh and a pattern of engagement across various sectors of the press that she sustained for the next three decades.[34]

Her initial step towards thus repositioning and establishing herself in the London-based press is evident in the first articles she published in any of the heavyweight intellectual quarterlies, a set of four essays that appeared in the *Westminster Review* over an eighteen-month period between late 1837 and the spring of 1839. Beginning in October 1837 with 'Miss Sedgwick's Works', she went on to contribute 'Domestic Service' that appeared the following August simultaneously with *How to Observe Morals and Manners*, 'The Martyr Age of the United States' the following December, and 'Literary Lionism', which appeared in April 1839, the month after *Deerbrook* came out. Individually, these four *Westminster* articles built upon the American visit, and they form responses to various aspects of the initial critical reception to *Society in America* as well as extending the work of this first book and the two others she published out of the visit even as she was beginning to write for the *Westminster*. Collectively, the articles thoroughly affirmed that 'masculine and unflinching intellect' of which the more conservative reviewers of *Illustrations of Political Economy* had complained and, in establishing Martineau as an important voice in the elite progressive liberal press, marked the first step in a career that eventually totalled more than thirty major contributions to the leading intellectual reviews. Martineau herself clearly understood, and revelled in, the significance of her newly achieved value in the London literary stock market and the influence that her appearances in the *Westminster* would confer upon her. Writing to William Ware in Boston in September 1837, shortly before her first article appeared, she exulted that the appearance of *Society in America* 'has brought to my feet the noble London & Westr Review, the proprietors of wh beg me to make it the vehicle of my entire moral philosophy, bringing my principles to bear on the great topics of the day'.[35]

Even as she recognised the significance of the standing she had thus earned as a major voice in the liberal cause, moreover, Martineau was also evidently well aware of the need to develop and deploy the survival skills essential to flourish within the often agonistic publishing networks of early Victorian London. For the resistance to her from conservative reviewers that had been evident ever since she began serialising the *Illustrations* continued throughout the decade. As late as May 1839, two full years after the publication of *Society in America*, for example, *Fraser's Magazine* published a notice that took the more personally directed attacks that had earlier greeted the *Illustrations* to a new level of rhetorical malice. Describing Martineau's alleged familiarity with the 'arcana of slave-state debauchery' and ridiculing those citizens of Cincinnati whom she had so praised as 'nothing more romantic than hard-working and industrious pork-butchers ... a very shrewd set of persons in the sphere to which God has called them',[36] *Fraser's* unidentified contributor demonstrated a remarkable level of animus. In anticipating both the sexist rhetoric of Dickens's assault in 'Our Wicked Mis-Statements' and the inadvertent but even more blatantly misogynist abuse Thackeray directed towards her in the *Cornhill* as late as 1860 and that is discussed in Chapter 7, however, the reviewer also implicitly acknowledges the extent to which Martineau had established herself in the position of authority she had claimed and testifies to the seriousness with which London's conservative critics had come to take her.

Martineau's ability to fend for herself in this rough-and-tumble, profoundly sexist world of early Victorian publishing, an ability that would stand her in good stead in those later clashes with both Dickens and Thackeray, was shaped during this period of her first major entry into the press and is apparent from early in her relationship with the *Westminster*. Even though she referred to *Retrospect* of *Western Travel* as a mere bagatelle, her 'chit chat book of travels',[37] for example, she evidently took some care to protect it from the hostility with which *Society in America* had already been treated by the more conservative reviewers. In January 1838, precisely as *Retrospect* was published, the *Westminster* carried a glowing review by its acting editor, John Robertson, of this second American book, one that followed 'the distinguished success of the first' and that was 'sure to be read by almost all our readers'.[38] Journals that had not had the pre-publication access to the book that Martineau must have provided the *Westminster* inevitably took longer to respond to its appearance. Not for another month, for example, would the *Athenaeum* come out with the first post-publication review, while the *Edinburgh* had to wait until the April issue to make up for its silence on *Society in America*, and both followed the *Westminster* in their enthusiasm.[39] Clearly, Martineau had ensured that the *Westminster* would be the journal to set the tone for her new book's critical reception and, presumably protective of its valued new contributor, the *Westminster* had obliged.

In her own first four contributions to the *Westminster*, Martineau further advances the liberal agenda for which her American books argue by making the nation a constant presence in her texts, regardless of whether it be the explicit subject of a review. Across the set of essays, that is, Martineau builds upon the concept of America as a prospective model of stadial progress, reiterates her emphasis on the deleterious effects of European 'aristocratic' and 'feudal' practices upon the fulfilment of the republican ideals of the United States, and incorporates into her discussion a theme necessarily omitted from the books focused upon the New World itself: the transatlantic ties uniting the community of progressive Anglo-American liberalism. In this way, the essays serve to build upon and intensify the connections between Martineau's three American books and the themes that, as Chapter 2 argued, were core to her representation of the liberal project in the United States: the structural position of women in both America and Britain; slavery and the abolitionist movement; and the role of education, literature and, especially, the press in forming national identity and furthering stadial development. Finally, in reflecting upon the emergence of early forms of mass culture through the ongoing expansion in print media, she speaks to the dangers of the new phenomenon of the author in an age of unprecedented celebrity, using the example of Emerson to valorise a countering model of authorial reserve and reticence. Taken together, the four essays thus push back against conservative resistance to the case her books made, consolidate and expand Martineau's account of America and expand upon her longstanding advocacy for the importance of print media in sustaining a healthy and dynamic public sphere that would foster liberal progress.

Martineau's reading of America as a potential exemplar of stadial development, a reading that, as Chapter 2 argued, was inscribed into her descriptions of the North American continent itself, is the focusing thesis of her first contribution to the *Westminster*. In reviewing the development of Catharine Sedgwick's fiction from the start of her career in 1822 through to her most recently published *The Poor Rich Man, and the Rich Poor Man*, Martineau uses the evolution of her friend's work to exemplify the progress of a recently formed national literature. Having outlined the principle of a three-stage stadial development from fiction 'which imitates itself' on to that which is 'a transcript of actual life' and finally to an ideal form that can 'be new to every mind, and in absolute harmony with all',[40] she goes on to suggest that the striking 'progression' evident in Sedgwick's writing has carried her firmly into the second phase and, offering 'the first true insight into American life', marks 'the first complete specimens of a higher kind of literature', 'the first distinct utterance of a fresh national mind'.[41] Though Sedgwick herself had been offended by Martineau's earlier and more robust appraisal of her novels' 'great and irretrievable faults as works of art'[42] and their friendship was irreversibly damaged as a result, the review thus confirmed the fundamentally affirmative vision of the United States that Martineau maintained throughout the antebellum period and extended the reading of the young nation that *Society in America* had offered by describing the potentially formative part its nascent literature had to play in furthering stadial progress.

Both the threats facing America's realisation of its potential as a stadial exemplar and the challenges to liberalism's advance at home unite in Martineau's second essay for the *Westminster*, 'Domestic Service'.[43] Moreover, in affirming the proposition that stadial progress, whether in America or Britain, is inseparable from the advance towards democracy, this second essay not only looks back to her review of Sedgwick's career but also anticipates her discussion of the abolitionist movement in 'The Martyr Age'. In her first article Martineau had identified an uneasy dualism in American culture, praising Sedgwick for waging 'war with the aristocratic spirit under various forms' but also noting a more general national tendency amongst the Americans towards a 'want of self-reliance, their proneness to imitate and vie with whatever they could ascertain of the old world' as the greatest check to their national progress.[44] Through identifying this American incapacity to emancipate the formation of opinion from Old World models Martineau points to larger constraints upon liberalism's foundational freedom to consent and in 'Domestic Service' she addresses this issue more explicitly. For, looking back to the concern she had expressed in her pre-American articles for the *Monthly Repository* over the potential for violent social unrest, the essay unites the issues of class antagonism in Britain and slavery in the United States. In Britain, that is, she attributes class conflict across the nation to 'the old Saxon enmity' that 'shows itself now in rick-burning, now in assassination-funds; here in frame-breaking or throwing vitriol; there in kitchen and nursery squabbles'.[45] Invoking the British working classes in terms of the stock image of the Norman Yoke that had brought a formerly free population into servitude, she repurposes the trope to her own ends as she connects the disposition towards violent unrest in Britain with the persistence of European models of 'feudal' practice in the United States. Noting that even 'the relation' of American domestic workers and their employers 'is impaired by the intrusion of European prejudices', she then moves to offer a larger diagnosis of more widespread corruption emanating from the slave-owning states: 'in the south the feudal prejudices on this subject are rank, and they poison the relation of employer and employed in the north'.[46] In doing so, Martineau thus merges an account of the failings of the emerging society in the New World with an attack upon the persistence and propagation of regressive Old World practices that prevent both nations from achieving their full liberal potential and that are contributing to the increasing social unrest occurring across Britain.

If 'Miss Sedgwick's Works' and 'Domestic Service' combine affirmation of the stadial potential of the American project with a diagnosis of the dangers posed by the young nation's 'proneness to imitate' and its tendency to subordinate its culture to that of the Old World, the two articles also show Martineau making use of the American experience to articulate a model of social activism potentially adoptable in Britain. Thus, in praising Sedgwick's portrayal of Americans 'as they are in their quiet homes, living in the atmosphere of their best affections',[47] she once again reminds her readers of the access to domestic life that had been an essential feature of her observation of American life and that would become even more central to her subject position in *Retrospect of Western Travel*. In 'Domestic Service', however, she also returns to the abolitionist trope of linking slavery and the cultural constraining of women into lives limited to the domestic sphere, adapting it from its American origins and applying it to conditions in British homes:

> The condition of women is the worst preparation for their use of power; and the power which they hold is abused as any wise observer would anticipate that it must be. The negro slave uses his dog and his ass as his master uses him; and women treat their servants as they have been treated by those who have the control of their lot.[48]

In this judgement, she reiterates that account of the 'political non-existence of women' from *Society in America* that had been so criticised by conservative reviewers and then goes on to describe ironically the effects of women's being excluded from 'the blessedness of work' and the ways in which 'the worst kinds of aristocratic tyranny are found among women who do not work; and they have it in their power to inflict more misery by their tyranny than their husbands can generally impose'.[49] By including this material in an essay that had for its nominal subject Charles Knight's latest volume in a series designed 'for the children educated in the work-house schools', the article achieves two significant ends for Martineau. On the one hand, it connects the *Westminster* itself with the work she was simultaneously undertaking for Knight's *Penny Magazine*, the focus of the next section of this chapter, suggesting a common cause uniting two periodicals positioned in very different parts of the public sphere and addressing very diverse readerships. On the other, by bringing the *Westminster* and Knight's venture together through her choice of subject and using transatlantic comparison as an essential part of that subject's treatment, she is able to model in her own work the kind of 'literary companionship'[50] between the two cultures in the cause of liberal progress that she had returned from America determined to achieve.

Such 'literary companionship' is realised most fully in Martineau's third *Westminster* essay, 'The Martyr Age of the United States', which appeared in the review's December 1838 issue and which extends the argument she had made in 'Domestic Service' for the essential role of women as agents of liberal progress. For although, as both Valerie Pichanik and Deborah Logan have suggested,[51] this extended article does serve to recapitulate major theses of Martineau's previous writing on America, 'The Martyr Age' does far more than simply restate the earlier case. Ostensibly an updating of the developments around the abolitionist cause in the eighteen months since her stay in Boston over the winter of 1835–6, the essay is Martineau's most developed statement to date of the interconnections between liberal progress, women's activism and the press. Moreover, in both its original version and then in the cheap reprint she arranged as a fundraiser for Oberlin College two years after the original publication and shortly before the first World Anti-Slavery Convention in June 1840, Martineau makes her own work an exemplar of transatlantic engagement and an embodiment of the active contribution to the public sphere women could, and, she implies, should make.

In bringing its readers up to date with developments in the abolitionist cause since late 1835, 'The Martyr Age' uses an account of the events following an 1838 court case over the issue of returning a slave child from Boston to New Orleans both to call out the role of women activists and to suggest the transatlantic nature of their progressive cause. By likening the court case and its outcome to 'Lord Mansfield's famous decision',[52] moreover, Martineau connects the work of abolitionism across the Atlantic and, in reminding her readers that it was Britain that first outlawed slavery, reverses the polarity of the point she had made to Abby Kelley just a few months earlier about the limitations of seeing stadial progress as simply linear in its development. If in this sense the Old World has shown the way forward to the New, however, by highlighting the role of Boston's female leaders and, in particular, the Boston Female Anti-Slavery Society (BFASS) in the abolitionist movement Martineau once again redirects the conversation to suggest the complex nature of progressive activism. For, as Debra Gold Hansen has shown, not only was the Society leadership unusual in the challenges it offered to conventional understandings of what was appropriate behaviour for women but, by the late 1830s, it was also becoming profoundly divided by a schism between supporters of Garrison and those who, more closely tied to the evangelical churches and alarmed by the racist riots in the city in 1834, were reluctant to challenge clerical authority and resisted Garrison's more assertive leadership.[53] As Martineau wrote to the British Quaker abolitionist Elizabeth Pease, she was well aware of these divisions and the painfulness of 'the exposure of the enmities of those whose first friendship sprang up in the field of benevolent labours'.[54]

In highlighting these tensions through publicly identifying the individual women at the head of the movement, however, Martineau's article made itself a form of activist intervention in political debate back across the Atlantic. Calling them out from the conventional anonymity of private life, Martineau names Maria Weston Chapman, Lydia Maria Child, Angelina and Sarah Grimké and Angelina Weld. Placing these Boston women alongside male leaders such as Garrison, emphasising their prominence, and stressing how it fell to them to accept 'the responsibility thrown of vindicating the liberty of meeting and of free discussion in Boston',[55] Martineau joins together female activism, social progress and the importance of the free circulation of ideas to suggest a model for the work of reform in Britain no less than the United States.

The significance of such naming, of bringing women's agency out of anonymity and into the public sphere, is especially apparent in the case of Angelina Grimké. Grimké and her sister Sarah, 'Quaker ladies of South Carolina',[56] had previously been described as exemplars of abolitionist leadership in *Society in America* for leaving their Southern home and upbringing to become champions of the cause in the North,[57] and Angelina herself was further notable for having married Theodore Weld, one of the forty faculty to secede from Lane Seminary in Cincinnati. In referring to her marriage, moreover, Martineau goes on to describe how the Lane faculty under Lyman Beecher 'forbade discussion and association on the question' of slavery, and she then connects their decision with a larger suppression of public discourse as she records sardonically how President Jackson, 'the people's man, who talked of liberty daily, with energetic oaths and flourishes of the hand', sought to persuade Congress to prohibit 'the transmission through the mails of anti-slavery publications, – or, as he worded it, of publications "intended to excite the slaves to insurrection"'.[58] Slowing the pace of the prose with iterative commas, Martineau makes her contempt for Jackson palpable to her readers and both reminds them of the case about constraints upon the press that she had made in *Society in America* and anticipates the account of Jackson and Amos Kendall that would appear in *Retrospect of Western Travel* when it was published just a month after this *Westminster* essay appeared. Having thus dismissed Jackson, Martineau counters with a vision of 'the moral aristocracy' constituted by the abolitionist movement, describes the breakaway group of faculty and students who left Lane in order to establish Oberlin as the first American college open to both women and people of colour and stresses the essential role of the abolitionists and of their press in acting as the conscience of the nation. Calling out Grimké, then, and her personal history of activist engagement in the cause of liberal progress, becomes a vehicle by which Martineau highlights the significance of women's leadership, restates the emphasis she placed upon the importance of educational institutions to the cause of progress and intensifies her criticism of those such as Caroline Gilman, who, as she argued in *Retrospect*, perpetuated the culture and practice of slavery through their accommodationist work in the Southern press.

Having explicitly called out Jackson's efforts to suppress the circulation of progressive newspapers and indirectly alluded to the case *Retrospect of Western Travel* would make against Gilman, *The Southern Rose* and other fellow-travellers, 'The Martyr Age' concludes with a twofold account of the abolitionist press. By comparing the fate of Elijah Lovejoy, an abolitionist newspaper editor in St Louis, Missouri, and Garrison's work in Boston on *The Liberator*,[59] Martineau creates a narrative for her *Westminster* readers that describes both the dangers facing a free press in a period of rising social unrest and the absolute necessity for such a press to resist the forces seeking to inhibit it. Recounting the repeated destruction of Lovejoy's press and types by pro-slavery mobs and ending with his being murdered in his office, Martineau's representation of his martyrdom as a 'sacrament . . . to his comrades till slavery shall be no more'[60] emphasises the need for heroic resistance to mob violence – the very activism that had, in part, so alarmed the anti-Garrison faction of the BFASS against which the article takes sides. For, speaking precisely to this issue, the article then describes how Garrison himself had to be rescued from the mob[61] yet had survived to advance the cause through his own work in the press:

> Garrison and his friend Knapp, a printer, were ere long living in a garret, on bread and water, expending all their spare earnings and time on the publication of the 'Liberator', now a handsome and flourishing newspaper; then a small shabby sheet, printed with old types.[62]

As Henry Mayer has discussed, Garrison had indeed been almost the single-handed creator of the abolitionist press: from the only paper in the nation that advocated immediate emancipation when he founded it in 1831, *The Liberator* had both doubled in size, been joined by more than thirty other papers that shared its commitment, and created pressure upon other journals to print articles in favour of the cause.[63] Setting Lovejoy and Garrison as exemplars against the work of pro-slavery mobs in not only predictable locations such as Charleston, South Carolina but even in that progressive Cincinnati she had made her exemplar of American stadial progress,[64] Martineau thus concludes the article by representing to her readers the paramount importance of the press in order to safeguard the course of liberal social development built upon the agency of activist individual leaders – with Garrison, both ecclesiastically and editorially, the pastor figure guiding the way forward, epitomising the fundamental role of the heroic journalist in shaping the public sphere, and joined in his work by the women of the BFASS.

If the thrust of these first three essays had thus been to emphasise the ties between liberal activism and a free press, the last of Martineau's 1830s *Westminster* articles offers a more ambivalent diagnosis of the role of print media in the modern age, one that picks up on the susceptibility to public opinion she had identified as a defining American weakness in both *Society in America* and 'Miss Sedgwick's Works'. For in 'Literary Lionism' Martineau simultaneously recognises the unprecedented growth of these media and of a new reading public yet also expresses a sense of unease over both that expansion and the appearance of another recently widespread phenomenon: the cult of the celebrity author. While she initially frames these changes in terms of her habitually affirmative move out of the medieval past – 'There was a time when literature was cultivated only in the seclusion of monasteries'[65] – she then picks up the concern with the 'vast spread of literature among our people' that her correspondence during this period consistently identifies as a more complexly problematic phenomenon:

> How great a number of readers is required to support, by purchase and by praise, a standing class of original writers! It testifies to the deterioration of literature as a whole. If, at any one time, there is a *class* of persons to whom the public are grateful for intellectual excitement, how *mediocre* must be the quality of the intellectual production![66]

Pointing to the concern Ian Haywood has identified among middle-class intellectuals with the rise of radical mass-market publications that did not conform to liberal ideology, the essay thus voices an anxiety that Martineau would both name and seek to address in her collaborations with Charles Knight during the 1840s. In this *Westminster* article, however, that concern is focused less upon the audience for such mass-market literature than its producers as the essay voices pointed antagonism towards the concomitant 'worship of popular authors' not simply as a form of dandyism but, and in terms which recall one of Martineau's major criticisms of Scott's fame, because 'it cuts off the retreat of literary persons into the great body of human beings. They are marked out as a class, and can no longer take refuge from their toils and their publicity in ordinary life'.[67] Thereby in danger of losing 'the very first necessity of his vocation [which] is to live as others live, in order to see and feel as others see and feel, and to sympathise in human thought',[68] the lionised author, according to Martineau, is liable to fancy 'that books govern the affairs of the world', attribute to himself far more importance than is warranted and move away from the pastoral role she privileged and saw represented, above all, in Garrison.

As Chapter 6 will show, this concern over the figure of the celebrity author (always referred to as masculine) and the influence he could wield over the reading public clearly became a factor in Martineau's difficult dynamic with Dickens. An author both lionised and yet remaining unique in his capacity to enter into the lives of 'the great body of human beings', Dickens generated a deep ambivalence in her. Allied with him in their shared broad commitment to the liberal project, she nevertheless struggled to reconcile the undeniable fact of his unmatched celebrity, his palpable ability to unite an extraordinary range of the population into a common readership and their fundamental differences over both the role of the state and the part to be played by women in advancing stadial progress. By contrast, and closing this set of articles, she is far more comfortable to offer Emerson, whose speech at Dartmouth is the ostensible subject of the review, as her model of the authorial selflessness she suggests is required to create 'a society of perfect sympathy'.[69] In so doing, she affirms once again the vitality of interchange between the Old World and the New and thereby reiterates a vision these four essays for the *Westminster* collectively lay out of a transatlantic progressive intellectual community, a vision that by the late 1830s had become, as it would remain throughout her career, a defining element in her sense of the role of the press in advancing liberal progress and of the part she herself would endeavour to play in that work.

'The liberal education of the people': Martineau, Charles Knight and the Popular Periodical Press

Martineau's next major act of repositioning after returning from America – the collaboration she established with Charles Knight – marks a second essential stage in her development as a journalist and in her influence upon shaping the early Victorian press. For, even as she was first appearing in the *Westminster*, so too Martineau was extending her established relationship with Knight, former superintendent of the Society for the Diffusion of Useful Knowledge (SDUK) and the leading publisher of 'improving' literature for working-class readers, whom she had first met in the early 1830s and who published both *How to Observe* as well as the three 'Guides to Service' that she wrote in 1838–9.[70] Always far more than a man with whom she was connected only by ties of business, Knight was for her 'a wise & benevolent publisher'[71] and became her ally and collaborator on a number of projects in the late 1830s and through the 1840s. As he did so, and testifying again to the close-knit nature of the networks of the Victorian press, he would also come to know Dickens and, just a few years later, join Martineau as another of the early contributors to *Household Words*. Examining her collaboration with Knight on, first, the SDUK's *The Penny Magazine* in the late 1830s and then the *Weekly Volume* in 1843 makes further evident Martineau's vision of the press and her own role in it, her sense of the vital importance of a transatlantic discourse in support of progress and her development of a vision of the liberal project that would both push her towards and eventually pull her away from Dickens.

Martineau's dozen or so articles for *The Penny Magazine* between 1837 and 1840 have been almost entirely overlooked in critical discussions of her work, with the most likely explanation being that they have been seen as little more than embodying the 'pacification' of its working-class readers that Ian Haywood has described as the periodical's 'prime ideological goal'.[72] Read through the lens of her other writing on the United States, however, this collection of pieces, above all her 'Account of Toussaint L'Ouverture', can be seen as an effort to extend her progressive agenda through the popularised treatment of material to reach a broader audience than either the American books or *Westminster* articles had targeted. The six-part 1840 series 'The Newcastle Improvements', for example, may well have modelled normative middle-class values for the working-class reader in the way Haywood describes. At the same time, however, in portraying the rise of Richard Grainger from humble origins into the master planner and builder of the modern city centre, parts of which still bear his name, the series also calls back to Martineau's accounts of Daniel Drake's combination of the pastoral and the entrepreneurial as he led the transformation of Cincinnati into an urban exemplar of civic progress. An even more explicit allusion to material previously treated in *Society in America* can be seen in 'The Shakers', which appeared in November 1837 and which shows how she and Dickens critiqued the sect on revealingly different grounds. As Chapter 3 noted, Dickens's attack on the Shakers in *American Notes* had been for the ways in which it made 'barren the imagination' and allowed itself to be led by a woman.[73] By contrast, having praised the Shakers' rich husbandry and their commitment to ensuring that everyone in the community has the basic means to live, Martineau then directs the reader's attention to the lamentable effects of the sect's anti-intellectualism: 'books are discountenanced; no such thing is dreamed of as the pursuit of science, literature or art. These noble intellectual occupations are regarded as toys with which the holy should have nothing to do.'[74] Emphasising again the importance of print culture and of both intellectual and creative pursuits, what her diagnosis of the Shakers ultimately faults is their having sequestered themselves from the wider world, cut themselves off from the advance of history and condemned themselves to 'being remembered only as an added example of man's social eccentricities'.[75]

Far and away the most significant of these *Penny Magazine* articles, however, is 'Account of Toussaint L'Ouverture', which appeared in February 1838 (Fig. 5.1). Having had the subject suggested to her by Charles Follen,[76] Martineau used the opportunity provided by Knight's venue to write a short biographical sketch of the Haitian revolutionary leader and so once again make that connection between enslaved people and the condition of the industrial working classes that becomes a recurring feature of her work in the press after the visit to America. Martineau's description of Toussaint's life and leadership provides an emphatic rebuttal to the question with which she rhetorically opens the article: 'whether negroes are constitutionally, and therefore irremediably, inferior to whites in the powers of the mind. Much of the future welfare of the human race depends on the answer which experience will furnish to this question.'[77] To argue against such implied racist assumptions, Martineau represents Toussaint as another exemplar of leadership towards stadial progress through having formed 'a nation of freemen out of a herd of negro slaves', 'made order take the place of licentiousness' and, by teaching 'that personal self-restraint is the only guarantee of social liberty', ensured that 'the waste country began to teem with fertility wherever he turned his steps'.[78] 'Licentiousness', of course, was the quality she had previously characterised as the fundamental flaw of Southern slave-owning masculinity in the United States and, as Elisabeth Arbuckle Sanders has noted, by the time the article appeared, Martineau's account of slavery in *Society in America* meant that her work no

Figure 5.1   Toussaint L'Ouverture.

longer circulated in the South.⁷⁹ In offering 'Toussaint L'Ouverture' to *The Penny Magazine*, however, Martineau was making deliberate use of the culture of reprinting to circulate her arguments to audiences to which she no longer had direct access. As she wrote to Fanny Wedgwood shortly after sending the article to Knight and before knowing whether he would accept it:

> Do you care about Toussaint L'Ouverture? I have been doing a life of him (much wanted) for the Penny Magne. My chief object is to get at the Southern States, where they reprint the P. M. fearlessly, and will never dream of meeting me. I hope a few hundred people there will learn what a negro has been, and what other negroes therefore may be.⁸⁰

Finally, the article also served to preview *The Hour and the Man*, Martineau's 1840 novel on the Haitian slave rebellion that would ultimately prove vital for developing her connection with the abolitionist movement in America. For, and as Susan Belasco has shown, *The Hour and the Man*, notwithstanding its disappointing initial sales in Britain, went on to become a key text for the abolitionist movement and thus was fundamental to Martineau's ongoing transatlantic engagement during a period of her career when she was not writing directly for American readers.⁸¹ Collectively, then, Martineau's contributions certainly contributed to *The Penny Magazine*'s strategy of containing working-class radicalism. At the same time, most notably in 'Toussaint L'Ouverture', they allowed her to put the periodical to the service of her own progressive liberalism and, in the way she used it as a vehicle to recirculate subversive material into the slave-owning states of America, to demonstrate the strategies she was developing to enact that 'literary companionship' and commitment to transatlantic discourse through the press she had unsuccessfully proposed to John Gorham Palfrey at the *North American Review* back in December 1835.

If Martineau's body of work for *The Penny Magazine* is in these ways more significant to her development as a journalist and commitment to transatlantic liberal activism than has been previously recognised, her second major partnering with Knight in the early 1840s reveals how she continued that activism and came to recognise the limitations of both her own abilities and the capacities of the venues with which she was involved. The *Weekly Volume*, a short-lived series launched by Martineau and Knight in 1844 and designed to republish a wide variety of texts in a form aimed at working-class readers, was, while not itself journalistic work, an attempt to use serial publication to advance the agenda of middle-class liberalism. Such ventures to improve the masses and offset the influence of radical publications were, as Richard Altick, Ian Haywood and Louis James have all shown,[82] a recurring phenomenon in the period between the end of the Napoleonic Wars and the mid-century. Martineau's engagement in this particular project, however, which has received almost no previous critical attention, is significant for my argument in three ways: first, it further evidences her commitment to effecting social change through the agency of print and periodical publication; second, it makes visible how, even as she addressed the needs of the working classes, she was simultaneously focused upon influencing other sectors of society, including the ruling elite, by increasing their awareness of the conditions of the masses; and third, it reveals her recognition of the inefficacy of class-based didacticism and shows that, even as she embraced this particular venture, she was increasingly aware of the limitations in her own understanding of the culture of its target audience. In these three ways, her involvement with the *Weekly Volume* is also an important precursor of her work during the 1850s, when she would fully emerge as the most influential woman journalist in the British press. For, on the one hand, her experience with Knight's project suggests why she would be drawn a few years later to *Household Words* and the branding power Dickens brought to reach a mass readership. On the other, it points to her ambitions to shape opinion among the more empowered sectors of British society and thus anticipates why Frederick Knight Hunt's 1852 invitation to join the *Daily News* as a leader writer would be so attractive to her. As intimated in the Introduction and as will be more fully explored in Chapter 6, Hunt's invitation would become an essential factor in Martineau's move away from Dickens's mass-market weekly magazine as, once again in her career, she would take a path that allowed her to develop professionally and extend her influence through shifting her primary publishing venue.

In 1844, however, the founding of both *Household Words* and the *Daily News* still lay in the future, and, for all her efforts with *The Penny Magazine*, Martineau remained deeply concerned over the growth of the unstamped radical newspapers that emerged to provide a voice for working-class unrest, particularly among the coal miners of northern England. Writing to Lord Howick in January 1844, she describes a visit from W. S. Tremenheere, Inspector of Mines, and notes his agreeing with her that 'that the minds of the adults must be got hold of, & the pernicious stuff they receive (from the Northern Star & other such papers) must be neutralized'.[83]

Writing further on this to both Howick and Tremenheere himself, she explores the possibility of herself editing such a newspaper for the miners that would 'be a quiet contradiction of the poor peoples' notion that all above them are their enemies'.[84]

Although she soon came to realise the impracticability of this project and turned away from the possibility of assuming an editorial role, Martineau quickly moved on to other options, making use of her publishing networks and established political relationships to advance a very different venture and one that would come to fruition in short order. Within weeks of her letters to Howick and Tremenheere, her correspondence shows her in the early stage of planning for what would become the *Weekly Volume* (Fig. 5.2). Soliciting financial support for the series among the aristocratic Whig families in the north of England with which she had long been connected, the goal she defined for it paralleled that which had been imagined for the newspaper for miners that had not materialised. She thus wrote to Lady Mary Lambton on 14 February describing the intended readers:

> Let us also remember that the chief mischief we have to combat is their persuasion that they are disliked & ill used by the classes above them. – Now nothing appears to me so likely to weaken this persuasion as their reading books <u>not written for them</u>, which picture forth the pursuits, ways & temper of the middle classes. – I am persuaded that such reading would do more to dislodge their painful & prejudiced feelings than any explanation aimed at them, or designed expressly for them.[85]

Repeatedly describing herself as 'a manufacturer's daughter', she also noted to R. H. Horne the opportunities afforded by her class and what she might elsewhere have defined as the limitations of her sex, given that she 'was of the middle class, – able to open a view for rulers into middle class life, – & safe, as being a woman, & therefore disinterested about office &c'.[86] Positioning herself as both unmarked and yet able to act as a bridge between the social classes, Martineau fostered the *Weekly Volume* project as a vehicle for creating that community of moral sympathy essential to stadial progress by addressing not simply the actual social divisions that she found so concerning but also the reciprocal ignorance she saw permeating Britain's highly stratified class structure.

The project moved ahead rapidly; Martineau and Charles Knight apparently corresponded about it extensively, determining by March that Knight's own biography of William Caxton would open the

Figure 5.2 *Knight's Weekly Volume.*

series, and in mid-April Knight travelled to Tynemouth 'for the especial purpose of conferring with Miss Martineau'.[87] Who actually originated the scheme remains unclear, but Knight's memoir apparently attributes it to Martineau as he credits her for 'arranging the details of a plan that mainly owes its origin to her unwearied solicitude for the good of her fellow-creatures' and, perhaps somewhat wryly, acknowledges the 'indefatigable zeal unabated by illness' with which she set out to seek support and to which her surviving correspondence amply testifies.[88] By late May the series was advertised, and by early June Martineau was able to share with Anna Horner, the wife of that Inspector of Factories who would later play a central part in her dispute with Dickens, the news that a cheque had even been received from the Privy Purse to pay for subscriptions for the libraries at the royal palaces.[89]

On the same day that Martineau corresponded with Mrs Horner about the project, Dickens was also in touch with Knight about it. Wrapping up the final number of *Martin Chuzzlewit* and about to leave England to spend a year in Italy and Switzerland, he had received a prospectus for the series from Knight. Writing back to offer his encouragement (and evidently initiating what would become their longstanding friendship and working relationship), Dickens commented favourably on the concept of the project and, specifically, on the second number, proofs of which Knight had shared with him:

> Many thanks for your proof, and for your truly gratifying mention of my name. I think the subject excellently chosen, the introduction exactly what it should be, the allusion to the International Copyright question most honourable and manly, and the whole scheme full of the highest interest. I had already seen your prospectus, and if I can be of the feeblest use in advancing a project so intimately connected with an end on which my heart is set – the liberal education of the people – I shall be sincerely glad.[90]

If Dickens shared in the passion for 'the liberal education of the people', those proofs to which he refers also foreshadow one of the key differences within his and Martineau's versions of liberalism that would eventually contribute to their great falling out in late 1855. For the *Weekly Volume*'s second issue, *Mind Amongst the Spindles*, consisted of a reprint of selections from that same *Lowell Offering* Dickens had celebrated in *American Notes*. But while the issue's introduction deploys Dickens's enthusiastic comments on the millworkers' literary miscellany as a means of enticing prospective readers, a portion of the prefatory matter explicitly identified with Martineau points towards a very different reading of Lowell and its women workers than that which *American Notes* had put into circulation less than two years earlier.

As Chapter 3 has shown, Dickens's account in *American Notes* renders the Lowell factories as a benignly feminised environment, the workers as simply compliant with the conditions provided them, and their literary magazine as working to 'inculcate habits of self-denial and contentment, and teach good doctrines of enlarged benevolence'.[91] Citing this passage in the earlier part of its own preface, *Mind Amongst the Spindles* at first appears to parallel Dickens's view as it goes on to claim that 'an improvement of the operative classes ... will be brought about in a parallel progression with the elevation of the operatives themselves in mental cultivation, and consequently in moral excellence'.[92] Almost immediately after this passage, however, the preface is taken in a different direction by the inclusion of a 'most interesting and valuable letter' from Martineau that the editor claims he has just happened to receive. Using this device to allow her an identified authorial voice in the text, the second part of the introduction to *Mind Among the Spindles* reiterates the claim about the value proposition of industrial employment for women that Martineau had made in both her American books and in the *Westminster* articles, and that had fundamentally differentiated her reading of the New World from Dickens's uncritical endorsement of republican motherhood:

> The institution of factory labour has brought ease of heart to many; and to many occasion for noble and generous deeds. The ease of heart is given to those who were before suffering in silent poverty, from the deficiency of profitable employment for women, which is even greater in America than with us.[93]

Arguing that even seventy hours a week of labour in the mills cannot tire minds 'kept fresh, and strong, and free by knowledge and power of thought',[94] Martineau uses an idealised interpretation of American industrial experience to reaffirm her longstanding expression of a commitment to the essential value of employment as the indispensable mechanism for achieving women's intellectual autonomy and allowing their agency as liberal subjects. Invoking Dickens's version of Lowell only to counter it in this way, Martineau's letter imagines *The Lowell Offering* as a foundational text, one that makes the larger case for the value of women's engagement in work beyond the home as an essential condition for the advance of a liberal society. As Chapter 7 will show, the enduring significance Lowell took on for Martineau would again be evident when, a decade and a half later, she returned to this subject and published her most extensive treatment of it with 'Female Industry' in the 1859 *Edinburgh Review*. Again, Lowell and its women workers serve as a focusing prism for her argument and demonstrate how Martineau's brief visit to the experimental Massachusetts factory town back in 1834 continued to serve her as an exemplar of how the economic conditions created by industrial capitalism had opened up new opportunities for women to work and contribute to stadial progress.

Martineau's enthusiasm for the *Weekly Volume* and her zeal in promoting it in 1844 are, then, deeply revealing of her own commitment to that 'liberal education of the people' in which both she and Dickens so deeply believed. At the same time, and as her correspondence reveals, Martineau was also coming to develop a more complex understanding of the difficulties involved in shaping the minds of the working classes through the use of popular literature. For herself, she clearly recognised that, while she may have been socially positioned to bridge between the industrial middle class and the progressive elite, by temperament and taste she faced much greater challenges in trying to connect to working-class culture. As she wrote to Milnes in April 1844, 'I cannot read James's novels & many popular books wh are to me as if they were written in Chinese characters, – so little impression do they leave if I try to read them.'[95] Although she described the *Offering* as 'the only existing literature in our language produced by the working class',[96] claimed that it was 'the most remarkable book of the age'[97] and asserted that the *Weekly Volume* project was destined to become 'the greatest boon in the history of the people',[98] she also sensed 'the hopelessness of operating on the minds of the working class in any degree as authors from their own order could do'.[99] Moreover, beyond her own challenges, the *Weekly Volume* itself soon struggled as a commercial venture. For all the enthusiasm and energy Martineau put into it and notwithstanding the underwriting support she had managed to build, it proved at 1/- a week to be priced too expensively to reach working-class readers, became commercially unsustainable and soon gave way to a short-lived monthly replacement.

Even though the *Weekly Volume* was fated to end as but one more of Charles Knight's valiant but precarious initiatives to provide cheap popular literature to a mass audience, however, the experiment reveals much about Martineau's ambitions for the press, the goals that she and Dickens shared and the underlying differences that would eventually push them apart. Indeed, the initial planning for the *Weekly Volume* began at a time when Dickens, too, was exploring new ways to forge cross-class unity and create that community of moral sentiment Martineau argued was fundamental to stadial progress. And, though *A Christmas Carol* would go on to become his single most influential expression of that effort, when it was first published in December 1843 it, like Knight and Martineau's series, was initially priced beyond the reach of many of the readers Dickens had hoped to affect. For both authors, then, and as Dickens's correspondence in the period before *Household Words* most clearly evidences, a recurring thread throughout their work of the 1840s was the effort to find a vehicle that would reach a broad mass-market readership and advance the liberal project.[100] The *Weekly Volume* project thus both suggests why Dickens would identify Martineau as a prospective contributor to his new magazine and why she would find value in joining forces with him. At the same time, however, the discrepancies the project reveals in their understandings of the relationship between industrial labour and women's role in the advancement of society, and the differences it points to in their identities and capabilities as writers seeking to connect with a readership drawn from across the social classes, also anticipate the fault lines along which their relationship at *Household Words* would ultimately fracture and dissolve in the bitter mutual recriminations of the winter of 1855–6.

'A periodical wh is neither conformable nor independent & consistent': Martineau and *The Leader*

As she and Dickens moved towards their collaboration at *Household Words*, Martineau's stature as a writer for cross-class audiences and for periodicals that advocated liberal causes was evident in two other start-up magazines' efforts to recruit her as a contributor: Howitt and Saunders' *People's Journal* in 1846, and *The Leader*, established by Thornton Leigh Hunt and G. H. Lewes in 1850. The limitations of both venues for Martineau quickly became evident to her, and her contributions to them have justifiably drawn little critical attention. Nevertheless both, and particularly *The Leader*, further illustrate why editors such as Dickens saw the value of having her write for them. They also reveal how, a little over a decade after returning from America, she had attained a position in the press not only where she was actively sought out as a contributor but also where she was free to resist being limited by editorial expectations at odds with her own sense of herself as a writer and the goals she had set out for her work.

When the *People's Journal* recruited her in 1846, for example, Martineau recognised that she was being solicited by editors who evidently wanted to replicate the success of *Illustrations of Political Economy* by having her write similar pieces for them. She lamented to Lord Grey that Howitt and Saunders

> so earnestly wish for fiction from me that, rather against my own judgment, I shall yield to their opinion of the popular desire for it, – pleasing myself too by sending didactic papers, reviews &c, when my prior engagements allow me time.[101]

Despite this expression of compliance, however, mindful of her own earlier assessment of the *Lowell Offering* and of 'the hopelessness of operating on the minds of the working class in any degree as authors from their own order could do',[102] and certainly aware that political economy had lost the power of popular appeal that it had enjoyed in the early 1830s, Martineau did not, in the end, provide the magazine with any such fiction. Instead, her contributions were limited to a single article and two series of pieces based on the region in which she had recently made her permanent home: the three-part 'Lake and Mountain Holiday' that appeared in 1846 and her monthly series, 'Survey from the Mountain'. As Alexis Easley has shown, Martineau's writing about the Lake District would over time become an important strategy in her 'capitalizing on celebrity culture as a way of ensuring her own enduring fame as a woman of letters',[103] and in this it suggests an intriguing response to the concern over the figure of the celebrity author she had voiced in 'Literary Lionism' back in 1839. In the mid-1840s, however, Martineau had just recently settled in the Lake District and not yet developed this aspect of her writerly persona. For my argument here, then, what is most significant about her engagement with the *People's Journal* is the ways in which it reveals her resistance to editorial expectations that did not align with her own sense of her professional strengths, a resistance that would become even more critical in her relationship with Dickens at *Household Words*.

Misalignment between her writerly identity, her ideological commitments and scepticism about a journal that sought her as a contributor were even more apparent in the last major engagement that she took on during this period – an article and then a series of twelve 'Sketches from Life' that appeared in *The Leader* between October 1850 and July 1851. Overlapping with her early contributions to *Household Words,* this series of pieces for Thornton Leigh Hunt and G. H. Lewes's start-up weekly indirectly confirms the attractiveness for her of the very different venue Dickens provided. Following a letter-article on the plight of impoverished middle-class women in London and the benefits of their living in communal homes, Martineau's series comprised twelve tales focused upon working-class and lower-middle-class characters.[104] Emphasising the injustices of the class system, the hardships inflicted on the working poor by the vagaries of the national economy and the marginalisation suffered by working women, the sketches aligned with *The Leader*'s efforts to position itself as a respectable voice of radical ideals. But, and even more than her work for *The Penny Magazine* a decade earlier, these are heavily didactic texts, often relying upon incidents or characters Martineau knew from her life in Ambleside, and they rarely venture beyond the kind of 'pacification' for which Ian Haywood has critiqued this class of improving literature. In their often leaden plotting, characterisation and style they are indeed a close match with *The Leader* itself, a paper that, as Laurel Brake has said, sought in vain to find a secure niche 'in a fragile and contested weekly space' and that, though radical in its ideology, was unable to succeed in sustaining the mass readership it sought.[105] Yet, even while she was well aware of the newspaper's limitations, Martineau also recognised the importance of the role it had attempted to perform. As she wrote to John Chapman in April 1851, even before her series had concluded:

> The failure (for so it is) of 'the Leader' tells nothing, as to the demand for liberal thought, for it has quailed, & is neither one thing nor another. In spite of its name, it is stumbling on <u>behind</u> the multitude for whom it was apparently intended, while it is too heretical for the rest of society. A periodical wh is neither conformable nor independent & consistent, cannot succeed: & this is very well.[106]

Encapsulating the conundrum she had faced throughout her work since returning from America, Martineau's letter defines the larger dilemma facing the liberal early Victorian press: how to make the progressive case and appeal sufficiently to the working classes without losing credibility among the more privileged segments of society. *Household Words*, which Dickens clearly intended to make conformable, independent and consistent in his own ways, represented the possibility of Martineau's at last finding a venue through which she could reach a cross-class readership and argue to it for the liberal causes to which she was committed. As the following chapter will show, however, the reality turned out to be more complex and problematic than either she or Dickens had anticipated or than the established critical narrative of their dispute over the magazine has made visible.

Notes

1. Hewitt, *The Dawn of the Cheap Press in Victorian Britain*, pp. 10–11.
2. See Dickens, *Letters*, vol. 6 for his invitations to women writers including Elizabeth Gaskell, Mary Howitt, Geraldine Jewsbury and Anne Marsh, none of whom had Martineau's stature or range of presence in the periodical press.
3. Haywood, *The Revolution in Popular Literature*, p. 5.
4. In addition to Haywood's work, studies of this phenomenon include Humpherys, *G. W. M. Reynolds: Nineteenth-Century Fiction, Politics and the Press*, Krishnamurthy, *The Working Class Intellectual in Eighteenth- and Nineteenth-Century Britain* and Rose, *The Intellectual Life of the British Working Classes*.
5. Haywood, *The Revolution in Popular Literature*, p. 125.
6. Ibid. p. 125.
7. Ibid. p. 195.
8. Logan, *The Hour and the Woman*, p. 103.
9. Martineau, *Letters*, vol. 3, p. 102.
10. [Dickens], 'A Preliminary Word', p. 1.
11. Martineau, *Autobiography*, p. 619.
12. Peterson, *Becoming a Woman of Letters*, pp. 45–7.
13. Martineau, *Letters*, vol. 2, pp. 159–60.
14. Martineau, *Further Letters*, p. 39.
15. This event is discussed by Budge, *Romanticism, Medicine, and the Natural Supernatural*, pp. 122–3; Pond, 'Harriet Martineau's Epistemology of Gossip', pp. 175–207; Roberts, *The Woman and the Hour*, pp. 56–60.
16. Martineau, *Further Letters*, p. 155.
17. Martineau, *Letters to Wedgwood*, p. 114.

18. Martineau, *Letters*, vol. 2, p. 325. Martineau's own efforts to address the needs of the rural working class in Ambleside, evident in the lecture series she offered and her establishing a building society to provide modern sanitary housing, are described respectively in Logan, *The Hour and the Woman*, pp. 308–9, and Webb, *Harriet Martineau*, pp. 261–3.
19. Martineau, *Letters*, vol. 3, p. 104.
20. Ibid. p. 148.
21. Martineau, *Illustrations of Political Economy No. IX Ireland*.
22. Martineau, *Letters*, vol. 2, p.13.
23. Martineau, *Letters to Wedgwood*, p. 72.
24. Martineau, *Letters*, vol. 2, p. 197.
25. Ibid.
26. Martineau, *History of the Peace*, in Logan (ed.), *Harriet Martineau's Writing on British History and Military Reform*, vol. 3, p. 307.
27. Martineau, *Letters*, vol. 3, p. 147.
28. Martineau, 'Female Education', p. 77. See also Logan, '"I Am, My Dear Slanderer, Your Faithful Malignant Demon"', pp. 171–91. Logan's account of Martineau's connection with the *Westminster* takes a more biographical approach than my discussion in this chapter.
29. Martineau, *Letters*, vol. 2, p. 316.
30. Dillon, *The Gender of Freedom*, p. 47.
31. Martineau, *Further Letters*, p. 154.
32. Martineau, *Letters*, vol. 3, p. 228.
33. Ibid. vol. 2, p. 316.
34. [Johnstone], 'Miss Martineau's Society in America'. As Joanne Shattock has shown, the consolidation of periodical journalism to London rather than Edinburgh was not limited to Martineau's decision to forsake *Tait's*. See her 'The Sense of Place and *Blackwood's (Edinburgh) Magazine*' for a discussion of Maga's relocation south in the early 1840s. Unlike Johnstone, who remained tied to Edinburgh and to *Tait's* for the remainder of her career, Martineau was thus freed to develop what would become a uniquely flexible and wide-ranging presence in the press.
35. Martineau, *Letters*, vol. 2, p. 7.
36. 'Practical Reasoning Versus Impracticable Theories', pp. 567, 564.
37. Martineau, *Further Letters*, p. 39.
38. [Robertson], 'Miss Martineau's Western Travel', pp. 470, 478.
39. 'Retrospect of Western Travel'; 'Miss Martineau's Travels in America'.
40. [Martineau], 'Miss Sedgwick's Works', pp. 43, 44.
41. Ibid. pp. 46, 59, 64, 65.
42. Martineau, *Society in America*, vol. 3, p. 213.
43. [Martineau], 'Domestic Service', pp. 405–32.
44. Martineau, 'Miss Sedgwick's Works', pp. 60, 65.
45. Martineau, 'Domestic Service', pp. 414, 415.

46. Ibid. p. 428.
47. Martineau, 'Miss Sedgwick's Works', p. 60.
48. Martineau, 'Domestic Service', p. 412.
49. Ibid. pp. 432, 431.
50. Martineau, *Letters*, vol. 1, p. 283.
51. Pichanik, *Harriet Martineau*, pp. 91–2; Logan, *The Woman and the Hour*, pp. 98–103.
52. Martineau, 'The Martyr Age', p. 34.
53. Hansen, *Strained Sisterhood*, p. 141. See also her extended discussion of the abolitionist movement in Boston, pp. 93–123.
54. Martineau, *Further Letters*, p. 51.
55. Martineau, 'The Martyr Age', p. 18.
56. Ibid. p. 24.
57. Martineau, *Society in America*, vol. 2, p. 341.
58. Martineau, 'The Martyr Age', p. 32.
59. Ibid. pp. 41–7, 4–7.
60. Ibid. p. 46.
61. Ibid. p. 23.
62. Ibid. p. 6.
63. Mayer, *All on Fire*, p. 209.
64. Martineau, 'The Martyr Age', p. 29.
65. [Martineau], 'Literary Lionism', p. 262.
66. Ibid. p. 264.
67. Ibid. pp. 264, 271.
68. Ibid. p. 272.
69. Ibid. pp. 279–80.
70. Knight, *Passages of a Working Life during Half a Century*, vol. 2, pp. 314–5.
71. Martineau, *Letters*, vol. 2, p. 245.
72. Haywood, *The Revolution in Popular Literature*, p. 123. Elisabeth Sanders Arbuckle's footnote on p. 17 of her edition of Martineau's letters to Wedgwood is the only previous discussion of this series of articles.
73. Dickens, *American Notes*, pp. 236–9.
74. Martineau, 'The Shakers', p. 447.
75. Ibid. p. 448.
76. Martineau, *Letters*, vol. 2, p. 71.
77. Martineau, 'Account of Toussaint L'Ouverture', p. 121. Alexis Easley describes the article as beginning 'with racist references to the presumed "inferiority of mind" among slaves in the New World', but also suggests that Knight's placing it in the issue's lead position and having it richly illustrated indicates his support for its abolitionist message ('Rewriting the Past and Present', p. 103). However, as the letter to Fanny Wedgwood cited below (n. 80) reveals, Martineau had submitted the article to Knight in the hope of making use of the magazine's being reprinted in the United States but with no certainty that the editor would in fact accept it.

78. 'Account of Toussaint L'Ouverture', pp. 126, 124.
79. Martineau, *Letters to Wedgwood*, p. 13, n. 16.
80. Ibid. p. 11.
81. Belasco, 'Harriet Martineau's Black Hero and the American Antislavery Movement', pp. 157–94.
82. Altick, *Writers, Readers, and Occasions*; James, *Fiction for the Working Man*; James, *Print and the People 1819–1851*.
83. Martineau, *Letters*, vol. 2, p. 223.
84. Ibid. p. 237.
85. Ibid. p. 246.
86. Ibid. p. 310.
87. Martineau, *Further Letters*, p. 71; Knight, *Passages of a Working Life*, vol. 2, p. 315.
88. Knight, *Passages of a Working Life*, vol. 2, pp. 314, 317.
89. Martineau, *Letters*, vol. 2, p. 307.
90. Dickens, *Letters*, vol. 4, p. 139.
91. Dickens, *American Notes*, p. 79.
92. *Mind Amongst the Spindles*, pp. xv–xvi.
93. Ibid. p. xix.
94. Ibid. p. xviii.
95. Martineau, *Letters*, vol. 2, p. 280.
96. Ibid. p. 246.
97. Ibid. p. 322.
98. Martineau, *Further Letters*, p. 71.
99. Martineau, *Letters*, vol. 2, p. 246. Maria Frawley reads Martineau's ongoing use of the *Lowell Offering* as a 'necessary weapon in her attempt to get her readers to acknowledge the need for a changed understanding of women's work in Britain', 'Behind the Scenes of History', p. 150. While largely in agreement with her argument, I note here the extent to which Martineau's utilisation of the text is offset by the recognition of the limits of her own ability to reach its target readership.
100. Drew, *Dickens the Journalist*, pp. 106–9, provides the fullest discussion of Dickens's ongoing effort to find a vehicle that would meet his goals for a periodical.
101. Martineau, *Letters*, vol. 3, p. 55.
102. Ibid. vol. 2, p. 246.
103. Easley, *Literary Celebrity, Gender, and Victorian Authorship, 1850–1914*, p. 69.
104. Martineau's first contribution to *The Leader* was 'Associated Homes', 19 October 1850, pp. 708–9. Under the title 'Sketches from Life', she followed this with 'I: The Old Governess',* 9 November 1850, pp. 788–9; 'II: The Collegian',* 23 November, pp. 836–7; 'III: The Maid-Servant', 7 December, pp. 883–4; 'III: The Maid-Servant', 14 December, pp. 907–8; 'IV: The Convert',* 28 December, pp. 955–6;

'V: The Factory Boy',* 11 January 1851, pp. 42–3; 'VI: The Farm-Labourer – The Father', 15 February, pp. 155–6; 'VII: The Farm-Labourer – The Son', 1 March, pp. 205–6; 'VIII: The Convict',* 15 March, pp. 252–3; 'IX: A Specimen of an Inferior Race', 5 April, pp. 324–5; 'X: The Despised Woman',* 19 April, pp. 372–3; 'XI: The Shopman',* 17 May, pp. 468–9; 'XII: The Stock Farmer', 5 July, pp. 637–8; 'XII: The Stock Farmer', 12 July, pp. 661–2. The seven articles marked * were reprinted in her 1856 collection, *Sketches from Life*, the role of which in her dispute with Dickens is discussed in Chapter 6.
105. Brake, '*The Leader* (1850–1859)'.
106. Martineau, *Letters*, vol. 3, p. 199.

Chapter 6

The Factory Controversy: 'What I dread is being silenced'

> What I dread is being silenced, and the mortification and loss of the manner of it . . . Yet, if it happens, I dare say it will become clear to me what I ought to do; and that is the only really important thing.[1]
>
> Harriet Martineau

Martineau's poignant comment in her *Autobiography* on the critical reception her work had regularly received voices the great challenge at the heart of her career and the force of her role as a model for the next generation of professional women writers. As she sought to find ways to speak into many of the major debates of her time and to advocate for the liberal causes to which she was profoundly committed, the one constant that she faced throughout her more than four decades of major publication was a struggle first to achieve and then to maintain a place in the public sphere. In that context, this chapter will argue, her bitter dispute with Dickens in the winter of 1855–6 takes a large part of its meaning from this enduring struggle. For, in the process of striving to make herself heard and resisting Dickens's efforts to extinguish her voice and erase her from view, the underlying differences in their understandings of liberalism and the role of the press in advancing its cause that this book has explored finally came to a head.

What made the eventual dispute so bitter and so disruptive, moreover, as Sally Ledger has shown, were the ways in which with the launch of *Household Words* in March 1850 Dickens created a brilliant response to the challenges Martineau and other liberals had seen developing in the 1840s through the rise of the unstamped radical press and the emergence of cheap mass-market entertainment of the kind offered by Reynolds and Lloyd. Bridging 'the incipient chasm that was opening up between popular and radical culture', his new weekly merged the tradition of popular miscellanies with that of campaigning journalism. Through its creation of 'a political and cultural hybrid', Ledger argues, Dickens's magazine wed 'an eighteenth-century conception of "the People" as a political entity to the emergent nineteenth-century category of the "populace" in a commercial culture'.[2] Indeed, that hybrid nature was explicitly called out in the 'Preliminary Word' with which Dickens opened the first issue. On the one hand, attacking what he defined as the exploitative mass-market weeklies associated with Reynolds and his ilk, and, on the other, emphasising the role of 'Fancy' and imaginative literature in a way that differentiated his own project from more overtly didactic periodicals such as *Chambers's Journal*, Dickens also told his readers that one of his main objects was 'to bring the greater and lesser in degree, together, upon that wide field, and mutually dispose them to a better acquaintance and a kinder understanding'.[3] Mirroring Martineau's commitment to the importance of creating a community of sympathy among a cross-class readership, Dickens thus explicitly positioned *Household Words* to resist the influence of those he termed the 'Bastards of the Mountain, draggled fringe on the Red Cap, Panders to the basest passions of the lowest natures'[4] who had given Martineau and other liberal progressives so much cause for anxiety over the preceding decade. Complementing this cross-class intent, even the magazine's material design, as Lorna Huett has shown, was designed to further the Dickensian agenda in the ways in which its 'proximity to the format of the cheap journal, combined with the vision and nature of its conductor . . . to create a new sort of middle-class audience'.[5] Bringing the unrivalled power of the Dickens brand into play and with the clear potential to reach a huge national readership, his magazine thus offered the promise of advancing liberal ideals by addressing many of the concerns about the condition of British society and the state of the press that Martineau had voiced in her own work and had been seeking to address ever since her return from the United States.

Even before she accepted his invitation to contribute to the new magazine, however, Martineau had documented her complicated, conflicted response to the phenomenon that was Dickens. In 1849, providing an overview of the major literary figures of the period since Waterloo in her continuation of Knight's *History of the Peace*, she recognised Dickens's unique standing in the age by devoting more space to him than any other living author. Describing him as 'last and greatest among the novelists . . . the Boz who rose up in the midst of us like a jin with his magic glass' and marvelling at his unrivalled capacity to 'carry all readers far away from critical thoughts, and give to the author the whole range of influence, from the palace library to the penny book-club', Martineau sees that Dickens was able to influence precisely the wide range of class readership she herself had hoped to reach with the *Weekly Volume* project. As a result, and possessing a profound sympathy with 'the suffering and the frail' that has made him an 'idol' among them and with no rival for the 'social influence [he] has in his power', Dickens, Martineau suggests, is indeed 'a man of a genius which cannot but mark the time, and accelerate or retard its tendencies'. And yet, for all the sense of wonder her language captures, it also records a clear measure of unease about this phenomenon. For Dickens, she fears, dwells too much 'on the grosser indulgences and commoner beneficence which are pleasant enough in their own place, but which can never make a man and society so happy as he desires them to become', and she wishes that he 'had a sounder social philosophy, and that he could suggest a loftier moral to sufferers'. Moreover, in terming him simultaneously a 'jin' and an 'idol' and thereby harking back to the alarm she had expressed over the ways in which both the charismatic rhetoric of Daniel O'Connell and the 'goblin' power of Amos Kendall could shape the public sphere, she gives expression to her anxiety over the power such a figure may have to be a force of either progress or stasis, either to 'accelerate or retard' the time. Although she does conclude by acknowledging and evidently accepting the irresistible power of Dickensian humour, observation, pathos and 'geniality of spirit',[6] her account of Dickens in *History of the Peace*, then, is revealingly complex. Most significantly of all for my argument here, and consistent with the mixed assessment evident in her incidental epistolary comments on Dickens ever since his rise to fame in the mid-1830s, it suggests that the collaborative dynamic at *Household Words* between two authors so close and yet simultaneously so divergent in their understandings of what comprised liberal progress, so different in their fundamental natures as writers and authorial figures and so willing to flare up against any opposition to the positions they had taken, would inevitably turn out to be a highly combustible mix.

Previous scholarly considerations of Martineau's work in *Household Words* have focused primarily upon her accounts of industrial capitalism or her representation of Ireland as a colonial subject. Catherine Waters and Tamara Ketabgian, for example, have written on the 'process' articles and described insightfully the effects of factory labour upon the working classes and the cultural significance of the commodities they produced, while Sabine Clemm and Teja Pusapati have explored the complex colonial identity of an Ireland that was simultaneously part of the United Kingdom and yet remained distinctively othered from the nation as a whole.[7] While my argument here will also speak to Martineau's engagement with the Irish issue, the focus of this chapter is on the ways in which *Household Words* became the site on which Dickens and Martineau's longstanding and ultimately incompatible representations of the liberal project and the role of the press in its advance finally came into direct conflict. Their interactions as editor and contributor and the cataclysmic dispute that ended their relationship during December 1855 and January 1856 express, then, the fundamental differences this book has explored in their understandings of the relationship between individual agency and the governmental state, authorial identity and gender and the idea of a transatlantic progressive community in which women held essential leadership roles. The unfolding of the dispute itself is also profoundly revealing of the nature and workings of mid-century publishing networks in the Victorian press and, once again, demonstrates the suppressive power of the forces that gave Martineau good cause throughout her career to 'dread being silenced' and that led her to develop strategies of resistance that have been largely masked by the established critical narrative of her conflict with Dickens.

To make this case, the chapter is organised into three parts. Book-ending its argument are discussions of Martineau's first and final contributions to *Household Words*: 'The Sickness and Health of the People of Bleaburn', published in four parts in May–June 1850, and 'How to Get Paper', which appeared on 28 October 1854 and which I read in the context of the campaign to repeal the 'taxes on knowledge' and place in contrast with Dickens's 1850 article, 'A Paper-Mill'. Martineau's two articles, which have received almost no previous critical attention, both address American subjects. In different ways, each reveals that, throughout Martineau and Dickens's collaboration at *Household Words* and even as each of them made use of the other to advance their own projects, the tensions underlying their relationship and agendas for the press were continuously in play and speak to the larger divergences within transatlantic liberalism that they respectively represent. Between these bookends, the chapter establishes a new narrative for the actual dispute of 1855–6 and does so in four subsections: first, it summarises the actual details of the quarrel itself, before moving on to contextualising the episode within, second, the professional circumstances of the two subjects' careers and, third, the acutely stressful personal situations in which each of them found themselves during 1855. In the fourth and longest subsection, the chapter then explores in close detail the development of the quarrel itself during 1855 and its aftermath during the following year. Through these four sections, this account demonstrates that, while there may have indeed have been much intemperance and remarkably personal invective on both sides, the quarrel was much more than a localised spat and, in speaking to the larger fissures within the liberal project and its goals for the press that this book has explored, it offers us a complex and revealing insight into the nature of mid-Victorian liberalism and its relationship to the formation of the nineteenth-century press.

'A noble example in an attractive garb for the instruction of the people': 'The Sickness and Health of the People of Bleaburn'

'The Sickness and Health of the People of Bleaburn', a four-part narrative that appeared in *Household Words* between 25 May and 15 June 1850, retells the events of an epidemic that occurred in the Yorkshire village of Osmotherly in 1811 – a minor local episode that has remained justifiably obscured to history. Describing a working-class population 'sodden with beer, and almost without ideas and interests'[8] and the failure of the nominal authorities within the community to respond effectively to the epidemic, the narrative looks back to both such earlier texts as *The Scholars of Arneside* and *Deerbrook* and to the concerns Martineau had expressed over the conditions of the rural proletariat in the years since her move to Ambleside. Into this parlous situation arrives a young American, Mary Pickard, who has come to visit an aunt but quickly takes charge of matters, becomes the moral centre of the beleaguered village and, dubbed 'the Good Lady... a sort of talisman in the people's possession', is translated into near saintly status as she sustains the population through to the epidemic's conclusion.[9] Counterpointing Mary's heroic domestic efforts against the 'many disasters and no victories'[10] in the war dragging out on the Iberian Peninsula, and drawing extensively on Martineau's own efforts to improve sanitation in Ambleside through her lecture series and the building society she established, the story makes use of the venue *Household Words* provided to reach a large, cross-class audience and thus becomes an extension of the work she had done with Knight almost a decade earlier.

Like those *Penny Magazine* stories, 'The Sickness and Health' has little aesthetic power and the fact that it has gone almost entirely undiscussed by both scholars of Dickens and those writing on Martineau is hardly surprising. The single exception to the critical lacuna consists of a short article by Anne Lohrli that examines the story in relationship to Martineau's ideas about 'what constituted an invasion of privacy in biographical writing'.[11] In the context of the argument of this chapter, however, the story can also be seen as marking Martineau's effort to once again use a periodical venue in service of her own agenda. Here, the first of what would become almost fifty contributions to Dickens's magazine extends and fuses together those two aspects of her liberal ideology that we have seen recurring throughout her work: the role of women as agents of social improvement, and the importance of a transatlantic community of reform.

For, in selecting the story of Mary Pickard Ware and offering her as an exemplar of activist moral leadership, Martineau was bringing before her readers a real-life figure from the abolitionist Unitarian community in New England with which she had formed such close ties during her American visit. Mary Lovell Pickard, that is, went on after her heroism in Osmotherly to marry Henry Ware Jr, Unitarian pastor in Boston, president of the Cambridge Anti-Slavery Society and one of Martineau's closest friends in New England. Retelling her story in Dickens's phenomenally successful new magazine offered readers on both sides of the Atlantic an idealised account of the power of an American woman to address urgent social crises and, while less intentionally disruptive in its messaging than had been her 'Toussaint L'Ouverture' in *The Penny Magazine* back in 1838, this debut contribution to *Household Words* thus modelled the kind of women's activism Martineau had consistently championed since her visit to the United States.

Uncollected until Deborah Logan's editions of the correspondence and so only partially available to Lohrli, moreover, are two letters from Martineau to Mary's daughter Anne Bent Ware that complicate the history of the story even further.[12] Evidently unhappy about the private details of her recently deceased mother's life appearing in a work of fiction that also identified her by name, Ware had written to express her concern to Dickens, and he in turn passed the note along to Martineau. Her replies, which testify clearly to the cordial ties between her and Dickens at this point in their relationship, express bemusement at the complaint, voice a concern lest it give Dickens a bad impression of America (for, Martineau notes, 'I love your country and people more than he does') and attempt to mollify her correspondent by saying that he 'worships the name of your mother' and was 'never in his life so moved before by any narrative'. Ultimately, however, Martineau insists both that she had intentionally written with a transatlantic audience in mind – 'as I told Mrs Follen and Mrs Chapman while writing it, we looked forward with great pleasure to the satisfaction your mother's children would have in seeing her so honoured. We kept her real name in her honour'[13] – and also that, for all her desire to respect privacy, 'It is the revelation of <u>the woman</u> in that scene of her life that we consider of such high social value, and a noble common social property.'[14] Though, as 'Literary Lionism' and her description of Dickens himself in *History of the Peace* clearly demonstrated, Martineau was uneasy about authorial celebrity and while she does acknowledge Anne Ware's concern over her mother's privacy, ultimately she insists that it was legitimate, and even incumbent upon her to make public use of this exemplar to offer a model of women's possibility. Pickard, Martineau implies, must be held up as a positive model of the abolitionist tradition of women's activism, a model countering someone like Caroline Gilman, whom Martineau had earlier covertly called out for her failings as an accommodationist but whom she would name explicitly in the *Autobiography* she would begin in 1855 and complete during the time of her quarrel with Dickens.

As Lohrli notes, moreover, the story's subsequent history is revealing. On the one hand, while Martineau reprinted almost half her contributions to *Household Words*, this was not among those she chose to reissue.[15] On the other, three years after it had appeared Henry Ware's brother-in-law published a memoir of Mary Lovell Pickard Ware, and, though his Introduction spoke to the family's concern over the making public of 'facts and thoughts so private and sacred', he yielded to the greater good and an unwillingness that 'the knowledge of such examples should be withheld from the many who crave it, and whom it would stimulate and bless'.[16] That Martineau had perhaps prompted the creation of a spiritual biography that treated a subject of whom she approved became further evident when her story was itself reissued in book form by the same Boston publishers as had published the Ware memoir. Acknowledging its origin in *Household Words* and lamenting the 'questionable propriety' of its revelations, they nevertheless seconded Martineau's representation of 'a noble example in an attractive garb for the instruction of the people'.[17] As had been the case with Toussaint L'Ouverture fifteen years before, Martineau had found an indirect mechanism that allowed her to recirculate her activist message back into the American reading public and again demonstrated her willingness to develop strategies in the press that would allow her to overcome resistance to achieving her goals. Though its fame was short-lived and it has remained largely invisible ever since, in the early 1850s, then, Martineau's rendering of Mary Ware's heroism connected readers across the Atlantic and, a decade and a half after her return from America, once again modelled the reciprocal connectedness of liberal progressives in the Old World and the New.

Back in the office of *Household Words* on Wellington Street, while Dickens evidently sided with his author over Anne Ware's complaint, his own reservations about the story were apparent in the fact that he had received Martineau's manuscript on 26 March 1850, come to the opinion within three days that it was 'heavy', and, though he immediately passed it on to his foreman printer,[18] did not find a place for it in the magazine until almost three months had passed. Moreover, though he may have had Martineau convey to Anne Ware that he 'worships the name of your mother' and was 'never in his life so moved before by any narrative', the sentimentalising terms of that praise speak to his habitual privileging forms of female agency that differ fundamentally from Martineau's conceptions and that certainly do not share her commitment to transatlantic activism in the cause of progressive social change.[19] While this first collaboration at *Household Words* has largely eluded critical attention, it thus offers a telling preview of the differences between Martineau and Dickens that, for all that they shared in common, would, less than five years later, emerge so cataclysmically in their attacks upon one another between December and January of 1855 and 1856.

'Weakness in a sick lady': The Factory Dispute

When that dispute broke out, the two combatants brought to bear upon one another a highly personalised rhetoric that has been often referenced in critical discussions of the quarrel and has come to take an important position within the received critical narrative of its meaning. Both the immediate rhetoric and the later scholarly narrative, however, obscure the dispute's origin in more fundamental ideological differences. Martineau herself made this evident when she published *The Factory Controversy* shortly before Christmas 1855 and in Manchester under the imprint of the National Association of Factory Occupiers as she positioned it from the outset within a larger conversation. For, although she indicates that her focus is upon a series of essays Henry Morley had written for *Household Words* on industrial safety and the need for parliamentary legislation to ensure appropriate fencing around factory machinery, she also presents this particular issue as part of an interwoven debate about the function of the state in regulating economic activity and the role of the press in shaping that discussion. For her, that is, factory safety should be seen as germane to determining 'the all-important point of the true sphere and proper duties of government'.[20] With these words, she connects her argument to the form of liberal progressivism most clearly identified with the *Westminster Review*, a journal in which she had begun to publish again in 1852, whose mortgage she had recently assumed to rescue it from chronic financial difficulty and whose editor was to play a crucial role in the dispute with Dickens.[21] For her phrasing explicitly references an article of the same title in the October 1854 issue, and she aligns herself with the journal's position on the limitations of the role of the state. As the *Westminster* article had argued:

> it may be inferred, that the limitation of the action of government, that is, of the application of force, at the point indicated, is truly suited to the nature of men, and is that at which enlightened experience will finally arrest that continual repression of governmental actions which distinctively marks, notwithstanding exceptions, the mass of our great modern movements.[22]

Martineau certainly was a manufacturer's daughter and, as Chapter 5 showed, she both took pride in describing herself as such and used this identity as an important part of her positioning in the public sphere.[23] Throughout the dispute with Dickens, moreover, her contention was that factory owners, motivated by their own self-interest to create efficient working conditions, were more effective than a state bureaucracy in enforcing industrial safety. Her resistance to the state, then, can be more fully understood not simply as the inhumane expression of Utilitarian values that Fielding and Smith suggest in their reading of the dispute with Dickens but, rather, should be seen as part of British liberalism's overarching emphasis upon individual agency and, in the words of the *Westminster* article, its sense that 'the nation is a mere convenient abstraction which affects nothing of the moral position, the duties, or the rights of the man'.[24]

On Dickens's part, the established critical narrative that has looked back to *Hard Times* to account for the terms of the dispute has drawn attention away from the novel he was actually writing when it occurred – *Little Dorrit*, which he began serialising on

1 December 1855, just two weeks before Martineau published *The Factory Controversy*. If we see the dispute in relation to *Little Dorrit*, however, the depth of difference between his and Martineau's visions of the role of the state and their hopes for liberal progress becomes evident. Building on Elaine Hadley's exploration of agency and accountability in texts from the 1850s, Sukanya Banerjee and Daniel Stout have explored a variety of ways in which, as Stout has said, the novel calls into question 'the belief that the world is susceptible to managed adjustment' as part of a broader reassessment of the viability of the liberal model in the wake of Crimea and the increasingly evident complexities of empire that would so soon manifest themselves in the Sepoy Mutiny.[25] That Dickens was increasingly uncertain over the possibility of such management is tellingly evident in a letter to Macready written just two months before *Little Dorrit*'s first number appeared. For, as he wrote despairingly to his old friend on 4 October, 'I do reluctantly believe that the English people are, habitually, consenting parties to the miserable imbecility into which we have fallen, *and never will help themselves out of it*'.[26] Almost two years later, in *Little Dorrit*'s final number, 'the best and brightest' of those Barnacles who maintain this imbecility through their unyielding control of the Circumlocution Office offers a more equable expression of Dickens's own sentiment: 'We must have humbug, we all like humbug, we couldn't get on without humbug. A little humbug, and a groove, and everything goes on admirably, if you leave it alone.'[27] Previewing the concluding sentence of the novel and its image of the London street into which Arthur and Amy Clennam are absorbed by the crowd of 'the arrogant and the forward and the vain [that] fretted, and chafed, and made their usual uproar',[28] Ferdinand Barnacle thus speaks to a Dickensian scepticism over the very possibility of liberal progress that underlies the 1855–6 quarrel with Martineau and that would, as Chapter 7 will explore, lead them to their final, even more deeply incompatible visons of the arc of historical narrative.

These larger differences, however, were simply overwhelmed for contemporary readers and for the *Household Words* team by the language into which Martineau's pamphlet slides. For she calls out both Dickens himself and their mutual friend Leonard Horner, the Chief Factory Inspector, and charges that they have 'taken up a ground which they do not pretend to establish on any principle; and they hold it in an objectionable temper, and by indefensible means'.[29] In thus targeting by name both the editor of a journal to which she had contributed extensively in its first five years and a member of the state bureaucracy with whose family she had enjoyed a long friendship,[30] she may have demonstrated her willingness to engage fully in the rough-and-tumble of Victorian journalism but she also opened up her text to be seen as a primarily personalised, vituperative attack. When she returns to address Dickens's role in the *Household Words* articles later in the pamphlet, she amply fulfils that promise (Fig. 6.1). For she offers a scathing indictment of her opponents, singles out Dickens's intellectual competence with a note of particular scorn – 'he should not meddle with affairs where rationality of judgment is required' – and then proceeds contemptuously to dismiss him as a mere 'humanity-monger'.[31] Building on the reservations she had expressed in *History of the Peace* and responding to the conductorial voice Dickens had claimed for himself in *Household Words*, she moves on to question his entire authority to speak into the public conversation on matters of social policy and so challenges the fundamental manifesto of his magazine:

> Mr Dickens himself changed the conditions of his responsibilities . . . when he set up 'Household Words' as an avowed agency of popular instruction and social reform. From that time, it was not only the right but the duty of good citizens to require from him some soundness of principle and some depth of knowledge in political philosophy.[32]

Since Dickens had asserted a role as public educator that she regards him as being fundamentally incompetent to perform, that is, she sees it as her social responsibility to critique him unreservedly. And, repeatedly, what she attacks both Horner and Dickens for are the 'representations' of the issue that, for her, reveal the pernicious nature and effects of their writing, especially, in Dickens's case, for publications aimed at the mass market:

> The mingled levity and fustian of the style of the specimens we have quoted will neutralise their mischief to educated people; but the responsibility of presenting such pictures, and offering such sentiment, to a half-educated order of readers, is such as few writers would like to be burdened with.[33]

Throughout his life Dickens was hardly noted for equanimity when the truthfulness of his writing was questioned, and, given that they had known each other for almost twenty years, that Martineau had contributed so extensively to *Household Words* in its first years and that this attack was so highly personalised, the pamphlet had to cent enterprise, in comparison with that which Mr. Dickens has undertaken on behalf of meddling and mischievous legislation like that of the fencing clauses of the Factory Acts. If we had room, and if our object was to convict the humanity-monger in "Household Words," of all his acts of unfairness and untruth, we should go into the case of the boy in Mr. Cheetham's factory, who, in defiance of remonstrance, thrust himself into the extremity of danger, and was killed on the instant; and of the overlooker at Bury, George Hoyle, aged 50, of whom his comrades said at the inquest, "It was entirely his own fault; the shaft was quite out of the way of everybody, and unless a person wilfully did something that he ought not to do, he could not be injured by that shaft." Again. "He was very venturesome; the shaft is quite entirely out of the way of every person, and could not do any harm, unless a person went wilfully into danger."—*Report of Association, page 21.* The people in the mill shouted to him to come down, and had done so often before; and when he was killed, the exclamation was, "It is just what I happened of." Such cases as these, set off with ironical descriptions of split brain, puddles of blood, crushed bones, and torn flesh, are exhibited as spectacles for which the masters are answerable, and which they obstinately prefer to an expenditure of a few shillings to make all safe. If Mr. Dickens really believes in such a state of things as he describes, he should not meddle with affairs in which rationality of judgment is required; and if he can be satisfied to represent the great class of manufacturers—unsurpassed for intelligence, public spirit, and beneficence—as the monsters he describes, without seeking knowledge of their actual state of mind and course of life, we do not see how he can complain of being himself classed with the pseudo-philanthropists whom he delights to ridicule. He has exposed philo-criminal, and philo-heathen cant; but his own philo-

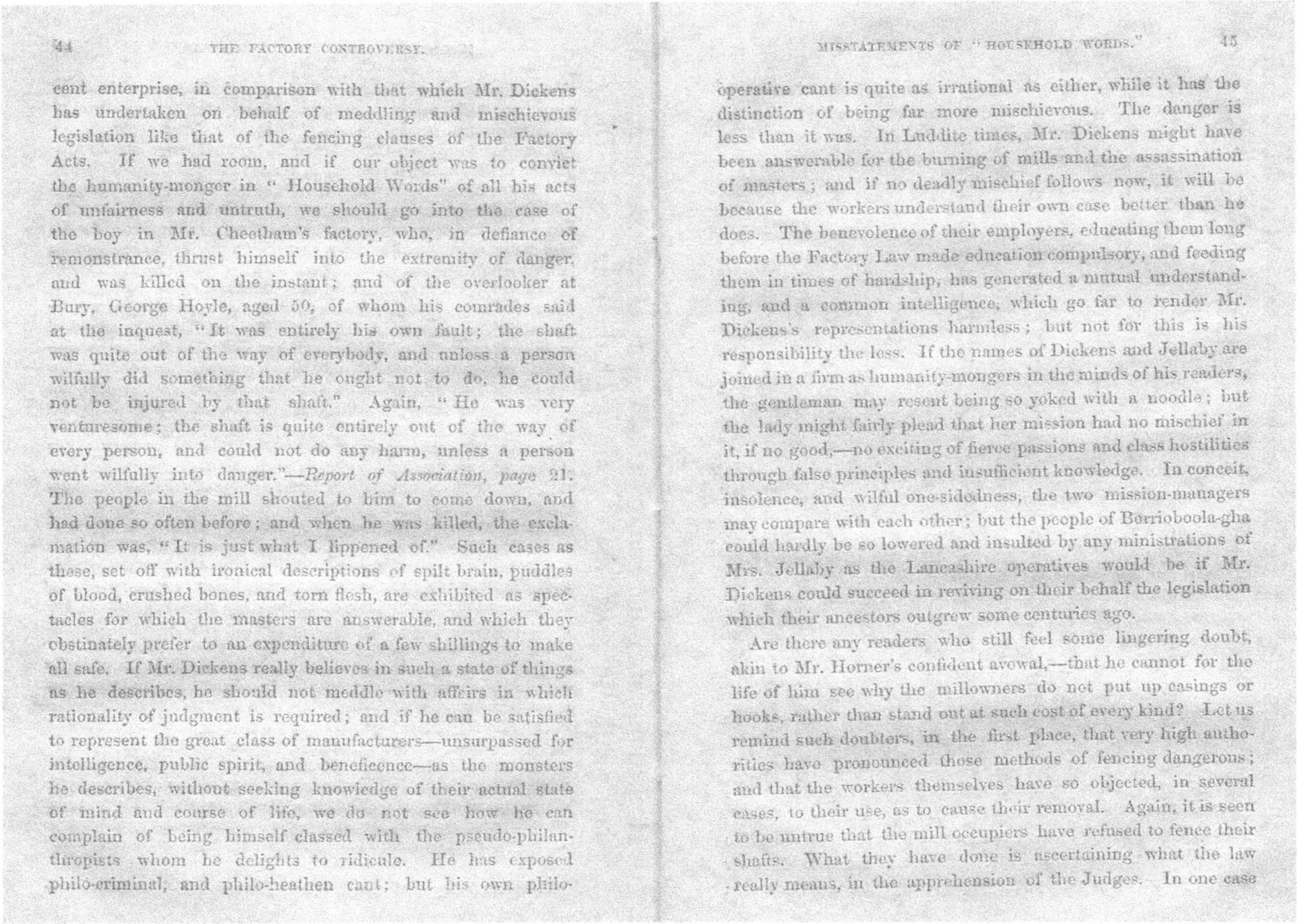

operative cant is quite as irrational as either, while it has the distinction of being far more mischievous. The danger is less than it was. In Luddite times, Mr. Dickens might have been answerable for the burning of mills and the assassination of masters; and if no deadly mischief follows now, it will be because the workers understand their own case better than he does. The benevolence of their employers, educating them long before the Factory law made education compulsory, and feeding them in times of hand-ship, has generated a mutual understanding, and a common intelligence, which go far to render Mr. Dickens's representations harmless; but not for this is his responsibility the less. If the names of Dickens and Jellaby are joined in a firm as humanity-mongers in the minds of his readers, the gentleman may resent being so yoked with a noodle; but the lady might fairly plead that her mission had no mischief in it, if no good,—no exciting of fierce passions and class hostilities through false principles and insufficient knowledge. In conceit, insolence, and wilful one-sidedness, the two mission-managers may compare with each other; but the people of Borrioboola-gha could hardly be so lowered and insulted by any ministrations of Mrs. Jellaby as the Lancashire operatives would be if Mr. Dickens could succeed in reviving on their behalf the legislation which their ancestors outgrew some centuries ago.

Are there any readers who still feel some lingering doubt, akin to Mr. Horner's confident avowal,—that he cannot for the life of him see why the millowners do not put up casings or hooks, rather than stand out at such cost of every kind? Let us remind such doubters, in the first place, that very high authorities have pronounced those methods of fencing dangerous; and that the workers themselves have so objected, in several cases, to their use, as to cause their removal. Again, it is seen to be untrue that the mill occupiers have refused to fence their shafts. What they have done is ascertaining what the law really means, in the apprehension of the Judges. In one case

Figure 6.1 Extract from *The Factory Controversy*. Hagley Museum and Library.

have been both unexpected and galling. Even so, the public response that he completed from a draft Morley developed managed to be still more hostile and even more vindictive than Martineau's initial assault. Published on 19 January 1856, 'Our Wicked Mis-Statements' is unique in its long and sustained assault upon the credibility of a *Household Words* contributor. Despite beginning by expressing reluctance to expose 'weakness in a sick lady whom we esteem',[34] Dickens goes on to build an unrelenting critique of both the substance and nature of her arguments, attacking her statistical data and her allies in the National Association of Factory Occupiers and using up almost a quarter of the entire issue to make his case. He then closes the essay by claiming his and Morley's own propriety and suggesting something very different about Martineau's virtue:

> We have done. We hope we have not been induced to exceed the bounds of temperate and moderate remonstrance, or to prostitute our part in Literature to Old Bailey pleading and passionate scolding. We thoroughly forgive Miss Martineau for having strayed into such unworthy paths under the guidance of her anonymous friend, and we blot her pamphlet out of our remembrance.[35]

More important even than this conclusion's effective termination of their relationship was the way in which the language of Dickens's reply thus worked to condemn all Martineau's hard-won authorial standing. For, not content with brutally labelling her as a fallen woman in need of guidance – a mere streetwalker of journalism – Dickens asserts his intent to exert an ultimate editorial authority, to 'blot' her into oblivion, to write her out of existence. For all the mercurial temper and readiness to take offence that led Dickens into a number of quarrels over the course of his life, there is nothing like this anywhere else in *Household Words*, or indeed in his journalism as a whole, no parallel attack upon another writer or a contributor. Clearly, both parties had lost sight of the larger underlying issues as they turned a wider cultural conversation into a highly personalised assault upon one another. How, then, did matters come to such a pass and conclude in this torrent of mutual recrimination? By turning, next, to the evolution of both Dickens and Martineau's work in the press in the early 1850s and then to the specifics of their life circumstances we can uncover not only what led them into this outburst of hostility but also understand more deeply how the local quarrel speaks back into the larger conversation about liberalism and the press and, ultimately, makes a substantial and previously unrecognised contribution to that conversation.

'A "gentleman of the press"': Martineau and the *Daily News*

While Dickens's invitation to contribute to *Household Words* offered a first resolution to the conundrum Martineau had faced throughout the 1840s in seeking a venue that would allow her to advocate for liberal causes, her career would, once again, soon be reshaped by the emergence of a completely different opportunity. In April 1852, she unexpectedly received an invitation from Frederick Knight Hunt to contribute leaders to the *Daily News* and, with it, the chance to develop a professional and editorial relationship quite unlike that she had with Dickens. She immediately recognised the potential for this to be a turning point, writing in her *Autobiography* just three years later how she 'saw that this might be an opening to greater usefulness than was likely to be equalled by anything else that I could undertake'.[36] Wrapping up her immediate commitments for Dickens, she seized the occasion and began to write for Hunt, relishing the chance to appear in the authoritative role of leader writer for the most progressive national daily and finally being able to achieve the goal of getting 'access to some widely read London newspaper' that she had first expressed back in 1849.[37]

Almost immediately, however, there was a hitch: the leader was a genre with which she had no prior experience, and, for all her wide-ranging experience with other journalistic forms, it presented her with new challenges. Clearly recognising that things were not going smoothly, just six weeks after her first piece had appeared, she wrote to Hunt:

> We are not getting on very well, – are we? My papers are not what you want: & yet, we both know that they might be, if I could have a lesson from you, & learn something of what your paper was before I saw it, – which I never did till I was connected with it.[38]

These early difficulties, however, became an opportunity for their relationship to develop, as Hunt responded actively to his new writer's appeal. Late that July, he travelled to visit her in Scotland and, as Martineau wrote in the *Autobiography*, 'for two half days he poured out so rich a stream of conversation that my niece could not stand the excitement'.[39] Evidently treating her as an intellectual equal and making this exceptional effort to tutor her in the requirements of the new genre, Hunt won her loyalty and initiated a close friendship that was broken only by his untimely death just two years later. Replicating her experience with her first editor back in the late 1820s and early 1830s, W. J. Fox at the *Monthly Repository*, he thus provided

Martineau with the kind of mentoring and intellectual friendship that she deeply valued, felt was invaluable for her professional growth and that she did not find in her relationship with Dickens.

Hunt's care with his new author was immediately and richly rewarded. Following his visit to Edinburgh, she travelled across the Irish Sea and began what would become a series of twenty-seven 'Letters from Ireland', published between August and mid-October 1852. Wide-ranging in their subjects and forcefully arguing that Britain should apply the principles of political economy in its Irish policy so as to stimulate growth and social progress, this series of leaders established Martineau in the daily press as what George Landow has termed a wisdom writer.[40] With its focus upon rational analysis and argument and using logos-driven language to persuade her readers, this role also evidences what Linda Peterson has noted as a larger pattern in Martineau's work of eschewing the more emotive role of the Victorian sage in an effort 'to gain access to traditional male domains and to prove that women can master those domains, both in style and content'.[41] As Teja Pusapati has shown, moreover, the series not only allowed Martineau to demonstrate her abilities as a foreign correspondent, a genre traditionally the preserve of male writers, but also reveals a fundamentally supportive view of British rule and of England 'as a well-meaning administration, whose few and rare errors are unintended and quickly remediable'.[42] Martineau's growing confidence in the ability of the state to enact liberal progress, even as she continued to emphasise the primacy of individual agency, becomes in the 1850s an increasing point of divergence with Dickens and, as Chapter 7 will show, leads towards their last, fundamentally incompatible visions of historical progress.

By its conclusion, 'Letters from Ireland' had established Martineau's position in a daily paper at the centre of British political life, given her a role at the *Daily News* that she would sustain for the next fourteen years and over 1,600 articles and allowed her to develop an authoritative voice on matters of social policy that was far more substantive than the part she had been asked to play at *Household Words*. Little wonder, then, that she wrote to Hunt to express her delight the following April:

> It is just a year now since you made me a 'gentleman of the Press' – or Maid-of-all-work to D. News. I have enjoyed it very much, – the finding utterance for so much that was on my mind: &, through your kindness & courtesy, it has been very easy. I have only one anxiety, – the being so entirely alone, – so far off, – that I can never be sure of being right, & doing what is best.[43]

Even here, however, as she acknowledges her debt and gratitude to Hunt as the editor who had guided her transition into daily journalism and become her friend, she gives voice to the ambivalence of her position as a professional woman author – gentleman of the press or maid-of-all-work? – and expresses the vulnerability both created by that position and reinforced by the fact that she worked primarily from her home in the Lake District, removed from the networks of literary and journalistic London. As will become clear in the third section of this chapter, that isolation, intensified by what she believed to be the terminal illness that reshaped her life in early 1855, would later come to play a significant role during the months leading up to her dispute with Dickens.

'Having a jolly time of it here': Dickens at *Household Words*

If Martineau's work for the press was significantly shaped by the constraints of geographical isolation from the political and publishing networks of London, Dickens in the early 1850s became, first, immersed in those networks and then, as the personal crisis that would lead eventually to his separation from his wife Catherine deepened, increasingly distanced himself from the capital. In the magazine's first years, however, and during the period when Martineau was most actively contributing to *Household Words*, Dickens was fully present in its daily operations as he constructed the homosocial team that constituted the world of the office in Wellington Street. But having built that team rapidly in response to *Household Words*'s immediate and sustained success, he then became increasingly dependent upon it. Specifically, during his own extended absences from London he ceded more and more authority to Wills to sustain the operations, and Wills in turn came to place ever greater reliance upon Morley. Writing to Miss Coutts in March 1855, for example, Dickens referred to his initial planning of the project that would become *Little Dorrit* and admitted the effects this was having upon his management of the journal: 'it makes me submit myself to Mr Wills whenever he can lay hold of me – that is to say, a little irregularly'.[44] Later that year, he would acknowledge that Wills had become his 'other self in Household Words',[45] and both his reliance upon and gratitude to the faithful 'Sub' are evident in his initially resisting the idea of Wills taking any other employment and then in giving way and facilitating his appointment as Miss Coutts's secretary at the handsome salary of £200 a year.[46]

Dickens's increased reliance upon Wills to keep the magazine going evidently had a knock-on effect as Wills, in turn, came to depend increasingly upon Morley, who thus became an ever more valued member of the editorial team. First writing for the magazine within months of its appearing, Morley quickly became a major contributor, was appointed to a staff position within a year and rapidly evolved into a key member of the inner circle. Moreover, as he became more important to the magazine, so he and Wills grew closer, and their correspondence offers considerable insight both into the younger man's increasing value to the editorial team as well as the growing friendship between the two. Wills's letters thus move from early cordial but formal transactions of business matters to a friendly correspondence that testifies to the intimacy of the circle of male friends and colleagues who ran the magazine. In August 1853, for instance, he wrote from Dickens's holiday home in Boulogne and describes the group invited to celebrate *Bleak House*'s final number:

> My Dear Morley,
> We are having a jolly time of it here, but our party is gradually dropping off. On Monday the dinner to emphasize the conclusion of Bleak House brought Forster, B & E [Bradbury and Evans] and Lemon but one by one they have left us. Last night Dickens read us his last number and a more affecting scene I never witnessed in real life.[47]

As Dickens's attention went elsewhere, then, the space created at *Household Words* was, by the mid-fifties, being filled by Wills, with Morley an ever more central member of the group, and these two were, in turn, becoming ever closer partners. Dickens's reliance upon his male friends and colleagues, together with his creation of an alternate home in the bachelor domestic space of the *Household Words* office, suggests powerfully the ways in which the lines between the professional and the personal blurred, especially as he grew increasingly uncertain about the direction of his life and ever more dissatisfied with his wife and family. When Martineau published *The Factory Controversy* as a direct response to Morley's series of essays on industrial safety, then, the pamphlet would become not simply an assault upon *Household Words* itself but an attack upon the close-knit team of male friends and colleagues who ran the magazine and to whose defense Dickens would leap.[48]

Crises

If these differences in the nature of both Dickens and Martineau's evolving understandings of the prospects for British liberalism and the directions of their individual work in the press contained the potential seeds of a larger divergence, additional material for the later conflagration developed in the courses each of their lives took during 1854. Dickens, who was clearly entering into a prolonged emotional crisis, thus described his state of mind to John Forster late that September:

> *Restlessness*, you will say. Whatever it is, it is always driving me, and I cannot help it. I have rested nine or ten weeks, and sometimes feel as if it had been a year – though I had the strangest nervous miseries before I stopped. If I couldn't walk fast and far, I should just explode and perish.[49]

As his biographers commonly note,[50] Dickens's response to this emotional disarray was to throw himself into what was, even by his standards, an extraordinarily frenetic range of activities. In 1854 and 1855 he found himself, for example, working with Angela Burdett Coutts on Urania Cottage, fighting to reform the Royal Literary Fund, staging *The Lighthouse*, beginning to experiment with public readings, seeking appropriate employment for his eldest son, Charley, completing *Hard Times*, negotiating to buy what would become his last home at Gad's Hill Place, and, finally, getting *Little Dorrit* under way. In addition, as was the case throughout his life, as the letter to Forster suggests and in a way that would become crucial to the quarrel with Martineau, Dickens's habitual response to an emotional crisis was to travel. In both 1854 and 1855, he moved his entire family out of England for extended periods. Much of the time between June and October 1854 was spent in Boulogne, while 1855 saw him take the family first to Folkestone from July through October, and then on to Paris, where they would stay until the end of April 1856. Although the record of his correspondence with Wills testifies to the level of his engagement with *Household Words*, these lengthy absences from England and his diminished presence in the office were to become a critical factor in the gestation of the dispute with Martineau.

For Martineau herself, despite the new level of authority that writing for the *Daily News* had conferred, a continuing sense of vulnerability is also evident at this period of her life. In particular, a series of four events that occurred at the end of 1854 and early in 1855 are germane to the breakdown in her relationship with Dickens. First, in the early fall of 1854 she wrote to Fanny Wedgwood about the latest development in the rupture that would irrevocably destroy the relationship between her and her brother James. Inseparable companions in childhood and youth, the two siblings had grown apart over the years. Their separation focused specifically around James's leadership of a new strain of Unitarianism that broke away from an early form that had its origins in the thought of Joseph Priestley. While Harriet remained, at least intellectually, faithful to the Priestleyan tradition, James fostered in Britain a form of the denomination that took its inspiration from the American Unitarian William Ellery Channing, and to which, incidentally, Dickens had adhered during his publicly Unitarian phase in the early 1840s. The division between brother and sister became public when James wrote an intensely critical review of Harriet's co-authored 1851 book, *Letters on the Laws of Man's Nature and Development*, a text widely taken to express her repudiation of conventional Christian belief. Following this definitive blow to their relationship, in 1854 James and an ally offered financial assistance to John Chapman and his ailing *Westminster Review*, a proposal Harriet thwarted when she herself took up the mortgage.[51] As she wrote to Fanny Wedgwood in September, she had thereby ensured that her rivals 'lost their scheme on the Review, and all future access to it'.[52] Second – and at the time apparently least significant – in November 1854 and after again soliciting a contribution from Martineau for the year's special Christmas issue, Dickens and Wills rejected her 'Father D'Estelan's Christmas Morning', a short story that had a self-sacrificing heroic Jesuit priest as its protagonist. This rejection, as would later become apparent, rankled considerably and played a major part in the dispute. Third, and a far deeper source of grief, Frederick Knight Hunt fell unexpectedly ill with typhus and, only forty years old, died suddenly that same November. Building upon the foundation established at the outset of their relationship, Hunt had become the closest and most influential of the several editors with whom she had worked, and, as she wrote to a friend, she was 'almost heart-broken' at his loss.[53] As the editor of the newspaper Dickens had founded and a fellow contributor to *Household Words*, Hunt had, of course, also been a vital node in the network of ties that connected Martineau and Dickens in the close-knit world of mid-century journalism – indeed, Wills was that friend who had written to her with the details of his death and to whom she had replied so poignantly – and, had he lived, the events of the following year would surely have gone somewhat differently. Finally, after several months of poor health, Martineau herself fell gravely ill and, in January 1855, her doctors told her – erroneously – that she had terminal heart disease. Anticipating that she had little time remaining, she suspended most of her professional commitments and dedicated what she assumed would be her final months to completing the *Autobiography* that she intended to appear after her apparently imminent death.

'Popular instruction and social reform': the Crisis of 1855

If this concatenation of personal circumstances created two subjects whose individual stresses contained abundant potential to activate their underlying ideological differences, Martineau's decision to target Dickens personally in *The Factory Controversy* was even more combustible than she knew, since the factory safety issue evidently mattered to him in ways that could not have been visible to her. In writing the pamphlet she singled out for discussion the four articles Morley contributed to *Household Words* between 14 April and 28 July 1855, all of which appeared in the journal's eleventh volume. She appears, as we shall see below, not to have been reading the magazine regularly and so to have been unaware that Dickens had already run two pieces by Morley on industrial safety back in Volume IX. One, 'Preventible Accidents', came out on 18 March 1854; the other, 'Ground in the Mill', appeared the following month, just three weeks after *Hard Times* had begun its serialisation. She also left out of consideration Morley's final essay in the series, 'Two Shillings Per Horse-Power', which appeared on 8 September 1855.[54] Moreover, if she thus apparently did not have a complete sense of the extent of *Household Words*'s treatment of the topic, she certainly could not have had any way of appreciating just how deeply Dickens merged an evidently sincere concern for the issue itself with a keen, proprietary awareness of the opportunity it provided for *Household Words* to give itself an edge in the marketplace. As he wrote to Wills in September 1854:

> – Reverting to H. W. I observed a paragraph, either in the Examiner or the Illustrated London News the other day, to the effect that there had been 'a large and influential meeting at Manchester' with a view to the prevention of Boiler explosions, and their consequent injuries to workpeople. Now, as we opened that subject, plainly and boldly, we

ought to pursue it: commending the Manufacturers for any endeavour in that wise that deserves commendation, and enforcing the principle of the workpeople being always protected from accident, by every human precaution. By losing or delaying so apposite an occasion for pursuing a subject we have opened, we lose a chance and waste our power.[55]

That Dickens should have expressed a desire not to be outflanked even by the *Examiner*, which was still being edited by his closest friend, John Forster, is revealing. For, as he sought to achieve an always elusive degree of financial security and was, throughout his career, mindful to find ways to maximise the income his work produced,[56] it suggests just how unsentimental he could be when it came to protecting his journal from competition. That he continued to be personally engaged with the safety issue itself is evident from a letter in June 1855 to David Roberts, the painter and another friend of long standing. There, he references a correspondence with one of the members of The National Association of Factory Occupiers (NAFO), 'angrily begun on his side, and temperately continued on mine'.[57] Unknown to Martineau, then, Dickens had developed a substantial engagement with the industrial safety issue and had a personal stake in it. Most significantly of all, he clearly saw *Household Words*'s championing it as a significant element in the journal's brand identity and as a way in which he could extend its 'power' and claim precisely the authority that she would call into question in *The Factory Controversy*.

Well into 1855, however, Martineau and Dickens were still on the good personal terms that had characterised their relationship since they met in the late 1830s, and in the spring of that year they corresponded again. In March 1855, that is, Dickens found himself writing to both Martineau and Angela Burdett Coutts about the latter's project to promote the teaching of domestic subjects at Whitelands College. In turn, two letters from Martineau to Dickens survive from this month, and neither he nor she says anything that would suggest the possibility of the appalling public outbursts against one another that would come later in the year. On 8 March, Martineau thus wrote from the Lake District using her own illustrated stationery as both the form and opening matter of her letter (Fig. 6.2):

> Dear Mr Dickens
>   I write on this paper that you may see where I sit in the sun, in these bright afternoons; – viz, in an easy chair before the porch; which porch is all grown over now with mixed evergreens & roses & honeysuckle, & really quite green already. You may understand the ladies on the terrace

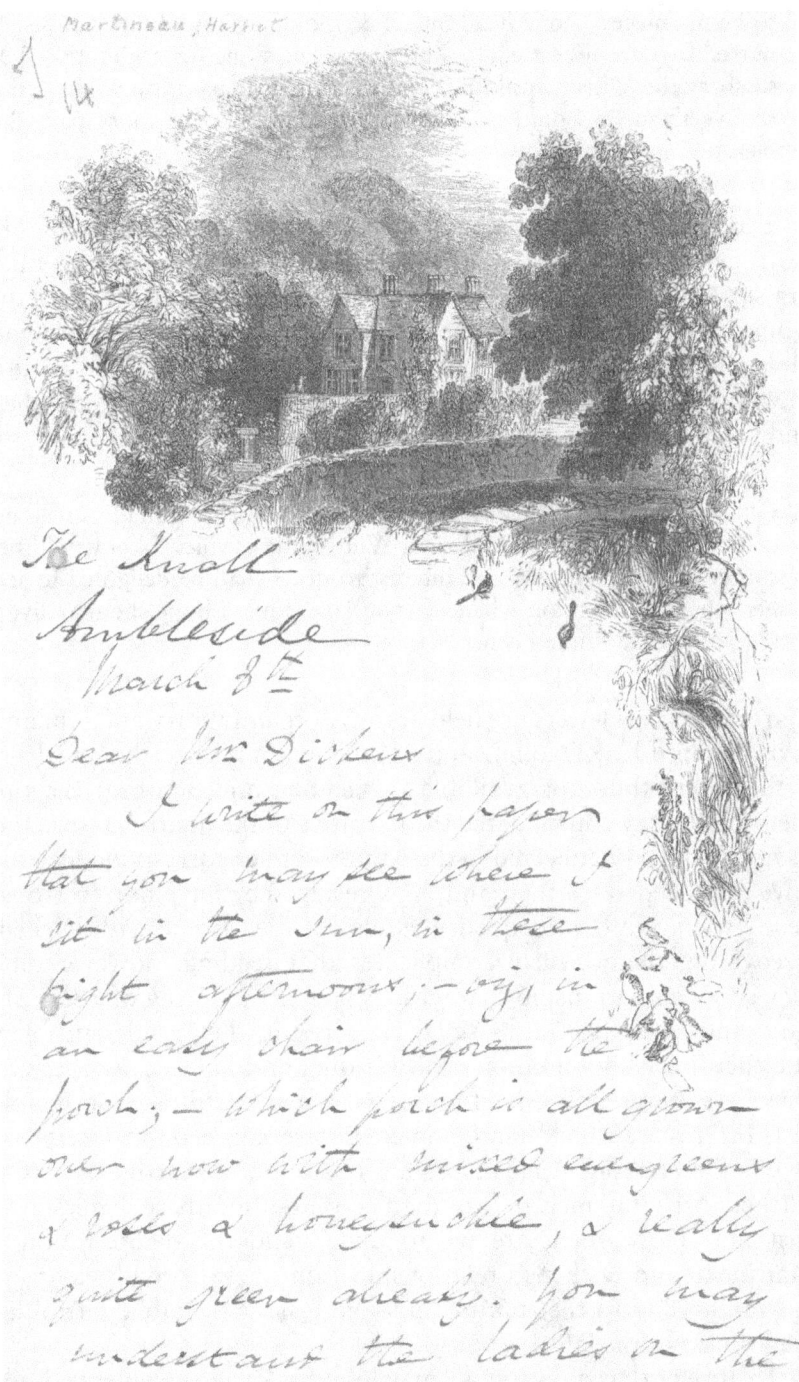

Figure 6.2 Harriet Martineau to Charles Dickens, 8 March 1855. The Morgan Library & Museum: MA 1352.653. Purchased with the assistance of the Fellows, 1951.

to be my nieces, – one head nurse, & the other housekeeper & second nurse. Two are necessary, as I am never left alone for a minute. – I am so sorry the Willses could not come to my little paradise while I could receive them. It would be no pleasure to them, – or more pain than pleasure, – to come now.[58]

Portraying even in her illness a bucolic feminine rural idyll, this reads as a letter to a trusted friend, one to whom she can go on to praise Miss Coutts's work by saying that 'I have always believed that <u>women</u> must do, or see done, what is wanted.'[59] While Dickens's replies to Martineau have not survived, his letters to Miss Coutts, to whom he wrote on 8 March, show that he was their intermediary and reveal his own regard for an ailing friend:

Only to day, I wrote again to Miss Martineau, explaining, as well as I could, the pains you had taken at Whitelands – which I know will be a source of great comfort and interest to her. I shall be delighted to send her what you mention whenever you give it me. I hope she may live to receive that additional cheer.[60]

Martineau's two letters are held at the Morgan Library and remained invisible until K. K. Collins and Alan Cohn published them in 1982. If they were thus not available to Fielding and Smith at the time their 1970 essay consolidated the narrative of the quarrel, so too they have remained uncollected in the editions of her correspondence that have appeared since then and, as a result, they have not previously been brought into subsequent readings of the dispute with Dickens. Recovering them clearly complicates that reading, however, since they show a relationship that was, as late as the spring of 1855, still close and cordial on both sides. As a result, they render problematic the direct line of connection Fielding and Smith draw between Dickens's representations of industrial life and Utilitarian principles in *Hard Times*, which had completed its serialisation in *Household Words* the previous August, and his assault upon Martineau in 'Our Wicked Mis-Statements' less than a year after these letters were written.[61] How, then, are we to understand the deterioration of Martineau and Dickens's relationship from these cordial exchanges in March 1855 to the rupture amid explosions of public vitriol less than nine months later?

To answer that question we may look back to the elements of ideological difference between Dickens and Martineau and the stresses within their respective life situations discussed above, and consider what all these together reveal about the nature of the world of letters of the time: for Dickens, the factory safety issue, his sense of its role in the branding of *Household Words* and his commitment to his team of colleagues all come into play. For Martineau, evident irritation at being excluded from the 1854 Christmas issue of the magazine is compounded by three factors: first, her being made aware of Morley's factory safety essays; second, Wills's insistence upon the ideological basis for rejecting her Christmas story; and third, John Chapman's refusal to publish her response to Morley in the pages of the *Westminster Review*. Given that this was also a time during which neither she nor Dickens was in a stable emotional state, the elements were all in place for the explosion that did indeed occur at the end of the year. Unpacking the details of their connections during the months after their friendly letters in March, then, reveals the chain of events that led to *The Factory Controversy*, Dickens's retaliatory response and Martineau's subsequent counter-attacks.

'Another paper from me? you ask': Martineau and W. H. Wills

In writing *The Factory Controversy* during October 1855 and as noted above, Martineau explicitly referenced that she was responding to only four of the seven essays Morley had by then written on industrial safety – those published between 14 April and 28 July that same year, all of which appeared in Volume XI of *Household Words*. Her expression of regret in her March letter to Dickens that the Willses could not come to Ambleside for a visit provides the clue as to why she only focused on these four articles, a focus that is itself additionally revealing about the evolution of the dispute. In September 1855, with her health somewhat more stable and the manuscript of her *Autobiography* ostensibly completed, she was finally able to host Wills, with whom she had had a cordial relationship ever since beginning to contribute to *Household Words*, and his wife Janet.[62] From letters written after the visit, it is evident that three things that must have happened during the Willses' stay in Ambleside: first, Dickens and his team still thought well enough of Martineau that Wills once again invited her to resume contributing to *Household Words*; second, there must have been some conversation about the rejection of her Christmas story the previous year; and, finally, Wills must have mentioned the recently published factory safety essays, essays of which Martineau had been previously unaware.

The invitation to contribute is apparent from Martineau's letter of 26 September 1855 that Wills found waiting for him when he got back to London and the *Household Words* office in Wellington Street and that began 'Another paper from me? you ask. – No, – not if I were to live twenty years.'[63] Not satisfied with simply declining, Martineau went on to accuse *Household Words* of anti-Catholic bias on the basis of a Philadelphia newspaper's review of Wilkie Collins's 'The Yellow Mask', which had appeared in the magazine during July. Replying on *Household Words* letterhead, Wills was, not surprisingly, somewhat taken aback by this letter from the friend in whose home he had just stayed, whom he had just invited to contribute again to the magazine. Having begun his reply by describing his wifeless return to London and himself as 'a desolate wanderer about deserted streets and empty clubs', he then asked her to thank her niece Maria for some seeds she had sent his wife. After this cordial beginning, he went on to enquire, not unreasonably, whether she had actually read Collins's story and chided her for building such a strong critique of *Household Words* on 'the slender foundation of a paragraph from an American newspaper'. From here, however, things went rapidly downhill, as, perhaps surprised and irritated by her letter, he proceeded to reiterate why he and Dickens had turned down 'Father D'Estelan's Christmas Morning' by saying that he felt 'perfectly justified in rejecting her Jesuit paper upon every principle, not only of duty, but of justice and common sense'.[64]

If Martineau responded, that letter has not survived, and the next to Wills that we have comes a full two months later on 30 November, when she begins:

> My dear friend
> I dare say you remember my mentioning to you here that I was going to write, for the Westminster Review, an art: on Meddling Legislation and the Factory case, and that you told me I ought to see the papers in 'H. Words' on the latter. I got them, and my sorrow and disgust were extreme. Mr Dickens mistakes the law, mis-states the facts, and shows a virulence of temper, and uses a brutality of language . . . wh will do him more injury than any of the many preceding mistakes he has made on social subjects.[65]

Clearly, then, while they had discussed the factory safety issue, she had not been following Morley's series until the hapless Wills brought it up in Ambleside. Clearly, too, while she shared an interest in the issues Morley's essays had raised, she responded negatively to the ways they had been represented. So how did she get those papers from *Household Words*, which she had evidently not been reading as they appeared?[66]

The answer seems to be that she did so very quickly after the Willses had left at the end of September and that she procured them from John Chapman, another close friend in the world of London publishing and the editor of the *Westminster Review*, to which she had been contributing again since July 1852 and the mortgage of which, as we have seen, she had previously assumed. Martineau's correspondence frequently indicates her indebtedness to friends for providing her with print materials not readily accessible in Ambleside, and it appears that, in this instance, she again drew upon her connections in the networks of London publishing for assistance. For, on 9 October 1855 Chapman wrote to her:

> I am sorry about 'Household Words'; more sorry that its policy is not peculiar. Were the papers which I sent what you wanted? I do not know of many books on your subject, and must therefore leave that matter in your hands.[67]

Even as he sent the articles, Chapman was evidently already sensing potential trouble ahead – and, if so, his concern was entirely justified. For Martineau quickly produced the essay that would become *The Factory Controversy* and sent it to him, surely expecting that, as the editor of a journal to which she had a long history of contributing and the mortgage of which she now held, he would have no difficulty putting it into print. There, however, she was to be disappointed, and in a series of six letters between 22 October and 11 November he stubbornly resists her repeated pressure to publish. On 6 November, he finally makes explicit the grounds for his refusal:

> I shrink from printing your article as it stands. I should not like to publish the personal attacks on Horner and on Dickens. An exposition of the law, of the difficulty of its application, and of its evil effects is valuable and telling and it seems to me that such an exposition would gain in force by being freed from all personal animadversion.[68]

Barred from publishing the essay in the London press, even in a venue that she technically owned, Martineau turned instead to Manchester, secured its acceptance within days of Chapman's final refusal,[69] and had it issued as a pamphlet by the NAFO – an organisation, as we have seen but as she could not have known, with which Dickens had already sparred over this very issue. More significant in terms of the evolving dispute, however, was the fact that, though it was friendly to her and her views, the Association was also one whose imprimatur could only have been seen as partisan and certainly one that aligned poorly with her hard-won status as an authoritative journalist whose writing was ordinarily in high demand.

To recap the series of events, then, following Dickens and Martineau's cordial correspondence of March 1855: between April and July, Morley had written four essays on industrial safety for *Household Words*; during his September visit to Ambleside, Wills had drawn Martineau's attention to them and bluntly restated his and Dickens's rejection of her Christmas story; and, during October and November, Chapman had first provided her with Volume XI of the magazine containing Morley's essays and then declined to publish her response to them. Where, though, was Dickens while all this was unfolding? The evidence suggests that, during this period of restless travel and having left London for Folkestone and then Paris, he was out of immediate contact with the office. As a result, he was evidently entirely unaware of the developing tensions or of Martineau's plans to write a response to Morley's essays. Although a large number of letters between him and Wills do survive from this period, they provide no inkling that Dickens had any knowledge of the burgeoning conflict – and indeed Wills himself may not have realised how serious it was until he received Martineau's letter of 30 November.

From that point, however, things moved rapidly: *The Factory Controversy* was published in mid-December; Morley evidently took it for the attack upon *Household Words* that it undoubtedly was; and, after doing the research and drafting a response, he and Wills brought Dickens up to speed. Even so, Dickens's first comment on the matter does not occur until a letter from Paris of 3 or 4 January, less than two weeks before issue 304 of *Household Words* appeared for sale. His comments, then, are surely much less considered than they have been taken to be in previous representations of the dispute:

> I am sufficiently irritable – though, as you know, the most amiable of men! – to desire to avoid reading Miss Martineau's vomit of conceit, unless I should feel myself positively obliged to do so. I have therefore put the precious packet by, without opening it. I will come to a decision upon Morley's notice of it, when I see the Proof of his article. But my present impression is, that I would rather (if only for the mortification it will cause her), not notice it at all. The Proof has not yet arrived.[70]

Notwithstanding that 'vomit of conceit' which has proved so irresistible to scholarly quotation, this passage as a whole is in fact much closer in spirit to that of his 8 March letter to Miss Coutts, and the Dickens we can see here is the one who has known Martineau for some twenty years, worked with her extensively and sympathised with her in her illness. Nevertheless, since she had recovered sufficiently to reward his earlier concern with a vituperative assault upon him, his collaborator and the authority of his magazine, he quickly set his reservations aside and focused upon revising Morley's draft response. Just two days later, he wrote again to Wills, demonstrating the tendency to revisionist representations of women who antagonised him that Lillian Nayder has shown to be a recurring pattern in his life:[71]

> Miss Martineau, in this, is precisely what I always knew her to be, and have always impressed her upon you as being. I was so convinced that it was impossible that she *could* be anything else, having seen and heard her, that I am not in the least triumphant at her justifying my opinion. I do suppose that there never was such a wrong-headed woman born – such a vain one – or such a Humbug.[72]

And he instructed Wills to make up the 19 January number and put his revised version of Morley's response 'into the opening . . . as I have arranged it in the enclosed proof'. Having thus dealt peremptorily with the matter, Dickens evidently left the dispute, and Martineau, behind him: not surprisingly, there were no further invitations to her to write for his journals; there are also no indications of any further contact with her or of reference to her – evidently, he did, indeed, 'blot her . . . out of our remembrance'.

'My secession from the corps of Mr Dickens's contributors': Martineau's Response

Martineau, however, could not so easily leave things there, for Dickens's attack was one she was bound to counter, if only to maintain her professional standing. Moreover, as several of her male friends and allies learned over the years and as this book has shown, she rarely hesitated to act on her sense of duty to correct what she perceived as error. In 1853, for example, even William Lloyd Garrison, whom she admired profoundly and with whom she had long worked closely, was thus reprimanded both publicly in a letter to *The Liberator* and with a private follow-up expressing her exasperation at his having intervened in the abolitionist debate in Britain without, according to her, understanding the issues involved.[73] In the case of Dickens, both since their dispute had been in print and because she could hardly continue a public slanging match with a man who had cast such toxic doubts upon her moral character and professional standing, her options were more limited. Nevertheless, she did find a variety of ways to respond extensively, both at once and overtly through the columns of the *Daily News* and then, in a more covert manner, through a management of her life story that has previously gone unrecognised.

Immediately and not surprisingly, Dickens's attack upon one of its principal contributors prompted a reaction from the *Daily News*, and Martineau played an extensive role in the paper's response. Having given only occasional attention to the factory safety issue during 1855, the paper came out with the first of several major articles on the matter on 31 January 1856. Using terms that could be read as applying to its founding editor as much as to the opponents of legal reform, it spoke both to the kinds of discourse appropriate to public discussion of such important social topics as well as to the gender politics Martineau's appearance in the debate had brought out into the open. Its leader thus noted how in her pamphlet 'inflated language and mawkish sentimentality are treated with the disregard they merit' and praised her as a writer on the subject who was 'not to be deterred from the free and sincere utterance of whatever opinions she may honestly entertain by deference to any set of men, however powerful or influential'.[74] While *Household Words* fell silent on the issue, the *Daily News* herewith announced its support for reform and, over the next four months, continued its coverage of the progress of the Factory Bill. At each critical stage as the Bill worked its way through the legislative process, the paper included a leader on the subject by Martineau herself and, though Dickens may have withdrawn from the fray, she continued her earlier line of attack upon his emotive rhetoric as she blasted the opposition for 'violence, an unfairness, and even a passionate malignity'[75] and labelled it as 'the usual course of cheap and vulgar philanthropy'.[76] Far from excluding her from the debate, then, Dickens may only have stimulated her and the *Daily News*'s engagement with it and intensified their attacks upon the rhetorical forms he favoured in the representation of issues of public policy – a deeply ironic consequence of his effort to 'blot' her out of his and his readers' view. With the Bill safely passed that summer, the extent and impact of Martineau's efforts were acknowledged when she received a letter on 19 July from Henry Whitworth, the NAFO Secretary, who congratulated her on her role in getting the legislation approved and praised the 'repeated evidences of the valuable service which your pen has rendered . . . and especially so in quarters where disinterested statements were needed'.[77] In reply, Martineau noted both her 'pure pleasure' at the legislative success as well as the 'overplus of gratification' brought by Whitworth's news that the NAFO had determined to pay her 100 guineas for her efforts[78] – a remarkable amount given both the overall modesty of her publishing income and the fact that she had already been paid by the *Daily News* for her leaders and, incidentally, a sum that was equivalent to forty per cent of her total earnings from the forty-seven articles she had written for *Household Words* over the four years she had contributed to the magazine.[79]

Martineau's response to Dickens, however, was not limited to her forthright contributions to the public debate, and, even as she was writing her leaders for the *Daily News*, so too she had been embedding a far less overt and much more complicated response to the dispute in the text of her *Autobiography*. For, just as Dallas Liddle has shown with Martineau's origination narrative as a published author,[80] here again she makes use of her life story to advance her project of self-definition as a professional woman writer in ways that reveal the complexity of the stresses to which she was subject. In this instance, however, she does so primarily by working to attack Dickens and thereby undermine the case he had made against her, as is evident from the account she provides in the *Autobiography* of her relationship with Dickens. Or, rather, the accounts, for late in the text and in close proximity to one another, come two fundamentally incompatible discussions of Dickens.

Martineau's first passage is warm and enthusiastic and aligns with the earlier history of their friendly and collaborative relationship, as she writes that 'Nothing could exceed the frank kindness and consideration shown by him in the correspondence and personal intercourse we have had' and praises him for a 'glowing and generous heart . . . kept steady by the best domestic influences'.[81] Consistent with her 1851 defense of *David Copperfield* as 'fiction of a high order . . . the direct produce of heart',[82] this passage both defines her grounds of praise for Dickens and yet, at the same time, anticipates her reservations about him. For she also sounds a characteristic note in her appraisal and one that looks both back to her account in *History of the Peace* and forward to her dismissive language in *The Factory Controversy*, when she comments that 'Nobody wants to make Mr Dickens a Political economist; but there are many who wish that he would abstain from a set of difficult subjects, on which all true sentiment must be underlain by a sort of knowledge which he has not.'[83] As Elaine Freedgood has noted in *Victorian Writing about Risk*,[84] Martineau is consistently drawn towards the certainties provided by the tenets of political economy and thus, even in her praise for Dickens, she never loses sight of what she sees as a fundamental difference in their approach to the debate around Utilitarian values: for her, Dickens sentimentalises issues that can only be addressed by the application of rational, analytic thinking and policies based upon such thinking, an intellectual liberalism rather than the more affective form to which she sees him as limited.

While their philosophical differences are evident in this initial passage, then, there is absolutely nothing here to prepare the reader for the shift that occurs thirty pages later when she announces that she 'must pause for a moment' to explain 'the grounds, and . . . the process, of my secession from the corps of Mr Dickens's contributors'.[85] She opens with a demurring comment that serves to establish her distance from the very type of authorship required by journals such as *Household Words*: 'I have observed above that Magazine writing is quite out of my way: and that I accepted Mr Dickens's invitation to write for his, simply because its wide circulation went far to compensate for the ordinary objections to that mode of authorship.'[86] As Chapter 5 has shown, however, to claim that writing for magazines is 'quite out of my way' is a wholly disingenuous representation of her journalistic ambitions and efforts during the 1840s, let alone in the years after she stopped contributing to *Household Words*. Moreover, what makes her tone here so remarkable is how strikingly different it is from the language she had used when she wrote to Fanny Wedgwood in late 1851, describing her proposal for the series of articles on industrial manufacturing that have been the principal focus of critical discussion of her work for the magazine: 'Mr D is so taken with the plan, and he has so *many* readers, and I shall learn so much, and the proceeds will build such a nice additional cottage, that I am sure it is right to do it.'[87] In the revisionist section of the *Autobiography*, however, and in keeping with what would become the received narrative of her dispute with Dickens, she goes on to explain her eventual 'secession' as triggered by a twofold demonstration of Dickens's ideological failings. First, she refers to his and W. H. Wills's rejection of the story she had offered for the 1854 special Christmas issue of *Household Words*. Secondly, she builds from that rejection to make a larger charge that the magazine is guilty of strident anti-Catholicism by contrasting her story's fate with Dickens's publication of Wilkie Collins's 'The Yellow Mask', the story that Wills chided her for judging from the account given in the Philadelphia newspaper. She glosses over the fact that she has not actually read Collins's text and, roundly decrying the magazine's alleged inconsistency, declaims, 'The last thing I am likely to do is to write for an anti-catholic publication; and least of all when it is anti-catholic on the sly.'[88] In closing, she magisterially expresses her revulsion: 'To a descendant of Huguenots, such total darkness of conscience on the morality of opinion is difficult to believe in when it is before one's very eyes.'[89]

Stepping away from the text of the *Autobiography*, however, places this latter statement in what at first appears to be a curious light. Even before Martineau wrote her life story in 1855, her religious beliefs had become other than conventionally Christian and, although she privately insisted on a continuing faith in a Prime Cause, her 1851 *Letters on the Laws of Man's Nature and Development* was widely viewed as at best agnostic in spirit and, as we have seen, had prompted hostile critical responses even from her own family. Nevertheless, and as 'Letters from Ireland' had revealed, she retained a keen sense of the institutional role of the church and its capacity to have enormous influence for good or ill. Her account of Ireland under British rule thus evidences sympathy for and condemnation of both the work of the native Catholic priesthood and the imported Anglican clergy. She held no specific brief for either but, rather, saw and described the corrosive effects of religious bigotry. If her assault on Dickens in the *Autobiography* seems out of place in terms of all that we know about their earlier relationship, her own evolving religious beliefs and her socio-political understanding of the role of the Catholic Church, however, there is a way in which charging him with an allegation of anti-Catholic bias in his editorial policy does make sense. For if the critique is seen in terms of her larger assessment of his weakness as a social analyst, it can be understood as part of her counter-attack against 'Our Wicked Mis-Statements'. That is, it enables her to label Dickens as the unreliable agent of public instruction that she had long considered him to be, someone whose brilliant emotional range she could admire in his work as a novelist while simultaneously suggesting that this very emotionality rendered him quite incapable of the dispassionate objectivity essential in an editor who claimed to shape the public sphere. Moreover, she thus defines him in stereotypically feminine terms, reversing the field of gendered attack and claiming for herself the position of masculine rationality that she had sought in her own professional development as a wisdom writer and that more broadly aligns with her privileging of modes of intellectual analysis that she associates with the value of Utilitarian approaches to the social issues liberals wished to advance.

Turning back to the actual manuscript of the *Autobiography* itself makes the point clearer, for this second section on Dickens is clearly an interpolation, consisting as it does of 5.5 pages of additional manuscript, prefaced by the direction 'Insert p. 241'.[90] The manuscript as a whole includes a number of inserted passages, but this one is among the longest. It was also written upon a paper stock that is unique to this part of the text, which suggests that it was not composed at the same time as the remainder of the manuscript, and that suggestion can indeed be confirmed by examining the history of the completion of the writing and printing of the *Autobiography* and setting both in the context of Martineau's falling out with Dickens. For, although she wrote in a letter to Fanny Wedgwood of 29 August 1855 that she had completed the manuscript two days earlier and sent it to be printed,[91] this second section on Dickens was clearly written somewhat later. That is, in illustrating her 'secession' from *Household Words* she quotes from the correspondence between her and Wills discussed above, specifically from their letters dated 26 and 28 September 1855, respectively. Moreover, this new section also offers an account of the ultimate fate of 'Father D'Estelan's Christmas Morning', an account that could not have been wholly true at the time of the manuscript's composition. For she writes that the story 'appears [present tense] in my volume of "Sketches from Life"'.[92] But that volume was not to be published until September 1856, more than a year after she claimed to have finished the manuscript, and some nine months after the *Autobiography* had been finally printed and sealed up to await publication after her death in 1876.[93]

An explanation for this curious sequence of claims and inconsistencies can be deduced by examining the history of the *Autobiography*'s manuscript and its conversion into the printed text that would be stored away for more than twenty years. The key figure in this explanation is one John Garnett, whose remarkable range of employment is listed in the *Guide to Windermere* that he had published for Martineau in 1854: 'railway superintendent, – Printer, bookseller, &c, Post Office'.[94] Described in her August letter to Fanny Wedgwood as the 'devoted printer' to whom she had sent the completed manuscript, Garnett had been her intended printer for *The Factory Controversy*. For unknown reasons, that had not happened, and the NAFO had instead had the pamphlet printed in Manchester, which may account for her response when Garnett contacted her in mid-December 1855, right between the appearance of *The Factory Controversy* and the publication of Dickens's response. For, to his enquiry whether she had 'any little Book not yet published' that he might bring out in time for the following year's Christmas market,[95] Martineau promptly responded that she did indeed 'have a little book to dispose of' and suggested republishing the series of a dozen tales of ordinary life that she had written for *The Leader*.[96] In also assenting to Garnett's request that she revise the tales as necessary, however, she resisted his suggestion that her niece Maria help with the project, noting that they were both agreed 'that it would not do for any work of mine to be edited by any one but myself during my life'.[97] She and Garnett signed a memorandum of agreement on 5 January 1856;[98] the revisions were completed during the spring, and the volume appeared on 1 September that year.

The book, however, is something of an oddity, both in its substance and in the ways in which Martineau represented it. For, as she firmly retained control over the process of preparing the text for the press, she made, but nowhere refers to or accounts for, a number of changes to the original line-up of its contents. She apparently had some difficulty in obtaining copies of the original stories from *The Leader*, and half of them do not appear in the collection at all. In their place, she added two new pieces, and she also chose to include 'Father D'Estelan's Christmas Morning'. Placed in a volume of simple narratives focused upon the lives, work and harsh living conditions of ordinary British working people, this story, with its thematic focus on the epic heroism of a Jesuit priest drowned on a voyage to China, is strangely out of place. Stranger still is the fact that the publisher's advertisements for the volume focus upon – indeed, name only – this particular story. And strangest of all, especially if the story had been included simply due to a need for material to fill out the volume, is that post-dated reference to its inclusion in her interpolated section of the *Autobiography*.

Accounting for these peculiarities, however, becomes easier when the gestation of the volume is placed within the context of the intersection between the interpolated passage in the *Autobiography* and the emerging dispute with Dickens. Since Garnett did not approach her about the book project until 17 December 1855, Martineau must have written the new section that refers to the *Sketches* somewhere between that date and before the printing of the *Autobiography* was completed in March 1856. Given that she and Garnett did not sign their contract until 5 January, it is probable that she composed the new section after that date and indeed perhaps after Dickens had published 'Our Wicked Mis-Statements' on 19 January. Writing to Fanny Wedgwood on 21 December 1855, she told her friend: 'I have just been presented with a ream of this paper by the Station Master [Garnett] of Windermere. I don't like it so well as the former.'[99] Given the timing and the connection with Garnett, this, then, may have been not only the paper used for her letter but also that on which she wrote the interpolated section on Dickens, which would account for the different stocks in the manuscript. More important than the precise date of composition, however, is the way in which thus constructing *Sketches from Life* as she did and revising the manuscript of the *Autobiography* in order to create a connection between the two texts allowed Martineau to realise a threefold response to Dickens's attacks on her professional standing. First, by foregrounding 'Father D'Estelan' in *Sketches from Life* she had the satisfaction of seeing it in print despite Dickens and Wills' reiterated rejection of its suitability for *Household Words*. Second, and more significantly, in publishing it, she created a contrast between the editorial team at *Household Words* and her own self-representation as an author willing to see and present a range of social values broader than her personal convictions. Third and most important of all, with her inserted passage in the *Autobiography*, she ensured that what would eventually become her final published representation of Dickens would be consistent with the position she had already taken in *The Factory Controversy*. For, by emphasising the allegations of anti-Catholicism and differentiating herself from them, she both strengthened her own self-representation as a voice of moderate reason and reinforced her version of Dickens as an agent of passionate bias, as unreliable in his self-proclaimed role as public educator as he had labelled her in 'Our Wicked Mis-Statements'. Little indeed, had Dickens known what he was in for when he tried to 'blot' her out of 'remembrance' and attempted unsuccessfully to silence a voice determined to be heard – which was, after all, 'the only really important thing' for a Victorian woman of letters.[100]

'Grimly bent upon the enlightenment of mankind': Paper, Print and the Press

If the very paper on which Martineau appears to have composed the interpolated section on Dickens for the *Autobiography* provides a previously unnoticed clue to the unfolding of their dispute, the inevitable end of the collaboration at *Household Words* had been anticipated in two articles dealing with the subject of paper itself. Both Dickens's August 1850 'A Paper-Mill' and Martineau's final contribution to the magazine, her October 1854 'How to Get Paper', were written within the context of the early 1850s campaign to complete the repeal of the 'taxes on knowledge', and the two authors' very differing attitudes to the campaign align with their contrasting positions on the role of the press as an agent of liberal progress that this book has explored. Dickens, as John Drew has shown, had a deeply 'ambivalent relationship' with the campaign,[101] and his account of paper production works to reconcile the modern industrial process with a nostalgic sense of English national identity while simultaneously taming the disruptive forces of political unrest into normative social patterns coded as domestic and female. Martineau, by contrast, was an unwavering advocate for repeal. In the months before her article in *Household Words* appeared, she wrote a number of leaders for the *Daily News* in which she described the various taxes as instruments of state constraint upon individual entrepreneurial agency and indicators of the nation's failure to achieve the full potential of its stadial advance. Consistent with this, her article for Dickens envisions paper production in transatlantic terms, unfavourably contrasting Britain and its limitations upon availability of the material and therefore access to printed matter against the laissez-faire conditions prevailing in the United States that were enabling the enthusiastic embrace of new forms of paper to meet the ever expanding demand of both manufacturers in need of packaging material and readers seeking print matter, both of which she defines as fundamental to the New World's continuing movement away from and ahead of the Old.

The movement to repeal the 'taxes on knowledge', which led to the repeal of advertisement duty and the stamp duty for monthly publications in 1853, that of the newspaper stamp duty in 1855 and finally of the paper duty in 1861, was, as Lucy Brown, Martin Hewitt and others have shown and as was discussed in the Introduction, foundational in enabling the growth of the mass-market press that came into being during the second half of the nineteenth century.[102] As Drew notes, Dickens's reluctance to join the campaign for repeal was tied to the concerns over the mass-market press that had been part of the motivation for establishing *Household Words* and that had been expressed in its manifesto's attack upon those 'Bastards of the Mountain, draggled fringe on the Red Cap, Panders to the basest passions of the lowest natures' discussed earlier in this chapter. Consistent with this position, even on 30 January 1851 when he joined William Chambers, Charles Knight and other leaders of the middle-class liberal press in lobbying the Chancellor of the Exchequer, Dickens, according to *The Times* report the following day, expressed his hostility towards the 'pernicious publications' to which repeal would give free rein and contempt for 'the most abject and degraded' of publishers who produced them.[103] Even more revealingly, in this public attack on the mass-market press Dickens was echoing a still more forceful statement he had made privately a year earlier. For, writing to Thomas Milner Gibson, who was leading Parliamentary efforts for repeal, he explained that his inability to offer his support arose from a concern lest 'we might be deluged with a flood of piratical, ignorant, and blackguard papers, something like that black deluge of Printer's Ink which blights America'.[104] Othering the American press as he had in both *American Notes* and *Martin Chuzzlewit*, suggesting an unease with its piratical energy that recalls his representation of the attractively repulsive Hannibal Chollop, Dickens codes his resistance to the very notion of a laissez-faire media marketplace into the apocalyptic material form of the ink that would itself constitute that unregulated world of print.

Set against these tirades, 'A Paper-Mill', which Dickens co-wrote with Mark Lemon as the lead for the 31 August 1850 issue of *Household Words*, counters that apocalyptic vision with a far more idealised representation of paper itself, the medium upon which shapeless, liquid ink is formed into print, turned into language, articulated into meaning. To this end, the first two columns of the article, almost half its total length, contextualise modern paper production into a historical narrative that is both monitory and comforting. Opening with the mill's location in Dartford, Dickens defines the Kent town not as it presently is but as the birthplace of its most famous historical figure, Wat Tyler, who had led the unsuccessful fourteenth-century Peasant's Revolt against Plantagenet rule. As he does so, and in what at first appears a gratuitous fixation upon feminine purity, he calls out the threat to the 'decency and honour' of working men's daughters under medieval social conditions, speculates on the unknown fate of the executed Wat's own daughter and imagines the 'king's fair daughters' who lived sequestered in the local nunnery.[105] Having established this historical foundation, the narrative then moves from the tumult of revolt and concomitant threats to feminine purity by recounting the founding of the first paper mill during the reign of Queen Elizabeth. Authorised by a royal license and soon thereafter gaining a patent that effectively granted him a monopoly over the production of white paper, German entrepreneur John Spielman is further celebrated by the Dickensian narrator for having introduced the lime tree to England and enabled his latter-day 'love of all the sweet-smelling lime-trees that have ever greeted me in the land, and all the writing-paper I have ever blotted'.[106]

Having established itself with this curious mix of images of revolt, rape and pastoral idyll, the article then turns to a celebratory account of the production of 'Paper! White, pure, spick and span new paper, with that fresh smell which takes us back to school and schoolbooks.'[107] Echoing Tom Pinch's delight in the smell of leather and paper in the Salisbury bookseller's, 'A Paper-Mill' goes on to describe the modern industrial production process through taking the point of view of the rags themselves as they are transformed from dusty bales into 'virgin paper', 'greatly purified – and gradually becoming quite ethereal',[108] and are turned by the power of steam machinery into an artefact that is simultaneously frail yet tender, its nurturing touch converting the text's earlier iterations of assaulted femininity into images of care and solicitude:

> how does it draw me out, when I am frailest and most liable to tear, so tenderly and delicately, that a woman's hand – no, even though I were a man, very ill and helpless, and she my nurse who loved me – could never touch me with so light a touch, or with a movement so unerring![109]

Cathy Waters has read this passage within the larger context of Dickens's treatment of factory processes and as, through its demonstration of 'the surpassing sensitivity of the machine', depicting 'an industrial scene in which objects start to usurp the subjectivity of those who work them'.[110] A different interpretation, however, Matthew Poland has argued, becomes available through focusing on the product rather than the process. Giving paper itself an embodied voice and concentrating upon the older, rag-based form of paper manufacturing rather than the emergent newer technologies that were beginning to shift the entire industry, 'A Paper-Mill', Poland suggests, resolves the socioeconomic threat of poor bodies and their rags and 'recovers social hierarchies from the levelling effects of industrial commodification'.[111] Drawing on each of these readings, my argument here is that pure, white, English, feminised paper functions, in this text, as an emblem of the form of Dickensian print culture that will as the article concludes, perform its 'mighty Duty' – a far higher duty than any that might be imposed by the excise office – and express 'love, forebearance, mercy, progress, scorn of the Hydra Cant with all its million heads!'[112]

Contrasted with both the implication of assault and rape associated with the forces of social unrest represented by Tyler's revolt and, more distantly, with the 'piratical' masculinity of the unregulated American press that continued to give Dickens so much cause for concern, this idealised image of paper thus becomes an emblem for his larger goals for the magazine itself – ironically, given the modest quality of newsprint permitted by the combination of *Household Words*'s own economic model and the paper duty.

Unlike Dickens, Martineau was entirely unambivalent where the campaign for the repeal of the 'taxes on knowledge' was concerned. Although she could not follow his example and join in directly lobbying political leaders, she expressed her clear support for the movement in a series of four leading articles she wrote for the *Daily News* during 1854. For Martineau, the 'dearth of paper' facing the nation epitomised the barriers to stadial progress created by an overly governmentalised state. Despite the manufacturing advances that had replaced wool with cotton and broadly improved longevity and the 'bodily ease' in which the population could live, and 'omitting all consideration of the spread of literary and political information among the people', the burden of the paper duty has frustrated progress and hampered Britain's economic development. Emphasising the same model of laissez-faire liberalism that was also evident in the course of the dispute with Dickens over factory safety, she goes on to note that 'the paper duty is truly a manufacturers' question', since it hinders their competitiveness against foreign competition by increasing the cost of paper packaging. The paper industry itself is but one instance of this wider pattern as, with 'no new paper mills' being constructed and innovation disincentivised by taxation, 'our papermakers go on sullenly and ploddingly making the white paper that is all that the public knows'. In Martineau's reading of the 'taxes on knowledge', then, there is no room for nostalgic sentimentality about lime trees planted around centuries-old paper mills or celebration of the purity of their snow-white product; instead, her entire focus is upon the damage caused by 'the whole plague ... of Government meddling' and the consequences, both designed and unintended, of the state's efforts to control the dissemination of knowledge and free formation of opinion in the public sphere.[113]

'How to Get Paper', which appeared in *Household Words* two months after the last of these articles, provides a shorter version for Dickens's audience of the case made in the columns of the *Daily News*, but replaces the attack against government 'meddling' with a focus upon paper as a synechdochic image of the entrepreneurial energy of the United States. After opening with an account of American ingenuity in finding ways to communicate in writing – and ironically counterposing the South Carolina slave guiding fugitives north by drawing on a sandy beach with plantation ladies composing notes to one another on magnolia petals, confident in their slaves' inability to read – Martineau proceeds to describe how, unrestricted by the state and unfettered by the kinds of cultural constraint Dickens's essay had expressed, America has fostered its stadial development through entrepreneurial innovation. Reiterating a point she had first made seventeen years earlier in *Society in America*, Martineau points out to the *Household Words* readers that not only is America a nation whose 'inhabitants use three times as much paper per head as we British do',[114] but that the growth of print is directly correlated with the expansion and development of the nation as a whole:

> Next to the church and the tavern, the printing-press is set up in every raw settlement; and a raw newspaper appears; probably on whity-brown paper, and in mixed type, with italics and Roman letters, capitals and diphthongs thrown together very curiously; but – still a newspaper.[115]

The 'miserable whity-brown paper . . . dingy uncomfortable print' for which Forster and Dickens had excoriated the *New York Herald* in their *Foreign Quarterly Review* essay back in 1842[116] thus becomes for Martineau an image of America's innovative energy, an emblem of its readiness to cast off European models of cultural value in pursuit of progress. For her, the virtues of American paper are quite different from the feminised qualities Dickens had prized in 'A Paper-Mill': 'Our American newspapers come to us in wrappers of brown and yellow, so tough, as never, by any accident, to arrive with the smallest rent in the edge, and bearing the ink as well as any paper whatever.'[117] The very advance that Dickens had celebrated in English paper-making through his nostalgic invoking of Spielman's innovation is thus inverted by Martineau as she celebrates American progress in terms of the expanding of the range of culturally acceptable material. What has enabled this expansion and led to the production of this 'tough' American paper, she goes on to argue to Dickens's readers, is the combination of a willingness to experiment with new sources of raw material together with freedom from the excise duties that have made British manufacturers uncompetitive with their American counterparts. Accordingly, returning to the account of American ingenuity in writing with which she had begun the essay, she concludes by praising the innovation of paper production across the Atlantic. Whether it be 'maize-stalks' or New England 'marsh-hay', or the 'flowering reeds' of the Gulf Coast,[118] all is grist to American paper mills in the effort to meet the insatiable demand for their products and drive the nation forward. Standing in stark contrast with Britain, where that pure white product Dickens had celebrated in 'A Paper-Mill' is both culturally privileged and maintained as the norm by an 'excise that will not allow experiments to be made, on fair conditions',[119] American paper thus becomes in Martineau's text an image that calls back to her American books' representation of the continent itself as an embodiment of stadial progress and an emblem of the nation's foundation upon a vision of liberal progress grounded in the circulation of ideas and formation of democratic opinion through the free propagation of print and, above all, the press.

The contrast between 'A Paper-Mill' and 'How to Get Paper' thus reaffirms the larger fissures we have seen in Martineau and Dickens's beliefs in the liberal project and the vital role in that project that the press had to play. Although the two writers were, as we have seen in this chapter, still on good personal terms and while, even seven months after 'How to Get Paper' appeared, Martineau reaffirmed her intention of continuing to contribute to *Household Words*,[120] the article was both symbolically and in fact her final appearance in the magazine. Revealing Dickens and Martineau's enduring differences on the relationship between the state and individual agency, and on their visions of the United States and the role of the press in the development of a society in which the governed could give their consent to the political conditions under which they lived, the two articles complete the terms of their separation that had underlain 'The Sickness and Health of the People of Bleaburn' and that would emerge most completely in the factory dispute. Though that separation has, as this book has argued, been incompletely understood for much of its history, Dickens himself anticipated its terms in his editorial comments to W. H. Wills on the proofs of 'How to Get Paper':

> Rather a gloomy No. Miss Martineau pretty well, but grimly bent upon the enlightenment of mankind, and quite absurdly overdoing American education. I have taken out that passage about paper instantly rising 20 percent if the Newspaper Stamp were taken off, for I think it a hazardous assumption to broach so very positively.[121]

'Gloomy', 'grimly bent' and committed to a vision of America as a model of liberal progress, the Martineau Dickens discerns offers none of the 'Fancy' he wanted to be *Household Words*'s distinctive feature – and which indeed had so richly infused 'A Paper-Mill'. Moreover, by silently removing one of Martineau's key points through his assertion of editorial privilege on the question of the newspaper stamp, Dickens not only imposed his view of the larger development and role of the press on her text but anticipated that far more destructive effort to 'blot her ... out of remembrance' with which their dispute, and their collaborative relationship, would end just fifteen months later. Resting, then, on major differences in their liberal visions for both progress and the press, the factory dispute pointed to a fundamental schism in Martineau and Dickens's understandings of the shape and movement of history, a schism that, as Chapter 7 will show, becomes most fully visible in the aftermath of their actual quarrel and the work they undertook in the years that followed.

Notes

1. Martineau, *Autobiography*, p. 569.
2. Ledger, *Dickens and the Popular Radical Imagination*, pp. 171–2.
3. Dickens, 'A Preliminary Word', p. 1.
4. Ibid. p. 2.
5. Huett, 'Among the Unknown Public', p. 64.
6. *Harriet Martineau's Writing on British History and Military Reform*, vol. 5, p. 309.
7. See Waters, *Commodity Culture*; Clemm, *Dickens, Journalism, and Nationhood*; Ketabgian, *The Lives of Machines*; Pusapati, 'Going Places'.
8. [Martineau], 'The Sickness and Health of the People of Bleaburn', p. 193.
9. Ibid. p. 283.
10. Ibid. p. 193.
11. Lohrli, 'Harriet Martineau and the People of Bleaburn', p. 101.
12. Martineau, *Letters*, vol. 3, pp. 161–2, 165–6.
13. Ibid. p. 161.
14. Ibid. pp. 161, 166.
15. Lohrli, 'Harriet Martineau', p. 101.
16. Hall, *Memoir of Mary L. Ware*, pp. 2, 3.
17. [Martineau], *The Sickness and Health of the People of Bleaburn* (1853), pp. iii, iv.
18. Dickens, *Letters*, vol. 6, pp. 73, 74.
19. Writing to Martineau in 1853 in an effort to persuade her to resume writing for *Household Words* after a lengthy interval, Dickens referred to the American reprinting of 'The Sickness and Health' in terms that

suggest only faint praise: 'how very starry and stripy our little Bleaburn experience appears to me to be', *Letters*, vol. 7, p. 67.
20. Martineau, *The Factory Controversy*, p. 5.
21. John Chapman, 'The Sphere and Duties of Government'. The John Chapman who wrote this article was a distant relative of the journal's editor, not that editor, the John Chapman who is discussed later in the chapter.
22. Ibid. p. 491.
23. Martineau, *Letters*, vol. 2, pp. 282, 300, 302, 320.
24. Chapman, 'The Sphere and Duties of Government', p. 487.
25. Stout, 'Little, Maybe Less'; Banerjee, 'Writing Bureaucracy. Bureaucratic Writing'; Hadley, 'Nobody, Somebody, and Everybody'.
26. Dickens, *Letters*, vol. 7, pp. 715–16.
27. Dickens, *Little Dorrit*, p. 770.
28. Ibid. p. 860.
29. Martineau, *The Factory Controversy*, p. v.
30. See *Letters*, vol. 2, pp. 70, 163, 307, 316.
31. Martineau, *The Factory Controversy*, pp. 44, 45.
32. Ibid. p. 36.
33. Ibid. p. 38.
34. [Dickens and Morley], 'Our Wicked Mis-Statements', p. 13.
35. Ibid. p. 19.
36. Martineau, *Autobiography*, p. 610.
37. Martineau, *Letters*, vol. 3, p. 139.
38. Ibid. p. 235.
39. Martineau, *Autobiography*, p. 611.
40. Landow, *Elegant Jeremiahs*, pp. 22–3.
41. Peterson, 'Harriet Martineau: Masculine Discourse, Female Sage', p. 178.
42. Pusapati, 'Going Places', p. 217.
43. Martineau, *Letters*, vol. 3, p. 276.
44. Dickens, *Letters*, vol. 7, p. 555.
45. Ibid. p. 694.
46. Ibid. pp. 746–8.
47. 'Morley Letters', Special Collections: University of Sussex.
48. Holly Furneaux's *Queer Dickens* provides the fullest account of the homosocial world in which Dickens lived and which evidently became increasingly important to him as his marriage moved towards its effective end. Martineau, by contrast, had since her move to Ambleside in 1845 created for herself a women-centred home with her close-knit group of servants and her niece and intellectual companion, Maria Martineau.
49. Dickens, *Letters*, vol. 7, pp. 428–9.
50. See, for example, Slater, *Charles Dickens*, p. 382.
51. Harriet Martineau Papers, Additional Materials III.2.
52. Martineau, *Letters to Fanny Wedgwood*, p. 128.

53. Martineau, *Letters*, vol. 3, p. 336.
54. The complete list of Morley's *Household Words* articles on factory safety is: 'Preventible Accidents', 18 March 1854; 'Ground in the Mill', 22 April 1854; 'Fencing with Humanity', 14 April 1855; 'Death's Cyphering-Book', 12 May 1855; 'Deadly Shafts', 23 June 1855; 'More Grist to the Mill', 28 July 1855; and 'Two Shillings per Horse-Power', 8 September 1855.
55. Dickens, *Letters*, vol. 7, p. 428.
56. Robert L. Patten's *Charles Dickens and His Publishers* remains the most systematic account of Dickens's efforts throughout his career to maximise his income and his struggles to meet his expenses. His 'Dickens Wills' paints a vivid picture of the extent to which Dickens took on responsibility for supporting his extended family from early in his career and the increasing range of demands upon him during the last fifteen years of his life. Lillian Nayder's *The Other Dickens* also provides extensive insights into the Dickenses' household finances and the high costs of their lifestyle.
57. Dickens, *Letters*, vol. 7, p. 655.
58. Collins and Cohn, 'Charles Dickens, Harriet Martineau, and Angela Burdett Coutts's *Common Things*'.
59. Ibid. pp. 409–10.
60. Dickens, *Letters*, vol. 7, p. 559.
61. Adding to the complication is correspondence in which Martineau refers to the editors of both the *Daily News* and *Household Words* taking shares in her Ambleside building society: *Letters*, vol. 3, p. 305.
62. Wills himself further evidences the close-knit ties within the networks of early Victorian journalism: having worked for *Chambers's Journal* in Edinburgh between 1842 and 1845, he then moved to London, married William and Roberts Chambers's sister and was at the *Daily News* until Dickens recruited him to help set up and run *Household Words*.
63. Martineau, *Further Letters*, p. 228.
64. Wills, ALS to Harriet Martineau, 28 September 1855. HM1026.
65. Martineau, *Letters*, vol. 3, p. 376.
66. Martineau's correspondence reveals that she regularly kept up with a wide range of the British and American press aimed at middle-class and elite audiences, but she nowhere mentions reading mass-market weekly magazines.
67. Chapman, ALS to Harriet Martineau, 9 October 1855. HM191.
68. Chapman, ALS to Harriet Martineau, 6 November 1855. HM193.
69. Martineau, *Letters*, vol. 3, p. 374.
70. Dickens, *Letters*, vol. 8, p. 6.
71. Nayder, *The Other Dickens*.
72. Dickens, *Letters*, vol. 8, p. 9.
73. Martineau, *Letters*, vol. 3, pp. 295–7.
74. 'The provisions of the Factory Acts'.

75. 'On Friday night'.
76. 'The Second Reading of the improved Factory Bill'.
77. Whitworth, ALS to Harriet Martineau, 19 July 1855. HM980.
78. Martineau, *Letters*, vol. 4, p. 15.
79. See Lohrli, *Household Words*, for details of the individual payments Martineau received for her contributions. In total, she earned a little under £260 for the forty-seven pieces she wrote for the magazine between 1850 and 1854.
80. Liddle, *The Dynamics of Genre*, pp. 48–58.
81. Martineau, *Autobiography*, p. 592.
82. Martineau, *Letters*, vol. 3, p. 187.
83. Martineau, *Autobiography*, p. 591.
84. Freedgood, *Victorian Writing about Risk*, pp. 39–40. Freedgood's exploration of the work done by Martineau's *Illustrations of Political Economy* to assuage early Victorian cultural anxiety over the developing industrial society has been invaluable to my thinking. My focus, however, is less upon the effects of Martineau's early work upon her readers and more on the ways in which, in the 1850s, she positions herself against Dickens and privileges the benefits of an industrial economy over its costs. The sentence quoted here from the *Autobiography* precedes Martineau's only recorded comments on *Hard Times*, as she describes Dickens's 'vigorous erroneousness about matters of science, as shown ... in "Hard Times", about the controversies of employers' (p. 591), a remark so vague that it may even raise doubts as to whether she had in fact read the novel, especially as she had evidently not been reading *Household Words* during its serial publication (see her letter to Wills quoted above, p. 244).
85. Martineau, *Autobiography*, pp. 619, 622.
86. Ibid. p. 619.
87. Martineau, *Letters to Wedgwood*, p. 121.
88. Martineau, *Autobiography*, p. 622.
89. Ibid. p. 621.
90. Harriet Martineau Papers, HM1418.
91. Martineau, *Letters to Wedgwood*, p. 132.
92. Martineau, *Autobiography*, p. 620.
93. Martineau, *Letters to Wedgwood*, p. 147.
94. Martineau, *Guide to Windermere*, p. 89.
95. Harriet Martineau Papers, HM321.
96. Martineau, *Letters*, vol. 3, pp. 382–3.
97. Ibid. p. 387.
98. Harriet Martineau Papers, HM330.
99. Martineau, *Letters to Wedgwood*, p. 142.
100. Martineau, *Autobiography*, p. 569.
101. Drew, *Dickens the Journalist*, pp. 183–7.
102. Brown, *Victorian News and Newspapers*, pp. 26–32; Hewitt, *The Dawn of the Cheap Press*, pp. 59–74.

103. *The Times*, 31 January 1851, p. 5.
104. Dickens, *Letters*, vol. 6, p. 36.
105. [Dickens], 'A Paper-Mill', p. 529.
106. Ibid.
107. Ibid. pp. 529–30.
108. Ibid. p. 530.
109. Ibid. p. 531.
110. Waters, *Commodity Culture*, pp. 90–1.
111. Poland, 'Bodies and Paper Production'; see also Inglis, 'Thomas Carlyle's Laystall', on Dickens's affirmation of the scavenger culture associated with rag-based paper production.
112. 'A Paper-Mill', p. 531.
113. Martineau's articles appeared in the editorial sections of the *Daily News* on 16 January, 1 March, 22 July and 12 August. She also wrote on the importance to the nation of its free press in the 12 December 1854 issue.
114. [Martineau], 'How to Get Paper', p. 242.
115. Ibid.
116. See above, p. 127.
117. [Martineau], 'How to Get Paper', p. 243.
118. Ibid. p. 244.
119. Ibid. p. 243.
120. Martineau, *Letters*, vol. 3, p. 359.
121. Dickens, *Letters*, vol. 7, p. 438.

Chapter 7

The End of Whig History: Dickens, Martineau and the Mid-Victorian Press

Martineau and Dickens's public falling out during the winter of 1855–6 inevitably brought their professional collaboration and personal relationship to an end. This, however, is not to say that the termination of their direct connection also marks an end to what we may learn from the dynamic between them – both about the development of the mid-Victorian press and about the core issues of liberalism with which they were both so profoundly engaged. Indeed, while Dickens may have sought to 'blot' his former contributor 'out of remembrance', Martineau not only continued to appear regularly in the leader columns of the *Daily News* but, in the decade following the quarrel, expanded her journalistic footprint substantially by making her debut in a wide range of venues, some long established, others newly founded.[1] Although there is no record of Dickens commenting on her ever again, as deeply involved in the mid-Victorian press as he himself was, he could hardly have been unaware of her unrivalled presence in it. For her own part, while she would have no further contact with the man himself, Martineau would continue to engage with the phenomenon that was Dickens. Her correspondence makes clear, for example, that despite their quarrel she evidently still read his new work, as a reference to *Little Dorrit* exemplifies. It also reveals, unsurprisingly, that she had a great deal to say about Dickens's separation from and treatment of his wife in 1858. Finally, and, more surprisingly, in a passing comment she indicates that her beloved niece and intellectual companion, Maria Martineau, was close to Charles Dickens the younger and his wife, remained so after the separation, and visited with them into the 1860s.[2] The close-knit connective ties of network and relationship that, as this book has argued, permeated the world of the Victorian press were, then, clearly evident during the final phase of the curious dyad that Charles Dickens and Harriet Martineau formed. Moreover, while they never again worked together, one of Martineau's major professional steps in her late career was taken in direct response to Dickens's most significant last contribution to the Victorian press – the replacement of *Household Words* with *All the Year Round*. In late 1859 she accepted an offer to contribute to Bradbury and Evans's new publication, *Once a Week*, turning down as she did so Thackeray's effort to recruit her for the *Cornhill Magazine*. As she made this decision, and as this chapter will discuss, she made it clear that it was shaped not only by doubts over Thackeray's editorial abilities and the new form of shilling monthly he was introducing, but also by the opportunity to write for a mass-market weekly established precisely as a direct competitor to Dickens's new journal.

Other than Deborah Logan's passing footnote on the relation of *Once a Week* to *All the Year Round*, however, there has been no critical discussion of the connection between Martineau and Dickens's last work in the Victorian press.[3] This concluding chapter fills that lacuna and, by examining the closing phase of the two journalists' careers, rounds out the argument this book has made in two specific ways. First, it builds on the previous chapters to show how Martineau and Dickens's competing visions for journalism as a shaping force in the public sphere contributed to the development of the press as it moved into the great era of growth following the final removal of the 'taxes on knowledge'. Second, it examines how, in these late years, their understandings of the liberal project, which had always been fraught by the competing emphases this book has explored, are ultimately subsumed into two very different conceptions of the evolving narrative of social history. On the one hand, until the end of her life and throughout her last working years as a professional journalist, Martineau remains committed to the core elements of a liberalism founded upon the unitary historical narrative of Enlightenment stadial theory, the limitation of state intervention and the essential role of individual volunteer activism in promoting that advance of women she argues is fundamental to broader social progress. On the other, Dickens, building upon the scepticism that began to emerge in *Little Dorrit*'s representation of the modern state, turns away from the forward-looking narrative that stadial theory offered, embraces instead the new models of comparative history that were coming to prominence during the 1850s and articulates a darker vision of a world that seems less and less susceptible to the kinds of managed adjustment upon which the hopes of liberalism were founded.

This contrast in their final conceptualisation of the historical arc defines the ways in which Martineau and Dickens were, for all their likeness, ultimately very different kinds of liberal thinkers and writers. It also points us towards a richer understanding of their subsequent fates in our own scholarly discipline than the established narrative of their quarrel over the far narrower issue of factory safety policy has allowed us to see. For, as Devin Griffiths has argued, the development of comparative history marked an intellectual shift that introduced 'a mode of contextual analysis that has become so fundamental to modern social inquiry that its nineteenth-century formulation has gone largely unnoticed'. Replacing 'both the liberal progressive thesis of Whig history and the stadial theories of the Scottish Enlightenment with a mixed understanding of the differential and contingent forces of historical change', comparative history emphasised instead 'indeterminacy', 'difference and divergence' and, as the French Revolution testified, 'a potentially limitless set of irruptions'.[4] Martineau's vision of stadial theory broadly aligned with the Whig assumption that the historical narrative was fundamentally progressive in its arc. Where she most notably differed with Whig ideology, as previous chapters have shown and this concluding part of my argument will explore one last time, was over its erasure of the case for women's identity as fully realised liberal subjects, a case she had argued throughout her work and that her own career as a professional author had modelled. That her now ongoing recovery in English studies should have had to wait until the 1980s when scholarship on women writers first became fully established within the discipline is, then, if unfortunate perhaps also understandable. Dickens, as we have also seen, made his own extensive contributions to the erasure of female agency, and, as the previous chapters have shown and this one will further touch upon, they mark a point of irresolvable difference in his and Martineau's visions of the liberal project. At the same time, however, his late work in the press also shows him moving away from the kind of stadial theory to which Martineau remained an adherent until the end of her life. Although earlier in his career, as Chapter 3 argued, *American Notes* had countered the disorder of democratic America with the potential of stadial development represented in British-ruled Canada, by the late 1850s Dickens's vision of the historical arc has tilted in a very different direction. Rather than the progressive forward impulse of stadial theory, Dickens moves increasingly towards the expression of an indeterminacy that, as Griffiths has suggested, makes him a profoundly modern author and surely contributed to the revival in his own critical fortunes that began in the uncertain decades after the Second World War. Examining, then, the concluding phase of what I described in the Introduction as Martineau and

Dickens's 'binary system of mutual proximity and influence' illustrates how their fundamental differences over liberal ideology and the narrative of historical movement both shaped their contributions to the mid-nineteenth century press and have contributed to the ways in which we have read them, individually and together, in our own scholarly accounts of their places within and impacts upon Victorian culture.

To make this case, the chapter is structured into three sections. First, it examines Dickens's final contribution to Victorian journalism, the creation of *All the Year Round*, and argues that his launching the new weekly with *A Tale of Two Cities* as its serial lead gives expression to the emergent model of comparative history and, in doing so, marks his own fullest statement on the liberal debate over the relationship between the individual and collective society. Drawing upon his longstanding connection with Thomas Babington Macaulay, the section concludes by showing how, through the combination of *All the Year Round* and the serialisation in it of *A Tale of Two Cities*, Dickens created an innovative journalistic form that represented a successor to both the ideology of Whig history and its embodiment in the *Edinburgh Review* with which Macaulay had been so closely associated. Second, pivoting to Martineau, the chapter shows how for her, too, Macaulay becomes a touchstone, a figure to whom she, like Dickens, responded in defining her vision of history and the press and a lens through whom we can understand more fully how both positioned themselves in the press and articulated ideologies that competed with Macaulay's as well as one another's. Martineau's essay 'Female Industry', which she published in the *Edinburgh* the same month that *A Tale of Two Cities* began its serialisation in *All the Year Round*, thus presents a vision of stadial social progress and the transformation of women's standing as liberal subjects through the expansion of access to employment. In doing so, it stands in contrast to both Dickens and Macaulay's diverging readings of the historical narrative as well as their shared marginalising of female agency. Emphasising the transformation of nursing in the period after Crimea into a formalised profession, Martineau's essay picks up on a form of female labour she had made the focus of her debut essay for *Household Words* and sets the precedent for what will become a recurring topic of attention in her late journalism. Third, while Martineau's differences with Macaulay are largely implicit in 'Female Industry', they become entirely explicit when, following two savage obituaries that Martineau published after his death in December 1859, William Makepeace Thackeray used his newly established *Cornhill Magazine* to launch a spectacularly ill-judged attack upon her. That attack and Martineau's subsequent relationship with the *Cornhill*, which have gone almost entirely unnoticed in the critical conversation, became an important factor in the series of choices Martineau made for own career as she adapted to the changing landscape of the mid-Victorian press and found multiple outlets through which to convey her liberal version of stadial progress to an expanding range of readerships. Examining those choices, the chapter ends by showing how Martineau closed out her active career as a professional woman writer by making her last arguments for a vision of stadial progress consistent with the master narrative of historical development to which she remained committed until the end. In particular, and building upon those articles in which she treats the training of women for the emerging profession of nursing, Martineau makes the case for a fundamental reconceptualisation of the ways in which girls should be educated as she argues for the value and necessity of preparing women to become autonomous liberal subjects able to take fully realised roles in society through entering the world of work.

'The alienation of the people from their own public affairs': *A Tale of Two Cities*, Comparative History and the Popular Press

In the spring of 1859, having outmanoeuvred his former publishers in a manner that would have done credit to Hannibal Chollop's editorial self-aggrandisement and gained control over both the legal entity that was *Household Words* and its remaining stock, Dickens launched its successor, *All the Year Round*.[5] Using *A Tale of Two Cities* to set the precedent, he established what would become his new magazine's ongoing strategy of using high-quality original fiction as the hook to draw in a mass-market readership and, in doing so, immediately achieved a level of success that eclipsed even his accomplishment with *Household Words*. As John Drew has noted, *All the Year Round* settled in to a regular sale of 100,000, while it also pioneered a new form of transatlanticism through the series of marketing arrangements Dickens and W. H. Wills negotiated with American agents and publishers.[6] This success, moreover, was achieved despite the brutal reception that the magazine's lead-off novel received at the hands of the critics. Largely ignored by the reviews, indeed, *A Tale of Two Cities* was, at best, dismissed briefly and, at worst, lacerated, most notably by James Fitzjames Stephens in the *Saturday Review*. Claiming that 'it would perhaps be hard to imagine a clumsier or more disjointed framework for the display of the tawdry wares which form Mr Dickens's stock-in-trade', Stephens goes on to pillory the foundation of the writer's methods:

> Mr Dickens is especially addicted to the cultivation of a judicious vagueness; but in his present work he affords an opportunity for instituting a comparison between the facts on which he relies, and the assertions which he makes on the strength of them.[7]

What contemporaries such as Stephens might have dismissed as 'judicious vagueness', however, has come to be understood by modern scholars as a far more nuanced reading of the historical narrative, one that resisted simpler dichotomies that had formed the conventional episteme and one that permeates Dickens's late journalism. Indeed, the novel becomes the most extended embodiment of the way in which, as Drew has suggested, *Household Words* and *All the Year Round* make evident the limitations of the models provided by Macaulay and Carlyle, 'the progressive line of development, versus the cyclical and prophetic', as Dickens used his magazines to suggest his 'apprehension as an editor of the relevance to readers of both kinds of patterning'.[8] Using *A Tale of Two Cities* as the lead to his new weekly, then, Dickens makes his final great contribution to the Victorian press as he fuses journalism and fiction to create a large-circulation hybrid magazine read across a wide range of social classes that combined popular entertainment with a richly complex representation of the nature of contemporary society and the historical narrative.

The complexity of that representation has been the focus of recent critical studies that have, in effect, recovered the contribution *A Tale of Two Cities* makes to mid-Victorian debates around the tensions between individual agency and collective social life. Devin Griffiths, Jonathan Grossman and Daniel Stout have each read the novel within its historical moment: Stout focusing upon its 'analysis of the surprisingly anti-individual implications of natural rights', Grossman exploring its positioning within an imaginary of 'a universalizing collective' made possible by the development of standardised forms of measurement and Griffiths, as suggested above, positioning it within a broader shift in paradigms of historical narrative.[9] For Stout and Grossman in particular, the essential point of focus becomes the guillotine, the instrument of death whose presence permeates the novel:

'How goes the Republic?' Sidney Carton asks the wood-sawyer outside La Force prison; 'You mean the Guillotine', is the response.[10] Dickens's capitalisation points to the all-importance of the machine of death and the ways in which, as Stout suggests, 'the purest republic is the republic that has done away with representation by doing away with all its representatives' and in which Grossman, building on Stout, argues that ultimately the guillotine should be seen 'not just from the perspective of the individuals it victimized but from that of the community it affirmed through standardizing executions'.[11] The irresistible, anonymous forces of the French Revolution, Stout has argued, are shown in Dickens's account to play a 'key role in the incorporation – the thoroughgoing corpororatization – of modernity',[12] displacing the power of individual agency with that of the collective.

The depth of this shift in the Dickensian vision becomes evident if we turn back to his first explorations of the nature of social life in a rapidly modernising world increasingly given shape by new forms of urban organisation that were discussed in Chapters 3 and 4. As Billie Melman has shown, for example, Dickens's earlier treatment of British history in *Barnaby Rudge* had already called into question the opposition between Macaulayan and Carlylean models that *A Tale of Two Cities* finally overthrows. Moreover, as Melman argues, the trepidations *Barnaby* expresses over mass violence (and, by extension of her case, the profound uncertainty in *Martin Chuzzlewit*'s representation of metropolitan life examined in Chapter 4) both speak to a larger sense of a 'labyrinthine character and structurelessness' that reveals how Dickensian London's 'chaotic and disordered past was alive and visible in its outlay, development, and lack of central government and was part and parcel of its modernity'.[13] Where *Barnaby* ends with the rioters defeated, order restored and the British state returned to its equilibrium, however, the degree to which Dickens's vision had become even more deeply problematised by the time he wrote *A Tale of Two Cities* can be reckoned from the passage of narrative commentary that opens the novel's third chapter:

> A wonderful fact to reflect upon, that every human creature is constituted to be that profound secret and mystery to every other. A solemn consideration, when I enter a great city by night, that every one of those darkly clustered houses encloses its own secret; that every room in every room one of them encloses its own secret; that every beating heart in the hundreds of thousands of breasts there, is, in some of its imaginings, a secret to the heart nearest it![14]

By contrast with both *Barnaby* and *Martin Chuzzlewit*'s representations of the burgeoning phenomenon of urban life, in *A Tale of Two Cities* entering the dark city is to put oneself in peril of death, the secrets in the darkly clustered houses are, whether stemming from the oppression of the ancien régime or the new tyrannies of the revolution, those of betrayal and condemnation, and the reflective melancholy of such a passage is soon drowned out by the epistemic violence of modernity. Even more than Melman's suggestion that Dickens's representation of both London and Paris consistently displays the ways in which the modern metropolis refuses to 'yield to grand narratives of order',[15] then, what *A Tale of Two Cities* depicts is the ultimate extension of the concern Dickens had voiced in a letter to Henry Austen back in April 1855: 'There is nothing in the present time at once so galling and so alarming to me as the alienation of the people from their own public affairs.'[16] For, finally, where the Dickens of the early 1840s had, in his account of New York, been intrigued and captivated by the spectacle of an American public so ambivalently immersed in their own affairs through the mass-market press, in *A Tale of Two Cities* we find him aligned with the broader intellectual shift that Griffiths has described occurring 'as post-1848 revolutionary histories struggled to reconcile the ongoing instability of European states with any sense of a general plan'. That the plot ends with Carton's act of self-sacrifice, then, marks neither such a general plan nor the triumph of individual agency but rather, in Griffiths's words, the deployment of 'the ethical solvent of melodrama to dissolve the moral ambiguity of social history'.[17]

Recent critical studies such as these have made freshly evident the rich historical complexity Dickens's second historical novel offers: in Griffith's words, it exemplifies 'the role his novels played in applying comparative methodology to the ethnographic and historicizing ambitions of nineteenth-century British fiction'.[18] In emphasising its achievements as a novel, however, something these studies have looked past is its initial identity as a serial component within the popular press. Building on these studies, my argument here is that, by publishing *A Tale of Two Cities* in his new mass-market weekly, Dickens not only called into question a prevailing conventional paradigm of historical narrative but simultaneously also disrupted established expectations for a cheap journalistic venue by making it the initial publishing vehicle for high-quality fiction. Writing a new kind of history in a new kind of magazine, the price for his bold experiment in popular fiction's enormous popular success may have been the negativity of its reception in a critical establishment unsure what to make of it. Through examining this experiment in the context of Dickens's connection with Thomas Babington Macaulay in the latter's dual role as principal spokesman for the unitary narrative of Whig history and magisterial gatekeeper of the *Edinburgh Review* that had been its elite journalistic outlet, we can understand more fully just how profoundly Dickens once again and one last time reshaped the Victorian press and used it to present his own vision of liberal history to the mid-century reading public.

'I know something of Macaulay': Dickens, Whig History and the Popular Press

Reactions to Macaulay's death in December 1859 point to the ways in which the model of history embodied in his life and work had become increasingly contested. Renowned as he had been for the eloquence of his parliamentary oratory and the magisterial style of both his essays for the *Edinburgh Review* and the three completed volumes of his *History of England*, his passing was nevertheless recorded by the London press in a remarkably diverse group of obituaries. These ranged from *The Times*'s expression of 'deep regret for such a profound loss which will universally be felt wherever the English language is spoken'[19] to the *Morning Chronicle*'s cryptic dismissal of him as 'the spoilt child of literature' along with its disparaging comment on 'that asceticism of opinion which exercised a fatal influence' over his political career.[20] Despite its differences with the more affirming views of Macaulay's life and career, however, even such a critical obituary as this recognised that he had been 'the interpreter of the views of the leaders of Whig principles, to whom, above all others, the nation delighted to listen' and that with his death 'another link in the chain of Whig traditions' had been broken. Notwithstanding the range of their assessments, then, the contemporary press was united in its view that the departure of the man who had celebrated the Great Exhibition as a triumphant culmination of the advance of British civilisation and 1851 itself as 'a singularly happy year of peace, plenty, good feeling, innocent pleasure and national glory'[21] marked the closing of a chapter in the ongoing Victorian debate over the nature of the Britain's past and the direction of its future.

The complexities suggested in these contemporary obituaries in the London press led into a longer-term debate over Macaulay's legacy that began, as Robert Sullivan has argued, soon after his death and has continued into modern scholarship. G. O. Trevelyan, his nephew and first biographer, 'carefully depicted his uncle as a Whig rather than as a mid-century liberal', for example, even as other contemporaries were eager to position him as Gladstone's ideological predecessor and a forefather to the Liberal Party.[22] Modern studies continue to echo the mixed assessment of Macaulay's contemporaries, affirming his role as the last great representative of the Whig tradition yet also interrogating his theory of British civilisation and its role in the project of empire. He has thus been variously described, for example, as 'the impresario of the Whig version of the constitution', 'the perfect spokesman for the practical secular center of English opinion', and as having, especially in his work for the *Edinburgh Review*, 'set a standard almost impossible of emulation'.[23] Focusing in particular on his contributions to the imperial project, Lauren Goodlad has read Macaulay's 'Minute on Education' as advocating a form of 'penetrative pastorship' that would deploy the canonical texts of English literature in the effort to create 'a seminal class through whom to advance the blood of Indian genealogy by dint of English mind'.[24] In Goodlad's interpretation, Macaulay's view of empire becomes less one to be identified with the Whig tradition and, instead, can be seen more fully as representative of one distinct form of liberalism that, marked by its 'antistatist and voluntarist governing philosophy', is to be differentiated from 'the centralized intervention favored by Benthamite rivals such as James Mill'[25] through its focus upon inculcating British ideology into the formation of a subaltern leadership cadre. Finally, extending the focus on Macaulay's influence on the imperial project through his role in the formation of this cadre through the education of Britain's male elite, Patrick Joyce has seen him as one of the key actors in 'the creation of Platonic Guardians for Britain and the Empire' through his efforts 'in promoting Greek civilization and history' to form a template for a model of 'a view of British society as an organic community held together by differences'.[26] Both Dickens and Martineau responded to the complexities Macaulay has come to embody for modern scholars as much as his contemporaries, reacting to differing aspects of the man, the historian and his legacy and, in so doing, illuminating their own ideological emphases within the liberal tradition and the ways in which these found expression in their late work in the press.

In the closely networked world of intellectual and literary London, Dickens did indeed 'know something of Macaulay',[27] with whom he became acquainted early in his career, and the two men evidently developed a cordial personal relationship, albeit one in which the balance of professional respect was heavily on one side. First meeting in the late 1830s, they both moved within the progressive network maintained by Lord and Lady Holland and occasionally overlapped in their charitable work, as in their efforts to secure a Civil List pension for Leigh Hunt in 1847.[28] Despite the fact that Dickens named Macaulay's *Lays of Ancient Rome* among the titles for a library his oldest son was putting together at his school and wrote of 'his brilliant History' in the very same issue of *Household Words* that included his assault on Martineau in 'Our Wicked Mis-Statements',[29] however, there was a significant differential in their mutual assessments. For Macaulay, while regarding Dickens as 'a man of genius and a good-hearted man', also detected in him 'some faults of taste' and in 1842 had been deeply disappointed by *American Notes*, which he found 'in spite of some gleams of genius, at once frivolous and dull'[30]. While, as Chapter 3 showed, such a response was typical of the critical reception to the travel book, the most significant outcome of Macaulay's appraisal was that it appears to have marked the decisive factor in ending a long courtship between the *Edinburgh Review* and Dickens as a prospective contributor.[31] For in his letter to Macvey Napier to indicate that he had changed his mind about reviewing *American Notes* for the Whig quarterly, Macaulay went on to express the sentiment that he still at least hoped to see Dickens 'inrolled in our blue and yellow corps, where he may do excellent service as a skirmisher and a sharp-shooter'.[32] Damning with such faint praise, however, Macaulay suggests that he could only imagine Dickens playing a subordinate, auxiliary role in the *Edinburgh*. Not surprisingly, no such role ever materialised and, indeed, was surely always an implausible match for the insurgently ambitious journalist who, as we have seen in Chapter 4, had returned from America with hopes of taking on a role that would provide him with the editorial authority to shape the public sphere as he saw fit. For all the success Dickens achieved over the following decade, Macaulay apparently never revised his judgement, however, as his late dismissal of *Hard Times* as nothing more than 'sullen socialism' reveals.[33]

That Dickens voiced no such reservations about Macaulay and that both *Household Words* and *All the Year Round* frequently cite him in glowing terms[34] should not, however, conceal the fundamental divergence in their visions of history and understanding of the role of the press in forming the public sphere. Although Macaulay had successfully kept the gates of the *Edinburgh Review* closed against him, Dickens had, as Chapter 6 discussed and Sally Ledger has noted,[35] created through the founding of *Household Words* his own brilliant mechanism through which to articulate a cross-class vision of national community. By the later 1850s, despite all his praise of Macaulay's work and its triumphant statement of progress towards the pinnacle of modernity that it found represented in mid-nineteenth-century Britain, Dickens, as we have seen, had become ever less assured that the legacy of the past had in fact created the foundation for the rising arc of progress Macaulay had propounded. Moreover, at the same time, and as John Drew has shown, as he developed *All the Year Round* away from *Household Words*, Dickens's late journalism also 'indexed the wider decline of radicalism in the 1860s'[36] through the magazine's reduced attention to the kind of specific social issues and concerns that had been a mainstay of its predecessor. Never revisiting the possibility of appearing in the great quarterly reviews, whose dominance of the press was over by mid-century, Dickens thus turned away from both the model of historical narrative and forms of journalism Macaulay had represented so powerfully and, in *All the Year Round*, its lead-off novel and the ethos of uncommercialism[37] created a mass-market, cross-class venue of his own through which to give voice to his own late representation of a Britain no longer simply marching down the confident path imagined in Macaulay's Whig vision.

'Society has outgrown illustration by fiction': Martineau, Macaulay and the *Edinburgh Review*

Just three months before Dickens launched *All the Year Round* by using *A Tale of Two Cities* to represent the emergent form of comparative history, Martineau expressed her own sense of the relationship between the arc of history and the role of fictional narrative in shaping the public sphere. In January 1859 she wrote to Florence Nightingale, responding, as Deborah Logan has noted, to her friend's desire to have the reports and statistics Nightingale had compiled on the reform of sanitary conditions in the military appear in a popular narrative form analogous to *Illustrations of Political Economy*. Martineau's letter voiced a more gradualist sense of historical development than the apocalyptic vision that Dickens's novel would reveal and downplayed the role of the novel as a genre: 'society has outgrown illustration by fiction . . . is now more solid, more practical, & more accustomed to political topics than ¼ of a century ago'. Continuing on to describe her own inability now to write such a narrative – 'I don't believe that any one who has successfully written History & "leaders" in a London "daily", cd ever again write fiction' – she simultaneously defines the kind of writer she believes herself to be and implicitly devalues the strategy Dickens had adopted for communicating his vision of 'political topics' to a readership that had clearly not 'outgrown illustration by fiction'.[38] Martineau's sense of herself as a writer focused upon analysis and exposition, a professional woman claiming forms of authority conventionally assigned to men, an author resisting merely fictional modes of representation and persuasion, is, as we have seen throughout this book, a recurring point of self-definition and differentiation from the forms of Dickensian power she both acknowledged and resisted. If her reiteration of this vision late in her career may have limited her ability to recognise the scope and significance of Dickens's innovative experiment with fictional form at *All the Year Round*, however, she was, as the contemporary reviews of *A Tale of Two Cities* show, far from alone in this. More significantly in terms of her own work, her perception of a society that had become 'more solid, more practical, more accustomed to political topics' points to her beliefs in continuing stadial progress and in her own role as a 'wisdom writer' seeking to support that advance, beliefs that are borne out in the choices she made about where she would publish during the last phase of her professional career and the ways in which she represented issues to her readers.

In Martineau's late journalism, those beliefs are most first and most fully exemplified in 'Female Industry', published in the *Edinburgh Review* at the beginning of the same month in which Dickens began serialising *A Tale of Two Cities* and the second of a dozen essays she published in the magazine. Following the collapse of her two-decade-long relationship with the *Westminster* following revelations of John Chapman's financial mismanagement, Martineau published her last article for it in October 1858 and, that same month, appeared for the first time in the *Edinburgh*. By the late 1850s, however, the Edinburgh was a very different review from the one over which Macaulay had ruled during the 1840s. Then, as Judith Newton has said, a significant component of its ideology had been a focus upon 'containing women and the impact of their written discourse to traditional domestic spheres'.[39] Now, with her cousin Henry Reeve as its editor, the review proved far more amenable to Martineau's agenda and open to her agency. 'Female Industry' thus shows how she was able to move the great Whig-founded quarterly into directions unimaginable during the era of Macaulay's domination, and it does so not simply through the choice of its subject but through the major rhetorical strategies Martineau deploys to make her case. Two of these in particular reveal how profoundly focused she is upon revising the established narrative of women's work that both Macaulay and an earlier iteration of the *Edinburgh* had done much to construct and that Dickens had also made part of his version of liberalism.

First, using in a new way the practice of authorial anonymity that Alexis Easley has shown was such an essential component of her professional positioning,[40] Martineau makes a two-part reference back to earlier publications of her own that had initially appeared in venues quite different from the lofty heights of the *Edinburgh* and does so in order to call out the importance of education for the advance of the working classes. She begins this move by returning to her longstanding interest in the exemplary community created by the women factory workers of Lowell, Massachusetts as she references a 'letter from Harriet Martineau' that had prefaced Charles Knight's 1843 reprint of the *Lowell Offering* for the *Weekly Volume* series she had been so instrumental in establishing. Calling back to the American women workers' miscellany and echoing the language of her preface, she argues for the importance of giving value to the intellectual lives of industrial workers: 'it is not the labour of the factory which hardens and brutalizes the minds of men or women, but the state of ignorance in which they enter upon a life of bustle and publicity'.[41] Then, as an exemplary model of how such a 'state of ignorance' can be addressed in the industrial context of the Old World, Martineau goes on to allude to one of her publications from almost a decade later – her 1852 piece for *Household Words*, 'The New School for Wives'. Reminding the *Edinburgh* readers of its account of factory-located educational provisions for women, she goes on to suggest that the article 'afforded great encouragement' about the potential of such initiatives, and so uses Dickens's venue to suggest to her readers that what was achieved in America may well be replicated in Britain.[42] Calling out her own earlier work to advocate for a cause Macaulay's *Edinburgh* would never have supported, and that Dickens himself would have resisted, Martineau thus uses anonymity not only to ruffle the pages of the once staid Whig quarterly with the presence of two mass-market publications but also to break through the cordon of gender policing Macaulay had so assiduously maintained during his time as its editor.

Second, having made this larger breakthrough, in the essay's final section Martineau deploys a strategy that becomes central to much of her late work in the press as she draws her readers' attention to the fact of women's employment beyond the home as a newly established norm and uses a particular category of labour to make her larger point. As she closes the essay by listing a number of women and their professional accomplishments across a variety of fields and even offers a touch of self-deprecating humour by implicitly acknowledging the opportunities her own career has provided – 'Our countrywomen have the free command of the press; and they use it abundantly'[43] – she calls out nursing for particular attention. In selecting nursing to exemplify for her readers the shift in women's employment that was taking shape in mid-Victorian Britain, Martineau fixed upon a particularly topical subject and one that offered an especially apposite model at the end of her career-long advocacy of the importance of female agency, work and the development of a fully liberal society. Beyond the ways in which public attention to the field had been intensified by the appalling conditions created during the Crimean War and the publicity that had been generated around Florence Nightingale's heroic efforts, nursing offered Martineau the opportunity to connect for her readers traditionally accepted domestic forms of women's labour with new kinds of professionalism. Describing it to her readers as 'an occupation combining the advantages which Adam Smith represents as alternatives – of social repute and pecuniary profit',[44] nursing allowed her to continue the process of adapting the legacy of Enlightenment stadial theory in light of British society's evolution in the second half of the nineteenth century. Basing her case upon a reiteration of the foundational liberal principle that the capacity of the state to effect such cultural and social change was neither significant nor indeed desirable, she once again built her argument upon strategies she had used throughout her career: the deployment of quantitative data that serve both as evidence for her case and as a means of positioning her outside the confines of conventionally feminine forms of discourse; adroit self-fashioning and manoeuvring within that 'dynamic of interlocking structures' Laurel Brake has named as a defining characteristic of Victorian journalism;[45] and the use of real-life case studies to provide exemplary narratives as illustrations of her claims. Combining these strategies in her late journalism, Martineau both made the argument for women's essential inclusion in the advancement of a liberal society and offered her readers a methodology of social-historical analysis that implicitly responded to those, including Macaulay, who had resisted the very notion of women's participation in the genre.

For the issue on which she most differed with Macaulay and the vision of Whig history he had forwarded was the subject of women's work she brought so forcefully to the attention of his journal's readers. As Catharine Hall has shown, Macaulay's understanding of history itself and his sense of the work for which women were suited were profoundly gendered – he was contemptuous of women as historians and believed that as writers they should restrict themselves to lesser genres.[46] Martineau, of course, spent her entire life defying such expectations, building a career in which she demonstrated unprecedented mastery of multiple genres and disciplines and modelling the role of professional author for the succeeding generation of women writers. Not surprisingly, then, she was enthusiastically receptive to the 'new discourse of women's work' that Linda Peterson has described developing during the 1850s and that was given specific voice by Anna Jameson in her 1856 *The Communion of Labour*. Challenging traditional binary distinctions between male and female work by arguing, as Peterson has said, that 'the duties of both men and women emerge from the home and radiate out into the public sphere', this was a discourse that aligned with Martineau's most fundamental ideological commitments and represented everything Macaulay opposed.[47]

To make her case in 'Female Industry', Martineau once again employs anonymous self-reference by alluding to the story of Mary Pickard, whose role as the subject of her very first article for *Household Words* was discussed in the previous chapter. In this second telling of Pickard's story, however, Martineau uses it to make new points and moves the focus on to another woman, one whose accomplishments both testify to the advances since the early years of the century when Pickard bravely intervened in the Osmotherly epidemic and also anticipate those still to come: 'Florence Nightingale and her disciples have inaugurated a new period in the history of working-women, and the manifest destiny of the nursing class will fulfil itself.'[48] Where just eight years earlier Martineau had been called on to defend naming a private individual in a public narrative, here and throughout her late journalism she evidently feels free to draw a contemporary female exemplar into the public sphere and offer her as a model for the wider cultural change she wishes to promote. For the contrast between the two women, which Martineau would revisit in an 1860 *Once a Week* article where she describes Pickard as 'a perfect example of a spontaneous, unprofessional nurse',[49] points to the particular value Nightingale assumes in her late journalism. That is, Martineau is able to capitalise upon Nightingale's heroic status in the years after the Crimean War and cast her as a metonymic representative for the changes in her field and a model for the contemporary professional woman. Drawing upon Dickens to support her case, she alludes to one of his best-known characters when she describes the monthly nurses of former years as 'scarcely caricatured even in Mrs Gamp'[50] and then singles out Nightingale's qualities in terms that recall those with which she had opposed Dickens's resistance to the Factory Act. For she, first, attributes Nightingale's success in Crimea to her capacity 'to lay open the case to the steady good sense of society, precisely when good sense was in most danger of being swamped by the mixture of a romantic egotism with a gush of genuine benevolence',[51] and, secondly, she describes the reforms Nightingale has championed as embodying a new paradigm for female professionalisation: 'her minute economy and attention to the smallest details are reconcilable with the magnitude of her administration, and the comprehensiveness of her plans for hospital establishments, and for the reduction of the national rate of mortality'.[52] As Elisabeth Sanders Arbuckle has noted, Martineau's campaign to promote the respectability of nursing as a profession for middle-class women certainly encountered considerable resistance and the success of Nightingale's efforts may have been limited.[53] Nevertheless, as Martineau emphasises to the readers of *Once a Week*, in Florence Nightingale she was presenting them with an example of a woman whose 'character was too strong, and its quality too real for any sympathy with shallowness and egotism'.[54] As such, Nightingale served as a model for the larger case about cultural transformation Martineau made throughout her late journalism, a case that culminates, as the final section of this chapter will show, in two *Cornhill* essays on education that argue the essential need for 'familiarising the mind of society with the idea of women becoming self-dependent'.[55]

'Thomas Macaulay wanted heart': Martineau, Thackeray and the *Cornhill*

Before she could write those essays and appear in the *Cornhill*, however, Martineau would pass through one more clash with the patriarchal structures of mid-Victorian journalism, a clash that resulted from her making brutally public her dissent from Macaulay and all that he represented. For, while she shared in the pleasure that Dickens and many other Victorian readers recorded they took from reading Macaulay's work, when it came to offering a summative appraisal of his contribution, she was decidedly less enthusiastic – both of the individual and the historian. In 1851, for example, she had dismissed him privately to Fanny Wedgwood: 'What Whig of the cold-blooded sort, – *his* sort – ever could see what was before his eyes, or could bear to look steadily at the future?'; four years later, in writing the *Autobiography* that would remain unpublished until after her own death, she had labelled his abilities as 'capable of nothing better than rearing gay kiosks in the flower gardens of literature, to be soon swept away by the caprices of a new taste, as superficial as his own'.[56] Although both of these dismissive comments would remain invisible until after her own death, there was no effort at concealment in the obituaries Martineau wrote for the *Daily News* and *Once a Week* following Macaulay's death on 28 December 1859.[57] Although she was certainly not unique in voicing criticism of the departed, her first piece was matched in its virulence only by her second article as she unsparingly dissected Macaulay's failings as a recorder of history. Writing in the *Daily News*, she noted that he had repeatedly demonstrated the 'radical inaccuracy of his habit of thought', was 'thoroughly deficient ... in moral earnestness', and, above all else, 'cold and barren as regards the highest part of human nature', he was 'wanting heart'. Her second notice two weeks later confirmed the judgement of the first since, while longer, more detailed and offering a more comprehensive account of the life and work, it also labelled Macaulay 'the greatest plagiarist of his time', condemned his 'indolence' and assumed that his not needing 'much human affection, within himself or towards himself' accounted for the 'deficiency in the coherence of his reasoning, and in his interpretation of much of human conduct in history'.[58] For Martineau, then, Macaulay combined more mechanical errors with a fundamental deficiency in that capacity for social sympathy that she had, since her writing on America more than two decades earlier, privileged as the combination of foundational methodological tool and as the essential characteristic of a progressive society.

The extraordinary vitriol of these final appraisals and their unstinting violation of the conventional expectations of the obituary genre made for anything but a valediction that would have given comfort to his grieving mourners. That she had accused him of wanting 'heart', for example, can only have caused pain amongst those who knew the extent and depth of Macaulay's emotional ties to his family, above all to his sisters.[59] Precisely when the *Daily News* obituary appeared, however, one of his closest friends found himself in an unusually opportune position to respond. Thackeray, who had known Macaulay since their time together at Trinity College, Cambridge, was in the thick of preparing copy for the second number of what had turned out to be his phenomenally successful new magazine, the *Cornhill*. He seized the moment and created a space both to reply to Martineau's charges and admonish her:

> The writer who said that Lord Macaulay had no heart could not know him. Press writers should read a man well, and all over, and again; and hesitate, at least, before they speak of those αιδοια. Those who knew Lord Macaulay knew how admirably tender, and generous, and affectionate he was. It was not his business to bring his family before the theatre footlights, and call for bouquets from the gallery as he wept over them.[60]

As Thackeray's daughter recorded more than thirty years later, this was an account of the late historian that moved his family deeply. Macaulay's brother Charles thus wrote to a friend that it was 'the outpouring of a tender, generous, noble nature' and went on to ask him to convey 'that the last book my brother read was the first number of "The Cornhill Magazine". It was open at Thackeray's story, on the table by the side of the chair in which he died.'[61]

Any satisfaction Thackeray may have felt at learning of this last connection with his late friend and the pleasure his response to Martineau had given the family was, however, to be short-lived, for he soon discovered that in his trenchant reply he had unwittingly committed a faux pas of monumental proportions, word of which quickly spread among London's literary circles. Late in March 1860, for example, it was discussed at one of the regular weekly dinners the senior staff of *Punch* held in the offices of Bradbury and Evans on Bouverie Street. Henry Silver, whose diary of these occasions provides a unique insight into the magazine and the literary world of which it was so central a part, recorded an exchange between Samuel Lucas, the editor of *Once a Week*, and John Leech, *Punch*'s best-known illustrator:

> Thackeray has not been seen since his αιδοια slip – no getting out of it, says Lucas, mistook it for private secrecies and thoughts. J. L. suggests that as it was Miss Martineau he was cutting up he used the Greek that she might enquire what it meant.[62]

Evidently, then, Thackeray was aware that Martineau had written the obituary and had intended to play upon her assumed lack of classical learning. Unfortunately, it was his own deficiencies as a classicist that were revealed, for what αιδοια actually meant was not 'private secrecies and thoughts' but, rather, 'the shameful parts', and it was the term that early Greek physicians had used to refer to the female genitalia.[63] Thackeray, an undistinguished scholar at Charterhouse who had gone on to university for just a single year, had clearly got it completely wrong. More significantly, the *Cornhill* had mapped itself on to the literary market place as a magazine intended to appeal to a broad and mixed audience, and Thackeray's own advertisement had described it as a 'social table' at which 'we shall suppose the ladies and children always present'.[64] Rather than adroitly putting Martineau in her place, then, his blunder undermined the very ethos of his publication, and it was no wonder that he buried himself out of sight in the weeks that followed.

The subject was not of course one suitable for public discussion, however, and so, although the incident clearly caused Thackeray considerable embarrassment in his circle, it had no discernible impact upon the magazine's meteoric success. Similarly, his blunder has been recorded just once in modern scholarship, and treated even there simply as matter for a passing footnote.[65] As was the case with her dispute with Dickens a few years earlier, had this later episode begun with Martineau's obituaries of Macaulay and ended with Thackeray's unfortunate response, it might have been simply a passing spat – one of some interest but perhaps not more broadly significant. But if we see it within the larger context of Macaulay's role as the principal custodian of Whig models of history, it reveals much more than Thackeray's linguistic ineptness. For, in addition to illuminating Martineau's particular version of the liberal project, the episode itself, the events that led up to it and its aftermath are richly indicative of Martineau's position in the world of the Victorian press, of the challenges she posed for the men who dominated that world and, finally, of her role as an essential model and mentor to the next generation of Victorian women authors, women whose work and careers were both anticipated and facilitated by the pioneering model she provided.

As Chapter 5 discussed in examining Martineau's career during the late 1840s and early 1850s, her ability to write on such diverse topics and for such different venues had made her an attractive recruit to start-up ventures in the rapidly expanding mid-century press. That appeal continued and, during the second half of the

1850s, she also developed a cordial relationship with George Smith, the publisher who would launch the *Cornhill* and who brought out four of her books as well as a new edition of *Deerbrook* in 1858. Indeed, Smith was to be literally her last publisher, since in addition to these books in the late fifties it was under his imprint that her posthumous *Autobiography* appeared in 1877, more than twenty years after she had completed it. Given both her professional record and her history with the firm of Smith, Elder, then, in the second half of 1859 when Thackeray began looking for writers to supply the *Cornhill* with matter for its 'discussion and narrative of events interesting to the public'[66] it was natural for him to consider her as a prospective contributor. But despite her ties to the firm and what she described as the 'noble terms' offered, she turned him down.[67] Her letters reveal that there were four factors to this decision: first, she was sceptical about the new model the *Cornhill* represented – as she cautiously wrote to Reeve, she distrusted 'Monthly Magazines set up all round in rivalship'.[68] In this, events quickly proved that she was too conservative in her appraisal of the journalistic marketplace, and her distrust turned out to be wholly misplaced. Second, and rather more accurately, she doubted Thackeray's 'power of industry for *such* work',[69] echoing doubts his own publisher had about the editor's resilience and anticipating what indeed turned out to be his short-lived tenure. Third, with her own health still poor, she claimed to be fully extended with her existing commitments to the *Daily News*, the *Edinburgh Review* and the *Anti-Slavery Standard*. Finally, she had also recently taken on another new commitment, again to an editor with whom she had a long relationship, when she agreed to write occasional pieces for Bradbury and Evans's new magazine, *Once a Week*, and this, she claimed, left her neither time nor energy for an additional responsibility.

Examining her decision to work for *Once a Week* more closely, however, adds yet another layer to the narrative and further complicates the gender politics of Martineau's position and self-positioning in the world of mid-Victorian journalism. In accepting the invitation from its editor – the same Samuel Lucas who just a few months later would find himself at the *Punch* dinner where Thackeray's gaffe was the subject of discussion – she was motivated by something more than simply enthusiasm for his new project. For what particularly drew her to it was her hostility towards Dickens and her readiness to seize the opportunity it provided to work against his interests. Two years after their quarrel over the Factory Act, Martineau had been further incensed by Dickens's public humiliation of his wife at the time of their separation and by the way he had retaliated against Bradbury and Evans for refusing to publish a self-serving account of his marital breakdown in the pages of *Punch*. Closing down *Household Words*, opening *All the Year Round* and returning to Chapman and Hall as his publishers, Dickens had blended self-righteousness with an opportunistic move to strengthen his own economic position, much to Martineau's disgust. As she wrote to Henry Reeve about Lucas's invitation: 'He asked me to write; & I was so indignant at Dickens's conduct to Bradbury and Evans, that I agreed – as have several other people with whom it is an honour to be associated.'[70] Clearly reluctant to venture onto the uncertain ground of a new kind of shilling monthly, especially under Thackeray's leadership, and relishing a chance to support a rival to *All the Year Round*, she concentrated her efforts on *Once a Week* and passed up the *Cornhill*'s offer.

If a variety of factors thus contributed to her turning Thackeray down, his blundering comment in the second issue can only have confirmed her in the decision. Her letters reveal that she did follow the *Cornhill*, so it seems reasonable to assume that she knew all about Thackeray's faux pas. Moreover, despite his assumption that she would have had to 'enquire what it meant', shortly before his article appeared she had coincidentally written to a correspondent that she 'had . . . a sound classical education'[71] and so certainly had the tools to find out for herself what he had said, if not the opportunity to discern what he had intended by it. While she was aware of the magazine's remarkable success, then, there clearly could have been no possibility of her contributing as long as he was its editor. Instead, she continued to appear in that wide variety of other outlets where she was already established and, with her reluctance to write for the new, and very successful, monthly magazines evidently overcome, also made an appearance in *Macmillan's* in June 1862.

Thackeray's death in December of 1863, moreover, reopened the possibility of her writing for the *Cornhill*. Indeed, given the extent and cordiality of the relationship she had developed with George Smith, it was not surprising that she did indeed contribute to what had become the most successful of the new magazines and, as it happened, the three articles she published with it in 1864 and 1865 were almost her last pieces of long-form journalism as her active career as a professional writer finally succumbed to the ill-health under which she had laboured so chronically. 'Nurses Wanted', the third of these articles, continues to make the case we have seen her begin with 'Female Industry' back in 1859, but, for the purposes of my argument here, it is her two-part essay on 'Middle-Class Education in England' that is particularly germane. For with 'Middle-Class Education: Boys' and 'Middle-Class Education: Girls', published in October and November 1864 respectively,[72] she engaged with a specific contemporary conversation about the conditions of upper- and middle-class schooling in England and used this as an opportunity to speak more generally to the issue of the cultural formation of the nation's next generation of elite leaders.

In engaging with this wider conversation, Martineau was both continuing her lifelong interest in education and taking into the public sphere a particular point of debate with which she and Matthew Arnold had been engaged since 1860. As Daniel Malachuk has noted, Martineau, long close with the Arnold family, whose Lake District home was close to her own in Ambleside, had corresponded with Matthew Arnold following the 1861 publication of his *Popular Education in France*. Continuing her longstanding emphasis upon volunteerism and individual agency as essential to liberal progress, Martineau took particular issue with 'Arnold's recommendation that the state intervene in the education of the middle class'.[73] Three years later, that private conversation would become part of a much broader public interest in the state of education in Britain. For the Clarendon Commission, which had been set up in 1861 to examine the condition of the public schools, then came out with a devastating analysis of the deficiencies of nine elite institutions. Arnold himself contributed further to the ongoing conversation, publishing two follow-ups to his own 1861 report: *A French Eton; or, Middle Class Education and the State*; and, in the April issue of the *Cornhill*, an essay on the role of the French Academy. Martineau, too, made use of her longstanding platform as a leader writer for the *Daily News* to add her support to calls for a study paralleling the Clarendon Commission's of the education available to middle-class families. Then, through her pieces for the *Cornhill*, she moved to engage further in the public conversation and respond, with a degree of diplomatic grace that as we have seen was not always a feature of her expressions of difference, to a diagnosis of the topic written by someone to whom she was close but with whose conclusions she also disagreed. Indeed, writing to Lord Fortescue between the appearance of the two essays, she explained that Arnold had urged her to publish her response, that they both wished 'to rouse the public to take some view', and that their one fundamental point of difference was that

> he assumes the best inspection can be provided only by the State, while I am confident that the highest security for the best quality. . . is in the provision being undertaken by the parties most nearly interested in the result.[74]

In addition, by choosing to appear in the *Cornhill* she made use of its highly popular venue to address the subject with an audience of middle-class family readers and was able to put behind her any residual awkwardness that may have lingered from the former editor's mishap. Even as she created the occasion to move forward, she nevertheless managed to find a way to embed within her contributions one final response to that now late editor, one last correction to the masculinist narrative that she had so often had occasion to resist.

At the heart of her argument in the articles are two central points that address her differences with both Arnold and Thackeray and yet that, more fundamentally, speak to the core principles of her liberalism and to the differences between her historical vision and those offered by both Dickens and Macaulay: the limitations of the state as an agent of change; and the essential expansion of the concept of employment so as to include women as agents of social progress. Connecting these two issues and speaking to the remaking of liberal education that Patrick Joyce has shown to be essential to mid-century 'grammars of governance', she focuses upon the particular importance of a classical education, and in so doing marks both a final point of dissent from the model of British history propagated by Macaulay and a closing comment upon the future leadership of the nation.[75]

Although Martineau had apparently originally conceived of the two essays as a single piece, in separated form the difference in their emphases becomes more clearly visible as each of them is built around one of the overarching theses. 'Middle-Class Education: Boys', which focuses largely upon the limitations of state agency in Britain, given the nation's religious diversity and its deep cultural resistance to any 'idea of a discipline so rigid and uniform, and locked in with the mechanism of the Government',[76] thus constitutes her final extended statement on that relationship between the authority of the state and the consent of the governed that she had explored throughout her career. Here, as she writes to educate the readers of the *Cornhill* about their collective class identity, she once again calls on Dickens as a touchstone for the episteme she wishes to shape in her own ways and, having praised *Oliver Twist* for its revelation of the 'unsuspected gradation of ranks in that great mass which is commonly spoken of as the lower orders',[77] she suggests that a similar diversity exists among the middle classes. In consequence, and given the impossibility of achieving a single satisfactory system of education, voluntary agency remains the only option for a society in which 'every Englishman will insist that no central administration can do anything for him and his neighbours that they ought not to do for themselves'.[78] Resisting Arnold's account of the Toulouse Lyceum and the model of centralised, state-organised education it represents, Martineau then affirms again her longstanding commitment to 'the energy which grows out of personal action and responsibility, and ... the liberty which is both the cause and effect of self-government' and reiterates in the context of the 1860s the belief in the liberal agency of the middle classes that had consistently been a fundamental element throughout her career and that had been an especially prominent aspect of her work in the press.[79]

Resisting statist solutions, yet also recognising the limitations of sectarian schooling and the challenges posed by the lack of a wide consensus upon pedagogical training and instructional methods, Martineau's second thesis is that, notwithstanding the new kinds of knowledge that had become essential to Britain's youth, classical learning remains 'an instrument for the training and cultivation of thought, by which other kinds of knowledge are to be obtained' and is 'the best, for the middle class, in all its gradations, if it is the best for any other'.[80] The significance of her emphasis upon what might appear to be a somewhat conservative approach to the curriculum becomes clearer in the light of Patrick Joyce's exploration of the central role of classical education in the formation of the British ruling class in the nineteenth century. As Joyce has shown, classical training was central to the formation of boys who would become the leaders of Britain and its empire, men who would 'regulate passion, suppress barbarism, and encourage character and public morality', and for whom, acting as the foundation of a shared episteme for 'the generalist civil servants and the elite political class, classical language and thought became in effect a private language binding them together and serving as a template for their own society'.[81] Profoundly affecting the development of both elite and middle-class education during the second half of the century, this model influenced men as diverse as Thomas Macaulay and Matthew Arnold, both of whom were, in their very different ways, shaped by a common vision of 'Greek civilisation subsisting in a sort of moral and intellectual empyrean beyond earthly criticism'.[82] There is no indication that Martineau subscribed to what Joyce calls the 'cultist terms' of this faith; however, her *Cornhill* essays make it clear that she certainly did recognise the degree to which the possession of a classical education provided access to the discourses of power and so argued for it taking a central role in the curriculum of the education provided to that middle class which was increasingly claiming political power commensurate with its economic might.

Characteristically, her radical modification to what begins as a largely uncontroversial claim is to extend the argument to include the education of girls. Having in her first article mentioned in passing the benefits that had accrued in the previous century to one exemplary woman, 'Mrs Barbauld, a woman of genius, had undergone the chastening discipline of a sound classical education',[83] she then makes girls' access to classical training a central point in her second. Citing Antioch College in Ohio as the forerunner in providing such opportunities,[84] she anticipates the forthcoming opening of Vassar as 'the women's University of the Republic', praises the degree to which that republic has come to conceive of a 'large intelligence and rich culture' as intrinsic to motherhood and argues that America's evolution into a society that now embraces women as educated professionals inevitably means that 'the order of attainment cannot but be higher, and the intellectual discipline more thorough and comprehensive than with us'.[85] A radically different representation of the United States from that which she had offered thirty years earlier, or even from her more recent accounts of the Civil War, this portrayal of education in America provides a model of encouragement for change in Britain that will result from the expansion of access for girls to education in the classics. Connecting this both to economic changes that have been 'familiarising the mind of society with the idea of women becoming self-dependent' and to 'a radical change in the principle and conduct of the intellectual culture of the educators of the next generation', Martineau concludes:

> Not all the ignorance, the jealousy, the meanness, the prudery, or the profligate selfishness which is to be found from end to end of the middle class, can now reverse the destiny of the English girl, or retard that ennobling of the sex which is a natural consequence of its becoming wiser and more independent, while more accomplished, gracious, and companionable. The briars and brambles are cleared away from the women's avenue to the temple of knowledge. Now they have only to knock, and it will be opened to them.[86]

She does not, of course, refer to Thackeray's hapless attempt to make use of his own classical education to assail a woman who had modelled the life of self-dependence and whose entire career had been devoted to shaping the intellectual culture of her times. Beyond the additional resonance that her language acquires through an awareness of his blunder, however, and even though she nods in the direction of conventional expectations of femininity with 'accomplished, gracious, and companionable', Martineau's larger point is twofold. First, that access to classical learning should become foundational to the education of the girls of the period; and second, that those such as Dickens, Macaulay and Thackerary, who simply assume education to be a masculine preserve, misunderstand the historical forces that are leading these girls to grow up to become women who will both take on an increasingly important role in professional life in Britain and give shape to the nation's culture.

'Nobody whose praise now, could be to me what Miss Martineau's is'

Although she did continue to contribute regularly to the *Daily News* for another year, Martineau's three articles for the *Cornhill* were almost the last of the long-form pieces that she wrote. They were clearly not, however, the end of her influence upon the generation of younger women writers that was emerging by the 1860s. For, even if her own extraordinary contribution to nineteenth-century letters was nearly complete, a larger transition had begun to take hold in the environment for aspiring women writers. The new understandings of labour and intellectual activity that Linda Peterson has described allowed female authors to claim their right to literary work and professional lives with a freedom unimaginable thirty years earlier when Martineau was beginning her own career, and it was the essential context in which a younger generation rose to prominence during the 1860s.[87] As they did so, however, it is clear that many of these women authors recognised the debt they owed their predecessor, even as she herself was in the process of withdrawing from public life.

Among the many examples of this recognition, the most poignant perhaps is offered by one of the new writers who had begun to establish herself in the 1860s and could hardly have had a closer connection to both Martineau and the *Cornhill*. For among the emerging women writers of the decade was Thackeray's own daughter, his beloved Annie, who had entered the 'temple of knowledge' with her father's encouragement and began her long literary career with a first contribution to the *Cornhill* while he was still its editor. If Thackeray was one formative influence, however, he might well have been disconcerted to know just how important to his daughter's professional growth Harriet Martineau had been. Citing Martineau's *Deerbrook* in a letter to a friend when she was just eighteen, Annie Thackeray anticipated the need she would face to make her own way through life as she referred to her father's chronically precarious finances: 'Papa says in a few years, we shall have only 200£ a year to live on & as my favourite Miss Martineau says it is far nobler to earn than to save.'[88] Some years later, when she had gone on to construct a modestly successful literary career of her own, she paid tribute to the role Martineau had played in inspiring her. For left among Martineau's papers after her death was a letter from Annie Thackeray to Henry Atkinson in which she describes the impact of Martineau's praise for her 1867 novel, *The Village on the Cliff*:

> Dear Mr Atkinson
> I am so touched and so grateful and glad and proud that I don't quite know in what words to write about it; & I do think it is so kind of you to have thought how glad I should be! I only could wish as I looked at the little scrap of paper that was so much to me that I could have shown it to my father, and that is the most grateful thing I can say to you and to the writer of those kindest words. There is nobody whose praise now, could be to me what Miss Martineau's is . . . I know I first came to life over a brown watered book called the Settlers at Home, walking up the Champs Elysées at Paris twenty years ago, when I was 8 or 9 years old. Her books haven't been books but friends & counsellors & comforters; & that <u>she</u> of all people should make me and my sister so glad by her praise seems like a delightful miracle on purpose to make us happy.[89]

Annie Thackeray's literary career was a modest one, but its very ordinariness is itself a testimony to the shift in the world of letters to which Martineau had contributed so much by helping to make it possible for women authors to work in both literature and journalism and to have the professional lives of their own for which she had so long campaigned. Martineau could certainly be a difficult character; Dickens was far from the only the male writer to find her exasperating, and it was indeed her own bluntness about Macaulay that prompted Thackeray's blunder. So too by the end of her life the intellectual paradigm of stadial theory had become outmoded, giving way to forms of indeterminacy to which Dickens was more responsive and to which his own particular genius was more receptive. But Martineau knew only too well how difficult it was for a woman author to negotiate the uncertain boundaries between public writing and private selves, as her depiction of Macaulay and her entire encounter with the *Cornhill* show, and, in adhering to her vision of the historical narrative, she remained to the very end of her career a writer who would not be silenced, one for whom it was invariably clear what she ought to do, and thus both a vital force in shaping Victorian liberalism and a pioneering model for the young writers who would become mid-Victorian women of letters.

Notes

1. Deborah Logan provides the most extensive listings in the Appendix sections to her five volumes of the *Collected Letters*. Those to volumes 4 and 5 show that, in her final decade as an active journalist, in addition to her ongoing work for the *Daily News* Martineau contributed to the *Edinburgh Review*, *The Spectator*, *Macmillan's Magazine*, *Atlantic Monthly*, the *National Anti-Slavery Standard*, the *Westminster Review*, *Once a Week*, *Chambers's Journal*, the *Quarterly Review* and the *Cornhill*.
2. Martineau, *Letters*, vol. 4, p. 207, pp. 97–8; vol. 5, p. 11. Martineau's ongoing indirect contact with the Dickens family may have led to her being aware of the attempt Dickens made to have his wife committed to a lunatic asylum (see John Bowen's 'Unmutual Friend'). If so, that in turn could explain her letter describing an 1872 visit she had from Arthur Penrhyn Stanley, who had preached Dickens's funeral sermon, and his wife. The Stanleys told her 'a pleasant & touching anecdote of Mrs Dickens'; Martineau, in response, 'told them not a little of Dickens . . . of the facts of his latter life' (Martineau, *Letters*, vol. 5, p. 310).
3. Martineau, *Letters*, vol. 4, p. 178, n. 2.
4. Griffiths, 'The Comparative History', pp. 813–16.
5. Patten, *Charles Dickens and His Publishers*, pp. 267–9.
6. Drew, *Dickens the Journalist*, pp. 140, 146–7.
7. [Stephens], 'A Tale of Two Cities', pp. 742, 742–3.
8. Drew, *Dickens the Journalist*, p. 142.
9. Stout, *Corporate Romanticism*, p. 136; Grossman, 'Standardization', p. 450; Griffiths, 'The Comparative History'.
10. Dickens, *A Tale of Two Cities*, p. 324.
11. Stout, *Corporate Romanticism*, p. 138; Grossman, 'Standardization', p. 468.
12. Stout, *Corporate Romanticism*, p. 137.
13. Melman, *The Culture of History*, p. 104.
14. Dickens, *A Tale of Two Cities*, pp. 14–15.
15. Melman, *The Culture of History*, p. 109.
16. Dickens, *Letters*, vol. 7, p. 587.

17. Griffiths, 'The Comparative History', p. 828.
18. Ibid. p. 815.
19. 'The Late Lord Macaulay'.
20. 'Lord Macaulay'.
21. Quoted in Peter Ackroyd, *Dickens*, p. 632.
22. Sullivan, *Macaulay*, p. 474.
23. See Burrow, *A Liberal Descent*, p. 37; Levine, *The Boundaries of Fiction*, p. 79; Shattock, *Politics and Reviewers*, p. 15.
24. Goodlad, *Victorian Literature and the Victorian State*, p. 127.
25. Ibid. p. 258, n. 6.
26. Joyce, *The State of Freedom*, pp. 248, 244.
27. Dickens, *Letters*, vol. 2, p. 279.
28. Ibid. vol. 5, p. 78.
29. [Dickens], 'Insularities', p. 3.
30. *The Letters of Thomas Babington Macaulay*, vol. 4, pp. 48, 61.
31. Collins, 'Dickens and the *Edinburgh Review*', p. 167.
32. *The Letters of Thomas Babington Macaulay*, vol. 4, p. 61.
33. *The Journals of Thomas Babington Macaulay*, vol. 4, p. 179.
34. See *Dickens Journals Online*, <http://www.djo.org.uk/>, where a simple search reveals ninety-five separate references to Macaulay (last accessed 12 June 2019).
35. Ledger, *Dickens and the Popular Radical Imagination*, pp. 171–2.
36. Drew, *Dickens the Journalist*, p. 138.
37. Ibid. p. 153. Drew's helpful term for the ethos generated through Dickens's irregular series of quirky essays that 'with its critique of "wholesale" and impersonal values of human nature such as utilitarianism and political economy and its recommendation of "retail" values and face-to-face confrontation, appears to embrace both reactionary and Utopian alternatives to liberal modernity'.
38. Martineau, *Letters*, vol. 4, p. 146.
39. Newton, *Starting Over*, p. 112.
40. Easley, *First Person Anonymous*, Chapter 2.
41. [Martineau], 'Female Industry', p. 323.
42. Ibid. p. 324.
43. Ibid. p. 334.
44. [Martineau], 'Nurses Wanted', p. 411.
45. Brake, 'Time's Turbulence', p. 115.
46. Hall, *Macaulay and Son*, pp. 301–4. As Hall points out, the dislike between Macaulay and Martineau was entirely mutual, he describing her as a 'hag' and 'that hideous woman'.
47. Peterson, *Becoming a Woman of Letters*, p. 46.
48. [Martineau], 'Female Industry', p. 331.
49. Scott [Martineau], 'Representative Women', p. 260.
50. 'Nurses Wanted', p. 413.
51. Martineau, 'Woman's Battle-Field', p. 476.

52. Scott [Martineau], 'Representative Women', p. 261.
53. Arbuckle, *Harriet Martineau in the London Daily News*, p. xvii.
54. Scott [Martineau], 'Representative Women', p. 261.
55. [Martineau], 'Middle-Class Education: Girls', p. 554.
56. Martineau, *Letters to Wedgwood*, p. 120; Martineau, *Autobiography*, p. 267.
57. [Martineau], 'Lord Macaulay', p. 5; I.S. [Martineau], 'Lord Macaulay', pp. 58–61.
58. [Martineau], 'Lord Macaulay', p. 60.
59. For discussions of Macaulay's unusually close family ties, see Hall, *Macaulay and Son*, especially Chapter 3, and Sullivan, *Macaulay*, pp. 95–100.
60. Thackeray, 'Nil Nisi Bonum', p. 134.
61. Ritchie, 'The First Number of "The Cornhill"', *Cornhill Magazine*, July 1896, p. 5.
62. H. Silver, *Diary*, British Library, Add MS 88937/2/13. See also Leary, *The Punch Brotherhood* for a full discussion of this group.
63. Pomeroy, *Women in Hellenistic Egypt*, p. 80.
64. Smith, 'Our Birth and Parentage', p. 7.
65. Ray, *Thackeray*, p. 481.
66. Smith, 'Our Birth and Parentage', p. 7.
67. Martineau, *Letters*, vol. 4, p. 197.
68. Ibid.
69. Martineau, *Letters to Wedgwood*, p. 182.
70. Martineau, *Letters*, vol. 4, p. 177.
71. Ibid. p. 213.
72. 'Middle-Class Education: Boys'. George Smith's accounts indicate that Martineau received £50 for the two articles, a level of payment consistent with the *Cornhill*'s generous payments to its contributors and a sum that must have been important to her during a period when the investment income upon which she depended was threatened by uncertainty over railway stocks. See the Smith, Elder Account Book at the National Library of Scotland, MS.23187, and Martineau's correspondence for details of her straitened circumstances at this time.
73. Malachuk, *Perfection, the State, and Victorian Liberalism*, p. 139.
74. Martineau, *Letters*, vol. 5, p. 84.
75. Patrick Joyce, *The State of Freedom*, Chapter 6.
76. [Martineau], 'Middle-Class Education: Boys', p. 410.
77. Ibid. p. 411.
78. Ibid. p. 422.
79. Ibid. p. 423.
80. Ibid. p. 415.
81. Joyce, *The State of Freedom*, pp. 239, 247.
82. Ibid. p. 248.
83. [Martineau], 'Middle-Class Education: Boys', p. 413.

84. [Martineau], 'Middle-Class Education: Girls', p. 562.
85. Ibid. p. 563.
86. Ibid. p. 567.
87. Peterson, *Becoming a Woman of Letters*, pp. 45–7.
88. Ritchie, *Journals and Letters*, p. 43.
89. Ritchie, ALS to Henry Atkinson, n.d. HM886.

Conclusion: 'Likeness in unlikeness'

Almost thirty years after he and Anne Smith published their foundational essay on the quarrel between Dickens and Martineau, Ken Fielding returned to the pair's complex relationship, rounding out a lifelong interest in both authors. Writing on this second occasion for the *Martineau Society Newsletter*, he emphasised similarity rather than difference: noting how much Martineau and Dickens had in common with one another, he described in particular their 'likeness in unlikeness', and the 'attraction of opposites' that had drawn them together, and he then went on to point to the ways in which their 'uneasy partnership in journalism is still a relatively under-researched area of scholarship'.[1] Fielding's second take on the Martineau/Dickens dynamic has not circulated as widely as his and Smith's remarkably influential essay in *Nineteenth-Century Fiction*, but, as much as this project has responded to that first reading of the quarrel, so too it has built gratefully from his later prompt and his call for further work into the 'uneasy partnership' on which this book has focused. In doing so, I have hoped to show how, while the established scholarly narrative of the dispute had tended to reduce it to a simple dichotomy, Martineau and Dickens's relationship is, as Fielding later suggested, more fully understood when we define it by its push and pull nature and the degree to which these two influential figures in fact had a great deal in common as they wrestled with the issues facing Victorian Britain. Drawing on the past half century of scholarship, I have also argued that new interpretations of nineteenth-century intellectual history, of the efforts by women authors to create a place for themselves in the world of Victorian letters and of the evolution of liberalism on both sides of the Atlantic have made visible understandings of Victorian culture and the role of the press in shaping public discourse that were not available when Fielding and Smith first addressed the Martineau/Dickens dispute. Finally, by placing not just the quarrel but the entire relationship within the contexts of early and mid-Victorian journalism, I have endeavoured to shed greater light on the closely knit networks that made up the nineteenth-century press and that played such an essential role in the formation of Anglo-American liberalism. Though it lay beyond the scope of this project, future investigation into Martineau's advocacy in the press on behalf of the Union cause and Dickens's complex representation of the Civil War in *All the Year Round*, especially in *Great Expectations*, offers the prospect of both increasing what Deborah Logan has described as our understanding of her essential 'role in American abolitionism as a literary liaison between Britain and America'[2] and shedding new light on his late-career representations of empire, race and slavery.

The intimacy of the early and mid-Victorian world of the press in which Martineau and Dickens played such a formative part is perhaps nowhere more visible than in the most explicit contemporary editorial comment on their quarrel. In April 1859, as Martineau was embarking on a new phase of her career at the *Edinburgh* and Dickens was preparing to launch *All the Year Round*, *The Critic* made the mistake of describing Martineau as a principal contributor to *Household Words* who had subsequently quarrelled with her old friend. Promptly writing in response to this assertion, Martineau noted dismissively that

> All these statements are false. I did not contribute to *Household Words* 'from the first'; I never was a 'principal contributor'; I never had the advantage of more than the slightest personal acquaintance with Mr Dickens, who was never therefore my 'Old Friend'; I have never 'quarrelled with Mr Dickens'; I withdrew from *Household Words* a year and a half before the disgraceful attack on the millowners appeared in it; and my withdrawal was for a reason which bore no relation to any views of Mr Dickens's on economical or social subjects.

All these statements, too, are false, as this book has shown. But, as *The Critic*'s editor astutely commented, in correcting the record so peremptorily Martineau had 'used language of precisely that degree of strength which only friends when they quarrel are known to use', and he went on to note that, for all their mutual recriminations, 'both worked honestly and conscientiously in their several and very different ways, to the promotion of the same ends in many respects'.[3] Martineau kept a cutting of this article among the papers she left at her death, and it speaks to us, as evidently it did to her, of that likeness in unlikeness she and Dickens shared, that both drew them together and plunged them so forcefully apart, and that makes the recovery of the full complexity of their relationship a valuable addition to our understanding of nineteenth-century culture and the press.

As Martineau's obscure final resting place suggests (Fig. C.1),[4] she did indeed long become blotted 'out of our remembrance' as Dickens had hoped, and largely remained invisible in English studies until the recovery that began with the work of scholars such as Elisabeth Sanders Arbuckle, Deirdre David and Valerie Sanders in the 1980s. What this project has also shown, however, is just how completely Martineau succeeded in fulfilling her lifelong ambition to shape the Victorian world through her work. Writing just a few months into the publication of *Illustrations of Political Economy* and even before she had escaped provincial life in Norwich, she told a correspondent of her hopes: 'I wish I was in London. I want to be doing something with the pen, since no other means of action in politics are in a woman's power.'[5] Galvanised by her visit to America and making a lifelong commitment to advancing liberal progress through writing on behalf of the conjoined causes of social agency for women and the abolition of slavery, Martineau's entire career certainly bore out that hope. Now, almost half a century after Fielding and Smith's essay appeared, her importance in Victorian culture is finally becoming more broadly recognised, as the growing body of scholarship upon her reveals.

Although Dickens's critical fortunes wavered during the middle of the last century, he, of course, has never been in any danger of being forgotten. A uniquely charismatic figure whose contribution to nineteenth-century life is amply attested by the thousands of studies of his work that modern scholarship has produced, he was the phenomenon that McCarthy and Robinson remembered in their memoir of the *Daily News*, a man who did so much to shape the early and mid-Victorian press: 'Younger people who did not know Charles Dickens, who perhaps never saw him, can have little idea of the moving power of his words, his appeals, his very presence over men. The mere thrill of his wonderful voice had a magic of persuasion in it.'[6] *Contested Liberalisms* has, I hope, shown that by bringing together Martineau and Dickens, utterly different in so many ways, profoundly similar in so many others, we can not only more fully understand the two of them as individual authors but also through them appreciate more deeply the complex intricacies of the world of early and mid-Victorian journalism, the importance of transatlantic discourse in the formation of that journalism and the tensions within

Figure C.1 Harriet Martineau's grave.

the progressive liberal tradition that was so fundamental to the shaping of nineteenth-century British culture and society and whose legacy remains with us to this day.

Notes

1. Fielding, 'Likeness in Unlikeness', p. 4. I am grateful to members of the Martineau Society, who first drew my attention to Fielding's enduring interest in the Martineau–Dickens relationship.
2. Logan, *Writings on Slavery*, p. xxiv.
3. 'Sayings and Doings', p. 339.
4. Martineau is buried with her mother in Key Hill Cemetery in the Jewellery Quarter in Birmingham. As the photograph shows, the gravestone is cracked and has been repaired, and the inscription on it is barely legible. There is no mention of Martineau on the informational sign listing the names of prominent occupants of the cemetery.
5. Martineau, *Letters*, vol. 1, p. 139.
6. McCarthy and Robinson, *The 'Daily News' Jubilee*, p. 13.

Bibliography

Ackroyd, Peter, *Dickens* (New York: HarperCollins, 1990).

Aling, Helen, 'Dickens's Unitarian Theology', PhD dissertation, University of Minnesota, 1996.

[Alison, Archibald], 'The Influence of the Press', *Blackwood's Edinburgh Magazine* 36 (September 1834), pp. 373–91.

Altick, Richard D., *Writers, Readers, and Occasions: Selected Essays on Victorian Literature and Life* (Columbus: Ohio State University Press, 1989).

'American Notes for General Circulation', *Edinburgh Review* 76 (January 1843), pp. 497–522.

'American Notes, for General Circulation', *Quarterly Review* 71 (March 1843), pp. 502–28.

'American Notes for General Circulation. By Charles Dickens', *North American Review* 56 (January 1843), pp. 212–37.

Arac, Jonathan, *Commissioned Spirits: The Shaping of Social Motion in Dickens, Carlyle, Melville, and Hawthorne* (New Brunswick, NJ: Rutgers University Press, 1979).

Archibald, Diana C., and Joel J. Brattin (eds), *Dickens and Massachusetts: The Lasting Legacy of the Commonwealth Visits* (Amherst: University of Massachusetts Press, 2015).

Bakker, Jan, 'Caroline Gilman and the Issue of Slavery in the Rose Magazines, 1832–1839', *Southern Studies* 2 (1991), pp. 369–80.

Banerjee, Sukanya, 'Writing Bureaucracy, Bureaucratic Writing', Dickens Universe, University of California Santa Cruz, July 2018.

Belasco, Susan, 'Harriet Martineau's Black Hero and the American Antislavery Movement', *Nineteenth-Century Literature* 55 (2000), pp. 157–94.

Bew, Paul, *Ireland: The Politics of Enmity 1789–2006* (Oxford: Oxford University Press, 2007).

Blaisdell, Lowell L., 'The Origins of the Satire in the Watertoast Episode of *Martin Chuzzlewit*', *Dickensian* 77 (1981), pp. 92–101.

Bourrier, Karen, 'Reading Laura Bridgman: Literacy and Disability in Dickens's *American Notes*', *Dickens Studies Annual* 40 (2009), pp. 37–60.

Bowen, John, *Other Dickens* (Oxford: Oxford University Press, 2000).

Bowen, John, 'Unmutual Friend', *Times Literary Supplement*, 19 February 2019, <https://www.the-tls.co.uk/articles/public/charles-catherine-dickens-asylum/> (last accessed 12 June 2019).

Boylan, Anne M., *The Origins of Women's Activism: New York and Boston, 1797–1840* (Chapel Hill: University of North Carolina Press, 2002).

Brake, Laurel, 'The Leader (1850–1859)', NCSE: *Nineteenth-Century Serials Edition*, <https://ncse.ac.uk/headnotes/ldr.html> (last accessed 12 June 2019).

Brake, Laurel, '"Time's Turbulence": Mapping Journalism Networks', *Victorian Periodicals Review* 44 (2011), pp. 115–27.

Brake, Laurel, and Marysa Demoor (eds), *Dictionary of Nineteenth-Century Journalism* (London and Gent: Academia Press and the British Library, 2009).

[Brougham, Henry], 'Progress of the People – The Periodical Press', *Edinburgh Review* 57 (April 1833), pp. 239–48.

Brown, Gillian, *Domestic Individualism: Imagining Self in Nineteenth-Century America* (Berkeley: University of California Press, 1990).

Brown, Gillian, *The Consent of the Governed: The Lockean Legacy in Early American Culture* (Cambridge, MA: Harvard University Press, 2001).

Brown, Lucy, *Victorian News and Newspapers* (Oxford: Oxford University Press, 1985).

Brown, Wendy, *Walled States, Waning Sovereignty* (New York: Zone Books, 2010).

Buckingham, J. S., *America: Historical, Statistic, and Descriptive* (London: Fisher, Son & Co., 1841).

Budge, Gavin, *Romanticism, Medicine, and the Natural Supernatural* (Basingstoke: Palgrave Macmillan, 2012).

Burrow, J. W., *A Liberal Descent: Victorian Historians and the English Press* (Cambridge: Cambridge University Press, 1981).

Button, Mark E., 'American Liberalism from Colonialism to the Civil War and Beyond', in Steven Wall (ed.), *The Cambridge Companion to Liberalism* (Cambridge: Cambridge University Press, 2015), pp. 21–41.

Carroll, Siobhan, *An Empire of Air and Water: Uncolonizable Space in the British Imagination 1750–1850* (Philadelphia: University of Pennsylvania Press, 2015).

Castillo, Larisa T., 'Natural Authority in Charles Dickens's *Martin Chuzzlewit* and the Copyright Act of 1842', *Nineteenth-Century Literature* 62 (2008), pp. 435–64.

[Chapman, John], 'The Sphere and Duties of Government', *Westminster Review* 62 (October 1854), pp. 473–506.

'Charles Dickens as an Editor', *The Bookman* 30 (October 1909), p. 111.

Claybaugh, Amanda, *The Novel of Purpose: Literature and Social Reform in the Anglo-American World* (Ithaca, NY: Cornell University Press, 2007).

Clemm, Sabine, *Dickens, Journalism, and Nationhood: Mapping the World in* Household Words (New York: Routledge, 2009).

Collins, K. K., and Alan Cohn, 'Charles Dickens, Harriet Martineau, and Angela Burdett Coutts's *Common Things*', *Modern Philology* 79 (1982), pp. 407–13.

Collins, Philip, 'Dickens and the *Edinburgh Review*', *Review of English Studies* 14 (1963), pp. 167–72.

[Croker, John Wilson], 'Miss Martineau's Monthly Novels', *Quarterly Review* 49 (April 1833), pp. 136–52.

Crouthamel, James L., *Bennett's* New York Herald *and the Rise of the Popular Press* (Syracuse, NY: Syracuse University Press, 1989).

Daly, Christopher B., *Covering America: A Narrative History of the Nation's Journalism* (Amherst: University of Massachusetts Press, 2012).

David, Deirdre, *Intellectual Women and Victorian Patriarchy: Harriet Martineau, Elizabeth Barrett Browning, George Eliot* (Ithaca, NY: Cornell University Press, 1987).

De Certeau, Michel, 'Practices of Space', in Marshall Blonsky (ed.), *On Signs* (Oxford: Blackwell, 1985), pp. 122–45.

De Certeau, Michel, *The Practice of Everyday Life* (Berkeley: University of California Press, 1984).

Dennis, Richard, *Cities in Modernity: Representations and Productions of Metropolitan Space, 1840–1930* (Cambridge: Cambridge University Press, 2008).

DeSpain, Jessica, *Nineteenth-Century Transatlantic Printing and the Embodied Book* (Farnham: Ashgate, 2014).

[Dickens, Charles], 'A Preliminary Word', *Household Words*, 30 March 1850, pp. 1–2.

Dickens, Charles, *A Tale of Two Cities*, ed. Richard Maxwell (London: Penguin Books, 2003).

Dickens, Charles, *American Notes*, ed. Patricia Ingham (London: Penguin Books, 2000).

Dickens, Charles, *Barnaby Rudge*, ed. John Bowen (London: Penguin Books, 2003).

[Dickens, Charles], 'Insularities', *Household Words*, 19 January 1856, pp. 1–4.

Dickens, Charles, *Little Dorrit*, ed. Stephen Wall and Helen Small (London: Penguin Books, 2003).

Dickens, Charles, *Martin Chuzzlewit*, ed. Margaret Cardwell (Oxford: Clarendon Press, 1982).

Dickens, Charles, *Sketches of Young Gentlemen and Young Couples* (Oxford: Oxford University Press, 2012).

Dickens, Charles, *The Letters of Charles Dickens*, ed. Madeline House, Graham Storey, Kathleen Tillotson et al., 12 vols (Oxford: Clarendon Press, 1965–2002).

[Dickens, Charles, and Mark Lemon], 'A Paper-Mill', *Household Words*, 31 August 1850, pp. 529–31.

[Dickens, Charles, and Henry Morley], 'Our Wicked Mis-Statements', *Household Words*, 19 January 1856, pp. 13–19.

'Dickens' First Words on America', *New York Herald*, 24 October 1842, p. 2.

'Dickens's American Notes', *Fraser's Magazine for Town and Country* 26 (November 1842), pp. 617–29.

Dillon, Elizabeth Maddock, 'Sentimental Aesthetics', *American Literature* 76 (2004), pp. 495–523.

Dillon, Elizabeth Maddock, *The Gender of Freedom: Fictions of Liberalism and the Literary Public Sphere* (Stanford: Stanford University Press, 2004).

Drew, John M. L., *Dickens the Journalist* (Basingstoke: Palgrave Macmillan, 2003).

Dzelzainis, Ella, 'Dickens, Democracy, and Spit', in Ella Dzelzainis and Ruth Livesey (eds), *The American Experiment and the Idea of Democracy in British Culture, 1776–1914* (Aldershot: Ashgate, 2013), pp. 45–60.

Dzelzainis, Ella, 'Feminism, Speculation, and Agency in Harriet Martineau's *Illustrations of Political Economy*', in Ella Dzelzainis and Cora Kaplan (eds), *Harriet Martineau: Authorship, Society and Empire* (Manchester: Manchester University Press, 2010), pp. 118–37.

Dzelzainis, Ella, 'Malthus, Women, and Fiction', in Robert J. Mayhew (ed.), *New Perspectives on Malthus* (Cambridge: Cambridge University Press, 2016), pp. 155–81.

Easley, Alexis, *First Person Anonymous* (Aldershot: Ashgate, 2004).

Easley, Alexis, *Literary Celebrity, Gender, and Victorian Authorship, 1850–1914* (Newark: University of Delaware Press, 2011).

Easley, Alexis, 'Rewriting the Past and Present: Harriet Martineau, Contemporary Historian', in Valerie Sanders and Gaby Weiner (eds), *Harriet Martineau and the Birth of Disciplines: Nineteenth-Century Intellectual Powerhouse* (Abingdon: Routledge, 2017), pp. 101–20.

Fawcett, Edmund, *Liberalism: The Life of an Idea* (Princeton and Oxford: Oxford University Press, 2014).

[Felton, Cornelius C.], 'American Notes for General Circulation. By Charles Dickens', *North American Review* 56 (January 1843), pp. 212–37.

Fielding, K. J., '*American Notes* and Some English Reviewers', *Modern Language Review* 59 (1964), pp. 527–37.

Fielding, K. J., '"Likeness in Unlikeness": Dickens and Harriet Martineau', *Martineau Society Newsletter* 12 (1999), pp. 4–10.

Fielding, K. J., and Anne Smith, '*Hard Times* and the Factory Controversy', in Ada Nisbet and Blake Nevius (eds), *Dickens Centennial Essays* (Berkeley: University of California Press, 1971), pp. 22–45. Originally published in *Nineteenth-Century Fiction* 24 (1970), pp. 404–27. Citations are to the collected volume.

Finlayson, Geoffrey, *Citizen, State, and Social Welfare in Britain 1830–1890* (Oxford: Clarendon Press, 1994).

[Forster, John], 'The Answer of the American Press', *Foreign Quarterly Review* 31 (April 1843), pp. 250–81.

Forster, John, *The Life of Charles Dickens*, 2 vols (London: Dent, 1969).

[Forster, John], 'The Newspaper Literature of America', *Foreign Quarterly Review* 30 (October 1842), pp. 197–222.

Franklin, Benjamin, *The Complete Works, in Philosophy, Politics, and Morals, of the Late Dr Benjamin Franklin, Now First Collected and Arranged: with Memoirs of His Early Life Written by Himself*, 3 vols (London: Johnson and Longman, Hurst, Rees, and Orme, 1806).

Frawley, Maria, 'Behind the Scenes of History: Harriet Martineau and *The Lowell Offering*', *Victorian Periodicals Review* 38 (2005), pp. 141–57.

Freedgood, Elaine, *Victorian Writing about Risk* (Cambridge: Cambridge University Press, 2000).

Freeman, Joanne B., *Affairs of Honor: National Politics in the New Republic* (New Haven: Yale University Press, 2001).

Furneaux, Holly, *Queer Dickens: Erotics, Families, Masculinities* (Oxford: Oxford University Press, 2009).

Gerhard, Joseph, 'The Labyrinth and the Library: A View from the Temple in *Martin Chuzzlewit*', *Dickens Studies Annual* 15 (1986), pp. 1–22.

Giles, Paul, *Transatlantic Insurrections* (Philadelphia: University of Pennsylvania Press, 2001).

[Gilman, Caroline], 'Miss Martineau's Attack on Miss Caroline Gilman', *Boston Daily Advertiser*, 20 June 1877, p. 1.

Gleadle, Kathryn, *Borderline Citizens: Women, Gender, and Political Culture in Britain 1814–1867* (Oxford: Oxford University Press, 2009).

Gleadle, Kathryn, *The Early Feminists: Radical Unitarians and the Emergence of the Women's Rights Movement, 1831–1851* (New York: St. Martin's Press, 1995).

Golden, Morris, 'Politics, Class, and *Martin Chuzzlewit*', *Dickens Quarterly* 10 (1993), pp. 17–32.

Goodlad, Lauren, *Victorian Literature and the Victorian State: Character and Governance in a Liberal Society* (Baltimore: Johns Hopkins University Press, 2003).

Greenberg, Kenneth S., *Honor & Slavery* (Princeton: Princeton University Press, 1996).

Grener, Adam, 'Coincidence as Realist Technique: Improbable Encounters and the Representation of Selfishness in *Martin Chuzzlewit*', *Narrative* 20 (2012), pp. 322–42.

Griffiths, Devin, *The Age of Analogy: Science and Literature Between the Darwins* (Baltimore: Johns Hopkins University Press, 2016).

Griffiths, Devin, 'The Comparative History of *A Tale of Two Cities*', *ELH* 80 (2013), pp. 811–38.

Gross, Robert A., 'Reading for an Extensive Republic', in Robert A. Gross and Mary Kelley (eds), *A History of the Book in America Volume 2: An Extensive Republic: Print, Culture, and Society in the New Nation, 1790–1840* (Chapel Hill: University of North Carolina Press, 2010), pp. 516–44.

Grossman, Jonathan, 'Standardization (Standardisation)', *Critical Inquiry* 44 (2018), pp. 447–78.

Hadley, Elaine, 'Nobody, Somebody, and Everybody', *Victorian Studies* 59 (2016), pp. 65–86.

Hall, Catharine, *Macaulay and Son: Architects of Imperial Britain* (New Haven: Yale University Press, 2012).

Hall, Edward B., *Memoir of Mary L. Ware, Wife of Henry Ware, Jr* (Boston: Crosby, Nichols, and Company, 1853).

Hansen, Debra Gold, *Strained Sisterhood: Gender and Class in the Boston Female Anti-Slavery Society* (Amherst: University of Massachusetts Press, 1993).

Haywood, Ian, *The Revolution in Popular Literature* (Cambridge: Cambridge University Press, 2004).

Henkin, David, 'City Streets and the Urban World of Print', in Robert A. Gross and Mary Kelley (eds), *A History of the Book in America Volume 2: An Extensive Republic: Print, Culture, and Society in the New Nation, 1790–1840* (Chapel Hill: University of North Carolina Press, 2010), pp. 331–46.

Henkin, David M., *City Reading: Written Words and Public Spaces in Antebellum New York* (New York: Columbia University Press, 1998).

Hewitt, Martin, *The Dawn of the Cheap Press in Victorian Britain: The End of the 'Taxes on Knowledge', 1849–1869* (London: Bloomsbury Academic, 2014).

Hill, Michael R., 'A Methodological Comparison of Harriet Martineau's *Society in America* (1837) and Alexis de Tocqueville's *Democracy in America* (1835–1840)', in Michael R. Hill and Susan Hoecker-Drysdale (eds), *Harriet Martineau Theoretical and Methodological Perspectives* (New York: Routledge, 2001), pp. 59–74.

Hobbs, Andrew, *A Fleet Street in Every Town: The Provincial Press in England, 1855–1900* (Cambridge: Open Book Publishers, 2018).

Holcroft, Thomas, *A Plain and Succinct Narrative of the Late Riots and Disturbances in the Cities of London and Westminster, and Borough of Southwark* (London: Fielding and Walker, 1780).

Howe, Daniel Walker, *What God Hath Wrought: The Transformation of America, 1815–1848* (Oxford: Oxford University Press, 2007).

Huett, Lorna, 'Among the Unknown Public: *Household Words, All the Year Round* and the Mass-Market Weekly Periodical in the Mid-Nineteenth Century', *Victorian Periodicals Review* 38 (2005), pp. 61–82.

Humpherys, Anne (ed.), *G. W. M. Reynolds: Nineteenth-Century Fiction, Politics and the Press* (Aldershot: Ashgate, 2008).

Hutchins, Zachary McLeod, *Inventing Eden: Primitivism, Millenialism, and the Making of New England* (Oxford: Oxford University Press, 2014).

'Illustrations of Political Economy', *The Literary Gazette*, 23 June 1832, pp. 386–90.

Inglis, Katherine, 'Thomas Carlyle's Laystall and Charles Dickens's Paper-Mill', *Carlyle Studies Annual* 27 (2011), pp. 159–76.

'Ireland', *The Times*, 7 July 1843, p. 3.

I.S. [Martineau, Harriet], 'Lord Macaulay', *Once a Week*, 14 January 1860, pp. 58–61.

James, Louis, *Fiction for the Working Man: A Study of the Literature Produced for the Working Classes in Early Victorian England* (London and New York: Oxford University Press, 1963).

James, Louis, *Print and the People 1819–1851* (London: Allen Lane, 1976).

Jameson, Anna, *Winter Studies and Summer Rambles in Canada*, 3 vols (London: Sanders and Otley, 1838).

John, Juliet, *Dickens and Mass Culture* (Oxford: Oxford University Press, 2010).

Jones, Aled, *Powers of the Press: Newspapers, Power and the Public in Nineteenth-Century England* (Aldershot: Scolar Press, 1996).

Jones-Rogers, Stephanie E., *They Were Her Property: White Women as Slave Owners in the American South* (New Haven: Yale University Press, 2019).

[Johnstone, Christian], 'Miss Martineau's Illustrations of Political Economy', *Tait's Edinburgh Magazine* 1 (August 1832), pp. 612–18.

[Johnstone, Christian], 'Miss Martineau's Society in America, and Grund's American Society', *Tait's Edinburgh Magazine* 4 (July 1837), pp. 404–24.

Joyce, Patrick, *The State of Freedom: A Social History of the British State Since 1800* (Cambridge: Cambridge University Press, 2013).

Kelley, Mary, *Learning to Stand and Speak: Women, Education, and Public Life in America's Republic* (Chapel Hill: University of North Carolina Press, 2006).

Ketabgian, Tamara, *The Lives of Machines: The Industrial Imaginary in Victorian Literature and Culture* (Ann Arbor: University of Michigan Press, 2011).

Knight, Charles, *Passages of a Working Life during Half a Century*, 3 vols (London: Bradbury and Evans, 1864; reprinted Shannon: Irish University Press, 1971).

Koss, Stephen, *Fleet Street Radical: A. G. Gardiner and the Daily News* (London: Allen Lane, 1973).

Krishnamurthy, Aruna (ed.), *The Working Class Intellectual in Eighteenth- and Nineteenth-Century Britain* (Farnham: Ashgate, 2009).

Landow, George, *Elegant Jeremiahs: The Sage from Carlyle to Mailer* (Ithaca, NY: Cornell University Press, 1986).

Leary, Patrick, *The Punch Brotherhood: Table Talk and Print Culture in Mid-Victorian London* (London: The British Library, 2010).

Ledger, Sally, *Dickens and the Popular Radical Imagination* (Cambridge: Cambridge University Press, 2007).

Levine, George, *The Boundaries of Fiction: Carlyle, Macaulay, Newman* (Princeton: Princeton University Press, 1968).

Liddle, Dallas, *The Dynamics of Genre: Journalism and the Practice of Literature in Mid-Victorian Britain* (Charlottesville: University of Virginia Press, 2009).

Litvack, Leon, 'The Politics of Perception: Dickens, Ireland and the Irish', in Neil McGaw (ed.), *Writing Irishness in Nineteenth-Century British Culture* (Aldershot: Ashgate, 2004), pp. 34–80.

Livesey, Ruth, *Writing the Stage Coach Nation: Locality on the Move in Nineteenth-Century British Literature* (Oxford: Oxford University Press, 2016).

Lloyd, David, and Paul Thomas, *Culture and the State* (New York: Routledge, 1998).

Logan, Deborah, *Harriet Martineau, Victorian Imperialism, and the Civilizing Mission* (Farnham: Ashgate, 2010).

Logan, Deborah, *The Hour and the Woman* (Dekalb: Northern Illinois University Press, 2002).

Logan, Deborah A., '"I Am, My Dear Slanderer, Your Faithful Malignant Demon": Harriet Martineau and the *Westminster Review*'s Comtist Coterie', *Victorian Periodicals Review* 42 (2009), pp. 171–91.

Lohrli, Anne, 'Harriet Martineau and the People of Bleaburn', *Studies in Short Fiction* 20 (1983), pp. 101–4.

Lohrli, Anne, *Household Words, A Weekly Journal 1850–1859, Conducted by Charles Dickens* (Toronto and Buffalo: University of Toronto Press, 1973).

'London, Saturday, July 8, 1843', *The Times*, 8 July 1843, p. 5.

'Lord Macaulay', *The Morning Chronicle*, 31 December 1859, p. 5.

Macaulay, John Allen, *Unitarianism in the Antebellum South: The Other Invisible Institution* (Tuscaloosa: University of Alabama Press, 2001).

Macaulay, Thomas Babington, *The Journals of Thomas Babington Macaulay*, ed. William Thomas, 5 vols (London: Pickering & Chatto, 2008).

Macaulay, Thomas Babington, *The Letters of Thomas Babington Macaulay*, ed. Thomas Pinney, 6 vols (Cambridge: Cambridge University Press, 1974–81).

McCarthy, Justin, and John R. Robinson, *The 'Daily News' Jubilee: A Political and Social Retrospect of Fifty Years of the Queen's Reign* (London: Samson Low, Marston and Company, 1896).

McGill, Meredith, *American Literature and the Culture of Reprinting, 1834–1853* (Philadelphia: University of Pennsylvania Press, 2003).

MacKay, Carol Hanberry, 'The Letter-Writer and the Text in *Martin Chuzzlewit*', *Studies in English Literature 1500–1900* 26 (1986), pp. 737–58.

McKnight, Natalie, 'Dickens, Niagara Falls and the Watery Sublime', *Dickens Quarterly* 26 (2009), pp. 69–78.

[Maginn, William,] 'Gallery of Literary Characters. No. XLII. Miss Martineau', *Fraser's Magazine for Town and Country* 8 (November 1833), pp. 576–8.

Magnet, Myron, *Dickens and the Social Order* (Philadelphia: University of Pennsylvania Press, 1985).

Malachuk, Daniel S., *Perfection, the State, and Victorian Liberalism* (Basingstoke: Palgrave Macmillan, 2005).

Marryat, Captain Frederick, *Diary in America* (Bloomington: Indiana University Press, 1960).

[Martineau, Harriet], 'Account of Toussaint L'Ouverture', *The Penny Magazine*, 31 March 1838, pp. 121–8.

Martineau, Harriet, *Autobiography*, ed. Linda H. Peterson (Peterborough, Ontario: Broadview Press, 2007).

Martineau, Harriet, 'Characteristics of the Genius of Scott', *Tait's Edinburgh Magazine* 2 (December 1832), pp. 301–14.

[Martineau, Harriet], 'Domestic Service', *Westminster Review* 31 (August 1838), pp. 405–32.

[Martineau, Harriet], 'Female Education', *Monthly Repository* (February 1823), pp. 77–81.

[Martineau, Harriet], 'Female Industry', *Edinburgh Review* 109 (April 1859), pp. 293–336.

Martineau, Harriet, *Guide to Windermere: With Tours to the Neighbouring Lakes and Other Interesting Places* (Windermere: John Garnett, n.d.; London: Whittaker and Co.).

Martineau, Harriet, *Harriet Martineau: Further Letters*, ed. Deborah A. Logan (Bethlehem, PA: Lehigh University Press, 2012).

Martineau, Harriet, *Harriet Martineau's Autobiography with Memorials by Maria Weston Chapman*, 3 vols (London: Smith, Elder, 1877).

Martineau, Harriet, *Harriet Martineau's Letters to Fanny Wedgwood*, ed. Elisabeth Sanders Arbuckle (Stanford: Stanford University Press, 1983).

Martineau, Harriet, *Harriet Martineau's Writing on British History and Military Reform*, ed. Deborah Anna Logan, 6 vols (London: Pickering & Chatto, 2005).

Martineau, Harriet, *History of the Peace* (London: Charles Knight, 1850). Reprinted in Deborah Anna Logan (ed.), *Harriet Martineau's Writing on British History and Military Reform*, 6 vols (London: Pickering & Chatto, 2005).

[Martineau, Harriet], 'How to Get Paper', *Household Words*, 28 October 1854, pp. 241–5.

Martineau, Harriet, *How to Observe Morals and Manners* (London: Charles Knight & Co., 1838).

Martineau, Harriet, *Illustrations of Political Economy: Selected Tales*, ed. Deborah Logan (Peterborough, Ontario: Broadview Press, 2004).

Martineau, Harriet, *Illustrations of Taxation. No. V. The Scholars of Arneside* (London: Charles Fox, 1834).

[Martineau, Harriet], 'Literary Lionism', *Westminster Review* 32 (April 1839), pp. 261–81.

[Martineau, Harriet], 'Lord Macaulay', *Daily News*, 31 December 1859, p. 5.

[Martineau, Harriet], 'Middle-Class Education in England: Boys', *Cornhill Magazine* 10 (October 1864), pp. 409–26.

[Martineau, Harriet], 'Middle-Class Education in England: Girls', *Cornhill Magazine* 10 (November 1864), pp. 549–68.

Martineau, Harriet, *Miscellanies*, 2 vols (Boston: Hilliard, Gray and Company, 1836).

[Martineau, Harriet], 'Miss Sedgwick's Works', *Westminster Review* 6 (October 1837), pp. 42–65.

[Martineau, Harriet], 'National Education', *Monthly Repository* 6 (October 1832), pp. 689–94.

[Martineau, Harriet], 'Nurses Wanted', *The Cornhill Magazine* 11 (April 1865), pp. 409–25.

[Martineau, Harriet], 'On the Duty of Studying Political Economy', *Monthly Repository* 6 (January 1832), pp. 24–34.

[Martineau, Harriet], 'On Friday night', *Daily News*, 4 March 1856, p. 4.

Martineau, Harriet, Papers. Cadbury Research Library, University of Birmingham.

Martineau, Harriet, *Retrospect of Western Travel*, 3 vols (London: Sanders and Otley, 1838).

Martineau, Harriet, *Sketches from Life* (London: Whittaker and Co.; Windermere: J. Garnett, 1856).

Martineau, Harriet, *Society in America*, 3 vols (London: Saunders and Otley, 1837; reprinted Cambridge: Cambridge University Press, 2009).

Martineau, Harriet, 'The Achievements of the Genius of Scott', *Tait's Edinburgh Magazine*, 2 (January 1833), pp. 445–60.

Martineau, Harriet, *The Collected Letters of Harriet Martineau*, ed. Deborah Anna Logan, 5 vols (London: Pickering & Chatto, 2007).

Martineau Harriet, *The Factory Controversy; A Warning Against Meddling Legislation* (Manchester: The National Association of Factory Occupiers, 1855).

Martineau, Harriet, 'The Martyr Age of the United States', *Westminster Review* 32 (December 1838), pp. 1–59.

[Martineau, Harriet], 'The Newcastle Improvements', 6 parts, *The Penny Magazine*, 14 March 1840, p. 99; 11 April, pp. 137–8; 18 April, pp. 148–9; 25 April, pp. 157–8; 2 May, pp. 169–70; 9 May, pp. 177–8.

[Martineau, Harriet], 'The Second Reading of the improved Factory Bill', *Daily News*, 27 March 1856, p. 4.

[Martineau, Harriet], 'The Shakers', *The Penny Magazine*, 18 November 1837, pp. 445–8.

[Martineau, Harriet], 'The Sickness and Health of the People of Bleaburn', *Household Words* 25 May – 15 June 1850, pp. 190–3, 230–8, 256–61, 283–8.

[Martineau, Harriet], *The Sickness and Health of the People of Bleaburn* (Boston: Crosby, Nichols, and Company, 1853).

[Martineau, Harriet], 'Theology, Politics, and Literature', *Monthly Repository* 6 (February 1832), pp. 73–9.

Martineau, Harriet, 'Woman's Battle-Field', *Once a Week*, 3 December 1859, pp. 474–9.

Martineau, Harriet, *Writings on Slavery and the American Civil War*, ed. Deborah Anna Logan (Dekalb: Northern Illinois University Press, 2002).

Mayer, Henry, *All on Fire: William Lloyd Garrison and the Abolition of Slavery* (New York: St. Martin's Press, 1998).

Meckier, Jerome, *Innocent Abroad: Charles Dickens's American Engagements* (Lexington: University of Kentucky Press, 1990).

Melman, Billie, *The Culture of History: English Uses of the Past 1800–1953* (Oxford: Oxford University Press, 2006).

[Merle, Gibbons], 'Journalism', *Westminster Review* 18 (January 1833), pp. 195–208.

Metz, Nancy Aycock, *The Companion to* Martin Chuzzlewit (Westport, CT: Greenwood Press, 2001).

[Mill, James], 'Periodical Literature', *Westminster Review* 1 (January 1824), pp. 206–49.

Miller, Elizabeth Carolyn, *Slow Print: Literary Radicalism and Late Victorian Print Culture* (Stanford: Stanford University Press, 2013).

Mind Amongst the Spindles: A Selection from The Lowell Offering (London: Charles Knight & Co., 1844. Reprinted Carlisle, MA: Applewood Books, n.d.).

Mineka, Francis E., *The Dissidence of Dissent: The Monthly Repository, 1806–1838* (Chapel Hill: University of North Carolina Press, 1944).

'Miss Martineau's *Society in America*', *North American Review* 97 (October 1837), pp. 418–60.

'Miss Martineau's Travels in America', *Edinburgh Review* 67 (April 1838), pp. 180–97.

Morgentaler, Goldie, 'Dickens in Canada', *Dickens Quarterly* 19 (2002), pp. 151–9.

Morrison, Kevin A., *Victorian Liberalism and Material Culture: Synergies of Thought and Place* (Edinburgh: Edinburgh University Press, 2018).

Moss, Elizabeth, *Domestic Novelists in the Old South: Defenders of Southern Culture* (Baton Rouge: Lousiana State University Press, 1992).

Nayder, Lillian, *The Other Dickens: A Life of Catherine Hogarth* (Ithaca, NY: Cornell University Press, 2011).

Nerone, John, 'Newspapers and the Public Sphere', in Scott E. Casper, Jeffrey D. Groves, Stephen W. Nissenbaum and Michael Winship (eds), *A History of the Book in America Volume 3: The Industrial Book 1840–1880* (Chapel Hill: University of North Carolina Press, 2007), pp. 230–48.

Newton, Judith, *Starting Over: Feminism and the Politics of Cultural Critique* (Ann Arbor: University of Michigan Press, 1994).

Nicholson, Bob, 'Transatlantic Connections', in Andrew King, Alexis Easley and John Morton (eds), *The Routledge Handbook to Nineteenth-Century Periodicals and Newspapers* (New York: Routledge, 2016), pp. 163–74.

O'Connell, Daniel, *Correspondence of Daniel O'Connell The Liberator*, ed. W. J. Fitzpatrick, 2 vols (London: John Murray, 1888).

Patten, Robert L., *Charles Dickens and 'Boz': The Birth of the Industrial-Age Author* (Cambridge: Cambridge University Press, 2012).

Patten, Robert L., *Charles Dickens and His Publishers* (Oxford: Clarendon Press, 1978).

Patten, Robert L., 'Dickens Wills', *Dickens Quarterly* 36 (2019), pp. 60–94.

Peterson, Linda H., *Becoming a Woman of Letters: Myths of Authorship and Facts of the Victorian Market* (Princeton: Princeton University Press, 2009).

Peterson, Linda H., 'Harriet Martineau: Masculine Discourse, Female Sage', in Thaïs Morgan (ed.), *Victorian Sages and Cultural Discourse: Renegotiating Gender and Power* (New Brunswick, NJ: Rutgers University Press, 1990), pp. 171–86.

Pichanik, Valerie, *Harriet Martineau: The Woman and Her Work, 1802–76* (Ann Arbor: University of Michigan Press, 1980).

Pocock, J. G. A., *Barbarism and Religion*, 6 vols (Cambridge: Cambridge University Press, 1999).

Poland, Matthew, 'Bodies and Paper Production in *Household Words* and *Our Mutual Friend*', RSVP/VSAWC Conference, July 2018.

Pomeroy, Sarah B., *Women in Hellenistic Egypt: From Alexander to Cleopatra* (New York: Schocken Books, 1984).

Pond, Kristen, 'Harriet Martineau's Epistemology of Gossip', *Nineteenth-Century Literature* 69 (2014), pp. 175–207.

'Practical Reasoning Versus Impracticable Theories', *Fraser's Magazine for Town and Country* 19 (May 1839), pp. 557–92.

Price, Kenneth M., and Susan Belasco Smith (eds), *Periodical Literature in Nineteenth-Century America* (Charlottesville: University Press of Virginia, 1995).

Pusapati, Teja Varma, 'Going Places: Harriet Martineau's "Letters from Ireland" and the Rise of the Female Foreign Correspondent', *Women's Writing* 24:2 (2017), pp. 207–26.

Rasmussen, Dennis C., 'Adam Smith and Rousseau: Enlightenment and Counter-Enlightenment', in Christopher J. Berry, Maria Pia Paganelli and Craig Smith (eds), *The Oxford Handbook of Adam Smith* (Oxford: Oxford University Press, 2013), pp. 54–76.

Ray, Gordon N., *Thackeray: The Age of Wisdom: 1847–1863* (New York: McGraw Hill, 1959).

'Repeal of the Paper Duty', *The Times*, 31 January 1851, p. 5.

'Retrospect of Western Travel', *The Athenaeum*, 3 and 10 February 1838, pp. 87–8, 102–4.

Rezek, Joseph, *London and the Making of Provincial Literature: Aesthetics and the Transatlantic Book Trade 1800–1850* (Philadelphia: University of Pennsylvania Press, 2015).

Rice, Thomas Jackson, *Barnaby Rudge: An Annotated Bibliography* (New York: Garland Press, 1987).

Ritchie, Anne Thackeray, *Anne Thackeray Ritchie: Journals and Letters*, ed. Abigail Burnham Bloom and John Maynard (Columbus: Ohio State University Press, 1994).

Ritchie, Mrs Richmond, 'The First Number of "The Cornhill"', *Cornhill Magazine* 1 (n.s.) (July 1896), pp. 1–16.

Rivlin, Joseph B., *Harriet Martineau: A Bibliography of Her Separately Printed Books* (New York: New York Public Library, 1947).

Roberts, Caroline, *The Woman and the Hour: Harriet Martineau and Victorian Ideologies* (Toronto: University of Toronto Press, 2002).

Rose, Jonathan, *The Intellectual Life of the British Working Classes* (New Haven: Yale University Press, 2002).

Sanders, Valerie, *Reason over Passion: Harriet Martineau and the Victorian Novel* (Brighton: Harvester Press, 1986).

'Sayings and Doings', *The Critic*, 9 April 1859, p. 339, and HM560 in the Martineau Papers.

Schneider, Matthew, 'Spitting At/As Abjection in Dickens's *American Notes* and *Martin Chuzzlewit*', *Symbiosis: A Journal of Anglo-American Literary Relations* 14 (2010), pp. 219–35.

Scott, Ingleby [Martineau, Harriet], 'Representative Women: The Free Nurse', *Once a Week*, 17 March 1860, pp. 258–62.

Seitz, Don C., *The James Gordon Bennetts* (Indianapolis: Bobbs-Merrill, 1928).

Shannon, Mary L., *Dickens, Reynolds, and Mayhew on Wellington Street: The Print Culture of a Victorian Street* (Farnham: Ashgate, 2015).

Shattock, Joanne (ed.), *Journalism and the Periodical Press in Nineteenth-Century Britain* (Cambridge: Cambridge University Press, 2017).

Shattock, Joanne, *Politics and Reviewers: The* Edinburgh *and the* Quarterly *in the Early Victorian Age* (London: Leicester University Press, 1989).

Shattock, Joanne, 'The Sense of Place and *Blackwood's (Edinburgh) Magazine*', *Victorian Periodicals Review* 49 (2016), pp. 431–42.

Silver, Henry, *Diary*, British Library, Add MS 88937/2/13.

Slater, Michael, *Charles Dickens* (New Haven: Yale University Press, 2009).

Smith, George, 'Our Birth and Parentage', *Cornhill Magazine* 10 (n.s.) (January 1901), pp. 4–17.

Steinlight, Emily, *Populating the Novel: Literary Form and the Politics of Surplus Life* (Ithaca, NY: Cornell University Press, 2018).

[Stephens, James Ftizjames], 'A Tale of Two Cities', *Saturday Review of Politics, Literature, Science and Art*, 17 December 1859, pp. 741–3.

Stockton, David, *The Gracchi* (Oxford: Clarendon Press, 1979).

Stoll, Steven, *Ramp Hollow: The Ordeal of Appalachia* (New York: Hill and Wang, 2017).

Stonehouse, J. H. (ed.) *Catalogue of the Library of Charles Dickens* (London: Piccadilly Fountain Press, 1935).

Stout, Daniel, 'Little, Maybe Less: Dickens's Vanishing Points', Dickens Universe, University of California Santa Cruz, July 2018.

Stout, Daniel M., *Corporate Romanticism: Liberalism, Justice, and the Novel* (New York: Fordham University Press, 2017).

Sullivan, Robert, *Macaulay: The Tragedy of Power* (Cambridge, MA: Belknap Press, 2009).

Tambling, Jeremy, '*Martin Chuzzlewit*: Dickens and Architecture', *English* 48 (1999), pp. 147–68.

[Thackeray, William Makepeace], 'Nil Nisi Bonum', *Cornhill Magazine* 1 (February 1860), pp. 129–34.

'The Late Lord Macaulay', *The Times*, 31 December 1859, p. 7.

'The New York Herald – Its Position, Prosperity, Circulation, and Prospects in Two Hemispheres', *New York Herald*, 7 November 1842, p. 2.

'The provisions of the Factory Acts', *Daily News*, 31 January 1856, p. 4.

Tucker, Andie, 'Newspapers and Periodicals', in Robert A. Gross and Mary Kelley (eds), *A History of the Book in America Volume 2: An Extensive Republic: Print, Culture, and Society in the New Nation, 1790–1840* (Chapel Hill: University of North Carolina Press, 2010), pp. 389–408.

Van Ghent, Dorothy, 'The Dickens World: A View from Todgers's', *Sewanee Review* 58 (1950), pp. 419–38.

Vetter, Lisa Pace, 'Harriet Martineau on the Theory and Practice of Democracy in America', *Political Theory* 36 (2008), pp. 424–55.

Walder, Dennis, *Dickens and Religion* (London: George Allen and Unwin, 1981).

Waters, Catherine, *Commodity Culture in Dickens's* Household Words (Aldershot: Ashgate, 2008).

Watts, Ruth, *Gender, Power, and the Unitarians in England, 1760–1860* (London: Longman, 1998).

Webb, Igor, 'Charles Dickens in America: The Writer and Reality', *Dickens Studies Annual* 39 (2008), pp. 59–96.

Webb, R. K., *Harriet Martineau: A Radical Victorian* (London: Heinemann, 1960).

Welsh, Alexander, *From Copyright to Copperfield: The Identity of Dickens* (Cambridge, MA: Harvard University Press, 1987).

Wiener, Joel, *The War of the Unstamped: The Movement to Repeal the British Newspaper Tax, 1830–1836* (Ithaca, NY: Cornell University Press, 1969).

[Wills, William Henry], 'The Appetite for News', *Household Words*, 1 June 1850, pp. 238–40.

Winch, Donald, *Wealth and Life: Essays on the Intellectual History of Political Economy in Britain, 1848–1914* (Cambridge: Cambridge University Press, 2009).

Winyard, Ben, and Hazel McKenzie (eds), *Charles Dickens and the Mid-Victorian Press 1850–1870* (Buckingham: University of Buckingham Press, 2013).

Wolfreys, Julian, *Writing London: The Trace of the Urban Text from Blake to Dickens* (Basingstoke: Macmillan, 1998).

Index

Note: Page numbers in italics refer to illustrations.

abolitionist movement, 9, 41, 52–3, 58–9, 88, 94n, 124, 180, 197–200, 205
   Martineau article on, 51
   see also slavery
Allegheny College, 64
All the Year Round
   American Civil War, 299
   Dickens as owner and editor of, 174
   and female autonomy, 16
   journalism and fiction, 138
   and Macaulay, 276–7
   Martineau and, 267, 287
   and *Once a Week*, 286–7
   A Tale of Two Cities in, 269, 270–1, 278
America
   and *Barnaby Rudge*, 97, 98–102
   education in, 64–9
   Martin Chuzzlewit, 142–56
   Martineau in, 50–94
   stadial theory, 53–9, 200
American Civil War, 299
American literature, 155–6
American newspapers, 259–60
   Forster, 119
   New York, 73, 128–9

American Notes
   American press in, 95–136, 256
   American women in, 152–6
   Canada, 107–8
   and female autonomy, 189
   New York Herald and, 143
   Irish immigrants in America, 116–17, 167, 187
   Juliet John, 96, 115, 139
   The Lowell Offering, 209–10
   Macaulay, 276
   and *Martin Chuzzlewit*, 137, 140–1, 144–9
   Mississippi, 55
   negative reviews of, 142
   O'Connell and, 173–4
   'The Passage Home', 109–10
   Shakers, 108–9, 203
   transatlantic reception of, 125–32, 142
   transatlantic voyage, 103–4
American press, 256
   in *American Notes*, 95–136, 256
   How to Observe Morals and Manners, 74–5
   Martin Chuzzlewit, 256

American women, 108–9,
    124–5, 225
  in *American Notes*, 152–6
  in *How to Observe Morals
    and Manners*, 56–7
  in *The Penny Magazine*, 196
  slavery and, 8–9, 67
  in *Society in America*, 196
Amherst College, 67
anti-Catholicism, 250–1, 254
Anti-Slavery Standard, 286
Arac, Jonathan, 139
Arbuckle, Elisabeth Sanders,
    203, 217n, 282
Arnold, Matthew, 288–9, 290
  Culture and Anarchy, 4
  *A French Eton; or, Middle
    Class Education and the
    State*, 288
  Popular Education in France,
    288
Athenaeum, 193
Atkinson, Henry, 293
Austen, Henry, 273
Autobiography, 239, 243
  critical reception of work, 220
  Caroline Gilman, 82, 86–7,
    226
  Daily News, 233
  Hard Times, 264n
  Macaulay, 283
  magazine writing, 184
  Martineau and Dickens, 13,
    249–55
  Smith, George, 286

Bakker, Jan, 83
Banerjee, Sukanya, 229
Barnaby Rudge
  and American visit, 97, 98–102
  and Canada, 108
  Catholicism in, 141–2, 166

Gordon Riots, 140, 158
  and radical press, 137
  and *A Tale of Two Cities*,
    272–3
  'taxes on knowledge', 149
Barrett, Elizabeth, 187, 190
Barton, Benjamin, 62
Beecher, Lyman, 198
Belasco, Susan, 205
Bennett, James Gordon, 120,
    127–8, 129
Bentley's Miscellany, 99
*Blackwood's Edinburgh
    Magazine*, 35
Blaisdell, Lowell, 168–9, 172
Bleak House, 6, 236
Boston, 22, 60–1, 81, 87, 111,
    115, 196–8
Boston Female Anti-Slavery
  Society (BFASS), 9, 81, 85,
    87–8, 197–8, 199–200
Bourrier, Karen, 109
Bowen, John, 99, 138, 139,
    164, 166
Boylan, Anne M., 9, 87–8
'Boz', 129–31, 173–4, 221–2
Bradbury and Evans, 267, 287
Brake, Laurel, 20, 214, 280
Bridgman, Laura, 109
Britannia, 103–4, 156
Brougham, Henry, 35, 123
Brown, Gillian, 8–9, 16, 57, 69
Brown, Lucy, 3, 255
Brown, Wendy, 5
Bryant, William Cullen, 73,
    119–20, 122–3, 174
Buckingham, James Silk, 50, 72
Budge, Gavin, 89–90
Burr, Aaron, 71

Calhoun, John C., 66–7
Canada, 97, 106–8, 146, 268

Carlyle, Thomas, 271–2
Carroll, Siobhan, 103
Castillo, Larisa, 154–5
Catholicism, 38–9, 140, 141–2, 166–7, 171, 189, 250–1
  anti-Catholicism, 13, 100, 189, 244
Chamber's Journal, 221
Chapman, John
  The Factory Controversy, 243, 245, 246
  The Leader, 214
  'The Sphere and Duties of Government', 262n
  Westminster Review, 238, 278
Chapman and Hall, 287
Charleston, South Carolina, 75, 80–1, 82–5, 86–7
Chartism, 72, 187
Child, Lydia Maria, 188
Chollop, Hannibal, 142, 174–6, 256, 270
A Christmas Carol, 212
Cincinnati, 22, 60–3, 68, 76, 116–17, 192, 198, 202
Clay, Henry, 56, 61, 62, 64, 78
Claybaugh, Amanda, 10, 96, 123
Clemm, Sabine, 222–3
Collins, Wilkie, 'The Yellow Mask', 244, 251
comparative history, 19, 25, 267–70, 273
Cornhill Magazine, 282–92
  'Middle-Class Education: Boys', 288, 289, 296n
  'Middle-Class Education: Girls', 288, 291
  'Middle-Class Education in England', 287–8, 290–1
  'Nurses Wanted', 287
  Thackeray, Annie, 292–4
  Thackeray, W. M., 192, 267, 270
Coutts, Angela Burdett, 235, 237, 240–2, 247
The Critic, 299
Croker, John Wilson, 44, 56

Daily News
  Dickens as editor, 37, 167, 169, 174
  Factory Bill, 248–9
  female education, 288
  Hunt, Frederick Knight, 19–20, 26n, 206
  Ireland, 189
  Macaulay, 283–4
  Martineau and, 233–5
  Martineau as leader writer, 182, 184, 237–8, 266, 286, 292
  memoir of Dickens, 300
  'taxes on knowledge', 255, 258–9
David Copperfield, 249
de Buffon, Comte, *Histoire Naturelle*, 105–6
de Certeau, Michel, 18, 59
Deerbrook, 186, 191, 286, 292–3
Dennis, Richard, 16, 17–18
DeSpain, Jessica, 10, 96, 129
Dickens, Charles
  'Boz', 129–31, 173–4, 221–2
  as editor of *Daily News*, 37, 167, 169, 174
  as 'humanity-monger', 11, 83
  Irish nationalism, 116
  letters to Forster, John, 17, 237
  New York, 103, 111–17, 119–22
  as owner and editor of *All the Year Round*, 174

Dickens, Charles (*cont.*)
    as owner and editor of
        Household Words, 37, 138,
        174, 235–6, 270–1, 287
    print and the press, 137–79,
        266–97
    and Whig history, 274–7
    Wills and, 235–6, 237, 263n
Dickens and Martineau, 11–15,
    241
    Autobiography, 13, 249–55
    Hard Times, 11–13, 228–9
    Household Words, 212, 213,
        237, 250, 254–5
    Logan on, 267
    Martin Chuzzlewit, 95
    New York, 97–8
    Westminster Review, 210, 228
Dickens Centennial Essays, 12
Dillon, Elizabeth Maddock, 8–9,
    16, 29, 32, 33, 57, 190
Drake, Dr Daniel, 61–3, 202
    'Remarks on the Importance of
    Promoting Literary and Social
    Concert in the Valley of the
    Mississippi', 63–4
Drew, John, 23, 96, 99–100,
    255, 270, 277, 295n
    Dickens the Journalist, 13
Dzelzainis, Ella, 18–19, 32,
    39–40, 44, 105–6

Easley, Alexis, 213, 217n, 279
Edinburgh Review
    American Notes, 142
    Brougham, 35
    'Female Industry', 211, 269,
        278–9, 281
    Macaulay, 274–7
    Martineau, 277–82, 286, 299
    Retrospect of Western Travel,
        193

Spedding, 130–1, 132
Whig history, 269
education
    in America, 64–9
    female, 189, 288
    Illustrations of Political
        Economy, 37–40
    Macaulay, 290
    Monthly Repository, 38
    Society in America, 68
Emerson, Lidian, 182–3,
    184, 201
Enlightenment, 42–3, 62
The Examiner, 43–4, 240
The Extra Boz Herald, 121

Factory Act, 248–9, 282, 286–7
The Factory Controversy, 11,
    220–65, 231
factory safety, 11, 140–1, 190,
    209–10, 279
'Father D'Estelan's Christmas
    Morning', 238, 243–4, 246,
    250–1, 252, 253
Fawcett, Edmund, 5
Fawkes, Guy, 159, 166
Felton, Cornelius C., 131, 143,
    151–2
female *see* women
feudalism, 57, 119, 193
Fielding, K. J., 140–1, 228,
    242, 298
    '*Hard Times* and the Factory
    Controversy', 11, 12–14
    Nineteenth-Century Fiction,
    298
Follen, Charles, 203
Foreign Quarterly Review,
    126–9, 131–2, 141, 147,
    148, 153, 259
'The Answer of the American
    Press', 143

Forster, John
  American newspapers, 119
  Dickens's letters, 17, 237
  The Examiner, 240
  Foreign Quarterly Review, 131–2, 139, 141–4, 147–8, 259
  Martin Chuzzlewit, 154
  'The Newspaper Literature of America', 126–9
Fortescue, Lord, 288
Fox, William Johnson, 187, 188, 233–4
France, 35–6
Franklin, Benjamin, 151–2
Franklin Institute, 64
Frasers's Magazine, 44, 130, 192
Frawley, Maria, 218n
Freedgood, Elaine, *Victorian Writing about Risk*, 250
Freeman, Joanne, 70
French Revolution, 5, 268, 271–2
Fuller, Margaret, 73
Furneaux, Holly, *Queer Dickens*, 262n

Garnett, John, 252–4
Garrison, William Lloyd, 61, 87, 88, 197–8, 199–201, 247–8
Gibson, Thomas Milner, 256
Giles, Paul, 9–10, 96
Gilman, Caroline, 80–7, 94n, 199, 226
  Recollections of a Housekeeper, 85
  Recollections of a Southern Matron, 83, 85–6
  'Religious Privileges of the Negroes in Charleston', 83–5

Gilman, Samuel, 80–3
Golden, Morris, 130
Goodlad, Lauren, 15, 35, 69–70, 275
  Victorian Literature and the Victorian State, 6–7
Gordon Riots, 99–101, 140, 158
Grainger, Richard, 202
Great Expectations, 299
Greenberg, Kenneth, 70
Grener, Adam, 164
Grey, Lady, 187
Grey, Lord, 213
Griffiths, Devin, 15, 19, 31, 42, 268, 271, 273
Grimké, Angelina, 124, 198–9
Gross, Robert, 66
Grossman, Jonathan, 271–2
Guide to Windermere, 252

Hadley, Elaine, 6, 229
Hall, Basil, 50
Hall, Catharine, 281, 287
Hamilton, Alexander, 71
Hansen, Deborah Gold, 9, 88, 197
Hard Times, 237, 239
  argument between Dickens and Martineau, 11–13, 228–9
  Macaulay, 276
  political economy and, 14, 264n
  Utilitarianism, 242
Harvard University, 66, 67–8, 87, 114–15, 151
Hawthorne, Nathaniel, 'Mrs Hutchinson', 29, 31, 43
Haywood, Ian, 125, 181–2, 200, 202, 206, 214

Henkin, David, 73, 113–14, 122, 141, 145
Hewitt, Martin, 34, 46, 180–1, 255
  The Dawn of the Cheap Press in Victorian Britain, 3–4, 26n
Hill, Michael, 'A Methodological Comparison', 26–7n
History of the Peace, 12, 221–2
Hobbs, Andrew, *A Fleet Street in Every Town*, 26n
Holcroft, Thomas, *Plain and Succinct Narrative of the Late Riots*, 100
Horne, R. H., 207
Horner, Anna, 209
Horner, Leonard, 229–30
The Hour and the Man, 205
Household Words
  anti-Catholicism, 13
  'The Appetite for News', 2–3, 16–17
  Dickens as owner and editor of, 37, 138, 174, 235–6, 270–1, 287
  Factory Bill, 248–9
  The Factory Controversy, 220–2, 239–40, 242–6
  factory safety, 11
  'Father D'Estelan's Christmas Morning', 254
  female autonomy, 16
  female employment, 269
  'Ground in the Mill', 239
  'How to Get Paper', 223, 255, 258–9, 260–1
  Hunt, Frederick Knight, 26n, 206, 238
  Ireland in, 189
  Macaulay, 276–7
  Martin Chuzzlewit, 169
  Martineau, 12–13, 181, 184, 202, 214–15, 234, 252, 299
  Martineau and Dickens, 212, 213, 237, 250, 254–5
  'The New School for Wives', 279–80
  'A Paper-Mill', 223, 255, 256–8, 259–61
  Pickard, 281
  'Preliminary Word', 220–1
  'Preventible Accidents', 239
  'The Sickness and Health of the People of Bleaburn', 223, 224–7, 260, 261–2n
  'Two Shillings Per Horse-Power', 239
How to Observe Morals and Manners, 51, 191
  American press, 74–5
  American women, 56–7
  Knight, 202
  Schiller, 33–4, 187
  stadial theory, 68–9
Howick, Lord, 187, 189–90, 206–7
Howitt and Saunders, 212–13
Hunt, Frederick Knight, 19, 26n, 206, 233–5, 238
  The Fourth Estate: Contributions towards a History of Newspapers and of the Liberty of the Press, 3
  History of the Peace, 249–50
Hutchinson, Anne, 29, 43

Illustrations of Political Economy, 181, 191–2, 300
  Croker, 56
  education, 37–40
  female excellence, 43
  female exclusion, 32

Freedgood, 264n
Ireland, 188
Nightingale, Florence, 277
The Pickwick Papers, 12
political economy and, 14
success of, 29–30, 45,
  80–1, 213
Illustrations of Taxation, 45
Ireland
  Act of Union, 168, 185
  Daily News, 189
  Famine, 185
  in *Household Words*, 189
  *Illustrations of Political
    Economy*, 188
  Logan on, 48n
  under British rule, 38–9, 48n,
    187–9, 222–3
Irish immigrants in America,
  115–17, 166, 167
  American Notes, 167, 187
Irish nationalism
  Barnaby Rudge, 158
  Dickens, Charles, 116
  Martin Chuzzlewit, 116, 137–8,
    140–2, 165, 166, 187–9
  Martineau on, 185
  The Times, 168–72
Irish temperance march, 116–17

Jackson, Andrew, 62, 66–7, 78,
  134n, 198
  press campaign, 78–80
Jacksonian America, 50–94
  press in, 69–88
Jameson, Anna, *The
  Communion of Labour*, 281
Jefferson, Thomas, 50, 51,
  59, 66
Jeffrey, Louisa, 80
Jerdan, William, 44
Jesuits, 166, 238, 244, 253

John, Juliet, 21, 23, 96, 102,
  115, 122, 139, 173
  Dickens and Mass Culture, 13
Johnstone, Christian, 40, 44, 191
Jones-Rogers, Stephanie E., 85
Joseph, Gerhard, 138, 162
Joyce, Patrick, 79, 275,
  289, 290

Kelley, Abby, 186, 197
Kelley, Mary, 7–8
Kendall, Amos, 79–80, 198, 222
Ketabgian, Tamara, 222
Knight, Charles
  'Account of Toussaint
    L'Ouverture', 217n
  biography of William Caxton,
    207–9
  History of the Peace, 188,
    221–2, 226, 230
  'improving' reading for
    working-class readers, 14
  'the liberal education of the
    people', 201–12
  The Lowell Offering, 279
  Martineau and, 183
  mass-market literature, 200
  political economy, 19
  'taxes on knowledge', 256
Knight's Weekly Volume, 208

Lambton, Lady Mary, 207
Landow, George, 234
The Leader, 24, 183, 253
  and Martineau, 212–15
  'Sketches from Life', 214
Lebanon, New York, 108, 117
Ledger, Sally, 220–1, 277
  *Dickens and the Popular
    Radical Imagination*, 13
Leech, John, 284
Lefebvre, Henri, 16

Leigh Hunt, Thornton, 183, 212–15, 276
Lemon, Mark, 256–8
'Letters from Ireland', 234, 251
Letters on the Laws of Man's Nature and Development, 238, 251
Lewes, G. H., 183, 212–15
Liberalism, definitions of, 5–9
The Liberator, 87, 248, 199
Liddle, Dallas, 81, 249
The Lighthouse, 237
The Literary Gazette, 44
Little Dorrit, 6, 228–9, 235, 237, 266, 267
Livesey, Ruth, 21, 138, 146, 161, 165, 178n
Lloyd, David, 75, 220
Locke, John, 8, 16, 69
Logan, Deborah, 182
  anti-Catholicism, 13
  Boston Female Anti-Slavery Society, 81
  female education, 189
  'Gallery of Literary Characters. No. XLII. Miss Harriet Martineau', 44
  Ireland, 48n
  Martineau and Dickens, 267
  Nightingale, Florence, 277
  slavery, 299
  Ware, Anne Bent, 225
Lohrli, Anne, 225, 226
  Household Words, 264n
London, 156–7, 158–60, 165
Lovejoy, Elijah, 199–200
The Lowell Offering, 119, 124–5, 147, 209–11, 213, 218n, 279
Lucas, Samuel, 284, 286–7

Macaulay, John Allen, 82
Macaulay, Thomas Babington, 25, 271–2
  All the Year Round, 276–7
  Edinburgh Review, 277–82
  education, 290
  'Female Industry', 269
  History of England, 274
  Lays of Ancient Rome, 276
  Martineau and, 283–5, 293–4
  'Minute on Education', 275
  Whig history, 19, 274–7, 289
McGill, Meredith, 10, 96, 123–4, 128, 138–9, 149
MacKay, Carol Hanbery, 163
McKnight, Natalie, 107
Macmillan's Magazine, 287
Macready, William, 229
Maginn, William, 'Gallery of Literary Characters. No. XLII. Miss Harriet Martineau', 44
Magnet, Myron, 105–6, 166
  Dickens and the Social Order, 99
Malachuk, Daniel, 288
Mansfield, Lord, 100–2
Marryat, Frederick, 50, 54, 72, 96, 107
Martin Chuzzlewit, 150, 209
  America in, 142–56
  and *American Notes*, 132
  England in, 156–65
  Felton in, 131
  Irish nationalism in, 116, 187–9
  Martineau and Dickens, 95
  metropolitan life in, 272–3
  print and press in, 97, 126, 137–79, 166–76, 256
  transatlantic voyage, 156–7

Martineau, Harriet
  All the Year Round and, 267, 287
  in America, 50–94
  and the American city, 59–64
  article on abolitionist movement, 51
  article on Sedgwick, Catharine, 51
  and *The Cornhill*, 282–92
  and the *Daily News*, 182, 184, 233–5, 237–8, 266, 286, 292
  'On the Duty of Studying Political Economy', 38
  Edinburgh Review, 277–82, 286, 299
  essays on Sir Walter Scott, 37, 39–43, 47n, 57, 190–1
  grave, *301*, 302n
  'Guides to Service', 202
  Household Words, 12–13, 181, 184, 202, 214–15, 234, 252, 299
  'improving' reading for working-class readers, 183
  'Ireland', 39, 46
  Irish nationalism, 185
  Knight and, 183
  and *The Leader*, 212–15
  and Macaulay, 277–82, 283–5, 293–4
  'A Manchester Strike', 46
  Monthly Repository, 29, 39, 40, 43, 190
  'National Education', 39
  The Penny Magazine, 202, 224–5
  and the press, 29–49, 180–219, 266–97
  'process' articles, 222–3
  reception of *American Notes*, 125–6
  rejection by Wills, 238, 243–7, 252, 254
  and stadial theory, 31–4, 38, 186
  and Thackeray, 282–92
  and *Westminster Review*, 51, 183, 190–201, 202
  and Wills, 243–7
Martineau, James, 238
Martineau, Maria, 266
Martineau and Dickens, 11–15, *241*
  Autobiography, 13, 249–55
  Hard Times, 11–13, 228–9
  Household Words, 212, 213, 237, 250, 254–5
  Logan, Deborah, 267
  Martin Chuzzlewit, 95
  New York, 97–8
  Westminster Review, 210, 228
Martineau Society Newsletter, 298
'The Martyr Age', 102
mass-market literature, 200
mass-market press, 97, 255–6
Master Humphrey's Clock, 99
material culture of the book, 160–5
Mayer, Henry, 199
Meckier, Jerome, 21
Melman, Billie, 272–3
Merle, Gibbons, 46, 74, 78, 129
  'Journalism', 35–6
Meteyard, Eliza, 190
Metz, Nancy, 177n
Mill, James, 35
Miller, Zane, 62
Milnes, Richard Monckton, 185, 188
Miscellanies, 89–90

Mississippi, 54–5, 63, 104–6, 109, 176
Monthly Repository
  education, 38
  female education, 189
  Fox, 233–4
  Gilman, Samuel, 80–1
  Martineau, 29, 39, 40, 43, 190
  Miscellanies, 89
  'A Parable', 82
  Schiller, 33
  social unrest, 195
  'The Solitary: A Parable', 82
  'Some Autobiographical Particulars', 82
Morgentaler, Goldie, 108
Morley, Henry, 227–8, 232, 236, 239, 243, 244–7
Morning Chronicle, 173, 274
Morrison, Kevin, 5
Moss, Elizabeth, 85

National Association of Factory Occupiers (NAFO), 227–8, 232, 240, 245–6, 249, 252–3
Native Americans, 115–16, 117–19, 134n, 135n
Nayder, Lillian, 16, 247
  The Other Dickens, 263n
Nerone, John, 72
New Orleans, 70–1, 76–7
New York
  American newspapers, 73, 128–9
  Dickens, 103, 111–17, 119–22
  Martin Chuzzlewit, 145–9, 152–3, 159–60, 167
  Martineau and Dickens, 97–8
New York Courier, 127, 144
New York Evening Post, 73, 119–20, 122–3, 127
New York Herald, 120, 127–9, 132, 143, 148, 161, 259
'The Newspaper Literature of America', 126
newspapers, 72–6, 119–22
Newton, Judith, 278
Niagara Falls, 54, 106–7
Nicholson, Bob, 1
Nightingale, Florence, 277–8, 280, 281–2
Nineteenth-Century Fiction, 12, 297
North American Review, 89, 131, 143, 205
nursing, 25, 269–70, 280–2

O'Connell, Daniel, 137–8, 166, 168–73, 185, 188–9, 222
Ohio, 61–2, 66, 76, 104, 107, 118, 291
Ohio River, 64, 65, 91n, 118, 153
Oliver Twist, 289
Once a Week, 267, 282, 283, 284, 286
'Our Wicked Mis-Statements', 192, 232, 242, 251, 254, 276

Palfrey, John Gorham, 89, 205
paper production, 255–61
Patten, Robert L., 99
  Charles Dickens and his Publishers, 263n
Pease, Elizabeth, 88, 197
The Penny Magazine
  'Account of Toussaint L'Ouverture', 202, 203–5, 204, 217n, 225

American women, 196
  'improving' reading for working-class readers, 183
  Martineau, 202, 224–5
  'The Newcastle Improvements', 202
  'pacification', 206, 214
  'The Shakers', 202–3
People's Journal, 183, 212–13
  'Lake and Mountain Holiday', 213
  'Survey from the Mountain', 213
Peterson, Linda, 16, 40, 44, 81, 234, 281, 292
  Becoming a Woman of Letters, 30
Philadelphia, 62, 111–12
Pickard, Mary, 224–7, 281–2
The Pickwick Papers, 12, 30
Pitchlynn, Peter, 118–19
Poland, Matthew, 257
Pope, Alexander, *Moral Essays*, 166–7
press, 201–12, 254–61
  formation of the, 19–20
  free press movement, 36–7
  'frightful engine', 95–136, 146–7
  growth of, 2–5
  in Jacksonian America, 69–88
  in *Martin Chuzzlewit*, 126, 137–79
  Martineau and the, 29–49, 180–219
  Society in America and the, 200, 259
  and Whig history, 274–7
Punch, 284, 286–7
Pusapati, Teja, 222–3, 234

Quarterly Review, 55–6, 130

Rasmussen, Dennis, 18, 31–2
Reeve, Henry, 278–9, 286–7
Reform Act, 3, 34–7, 72
Repeal Associations, 166, 187–8, 188
Republican motherhood, 8, 51, 57–9, 69, 95, 98, 109, 125, 137, 153, 180, 210
Retrospect of Western Travel, 51
  Boston, 60
  Cincinnati, 61
  duels, 71
  Gilman, Caroline, 86
  Jackson, 198–9
  'Mississippi Voyage', 55
  reviews of, 192–3
  slavery, 195
Reynolds, G. W. M., 220–1
Rezek, Joseph, 10, 96, 118
Roberts, Caroline, 58
Roberts, David, 240
Robertson, John, 193
Robinson, Henry Crabb, 126, 300
The Rose Bud, 83
rural society, 186–7
Rush, Benjamin, 62

St Louis, 112
The Salem Gazette, 29
Salisbury, 157–8, 160–2
Sanders, Elisabeth Arbuckle, 203–5
Satirist, 120
Saturday Review, 271
Saunders, John, 17
Schiller, Friedrich, 22, 31, 32–3, 47n, 75, 187
Schneider, Matthew, 139, 140
The Scholars of Arneside, 45–6, 51, 78, 186

Scott, Sir Walter, 118–19, 200–1
  Marmion, 118–19
  Martineau essays on, 37, 39–43, 47n, 57, 89–90, 190–1
Scottish Enlightenment, 18, 31, 268
Sedgwick, Catharine, 74–5, 194–5
  Martineau article on, 51
  The Poor Rich Man, and the Rich Poor Man, 74, 194
Shannon, Mary L., 20
Shapiro, Henry, 62
Silver, Henry, 284
'Sketches from Life', 252, 254
Slater, Michael, *Charles Dickens*, 13
slavery
  abolitionist movement, 51, 52, 58–9, 205
  'Account of Toussaint L'Ouverture', 203–5
  American Notes, 123–5
  American women and, 8–9, 67
  'Domestic Service', 195–6
  Gilman, Caroline and, 81–3, 86–7
  Harvard University, 67–8
  'How to Get Paper', 259
  'The Martyr Age of the United States', 196–1
  Society in America, 60–1, 76–8, 196–9
Smith, Adam, 22, 31, 33, 280
  Lectures on Jurisprudence, 32
  The Theory of Moral Sentiments, 32
  The Wealth of Nations, 32
Smith, Anne, 140–1, 228, 242
  '*Hard Times* and the Factory Controversy', 11, 12–14
  Nineteenth-Century Fiction, 298

Smith, George, 286, 287, 296n
Smith, Thomas Ruys, 55
Society for the Diffusion of Useful Knowledge (SDUK), 202
Society in America
  'Allegiance to Law', 60–1
  American women, 196
  Boston, 60
  'Civilisation', 50–1, 59
  education, 68
  female alcoholism, 57–8
  Grimké, Angelina, 198
  'Morals of Slavery', 58–9
  Palfrey, John Gorham, 89
  press, 200, 259
  Sedgwick, Catharine, 75, 194
  Shakers, 202–3
  slavery, 203–5
  Westminster Review, 192–3
Southern newspapers, 76–7
The Southern Rose, 80–1, 83–6, 84, 87, 199
The Southern Rose Bud, 83
Spedding, James, 130–1, 132
stadial theory, 31–4, 118, 146, 268
  America, 53–9, 200
  anti-stadial, 105–6
  Martineau, 38, 186
  Nightingale, Florence, 280
  Scott, Sir Walter, 42
stamp duty, 31, 34, 36–7, 98, 131, 177n, 255–6, 260–1
Stapleton, Anne, 90
Steinlight, Emily, 6
Stephens, James Fitzjames, 271
Stockton, David, 155
Stoll, Steven, 134n
Stout, Daniel, 5, 229, 271–2
Sullivan, Dora, 39
Sullivan, Robert, 274–5
Sun (New York), 73, 120

Tait, William, 40–1
Tait's Edinburgh Magazine, 37, 39, 40–1, 44, 47n, 89–90, 190–1
'A Letter to the Deaf', 82
A Tale of Two Cities, 269, 270–4, 277, 278
Tambling, Jeremy, 166
'taxes on knowledge', 4, 21, 31, 36–7, 45, 181, 122, 223, 255, 255–6
Ten Hour Bill, 190
Thackeray, Annie, 292–3
  The Village on the Cliff, 293
Thackeray, W. M., 25, 192, 267, 269–70, 282–92, 292
Thomas, Paul, 75
The Thunderer, 100, *101*
The Times, 3, 143, 166, 168–72, 256, 274
Tocqueville, Alexis de, 7, 26–7n
Toussaint L'Ouverture, *204*
Transylvania University, 63, 64
Tremenheere, W. S., 206–7
Trevelyan, G. O., 275
Trollope, Frances, 54, 60, 61–2, 72, 79, 96
  Domestic Manners of the Americans, 55, 62–3
Tucker, Andie, 78

Unitarianism, 14–16, 27–8n, 45, 60, 82, 238
University of Virginia, 66
Utilitarianism, 6, 140–1, 228, 242

van Ghent, Dorothy, 158–9
Vetter, Lisa Pace, 33
voluntarism, 7, 15–16, 275, 288

Ware, Anne Bent, 225–7
Ware, Henry, *Sober Thoughts on the State of the Times*, 71
Ware, Mary Pickard *see* Pickard, Mary
Ware, William, 57–8, 192
Waters, Catherine, 222, 257
Wedgwood, Fanny
  'Account of Toussaint L'Ouverture,' 205, 217n
  Garnett, 252–4
  industrial manufacturing, 250
  Macaulay, 283
  Martineau, James, 238
  O'Connell, 188
  rural society, 187
Weekly Volume, 183, 202, 205–10, 211–12, 222, 279
Mind Amongst the Spindles, 209–10
Weld, Theodore, 198
  American Slavery As It Is, 123–4
Welsh, Alexander, 163
Western Museum, 62–3
Westminster Review
  Chapman, John, 243, 245, 278
  'Domestic Service', 191, 194–6
  Forster, John, 132, 143
  'Literary Lionism', 191, 200, 226
  and Martineau, 51, 183, 190–201, 202
  Martineau and Dickens, 210, 228
  Martineau James, 238
  'The Martyr Age of the United States', 88, 191, 194, 196–9
  Merle, Gibbons, 35, 74, 78
  Mill, James, 35
  'Miss Sedgwick's Works', 74–5, 191, 194–5, 200
Wills, 244

Whig history, 19, 266–97
Whitworth, Henry, 249
Wills, William Henry
  All the Year Round, 270
  anti-Catholicism, 13, 250–1
  'The Appetite for News', 3, 16–17, 19–20
  Dickens and, 235–6, 237, 263n
  factory safety, 239–40
  'How to Get Paper', 260
  rejection of Martineau, 238, 243–7, 252, 254
Winch, Donald, 14
Wolfreys, Julian, 164
women
  access to employment, 68, 185, 189–90, 193, 195–6, 269, 279–81
  alcoholism, 57–8
  American, 108–9, 124–5, 225
  in *American Notes*, 152–6
  autonomy, 16, 189
  education, 189, 288
  excellence of, 43, 43–4
  exclusion of, 32, 67, 196
  in *How to Observe Morals and Manners*, 56–7
  leadership, 196–9
  mill workers, 209–11
  in *The Penny Magazine*, 196
  rights of, 41
  slavery and, 8–9, 67
  in *Society in America*, 196
  subjection to coverture, 8–9
working classes, 184–6
  'improving' reading for, 183, 202–12

EU representative:
Easy Access System Europe
Mustamäe tee 50, 10621 Tallinn, Estonia
Gpsr.requests@easproject.com

www.ingramcontent.com/pod-product-compliance
Lightning Source LLC
Chambersburg PA
CBHW071827230426
43672CB00013B/2777